CLASSICS IN THEORY

General Editors

Brooke A. Holmes
Miriam Leonard
Tim Whitmarsh

CLASSICS IN THEORY

Classics in Theory explores the new directions for classical scholarship opened up by critical theory. Inherently interdisciplinary, the series creates a forum for the exchange of ideas between classics, anthropology, modern literature, philosophy, psychoanalysis, politics, and other related fields. Invigorating and agenda-setting volumes analyse the cross-fertilizations between theory and classical scholarship and set out a vision for future work on the productive intersections between the ancient world and contemporary thought.

Metalepsis

Ancient Texts, New Perspectives

Edited by

Sebastian Matzner
and Gail Trimble

OXFORD
UNIVERSITY PRESS

OXFORD

UNIVERSITY PRESS

Great Clarendon Street, Oxford, OX2 6DP,
United Kingdom

Oxford University Press is a department of the University of Oxford.
It furthers the University's objective of excellence in research, scholarship,
and education by publishing worldwide. Oxford is a registered trade mark of
Oxford University Press in the UK and in certain other countries

Published in the United States of America by Oxford University Press
198 Madison Avenue, New York, NY 10016, United States of America

British Library Cataloguing in Publication Data

Data available

Library of Congress Control Number: 2020934974

ISBN 978-0-19-884698-7

Printed and bound by
CPI Group (UK) Ltd, Croydon, CR0 4YY

Acknowledgements

From: Gail Trimble <gail.trimble@trinity.ox.ac.uk>
Date: Monday, 5 May 2014 at 14:08
To: Sebastian Matzner <sebastian.matzner@classics.ox.ac.uk>
Subject: Metalepsis begins

Dear Sebastian,
It was great to talk today; thanks for being keen to begin to get things going. Here are some ideas to get our exchange started. Everything (with the possible exception of dates) is very tentative!

This is how 'Metalepsis begins'. Or, at least, how it began for us. The pages that follow contain the explorations that took their cue from this exchange—and a first thank you must go to Tim Whitmarsh who introduced us to each other and sparked such a fruitful and enjoyable collaboration.

A major milestone was the conference 'Breaking and Entering: Metalepsis in Classical Literature', jointly organized by the editors, which took place at the University of Oxford's Faculty of Classics on 3–5 September 2015. The conference was financed by the Arts and Humanities Research Council as part of a Research Fellowship (Early Career) awarded to Gail Trimble (grant number AH/K008145/1), with further support from the Lingen Fund of Trinity College, Oxford: we wish to thank our funders who made this event—and thereby this whole project—possible. Over the three days of the conference, our international speakers spiritedly engaged with the topic in ways that exceeded our expectations, prompting an intense, sustained discussion, and a productive wrestling with the very notion of metalepsis and what this concept is and does, both in general and in its particular instantiations in ancient works. This confirmed us in our sense that metalepsis deserves more attention from the perspective of classical scholars and from the perspectives of classical literature, art, and thought. We are very grateful to all who contributed to making the conference a success, in particular: the original cast of speakers; the engaged and intellectually generous members of the audience; our graduate assistant, Calypso Nash, who took much of the weight of logistics off our shoulders; and the Classics faculty's wonderfully supportive staff.

Emboldened and enthused by the conference, we were delighted when our proposal for a volume on the critical concept of metalepsis in the light of classical literature was met with equal enthusiasm by the general editors of OUP's Classics in Theory series and by OUP's Classics Commissioning Editor and Assistant Commissioning Editor. Our heartfelt thanks to Brooke Holmes, Miriam Leonard, Tim Whitmarsh, Charlotte Loveridge, Georgina Leighton, and Hannah Chippendale for their encouragement, commitment, and hands-on support in developing the book and steering it through the publication process, and to Kim Richardson for his scrupulous copyediting. Our thanks also to the anonymous Press readers, who helped to further clarify our editorial thinking.

For support in preparing the volume for publication, a big thank you must go to our research assistant, Francesca Modini, for her excellent help in putting together the two indices, as well as to the King's College London Comparative Literature Research Fund for supporting this book project with a grant for indexing. We also want to say 'Dankeschön!' to Sabine Hug, whose support from Heidelberg's Classics department made obtaining the illustrations and image rights for Jonas Grethlein's chapter a breeze. Our special thanks belong to the people without whom none of what follows would have been possible, the contributors to this volume, for being so responsive, patient, and reflective in our continued trialogue over each of their chapters. Needless to say, any remaining errors or infelicities must be attributed to us (and are, obviously, part of a sophisticated poetics of unreliable narration in academic prose).

As our initial ideas turned into a conference, a conference into a book proposal, and a book proposal into this book, the cast of characters in another—if certainly not unrelated—narrative world has changed considerably, in plot twists that neither of us quite saw coming. Gail's family grew as she and her husband Tom became the parents, first of Roger and then of the twins Jonathan and Felicity; Sebastian met and not long after eloped with Christoph to embark on a life together as husbands. Our days have grown infinitely richer since these (co-)authors made their first interventions into the stories we tell of our lives. We could not be more grateful for these, the most marvellous of all metalepses in our universes.

Sebastian Matzner and Gail Trimble

London and Oxford
December 2019

Copyright and Permissions

The editors and publisher wish to thank the following for their kind permission to reproduce short extracts as epigraphs to the following chapters:

Chapter 4: From: THE PURSUIT OF SIGNS: SEMIOTICS, LITERATURE, DECONSTRUCTION by Jonathan Culler, Copyright © 1981, Routledge. Reproduced by permission of Taylor & Francis Group. Reproduced with permission of the Licensor through PLSclear

Chapter 10: From: HISTORICAL ONTOLOGY by Ian Hacking, Cambridge, Mass.: Harvard University Press, Copyright © 2002 by the President and Fellows of Harvard College. Reproduced with permission of Harvard University Press.

Chapter 11: From: NARRATIVE DISCOURSE: AN ESSAY IN METHOD by Gérard Genette. Copyright © 1980 Cornell University Press. Reprinted by permission of Georges Borchardt, Inc., on behalf of the author's Estate, and by permission of Cornell University Press.

Contents

List of Illustrations

Note on Abbreviations

Classical authors and works are usually abbreviated following the practice of the *OLD* and *LSJ*, and journals according to that of *L'Année Philologique*.

List of Contributors

Peter Bing is Professor of Classics at the University of Toronto. His research focuses on Hellenistic poetry, a field in which he has published widely, with key works including *The Well-Read Muse: Present and Past in Callimachus and the Hellenistic Poets* (Göttingen, 1988, 2nd edn. Michigan Classics Press, 2008), *Games of Venus: An Anthology of Greek and Roman Erotic Verse from Sappho to Ovid*, co-authored with R. Cohen (New York, 1991), *The Scroll and The Marble: Studies in Reading and Reception in Hellenistic Poetry* (Ann Arbor, 2009) and *Aristaenetus: Erotic Letters. Introduced, Translated and Annotated*, co-authored with Regina Höschele (Society of Biblical Literature, 2014).

Felix Budelmann is Professor of Greek Literature at the University of Oxford and Tutorial Fellow at Magdalen College. He works on Greek literature, especially lyric and drama, and has an interest in approaches drawn from the cognitive sciences. He is the author of *The Language of Sophocles: Communality, Communication and Involvement* (Cambridge, 2000) and *Greek Lyric: A Selection* (Cambridge, 2018), as well as editor of *The Cambridge Companion to Greek Lyric* (Cambridge, 2009) and co-editor of *Choruses, Ancient and Modern* (Oxford, 2013; with J. Billings and F. Macintosh) and *Textual Events: Performance and the Lyric in Early Greece* (Oxford, 2018; with T. Phillips).

Laurel Fulkerson is Associate Vice President for Research and Professor of Classics at Florida State University where she specializes in Latin and Greek poetry and gender in antiquity. Her recent works include the monographs *The Ovidian Heroine as Author: Reading, Writing, and Community in the Heroides* (Cambridge, 2005), *No Regrets: Remorse in Classical Antiquity* (Oxford, 2013), and *A Literary Commentary on the Elegies of the Appendix Tibulliana* (Oxford, 2017) as well as articles on Latin and Greek poetry and prose. Her ongoing research interests cluster around the representation of emotions in the ancient world, the relationship of epic and history, and Latin elegy.

Jonas Grethlein is Professor of Classics at Heidelberg University. His scholarship covers a wide range of topics in Greek literature, art, and culture, with key monographs including *Experience and Teleology in Ancient Historiography: Futures Past from Herodotus to Augustine* (Cambridge, 2013) and *Aesthetic Experiences and Classical Antiquity: The Content of Form in Narratives and Pictures* (Cambridge, 2017). He is co-editor of *Time and Narrative in Ancient Historiography: The 'Plupast' from Herodotus to Appian* (Cambridge, 2012; paperback 2016; with C. Krebs) and *Narratology and Interpretation: The Content of Narrative Form in Ancient Literature* (Berlin 2009, paperback 2016; with A. Rengakos) and Principal Investigator of the ERC-funded research project Experience and Teleology in Ancient Narrative (AncNar).

Irene J. F. de Jong is Professor of Ancient Greek at the University of Amsterdam. A pioneer in applying concepts from narratology to ancient texts, notably Homer, Herodotus, Sophocles, and Euripides, she has opened new areas of research, refined interpretations, and modernized philological tools such as commentaries and literary histories. Her books include the monographs *Narrators and Focalizers: The Presentation of the Story in the Iliad* (Amsterdam, 1987; 2nd edn. London, 2004), *A Narratological Commentary on the Odyssey* (Cambridge, 2001), *Homer Iliad Book XXII* (Cambridge, 2012), and *Narratology and Classics: A Practical Guide* (Oxford, 2014) as well as the edited volumes *Narrators, Narratees, and Narratives in Ancient Greek Literature* (Leiden, 2004; with R. Nünlist, A. Bowie), *Time in Ancient Greek Literature* (Leiden, 2007, with R. Nünlist), and *Space in Ancient Greek Literature* (Leiden, 2012). She is currently writing a narratological commentary on Herodotus.

Talitha Kearey is a Junior Research Fellow at St John's College, Cambridge, following a position as Stipendiary Lecturer at Magdalen College, Oxford. Her research focuses on interactions between authorial self-fashioning and readers' creative reception: she is currently preparing her doctoral thesis, *The Poet at Work: Concepts of Authorship in the Ancient Reception of Virgil*, for publication, and has recently published articles on the pseudo-Virgilian *Culex* and on acrostics in Horace's *Satires*. Her wider research interests include poetics and metapoetics, literary and cultural theory, and the history of scholarship.

Duncan Kennedy is Emeritus Professor of Latin Literature and the Theory of Criticism at the University of Bristol. His publications cover a wide range of Latin writers and their reception in later periods and frequently address topics at the intersection of literary criticism, critical theory, and philosophy. In addition to numerous journal article and book chapters, he has published *The Arts of Love: Five Studies in the Discourse of Roman Love Elegy* (Cambridge, 1993) and *Rethinking Reality: Lucretius and the Textualisation of Nature* (Ann Arbor, 2002), and *Antiquity and the Meanings of Time: A Philosophy of Ancient and Modern Literature* (London, 2013).

Helen Lovatt is Professor of Classics at the University of Nottingham. Her research focuses on Latin epic and its reception, with broader interests in Greek and Latin epic, other aspects of Latin literature, Roman social and cultural history, and the reception of classical antiquity, especially in detective fiction and children's literature. Key publications include the monographs *Statius and Epic Games: Sport, Politics and Poetics in the Thebaid* (Cambridge, 2005) and *The Epic Gaze: Vision, Gender and Narrative in Ancient Epic* (Cambridge, 2013) and the edited volume *Epic Visions: Visuality in Greek and Latin Epic and Its Reception* (Cambridge, 2013; with C. Vout). Her current research project is a cultural history of the Argonautic myth, from its earliest beginnings up to its most recent reworkings.

Sebastian Matzner is Senior Lecturer in Comparative Literature and Director of Queer@King's at King's College London. His research focuses on interactions between ancient and modern literature and thought, especially in the fields of poetics and rhetoric, literary and critical theory, history of sexualities, and LGBTQ studies. He has published several articles and book chapters in these fields and is the author of *Rethinking Metonymy: Literary Theory and Poetic Practice from Pindar to Jakobson* (Oxford University Press, 2016) as well as co-editor of *Complex Inferiorities: The Poetics of the Weaker Voice in Latin Literature* (Oxford University Press, 2018; with S. Harrison).

Gail Trimble is Associate Professor in Classical Languages and Literature at the University of Oxford and Brown Fellow and Tutor in Classics at Trinity College. Her commentary on Catullus 64, with newly edited text, is forthcoming in the Cambridge University Press 'orange' series Cambridge Classical Texts and Commentaries. Her wider research interests focus on Latin poetry and literary form, and she has published book chapters on Catullus, Virgil, and Ovid as well as work interrogating the history of scholarship as reception. She is planning a future project on the personal names of pastoral literature.

1

By Way of Introduction

Back to the Future?

Problems and Potential of Metalepsis *avant* Genette

Sebastian Matzner

'At the beginning of the twentieth century, "metaphor" was one of the rare terms to survive the great shipwreck of rhetoric, and this survival is obviously neither fortuitous nor insignificant.'[1] What Genette said about metaphor in his polemic on the decline of rhetoric, 'La rhétorique restreinte' ('Rhetoric restrained') of 1970, could be said about metalepsis at the beginning of the twenty-first century. If anything, metalepsis not only survived but flourished more than ever. Its core characteristics and features seem to strike a chord with contemporary thought in a way that metaphor does not, making metalepsis appear especially attuned to high postmodern sensitivities. Whether one thinks of postmodernism's predilection for dismantling solidly ordered narratives (meta- or otherwise); its democratic impulses of participatory co-construction of meaning (not by one all-powerful, but through several interacting and interdependent agents); or its joyful overturning of ontological and epistemological one-time certainties—it is easy to see how all of these resonate strongly with the dynamics that lie at the very heart of metalepsis. Yet whatever its timeliness in the landscape of contemporary critical thinking, the very fact that metalepsis should have been granted such a new lease of life through its narratological reinvention is in itself remarkable. After all, the phenomena discussed today under the lemma 'metalepsis' could have easily been

---

[1] Genette (1970: 114).

Sebastian Matzner, *By Way of Introduction: Back to the Future?: Problems and Potential of Metalepsis* avant *Genette* In: *Metalepsis: Ancient Texts, New Perspectives.* Edited by: Sebastian Matzner and Gail Trimble, Oxford University Press (2020). © The editors and Oxford University Press.
DOI: 10.1093/oso/9780198846987.003.0001

grouped under an altogether new heading, something with the typical Genette ring to it, like 'transdiegetic intrusion'. Instead, Genette appeals to a term from the rhetorical tradition, and takes it into a decidedly new direction. And this is not a singular event in twentieth-century criticism, quite the contrary: the debris and flotsam of the great shipwreck of rhetoric has been repeatedly put to constructive use. Whether we think of metalepsis, metaphor, metonymy, or allegory—all of these have been subject to what we might call 'conceptual squatting'. Once more or less clearly circumscribed forms of stylized language, elaborated in the rhetorical treatises of antiquity and the classical tradition, twentieth-century theoreticians deemed them sufficiently disused to be ripe for occupation. Genette, Jakobson, de Man, Lodge, and many other theoreticians (re)turned to these tropes, and filled them with new meanings. More often than not, they did so by way of radically extending their original scope to incorporate further dimensions or levels of verbal expression (or indeed further varieties of both verbal and non-verbal discourse).[2] While never entirely without some sort of genealogical connection to their prehistory in poetics, rhetoric, and stylistics, these structuralist and post-structuralist reinventions of terms from classical tropology often sit somewhat awkwardly and uncomfortably next to their classical counterparts, which they have frequently sidelined and eclipsed in critical discourse and parlance. The case lies a bit as with those comparative 'before' and 'after' pictures, popular in advertising: one is somewhat unsure whether it is actually the same person that is portrayed in the two images, but it is certainly apparent which one is supposed to be the more attractive one. Picking up Genette's deliberations on the fate of metaphor in the more recent history of rhetoric, it therefore seems a valid question to ponder whether the survival of metalepsis in this context is to be considered 'fortuitous' and 'significant'—or not.

What this introductory chapter offers is not a history of ideas. Rather than unfolding a genealogy of the concept's development and transformation from classical rhetoric to structuralist and post-structuralist criticism, the preliminary considerations set out here instead seek to mobilize earlier theorizations of metalepsis for a critical reappraisal of current thinking about metalepsis. Returning once more to metalepsis *avant* Genette thus serves the purpose of casting into relief (and tentatively addressing) some of the fault lines that have emerged in recent debates

[2] See e.g. Genette (1966–2002), Jakobson (1956), de Man (1979), Lodge (1977), White 1973.

and publications on the topic, which necessarily involves looking ahead at several of the issues that the subsequent chapters will investigate in much greater detail.

Before turning to earlier conceptualizations of metalepsis to problematize some issues in current theorizing, it is useful to begin with a very brief sketch of the common starting position of scholarly debate in this field by revisiting the types of metalepsis discussed by Genette in *Discours du récit* ('Narrative Discourse', 1972).[3] Once these are before us, the discussion will centre on what *sort* of phenomena we are looking at here and what they might have in common with metalepsis *avant* Genette. In particular, I will draw on the classical differentiation between tropes and figures—now often, and unhelpfully, blurred or abandoned—which, I think, can serve as an important criterion to get a better handle on some of the tensions that underlie contemporary conceptualizations of metalepsis.

In the context of his famous definition of metalepsis as 'any intrusion by the extradiegetic narrator or narratee into the diegetic universe (or by diegetic characters into a metadiegetic universe, etc.), or the inverse,'[4] Genette discusses five expressions which this general principle can assume:[5]

Author(ial) metalepsis—classic example: 'Vergil has Dido die'[6]—points to the author as an involved narrator, actively shaping the plot, rather than telling a story over which they have no power. The conveyor *of* the story here becomes visible as a formative force active *in* the story world, equivalent to 'god'/'fate'/'chance'/'history'/'natural or social laws' and the like in the extrafictional world. This is often considered to be undermining realistic expectations of literal truth-telling,[7] but it can also be seen as an

---

[3] It goes without saying that notions and typologies of metalepsis have proliferated since Genette's seminal publication. A round-up of recent theoretical contributions that, to varying degrees, build on and/or diverge from Genette is offered by Grethlein and Kearey in this volume: see below, p. 28 n. 7 and p. 197 n. 9, respectively. Given its foundational status and lasting influence as a touchstone for thinking about metalepsis, it still seems legitimate to return here to Genette as the archete of modern theorizing of metalepsis before attempting to probe modern theory from the perspectives of ancient critics.

[4] '[Metalepsis is] any intrusion by the extradiegetic narrator or narratee into the diegetic universe (or by diegetic characters into a metadiegetic universe, etc.), or the inverse (as in Cortázar), [and] produces an effect of strangeness that is either comical (when, as in Sterne and Diderot, it is presented in a joking tone) or fantastic.' Genette (1972 = 1980: 234–5).

[5] The following exposition broadly follows Fludernik (2003b: 383–9).

[6] It is worth pointing out that such English translations of 'Vergile fait mourir Didon', famously cited and popularized by Genette (1972: 244), flatten out the crucial ambivalence of 'kills her' and 'has her die' that characterize 'faire mourir' and constitute the metaleptic pun(chline) in the French original. For further discussion of the complexities this entails, see below, pp. 6–8ff. as well as Kearey, Lovatt, Trimble, and Matzner/Trimble in this volume.

[7] Fludernik (2003b: 384).

epistemological reality check, given that it foregrounds and highlights two things: (*a*) the hierarchical structuredness of truth statements that we pragmatically engage with as 'truths', but as truths relative to each other (namely according to the different levels and layers of 'reality' on which we encounter them); and (*b*) the presence of validating entities—be they agents, scripts, or premises—that underwrite and shape 'truths' on each of these levels. The chapters by Kearey and Kennedy in particular offer further exploration of these issues: Kearey by examining the narrativization of authors themselves, as characters and narrative agents or presences, that occurs when critics engage with their narratives; Kennedy by probing the metaphysical implications of the acts of narrative framing by which all human subjects-as-authors process, order, and project their empirical experiences—and break in on each other's narratives as we establish what to accept as our 'reality'.

Closely related to this, but removed from the threshold between extra-fictional reality and story world, is *narrator metalepsis*, in which a narrator moves down a narrative level within the story world. Apostrophes by the narrator addressed to characters in the narrative they tell, such as the ones in Pindar discussed by De Jong and those in Catullus discussed by Trimble in this volume, are prime examples. Narrator metalepsis thus consists in the consolidated presence of the narratorial voice on the level of the story, so much so that it seems, as Fludernik puts it, 'physically present in the story world by means of an implicit anthropomorphic metaphor'.[8] 'Metaphor' is an interesting word to use in this context, and I will come back to this later.

Conversely, in *narratee metalepsis*, it is a narratee who shifts to another story level, such as in moments when the extradiegetic narratee becomes implicated on the story level, for instance when the extrafictional reader is directly addressed by a protagonist or when a diegetic protagonist becomes an intradiegetic narratee on a further narrative level. A particular issue that arises here is that of the underdetermined personal pronouns 'I' and 'you'. Irrespective of their contextual use, both lend themselves to being (also) inhabited by the extradiegetic reader: for the (extraliterary) 'I' that reads also vocalizes the text, and thereby aligns itself—at least temporarily, partially, or potentially—with the (literary) 'I' that speaks—while occupying

---

[8] Fludernik (2003b: 385). According to Fludernik (2003b: 384–5), the arising effect is illusionistic rather than anti-illusionistic: 'imaginative projection of the narrator into the story draws the reader more closely into the fiction' (385).

in the same act of reading also and simultaneously the position of the immediate opposite number, the directly addressed 'you' of that speaking 'I'.[9] The resulting complications and complexities find further discussion and analysis in Budelmann's and De Jong's chapters.

Not so much agents in their relation to narrative levels, but actions and their temporal relation take centre stage in *discourse metalepsis*. Here, the narrator fills either 'empty' or 'frozen' time during a narrative with an intervention that acknowledges both the pause in narrative action and its filling by the narrator (for instance with further background information). What thereby becomes palpable is a peculiar temporality, namely the simultaneity of the narrated events and the act of narration. This is often realized through the use of 'while' to connect narrative action and narratorial intervention, which, with the chronological alignment of the two on a shared temporal plane, facilitates an approximation of two narrative levels to the point of a perceived merger.[10] Bing's chapter investigates related phenomena and ponders how far strategically deployed anachronisms can facilitate metaleptic effects.

Lastly, Genette spends considerable time on pseudo-diegetic or reduced metadiegetic narrative constellations; for short, one might simply say: *pseudo-metalepsis*. This is a sort of 'metaleptic creep' in which an embedded narrative gradually usurps the status of a higher-level narrative, typically with the frame narrator assuming the role of the intradiegetic narrator.[11] Classic examples from ancient literature are extended ekphraseis, such as in Catullus 64, whose multiple metaleptic manoeuvres receive a fresh examination in Trimble's chapter, but also other multilayered

---

[9] See Genette (2004: 109–11). Compared to his earlier notions of narrative metalepsis, Genette here significantly broadens the scope of this phenomenon, going so far as to suggest that '[o]ne can, therefore, consider as metaleptic any statement about oneself/a self [tout énoncé sur soi]...including any narrative...that includes or develops such a statement. This form of metalepsis is without doubt less obviously fantastic than the others, but in a sly manner it is at the heart of everything we can say or think of ourselves, if it is true—and it is—that I am always also an other [que *je* est toujours *aussi* un autre].' Genette (2004: 110; unless otherwise indicated, translations are my own).

[10] The nexus of temporal-spatial-narrative transgressions at issue here is very subtle, elusive, and hard to rationalize. Fludernik's reflections are instructive: 'I realized that the projected simultaneity metaphorically moves the narrator into the realm of the fictional world that I started to see that where the boundary crossing might be located. In order to be able to talk while the cleric is climbing the stairs, the extradiegetic narrator [in Balzac's *Illusions perdues*, discussed by Genette (1972 = 1980: 65)] would have to be located *in* the story, otherwise the *while* cannot link the same kind of temporality.' Fludernik (2003b: 387).

[11] Some critics have reservations as to whether this type of metalepsis should feature in critical discussions of the phenomenon. Thus Fludernik decides: 'I will from now on eliminate type 5 from discussion because I do not consider it to be properly metaleptic.' Fludernik (2003b: 388).

narratives, such as in the second book of Vergil's *Aeneid*, whose various slippages (notably the shift in focalization from Aeneas' story to Sinon's story) Lovatt examines as part of her broader exploration of the emotional work metalepsis can enable and facilitate.

A good starting point for moving backwards from here to look at metalepsis *avant* Genette is to examine Genette's own connection of his notion of metalepsis with that of the classical rhetorical tradition, that is, the Greco-Roman classics as mediated by the French classics; in his case specifically Fontanier revising Dumarsais. In *Discours du récit*, Genette takes Cortázar's story 'Continuidad de los parques' and the expression 'Vergil "has Dido die" in Book IV of the *Aeneid*' as his point of departure:

> Cortázar tells the story of a man assassinated by one of the characters in the novel he is reading; this is the inverse (and extreme) form of the narrative figure the classics called author's metalepsis, which consists of pretending that the poet "himself brings about the effects he celebrates", as when we say that Virgil "has Dido die" in Book IV of the *Aeneid*...[12]

As Nauta has pointed out, Genette's move of framing metalepsis as a 'narrative figure' facilitates a seemingly smooth derivation of the term from rhetoric for subsequent use in narratology,[13] and he repeats this manoeuvre in the very subtitle and the opening pages of his more recent work on metalepsis, the 2004 monograph *Metalépse: De la figure à la fiction* ('Metalepsis: From Figure to Fiction'), where he expounds at greater length on the purported connection between the metalepsis of classical French rhetoric and modern narratology. I want to put some pressure on his line of argument in making this connection and problematize some of the consequences this proposed connection has for critical practice.

Genette's argument revolves, as it were, around two pivots which he is keen to bring to the point of convergence: one etymological, one tropological. On the etymological side, he plays with the root of *fingere* that stands behind both *figure* and *fiction*:

[12] Genette (1972 = 1980: 234). The citation is from Fontanier (1818: 116). On the ambivalence of the expression in the French original, see above, p. 3 n. 6. For further discussions of this sentence and its implications, see also Kearey, Lovatt, Trimble, and Matzner/Trimble in this volume.
[13] Nauta (2013a: 479). On the rhetorical trope metalepsis and its narratological reception and reinvention in the late twentieth century, see also Hanebeck (2017: 11–22).

When I consider… 'to follow some of the paths theoretically opened by this definition', I essentially mean extending the investigation from the simple *figure*, even in several words (*figurative* metalepsis), to what we must call *fiction* (*fictional* metalepsis), and which is for me a widened mode of the figure… I do not need to recall the common root of these two words, which is found in the Latin verb *fingere*, which means to 'shape', 'represent', 'pretend' and 'invent'; the names *fictio* and *figura*, ancestors of our 'fiction' and 'figure', both derive from this verb… Without abusing the etymological argument, it is not adventurous to find a kinship between these two notions. I have just said that fiction is 'a wider mode of the figure' because I propose to pass from one to the other by extensions, but we shall see that it is rather a reinforced or aggravated mode. It is doubtless easier to conceive the thing in the other direction: a figure is (already) a little fiction, in that double sense that it usually holds in a few words, even in a single word, and in that its character is fictitious and somewhat attenuated by the smallness of its vehicle and often by the frequency of its use, which prevent one from perceiving the boldness of its semantic motif: only use and convention make us accept as banal a metaphor like 'to declare one's flame', a metonymy like 'to drink a glass', or a hyperbole like 'to die of laughter'. The figure is an embryo, or, if one prefers, a sketch of fiction.[14]

---

[14] 'Quand j'envisage… de "suivre quelques-unes de voies théoriquement ouvertes par cette définition", j'entends essentiellement par là étendre l'enquête en passant de la simple *figure*, fût-elle en plusieurs mots (métalepse *figurale*), à ce qu'il faut bien appeler la *fiction* (métalepse *fictionnelle*), et qui est pour moi un mode élargi de la figure… Je n'ai pas besoin de rappeler la racine commune de ces deux mots, qu'on trouve dans le verbe latin *fingere*, qui signifie à la fois "façonner", "représenter", "feindre" et "inventer"; les noms *fictio* et *figura*, ancêtres des nos *fiction* et *figure*, dérive tous deux de ce verbe… Sans abuser de l'argument étymologique, il n'est pas aventureux de trouver une parenté entre ces deux notions. Je viens de dire que la fiction était "un mode élargi de la figure" parce que je me propose de passer de l'une à l'autre par extensions, mais nous verrons qu'elle en est plutôt un mode renforcé, ou aggravé. Il est sans doute plus facile de concevoir la chose en prenant dans l'autre sens: une figure est (déjà) une petite fiction, en ce double sens qu'elle tient généralement en peu de mots, voire en un seul, et que son caractère est fictionnel et en quelque sorte atténué par l'exiguïté de son véhicule et, souvent, par la fréquence de son emploi, qui empêchent de percevoir la hardiesse de son motif sémantique: seuls l'usage et la convention nous font accepter comme banale une métaphore comme "déclarer sa flamme", une métonymie comme "boire un verre", ou une hyperbole comme "mort de rire". La figure est un embryon, ou, si l'on préfère, une esquisse de fiction.' Genette (2004: 16–17). Both the reuse and reinvention of available critical categories and the expansionist move from a micro-level category to macro-level considerations here mirror Genette's mode of thinking in his earlier work, notably the description of any narrative as the expansion of an action and, therefore, of a verb, which triggers the recasting of the grammatical categories of 'tense', 'mood', and 'voice' in narratological terms; cf. Genette (1972 = 1980: 30–1).

On the tropological side, he plays with metonymic expressions that variously implicate authors and/or narrators on the story level. Thus, the aforementioned 'Vergil has Dido die in Book IV' can be read metonymically as 'Vergil's narrative of the *Aeneid* has Dido die in Book IV'; just as a passage from Boileau's *L'art poétique*, cited by Genette as a further illustrative example,[15] in which the critic chides the poet Saint-Amant for his dry-as-dust epic *Moyse sauvé* (1653) with the words 'He [sc. the author] followed Moses over desert sands | and drowned, both he and Pharaoh, in those lands',[16] can be read metonymically as 'The narrative of *Moyse sauvé* followed Moses over desert sands' and 'both the pharaoh in the narrative and the narrative itself are hapless and ill-fated'.[17] The association of metalepsis with metonymy can be traced over the course of the rhetorical tradition,[18] and the connection drawn between metalepsis, metonymy, and examples like the ones mentioned by Genette consists in the relationship of producer and product.[19] This relationship is one of the countless relationships that can be detected in metonymic expressions, and Genette argues that metalepsis can be understood as the specific case in which the producer of a representation is united with that representation itself:

[15]   Genette (1972 = 1980: 234 n. 49).

[16]   'Et, poursuivant Moïse au travers des déserts, | Court avec Pharaon se noyer dans les mers'. Boileau (1674 = 2007), *L'art poétique* 1.25–6; trans. Raffel.

[17]   Admittedly, something more complex than straightforward metonymy on its own is at play in the second part of the sentence: it hinges on the conditional metaphor 'drowned'—literal for the character ('pharaoh') *within* the narrative, metaphorical for the author ('he') *of* the narrative—but the authorial 'he' itself nevertheless clearly points metonymically to the *product* of the author's work, i.e. the criticized epic poem, rather than to the *producer* himself.

[18]   Quintilian addresses metalepsis as the last of the 'tropes that modify signification', which subsume inter alia also metonymy (*Inst.* 8.6.37–8; see below, p. 15 for further discussion of this passage) and Donatus addresses metalepsis in his chapter *De tropis* between metaphor/catachresis and metonymy (Don. *Ars Gramm.* 400 (*Grammatici Latini*, ed. Keil, vol. iv); also discussed in more detail below, see p. 16). Looking back to this classical tradition, Dumarsais states: 'Metalepsis is a kind of metonymy, by which one explains what follows in order to convey that which comes first; or [one explains] what comes first in order to convey that which follows: metalepsis opens, so to speak, the door, says Quintilian, in order that you may move from one idea to the other; *ex alio in aliud viam praestat* ['makes a path from one thing to another' = Quint. *Inst.* 8.6.37]: and it is always the play of associated ideas from among whom one gives rise to the other' ('La métalepse est une espèce de métonymie, par laquelle on explique ce qui suit pour faire entendre ce qui précède; ou ce qui précède pour faire entendre ce qui suit: elle ouvre, pour ainsi dire, la porte, dit Quintilien, afin que vous passiez d'une idée à une autre; *ex alio in aliud viam praestat*: c'est l'antécédent pour le conséquent, ou le conséquent pour l'antécédent, et c'est toujours le jeu des idées accessoires, dont l'une reveille l'autre'). Dumarsais (1730: 110).

[19]   Cf. also Genette (2004: 11–12) as well as the discussion of the metonymic use of 'author' for 'work' in Servius and Fulgentius by Kearey in this volume, p. 211.

But first of all, and since the concept of metonymy includes, among other modes or motives of transfer, the designation of the effect by the cause, or vice versa, I think it is reasonable to reserve the term metalepsis henceforth for a manipulation—at least figurative, but sometimes fictional (I shall come back to this gradation)—of this particular causal relationship, which unites, in one sense or the other, the author and their work, or more widely the producer of a representation and this representation itself. I therefore leave aside, in the broader field of metonymy, other well-known cases of the relationship between producer and production, such as that which makes it possible to designate an invention by the name of its inventor...and I say 'representation' to cover both the literary domain and some others: painting, theatre, photography, cinema...A special case of metonymy, metalepsis thus defined has therefore as its canonical investment the aforementioned 'author(ial) metalepsis', but its field... extends to other modes of transgression, figurative or fictional, at the threshold of representation.[20]

Nauta has taken issue with Genette's appeal to metonymy as a way of connecting rhetorical metalepsis and narrative metalepsis by arguing that the 'manipulation' of causal relations that occurs in narrative metalepsis is different from the 'substitution' of cause for effect (and vice versa) in rhetorical metalepsis, with the former constituting a disruptive, interfering *modification* of conventional narrative procedures, and the latter constituting a *replacement* of words.[21] A problem with this line of criticism arises from its underpinning commitment to a substitutionalist understanding

---

[20] 'Mais tout d'abord, et puisque le concept de métonymie comporte, entre autres modes ou motifs de transfert, la désignation de l'effet par la cause ou réciproquement, je crois raisonnable de réserver désormais le terme métalepse à une manipulation—au moins figurale, mais parfois fictionnelle (je vais revenir sur cette gradation)—de cette relations causale particulière qui unit, dans un sens ou dans l'autre, l'auteur et son ouvre, ou plus largement le producteur d'une représentation à cette représentation elle-même. Je laisse donc de cote, dans le champ plus vaste de la métonymie, d'autres cas bien connu de la relation entre producteur et production, telle que celle qui permet de désigner une invention par le nom de son inventeur, comme le cardan ou la poubelle, et je dis "représentation" pour couvrir à la fois le domaine littéraire et quelques autres: peinture, théâtre, photographie, cinéma, et j'en oublie sans doute. Cas particulier de la métonymie, la métalepse ainsi définie a donc pour investissement canonique ladite "métalepse de l'auteur", mais son champ, nous le verrons, s'étend bien d'autres modes de transgression, figurale ou fictionnelle, du seuil de la représentation.' Genette (2004: 13–14).

[21] 'When an author is represented as causing what he narrates, this may be called a "manipulation" of the "causal relation that unites...the author and his work", but it is not a substitution of the author for the work (at most it is a substitution of one metonymical relation—causing—for another—narrating).' Nauta (2013a: 479).

of tropes. In theory of metaphor, notions of replacement and substitution—with their undesirable associations of one-to-one equivalence and quasi-synonymy—have long given way to theories that highlight the importance of interaction that occurs in tropes. This change in approach allows us to give due account of the semantic and aesthetic surplus such interaction generates through its concomitant terminological and conceptual frictions;[22] something that notions of substitution generally fail to do. For the same reason it is highly desirable that we should also move beyond a substitutionalist understanding of metonymy in order to better appreciate the various effects caused by metonymic shifts.[23] Adopting this perspective in fact results in a notion of metonymy that comes relatively close to Genette's formulations: metonymy as a disruptive 'manipulation' of lexical choices, rather than a 'substitution' of words. Yet Nauta is undoubtedly right to insist that this particular passage in Genette requires scrutiny and that Genette's manoeuvre here is slippery—but the crucial slippage appears to me to lie elsewhere: if metalepsis is indeed a variant of metonymy (as Genette holds), and if metonymy is a trope, then Genette moves here from *trope* to fiction, not from *figure* to fiction. The slippage between trope and figure may seem insignificant and perhaps barely noticeable, given how the two are used virtually interchangeably in much contemporary critical discourse (including Genette's own writings), but an important distinction gets lost if we give up this differentiation. The point here is not to be a stickler about terminology and to rain on Genette's etymological parade, but to draw out a fundamental ambiguity that can be seen as a covert source of complications in the conceptual development of metalepsis.

So what is the difference between a trope and a figure, and why does it matter?[24] When viewing poetic language in a formalist manner as a phenomenon of aesthetically and/or semantically effective defamiliarized language usage, it becomes possible to explore and differentiate further how such defamiliarizing deviation from ordinary language usage may occur on various levels and in different ways. Shklovsky's introduction of the term and concept of defamiliarization includes a mapping out of the different areas in which this poetic activity can take place:

In studying poetic speak [sic] in its phonetic and lexical structure as well as in its characteristic distribution of words and in the characteristic

---

[22] See Richards (1936), Black (1962), and Silk (1974).   [23] See Matzner (2016b).
[24] For a more detailed exposition of the argument summarized in what follows, see Matzner (2016b: 30–6).

thought structures compounded from the words, we find everywhere the artistic trademark—that is, we find material obviously created to remove the automatism of perception; the author's purpose is to create the vision which results from that deautomatised perception.[25]

From early on ancient critics were sensitive to this 'artistic trademark' of deviance from ordinary usage and worked towards a systematic understanding of the different forms such deviation could take.[26] Building on an already established tradition,[27] Cicero offers the following contrastive definitions of tropes and figures:

The Greeks consider that language is embellished if such changes of words [*uerborum immutationibus*] are employed as they call tropes [τρόπους], and such formations of thought and language [*sententiarum orationisque formis*] as they call figures [σχήματα]...[28]

Now there are almost countless ways of shaping both words and thoughts into figures, as I am well aware that you know. But between the formations [*sc.* figures] of speech and of thought [*conformationem uerborum et sententiarum*] there is this difference, that those of speech disappear if you change the words, while those of thought remain no matter what words you choose to employ.[29]

---

[25] Shklovsky (1917: 19); emphasis added.

[26] The terms most frequently used in ancient Greek criticism that give evidence of this sensitivity are κύριος/κυρίως ('having power/authority (like/of a ruler)', hence 'authoritative', 'legitimate', 'valid', 'proper', 'principal/important'; cf. e.g. Arist. *Rhet.* 1404b6, 1410b12; Arist. *Poet.* 1457b3; D.H. *Comp.* 21) and κυριολογία/κυριολεξία ('ruling/authoritative/proper speech', that is, 'proper (*sc.* literal) usage/meaning of a word'; cf. e.g. Tryph. *Trop.* [= *Rhetores Graeci*, ed. Spengel, vol. iii] 728.5; Longin. *De Subl.* 28.1), all of which denote ordinary, standard language usage as the foundational framework and foil against which deviant usages can be discerned, described, and analysed.

[27] The exact historical development of the distinction cannot be reconstructed for lack of surviving textual evidence. As Innes (1995: 313-4) rightly notes, 'We have only fragmentary knowledge of literary and rhetorical theory between Aristotle and authors of the first century BC, a period including Theophrastus' *On Style* (περὶ λέξεως) and the development of the theories of styles, tropes, and figures, which we see in the works of Cicero and his contemporaries.' It seems most likely that the theory of tropes was a Hellenistic development; see Barwick (1957: 88-111) and Russell (1981: 143-7). While the distinction between tropes and figures is not present in early theory, it appears fairly clearly defined in the rhetorical writings of Cicero and Dionysius of Halicarnassus (see Schenkeveld 1964: 147) and then features as a—critically discussed—orthodoxy in Quintilian (see Quint. *Inst.* 9.1.1-18).

[28] *ornari orationem Graeci putant, si uerborum immutationibus utantur, quos appellant τρόπους, et sententiarum orationisque formis, quae uocant σχήματα*...Cic. *Brut.* 69; trans. Hendrickson (adapted).

[29] *formantur autem et uerba et sententiae paene innumerabiliter, quod satis scio notum esse uobis; sed inter conformationem uerborum et sententiarum hoc interest, quod uerborum*

What differentiating characteristics between tropes and figures emerge here? Tropes are based on some sort of 'change' that affects individual words while figures (both of thought and of speech) are all about the arrangement of a given idea into a specific form that follows a describable shape or pattern. Figures of thought thereby follow and exhibit a shape or pattern that finds expression in (the meaning of) a larger unit—a sentence or comparable sequence—without being dependent on the concrete individual words used. Existing at a certain remove from the specificities of linguistic expression, they are chiefly abstract, intellectual structures.[30] Figures of speech, by contrast, depend on the precise word(s) used, since the characteristic figurative conformation is achieved here by exploiting the phonetic, syntactic, etymological, and other linguistic properties of the concrete words used.[31] Tropes are different from both of them. Quintilian defines tropes as 'a shift of a word or phrase from its proper meaning to another, in a way that has positive value'[32] and sets them apart from the figures:

> The name of trope is applied to the transference of expressions from their natural and principal signification to another (*a naturali et principali significatione tralatus*), with a view to the embellishment of style or, as the majority of grammarians define it, the transference of words and phrases from the place which is strictly theirs to another to which they do not properly belong (*dictio ab eo loco tralata in eum in quo propria non est*). A figure, on the other hand, as is clear from the name itself, is the term employed when we give our language a conformation (*conformatio quaedam orationis*) other than the obvious and ordinary.[33]

---

tollitur, si uerba mutaris, sententiarum permanet, quibuscumque uerbis uti uelis. Cic. *de Orat.* 3.200; trans. May and Wisse (adapted).

[30] Cf. Auct. ad Her. 4.18: *sententiarum exornatio est quae non in uerbis, sed in ipsis rebus quandam habet dignitatem* ('A figure of thought derives a certain distinction from the idea, not from the words'; trans. Caplan; or rather: 'Embellishment of ideas is that kind of embellishment which involves a certain distinction not in the words used but in the content itself').

[31] Cf. Auct. ad Her. 4.18: *uerborum exornatio est quae ipsius sermonis insignita continetur perpolitione* ('It is a figure of diction if the adornment is comprised of the fine polish of the language itself'; trans. Caplan). Note that neither this passage nor the one quoted in the note above has the technical term *figura* ('figure') in the Latin original, which instead speaks of *exornatio* ('embellishment') of either *sententiae* ('ideas', 'thoughts') or *verba* ('words'); however, this terminological issue does not affect the principle behind the distinction, which is what matters here.

[32] Quint. *Inst.* 8.6.1; trans. Russell.

[33] *est igitur tropos sermo a naturali et principali significatione tralatus ad aliam ornandae orationis gratia, vel, ut plerique grammatici finiunt, dictio ab eo loco in quo propria est tralata in eum in quo propria non est: 'figura', sicut nomine ipso patet, conformatio quaedam orationis remota a communi et primum se offerente ratione.* Quint. *Inst.* 9.1.4; trans. Russell.

Like Cicero, Quintilian, too, suggests that the key characteristic of tropes consists in a shift or change in the meaning of words that results from their usage outside their usual context, which makes it impossible to understand them as one would according to their standard usage. The common feature and signature trait of figures, on the other hand, is that they transform the mode of expression; that is to say, a figurative expression differs noticeably from ordinary forms of unstructured or unstylized usage, but not in a way that would affect the meaning of any of the words it contains.[34] Unlike tropes, which are characterized by such deviance from and subversion of the usual semantic order of standard language, figures, so Quintilian, rather assume the natural properties of words:

> We speak as if every kind of language possessed a figure: for example 'cursitare' and 'lectitare' are said to have the same figure, that is to say, they are identical in formation. Therefore in the first and common sense of the word everything is expressed by figures.[35]

It is the orchestrated exploitation of the natural, unchanged properties of words (including their meanings in ordinary language) that constitutes figurative language in the narrow sense:

> If, on the other hand, the name ['figure'] is to be applied to certain attitudes, or I might say gestures of language, we must interpret *schema* [sc. figure] in the sense of that which is poetically or rhetorically altered from the simple and obvious method of expression.[36]

Building on these ancient efforts to differentiate and characterize the two main modes of poetic language, 'tropes' and 'figures' might be defined as follows:

Figures prominently deploy a given word or group of words while assuming their current meaning, whereas tropes redefine their meaning, since they entail a 'turn' away from their meaning in ordinary usage to an

---

[34] Cf. Quint. *Inst.* 9.1.7: *nam et propriis uerbis et ordine conlocatis figura fieri potest* ('For a figure does not necessarily involve any alteration either of the order or the strict sense of words'; trans. Russell).

[35] *ita loquimur tamquam omnis sermo habeat figuram. itemque eadem figura dicitur 'cursitare' qua 'lectitare', id est eadem ratione declinari. quare illo intellectu priore et communi nihil non figuratum est.* Quint. *Inst.* 9.1.12; trans. Russell.

[36] *sed si habitus quidam et quasi gestus sic appellandi sunt, id demum hoc loco accipi schema oportebit quod sit a simplici atque in promptu posito dicendi modo poetice uel oratorie mutatum.* Quint. *Inst.* 9.1.13; trans. Russell.

unforeseen, new meaning that must be inferred to render the sequence comprehensible. While both of these two modes of poetic usage tend towards defamiliarization through deviance from ordinary language usage, the semantic surplus of figures is external to the meaning of the words in question; it is generated by exploiting, and thereby rendering visible, their given properties (phonetic structure, syntactic position, conventional denotative meaning, and so on) in correspondence with their context and in amplification of the ordinary meaning of these words. The semantic surplus of tropes, on the other hand, is internal; it affects the meaning of the words and is generated by using words in a way and context that invests the ordinary word with a new, extraordinary meaning without which no sense can be made of the sequence.

What does this mean for our understanding of metalepsis? In ancient rhetoric, where not concerned with metalepsis as a *status* in legal proceedings, that is, with the raising of an 'issue' regarding the 'state' of a legal case,[37] metalepsis is discussed as a trope rather than as a figure: the various classical discussions make clear that what is at issue here is a non-ordinary usage of words. Trypho's definition, 'metalepsis is an expression that explains a homonym through a synonym, like "and from there in turn he directed the course to the sharp islands"'[38], portrays it as the mirror image of metonymy, which he defines as 'an expression that explains a synonym through its homonym'[39]—a definition of metonymy that is rather far removed from anything one would readily recognize as a metonym and, much like his definition of metalepsis, rather difficult to understand in the abstract. The underlying logic of the metalepsis definition is that metalepsis facilitates a connection between A and D while skipping over the intermediary steps of B and C. The operative principle here resembles that of Cockney rhyming slang: an expression like 'lend me your Britneys' draws on the familiar connection of 'Britney' with 'Spears' and the aural connection of 'Spears' with 'ears'—so that 'lend me your Britneys' can signify 'lend me your ears'. What Cockney rhyming slang achieves through, first, a shift on the lexical level (words that usually occur together: Britney and

---

[37] See below, pp. 23–4.

[38] μετάληψίς ἐστὶ λέξις ἐκ συνωνυμίας τὸ ὁμώνυμον δηλοῦσα οἷον "Ἔνθεν δ'αὖ νήσοισιν ἐπιπροέηκε θοῆσει.' Tryph. *Trop.* [= *Rhetores Graeci*, ed. Spengel, vol. iii] 738.10–12; the example is from *Od.* 15.299; cf. schol. *Od.* 15.299: θοῆσιν· μεταληπτικὸν ἐκ τοῦ κατὰ κίνησιν ὀξέος ἐπὶ τὸ κατὰ σχῆμα ('"θοῆσιν" ['sharp', 'swift', 'pointed']: metaleptic transference from sharpness in terms of movement to sharpness in terms of shape').

[39] Cf. Tryph. *Trop.* [= *Rhetores Graeci*, ed. Spengel, vol. iii] 739.20–1: μετωνυμία ἐστὶ λέξις ἀπὸ τοῦ ὁμωνύμου τὸ συνώνυμον δηλοῦσα.

Spears) and then a leap on the phonetic level (words that rhyme: Spears and ears), metalepsis achieves through a twofold shift on the semantic level, as Quintilian's examples illustrate:

> There remains one trope involving a change of meaning, namely meta-lepsis or transumption, which, as it were, makes a path from one thing to another. <Except in comedy> it is very rare and highly incorrect, but commoner with the Greeks, who call Chiron the Centaur Ἥσσονα, and use θοαί and ὀξεῖαι of islands. Who would tolerate it if we were to call Verres 'Pig' or Aelius <Catus> 'Doctus'?[40]

The centaur's name (Χείρων) is a homonym of the Greek word for 'worse' (χείρων), for which ἥσσων (also 'worse') is a synonym. All of these inter-vening steps are elided when simply calling the centaur, metaleptically, Ἥσσων. Similarly, θοός and ὀξύς are partly synonymous in their (some-times) shared meaning of 'swift', but they do not fully overlap in their semantic scope, where ὀξύς can also denote 'sharp, pointed' but θοός, in ordinary usage, cannot—yet is made to mean just that in its deviant, meta-leptic usage here. In like manner, calling *Verres* a *sus* or *Catus doctus* capit-alizes on the polysemy of words by, first, drawing on a semantic dimension of a word which in the given context is *not* at issue (Verres not as proper name but as plural of *uerris*, 'boar'; and Catus not as proper name but as adjective *catus*, 'wise'); and by then performing a second, sideways shift by deploying a semantically equivalent synonym that further enhances the felt abrasiveness (from *uerris*, 'boar', to *sus*, 'pig'; and from *catus*, 'wise', to *doctus*, 'learned'). Again, the proximity to metonymy, which is based on a lateral shift within a semantic field, is apparent. It may seem as though this twofold shift in rhetorical metalepsis sets it apart from the shift in mean-ing in metonymy, but this is not a difference in kind: after all, in meton-ymy, too, one frequently finds cases, often the most powerful and interesting ones, in which a metonym involves precisely not just one indir-ectly evoked term but rather a chain of associated terms that all inform to different degrees what is at issue. That is to say: directional aesthetics and multiple internal shifts are something that rhetorical metalepsis and

---

[40] *superest ex his quae aliter significant metalempsis, id est trasumptio, quae ex alio [tropo] in aliud uelut uiam praestat, <cuius usus nisi in comoedia> et rarissimus et improbissimus, Graecis tamen frequentior, qui Centaurum, qui Chiron est, Ἥσσονα et insulas ὀξείνας θοάς dicunt. nos quis ferat Verrem 'suem' aut Aelium <Catum> 'doctum' nominemus? est enim haec in metalempsi natura, ut inter id quod tranfertur <et id quo transfertur> sit medius quidam gradus, nihil ipse significans sed praebens transitum.* Quint. *Inst.* 8.6.37–8.

rhetorical metonymy certainly do have in common. What is more, precisely this feature is also highly relevant to a second ancient strand of thinking about metalepsis that has given rise to a further extended notion of metalepsis—namely metalepsis as allusion. This strand runs parallel to the one of Trypho and Quintilian, just discussed, and can be traced back to Donatus, who discusses metalepsis in his *Ars Grammatica* right after metaphor and right before moving on to metonymy. His definition of metalepsis as 'a mode of expression that arrives step by step at what it presents, such as "he hid them in *gloomy* caverns" and "Shall I, after a long time, looking at my kingdom, marvel at *corn ears*?"'[41] focuses precisely on the chain of associations that is, in principle, at the core of metonymy. Charisius (who, like Diomedes and Pompeius, follows in Donatus' footsteps) explains the inner logic at work here:

> Metalepsis is the deferral (*dilatio*) of proper signification (*dictionum proprietatis*) by way of taking one thing for another (*per transumptionem*), a mode of expression that step by step comes down to the proper signification, such as 'he hid them in gloomy caverns'; because from 'gloomy' one infers 'dark', from 'dark' 'filled with darkness', and from that '[possessing] extreme depth'.[42]

Metalepsis is portrayed here as a suggestive, long-distance version of metonymy: from gloomy to black to holding darkness to having depth; or from ears to crops to summers to years gone by.[43] And herein lies the link to metalepsis (or, latinized, *transsumptio*) as appealed to in studies of intertextuality by Hollander, Conte, Barkan, and Hinds. Barkan's influential definition, for instance, reads: 'My transsumption, then, is the figure that renders into explicit consciousness the cultural activity of figuration and thus the existence of a diachronic cultural tradition as well as the gap across which figures may be constructed.'[44] As with the directional

---

[41] *metalepsis est dictio gradatim pergens ad id quod ostendit, ut 'speluncis abdidit atris'* [= Verg. *Aen.* 1.60] *et 'post aliquot mea regna uidens mirabor aristas?'* [= Verg. *Ecl.* 1.69]. Don. *Ars Gramm.* 400 [= *Grammatici Latini*, ed. Keil, vol. iv].

[42] *metalepsis est per transsumptionem dictionum proprietatis dilatio, dictio gradatim homonymiae ad propriam significationem descendens, ut 'speluncis abdidit atris'; ab atris enim nigrae intelleguntur, ex nigris tenebras habentes, et per hoc in praeceps profundae.* Charisius, *Inst. Gramm.* 273 [= *Grammatici Latini*, ed. Keil, vol. i]. Cf. Diomed. *Gramm.* 458 [= *Grammatici Latini*, ed. Keil, vol. i].

[43] So Pompeius in his explanation of this example s.v. *metalepsis: per aristas segetes significat, per segetes aestates, per aestates annos. ergo post aliquot aristas id est post aliquot annos.* Pomp. *Comm. Artis Donati* 306 [= *Grammatici Latini*, ed. Keil, vol. v].

[44] Barkan (1991: 45–6).

semantics of metalepsis and metonymy, it is here a range of intertextual echoes, traces, and intermediate layers of connections that may inform the reading of an individual passage and it is the context that determines which information beyond the text is mobilized to enable a meaningful reading (which, again as with metalepsis and metonymy, can involve just one or any number of relevant associations).

Rhetorical metalepsis, allusive metalepsis, and narrative metalepsis, then, all do share some central core characteristics—characteristics which themselves have broadly metonymic traits: they are all about shifts, associations, and realignments of elements within a broader, internally coherent field: the field of language in rhetorical metalepsis, the field of literature and literary traditions in allusive metalepsis, and the field of narration in narrative metalepsis.

Yet does this overlap in a shared conceptual principle also suggest that all of these different manifestations of metalepsis can be uniformly aligned with the distinctive features of either tropes or figures, as distinguished in ancient criticism? The question matters, because metalepsis itself has carried these terms along with it into new domains of critical discourse, specifically narratology and intertextuality, even though these are somewhat removed from stylistics strictly speaking; and if speaking of tropes and figures in these domains is to have any concrete meaning that goes beyond a not further specified 'manner of speaking', then it is important to think about (*a*) what 'trope' and 'figure' might mean in these contexts; (*b*) whether metalepsis in each of its various incarnations belongs to the former or to the latter; and (*c*) what implications this has for our understanding of what metalepsis is and does.

As we have seen, ancient criticism considers rhetorical metalepsis to be a trope and it considers tropes to be deviantly used words, that is, instances in which the usage of a given word deviates from its usage in ordinary language. As Trypho observes, tropes are not just any manner (τρόπος) of speaking that differs from the daily usage of language but one that is marked by a characteristic turn (τροπή): 'a trope is an utterance of speech that involves a turning away from the ordinary' (τρόπος δέ ἐστι λόγος κατὰ παρατροπὴν τοῦ κυρίου λεγόμενος).[45] So what about allusive and narrative metalepsis? Since we are dealing here with different dimensions of textual realities, any appeal to 'metalepsis', 'trope', and 'figure' must take account of

---

[45] Tryph. *Trop.* [= *Rhetores Graeci*, ed. Spengel, vol. iii] 728.12–13.

the new framework within which the structural principles of these critical concepts are put to work.

In allusive metalepsis, for instance, we observe a gliding from intertext to intertext that resembles the semantic shift from term to term characteristic of rhetorical metalepsis as a variant of metonymy; yet we would not say that allusions in a text constitute a deviation from how texts ordinarily function: the appearance of an allusion is not perceived as disruptive or abrasive because it does not negate the meaning of the passage as it stands— it does not force us to make an inference in order to arrive at a meaningful reading. Yet precisely this would be the case if we were dealing with a trope-like phenomenon here. Tropes, after all, are by definition based on a noticeable turning away from the ordinary—but no breach of rules or conventions that ordinarily apply can be detected here and some such case would have to be made if we were to think of allusive metalepsis as a trope of (inter-) textuality. As a figure of (inter-)textuality, on the other hand, allusions can be seen as powerfully and meaningfully foregrounding an always already existing property of texts: their connectedness with other texts. In allusive metalepsis, this general feature of texts gains greater significance and becomes more visible—just as, say, the general phonetic properties of words become more foregrounded in the figure of alliteration. In principle, I would therefore err on the side of thinking of allusive metalepsis as a figure—because it lacks, on the level of reading experience, the moment of an inevitably perceived startling abrasiveness that is characteristic of tropes. And yet in our analyses we often employ a language that makes allusions sound far more transgressive, as if encountering an allusion in a text suddenly destroyed the otherwise carefully sustained illusion of a text being an entirely autonomous, self-contained utterance, whose integrity, ordinarily uncompromised by other texts, is suddenly broken into. On reflection, one can of course entertain such a view—and much is to be said for the critical insights into intertextual dynamics that can be generated from this perspective—but the thereby perceived intrusion is the result of a shifting of goalposts: it is only against a somewhat artificially assumed integrity and autonomy of texts that these intrusions emerge as such.

And this, I would argue, also applies to a certain extent, *mutatis mutandis*, to narrative metalepsis, especially in the light of the progressive expansion of the term's usage to denote an ever-increasing set of narrative scenarios and events. Genette himself shows an awareness for the distortions that can be introduced by the critic as a participating observer. In *Discours du récit* he writes:

A narrating situation is, like any other, a complex whole within which analysis, or simply description, cannot *differentiate except by ripping apart a tight web of connections among the narrating act*, its protagonists, its spatio-temporal determinations, its relationship to other narrating situations involved in the same narrative, etc. The demands of exposition constrain us to this *unavoidable violence* simply by the fact that critical discourse, like any other discourse, cannot say everything at once.[46]

The tendencies of critical discourse towards dissection are thus prone to introduce, as it were, an external violence to the discussion of texts that can obscure or misrepresent where actual violations within the text are played out. For here, too, the difference between figures and tropes applies and is relevant: there is a difference between a textual dynamic that lays bare and strategically foregrounds the narrative structure of a text (a narrative figure), and a textual dynamic that causes a deviation from what is considered coherent narrative (a narrative trope). The latter, arguably, always involves the former since breaking a rule renders that rule (somewhat) visible through its violation; but the former does not necessarily entail the latter.

What these reflections on tropicality and figurality bring to the fore is the importance of the framework within which we detect and discuss metalepsis. Metalepsis as a narrative figure falls back on the workings of narrative and narration per se; metalepsis as a trope requires a framework, a set of expectations and norms, that is transgressed by the narrative trope. If no such transgression takes place, we are dealing with a narrative figure rather than a trope.[47] Genette's discussion of the functions of the narrator is very helpful here: in addition to the most obvious function, narrating the story ('narrative function'), he refers to the 'directing function', references by the narrator to the progress of story and text which create

---

[46] Genette (1972 = 1980: 215); emphasis added.

[47] My notion of metalepsis as a narrative figure, as set out above, differs considerably from Hanebeck's (2017: 84–92) 'figurative metalepsis', which has little substantive connection with what a figure—in the traditional sense—is and does, even if his notion also involves a reduced aesthetic effect: 'It [*sc.* metalepsis] is a transgression in the figurative sense when the transgression between the domains of the signifier and the signified is *implied* or *suggested*—thus realizing only limited metaleptic potential. The transgression is neither complete (there is no narrative entity that moves "physically" and *illicitly* from one diegetic universe to another), nor does it deny the logic of the act of narrative representation in a fundamental manner.' Hanebeck (2017: 84).

connections or signposts in the internal organization of the narrative; the 'communicative function', which consists in maintaining a relationship with the audience (beyond the mere articulation of the narrative itself), akin to Jakobson's phatic and conative functions of language; the 'testimonial function', which covers the relationship the narrator maintains with the narrative told (be it an emotional or intellectual relation to it); and, lastly, the 'ideological function', which refers to the directly or indirectly conveyed evaluations of actions in the narrative that colour the narrative with a certain ideological point of view.[48] As Genette says, 'none except the first is completely indispensable, and at the same time none, however carefully an author tries, can be completely avoided'.[49] If we follow Genette in seeing all of these functions as parts of the act of narration per se, as a collorary of the fact that all narrative is representational, then we are reminded that it is not only striking cases of metalepsis that render these functions visible; rather, narrative is always somehow visible as narrative because it is always a representation of a reality (of whatever sort).

Two things follow from this for thinking further about metalepsis. The first is, perhaps, a word of caution. There seems to be a recurring tendency of criticism to become so intrigued by the perspectives yielded by critical concepts that these concepts are pursued and pushed so far that they, ironically, lose perspective and critical rigour. Quintilian's comments on figures, discussed earlier, are a case in point:[50] he begins with the valuable insight that figures are, as opposed to tropes, operative on the basis of the properties of ordinary language, and then ends up declaring that all language is in a way figurative, which renders the entire category of figurality useless for criticism. Likewise, the great infatuation of Western criticism with metaphor, especially pronounced from Romanticism onwards, has led to an increasing perception not just of all poetic language as metaphorical, but of all language as metaphorical.[51] The inevitable consequence is, again, a

---

[48] See Genette (1972 = 1980: 255–7).   [49] Genette (1972 = 1980: 257).

[50] See above, p. 13.

[51] Witness, for instance, Sojcher's remark that '[i]f poetry is a space that opens up in language, if through it words speak again and meaning becomes significant again, it is because there is between everyday language and rediscovered speech a shift of meaning, metaphor. Metaphor is no longer, from this point of view, a figure among others, but the figure, the trope of tropes' (Sojcher 1969: 583) or de Man's claim that '[a]ll language is language about denomination, that is, a conceptual, figural, metaphorical metalanguage' (de Man 1979: 152–3). De Man stands in the tradition of Nietzsche: 'What then is truth? A movable host of metaphors, metonymies, and anthropomorphism: in short, a sum of human relations which have been poetically and rhetorically intensified, transferred, and embellished, and which, after long usage, seem to a people to be fixed, canonical, and binding. Truths are illusions which we have forgotten are illusions; they are metaphors that have become worn out and

significant loss of critical acumen—all for the dubious 'gain' of restating that language stands indeed in a mediating, representational relation to extralinguistic reality. And tendencies of this very sort can also be observed in postmodern metalepsis criticism, so for instance in McHale's extension of metalepsis to include any kind of engagement of the addressee/reader with the story level: mere immersion and affective involvement are taken as sufficient to constitute a transgression of an ontological boundary.[52] From here it is not far to Fludernik's suggestion that 'one could perhaps see this device [*sc.* metalepsis] as...a master trope of the narratological imaginary'[53] and to Genette's declaration that all fictions and all reality are woven through with metalepses. Given this observable, recurring pattern in the development of critical discourse, I would caution us against attaching the label 'metalepsis' to an increasing number of instances in which narration merely becomes at all recognizable as, well, narration. A differentiation between instantiations of metalepsis as a figure that meaningfully foregrounds already present features of narrative acts and as a trope of narrative that breaks with conventional expectations towards narrative may be a helpful step towards preserving the value of metalepsis as a critical concept and to safeguarding us against the risks of overextending it to the point where it designates any manner of speaking that makes narrative recognizable as narrative.

Conversely, and this is the second conclusion I would draw, where we are concerned with metalepsis as a trope of narrative, we need to carefully consider what exactly we posit as the narrative framework from which the metaleptic trope in question deviates. Just a few points for consideration: Whitmarsh has suggested that we should differentiate between strong and weak metalepses, depending on whether they transgress a frame that separates a fictional from the real world, thereby causing a strong shock, or whether they are non-intrusive stylistic features, such as temporal convergences between the act of narration and the events described.[54]

---

have been drained of sensuous force, coins which have lost their embossing and are now considered as metal and no longer as coins' (Nietzsche 1873: 84). More broadly speaking, the view that all language is metaphorical can be traced back to *c.*1880 and then quickly becomes more and more prominent over the course of the following century; see Nerlich and Clarke (2001). For a critique of this over-expended notion of metaphor, in part similar to the one articulated above, see Cornell Way (1991: 17–20).

[52] McHale (1987: 222).
[53] Fludernik (2003b: 392). Notably, this is achieved within a conceptual framework that is itself metaphorical in nature; see Fludernik (2003b: 393) and cf. below, p. 22.
[54] See Whitmarsh (2013b: 5–6).

The differentiation ultimately rests on an ontological distinction (a distinction challenged by the metaphysical considerations offered in Kennedy's chapter). Fludernik, on the other hand, going in almost the opposition direction, has suggested that these metaleptic transgressions are themselves metaphoric in character, that is, they only appear as 'transgressions' under the imposition of a relatively strict analogy between narrative representations and extrafictional reality:

> What I am suggesting here is that many examples of metalepsis, especially the illusion-enhancing ones, need to be treated as metaphoric transgressions of narrative boundaries; they are part of a narratorial metaphorics of immersion in the fictional world that attempts to make believe that this fictional world is real—at least for the time while readers are engaged in the reading process. What I am therefore saying is that the device of metalepsis in many instances need not actually be literally treated as an ontological contradiction (and therefore transgression), but could be regarded as an imaginative transfer into the impossible in parallel with authorial omniscience or autodiegetic narrators' precise memory of dialogues and thoughts in the past.[55]

At this point, it becomes apparent how the problems arising from extremely broad notions of metaphor on the one hand and of metalepsis on the other converge, yet again, around a restatement of the representational character of narrative—an outcome that strikes me as selling us rather short on the critical work that the concept of metalepsis can do for us. From the more intra-narratological perspective pursued and developed here by way of revisiting metalepsis *avant* Genette, the relative strength and weakness of metaleptic 'shocks' would be determined by the intensity of their violation of expectations—expectations which are bound to vary and change. For one thing, the mere visibility of the mechanics of narration will be perceived as all the more unsettling, the greater an expectation of their *in*visibility is—but this is not an expectation that we should always posit as a given. The artful presence of visible 'gear changes' in the act of narration might itself be part of the repertoire of characteristic features of forms of narrative,[56] in which case it would be difficult to appeal here to metalepsis as a narrative trope. Likewise, audience expectations about what

---

[55] Fludernik (2003b: 393); cf. also p. 4 and p. 5 n. 10 above.
[56] Cf. Fludernik (2003b: 391–2): '[M]etalepsis, irrespective of its illusionistic or anti-illusionistic qualities, may perhaps be linked to the necessity of functional gear-shifting, to

is considered narratively coherent are bound to differ from genre to genre, from period to period, and from reception context to reception context. If, for instance, metalepsis is such a widespread phenomenon in postmodern literature, might this indicate that it is less rather than more powerful when it appears in this period, precisely because it is an important and established part of the novelistic repertoire? In the light of such considerations one might want to ask whether there is such a thing as 'dead metalepsis' (in analogy to dead metaphors): a narrative move that has become so commonplace that it has lost its shocking effect, even if it can still be described and analysed in its structure as metaleptic. Conversely, a change in performance context and/or medium—for instance, a sung monodic ode as opposed to a read one—is likewise bound to change the degree to which an audience perceives an expression as metaleptic. Grethlein's chapter, which discusses the important differences as well as parallels between metalepsis in ancient poetry and vase-painting, highlights the significance of the medium-specific realizations and perceptions of metaleptic moments. Once we are aware of the importance of such variables, it becomes increasingly problematic to consider deictic markers, the use of the present tense, or inherent referential ambiguities in the first and second person *categorically* as elements of a supposed 'grammar of metalepsis', that is, as linguistic means that facilitate small- or large-scale metaleptic moments; because they are, like the traces of the narrator and the narratee found in all narrative (as highlighted in Genette's discussion of the functions of the narrator), ultimately part and parcel of the given *factum brutum* of the representational character of all narrative and all language. To productively discuss the figurative foregroundings and tropical deviations through which literature metapoetically reflects, negotiates, and plays with this fact requires an acute awareness of both the mechanics of narration and the frames and framing assumptions that underwrite—historically contingent—notions of 'ordinary' narrative and narrative coherence.

Raising these very questions, drawing out such assumptions, and probing their implications and consequences, as the chapters of this volume do from a wide variety of angles and perspectives, is one of the most important ways in which thinking about metalepsis in ancient literature can enrich classical scholarship and literary criticism *tout court*. It is also, incidentally, very close to what metalepsis in its little-discussed notion as a *status* in *genus iudicale* is all about: namely to pose questions about the

the mechanics of telling that remain visible at times, allowing the reader a brief glimpse into the machinery producing the story through the technology of narration.'

jurisdiction of the presiding court and the legitimacy of the proceedings.[57] Driven by that same inquisitive-metaleptic spirit, this volume probes the validity and viability, problems and potential of recent theorizations of 'metalepsis' when brought to bear on classical literature and, in the chapter by Grethlein, also classical art and visual culture. By bringing modern theory and ancient material into a critical dialogue, the individual chapters and the volume as a whole simultaneously seek to advance literary-theoretical debate—both within and beyond the discipline of Classics—and to shed new light on familiar and less familiar Greek and Roman texts and artworks.

While the chapters assembled here are diverse in outlook and do not converge altogether frictionlessly on a consolidated, monolithic view and notion of metalepsis (as the summary reflections on the volume's collective insights in the epilogue duly acknowledge), they are all bound by the shared desire to refine and rethink this concept in order to capitalize more fully on its promise and acumen in the study of classical antiquity—by way of working towards a greater precision, a broader consensus, and a more rigorous methodological framework for its mobilization and invocation in classical contexts and beyond. Metalepsis, after all, is a genuinely slippery concept; its very point, as this introductory chapter has sought to show, in all its many guises, both ancient and modern, is to denote slipperiness: of the semantic range and connections of words, of the allusive dimensions of literature across time, of the relations between agents and parameters involved in narration. It would be a pity if, in talking about this slipperiness, the concept itself slipped into signifying first everything—and then nothing.

---

[57] For metalepsis as a status, see e.g. Hermagoras *Stat.* 2.16 and Quint. *Inst.* 3.6.83–4. See also Heath (2003).

2

Representation Delimited and Historicized

Metalepsis in Ancient Literature and Vase-Painting

Jonas Grethlein

The Transmedial Dimension of Metalepsis

The *Imagines* of Philostratus, the description of an imaginary gallery from the beginning of the third century CE, contains the ekphrasis of a painting showing a group of hunters. The old rhetor, who explains the pictures to a young boy and a crowd of adolescents, begins this ekphrasis (1.28.1, trans. Fairbanks):[1]

> Do not rush past us, hunters, and do not urge on your horses till we track you down (ἐξιχνεύσωμεν), what you want and what you are hunting. For you say that you pursue a fierce wild boar, and I see the actions of the animal; it has burrowed under the olive trees, cut down the vines, and has left neither fig tree nor apple tree or branch, but has torn them all out of the earth, partly by digging them up, partly by hurling itself upon them, partly by rubbing against them. I see the creature, its mane bristling, its eyes flashing fire, and it is gnashing its tusks at you, gentlemen; for such wild animals are capable of hearing the din from far away.

* I am grateful to Nikolaus Dietrich for illuminating discussions about ancient vase-painting and its intricate logic of representation, and I wish to thank Sebastian Matzner and Gail Trimble, whose insightful comments and suggestions were very helpful.

[1] On the *Hunters*, see, e.g., Elsner (1995: 33–5); Baumann (2011: 69–76; 2013: 264–5, 268–70); Squire (2013: 113–15).

Jonas Grethlein, *Representation Delimited and Historicized: Metalepsis in Ancient Literature and Vase-Painting*
In: *Metalepsis: Ancient Texts, New Perspectives.* Edited by: Sebastian Matzner and Gail Trimble,
Oxford University Press (2020). © The editors and Oxford University Press.
DOI: 10.1093/oso/9780198846987.003.0002

The speaker appears to have plunged into the painted scene. He seems to stand right inside the devastated orchard, not only seeing the boar, but even hearing the grinding of his tusks. So intense is his immersion that he addresses the hunters directly. Here as in other *Imagines*, Philostratus drives home the point that painting has the capacity to transport its recipients into the world it represents.

Continuing his exegesis, the rhetor speculates about the true object of the hunt: are they really hunting the boar (in the picture) and not rather the beautiful boy (who stands amidst the listening spectators in front of the picture)? Then, the speaker's illusion breaks (1.28.2, trans. Fairbanks):

> How I was deceived! I was deluded by the painting/description (γραφῆς), thinking that they were not painted/described (γεγράφθαι), but were real beings and actually moved and loved—I tease them as though they hear me, and I think that I hear some response—and you did not utter a single word to avert me from my mistake, overcome as much as I was, unable to free yourself from the deception and the slumber induced by it. So let us look together at the things painted/described (γεγραμμένα); for it is a painting/description (γραφῇ) before which we stand.

The rhetor notes that what he is seeing is only a picture and starts to muse on his initial deception. His absorption was only temporary and is now counterpoised with reflection. At the same time, the rhetor's comment features a pun that is widely popular in imperial ekphrasis and that here, as in other cases, juxtaposes the mimesis of pictures and words. No less than four times does the rhetor use the word γράφειν and its cognates, which signify both painting and writing.[2] Philostratus hereby blends together verbal and pictorial representation. He highlights the mimetic recession with which the *Imagines* delightfully toys: its descriptions represent what itself is a representation. The ekphrasis repeats the mimesis of the picture. Aligning the verbal with the visual representation, the emphatic use of γράφειν makes the painting a mirror for its description. The response of the rhetor to the painting becomes a model for the spell that Philostratus hopes to cast on the readers of the ekphrasis.

What is more, the lexical ambiguity collapses the boundary between the two levels of mimesis. Meaning both painting and description, γραφή

---

[2] Prominent examples of the ambiguity of γραφή outside Philostratus include Longus, *Daphnis and Chloe*, pr.; Lucian, *De Domo* 21; *Imagines* 3. See also Servius *ad Aen.* 6.34 (for an ancient comment on it). Cf. Lissarrague (1992).

intimates that, although only a verbal rendering, the ekphrasis lets us readers actually see the picture. The very words with which the rhetor distances himself from his absorption suggest that the reader has unmediated access to the painting; when he comments on his delusion, his reference to γραφή erases the boundary between text and picture. Pointing out his deception, the speaker himself enacts another deception which is palpable in the second-person plural form: 'You did not utter a single word to avert me from my mistake.' As commentators have noticed, the words directed to the internal audience, the boys in the gallery, can also address the external audience, that is the readers, who, too, did not, in fact could not, intervene to stop his delusion.[3] The readers thereby find themselves at the same level as the characters in the text.[4] The meditation on the gap separating the spectators from the world of the picture simultaneously draws the readers into the world of the text.

Philostratus' sophisticated play with pictorial and verbal representation invites a transmedial exploration of metalepsis.[5] Both pictures and words, it suggests, have the capacity to make their recipients step into the worlds of their representation, if only for a moment. Just as the rhetor has the feeling of being face to face with the hunters, his reference to γραφή and the ambiguous address to his audience insinuate that his description jolts the reader to the gallery right in front of the picture. In this chapter, I would like to follow up on this parallel and compare metalepsis in Greek literature and vase-painting. Needless to say, my exploration is highly selective and its samples will not be able to cover the large field systematically. However, the broad view taken will permit us to approach metalepsis as more than a textual device, as something that is a transmedial phenomenon and can occur in images whether they are narrative or not.[6] Observing differences and parallels between media will deepen our understanding of how metalepsis works. Moreover, the common ground shared by ancient texts and pictures may help us identify features that render the ancient use of metalepsis distinct. The crossing of boundaries that are otherwise deeply entrenched in the disciplines of literary studies and art history may make scholars on both sides of the fence feel uncomfortable,

---

[3] Cf. Elsner (1995: 35); Squire (2013: 115).

[4] The blurring of medial boundaries extends into the other direction when later a character is described 'as though he were painted/described' (οἷον γραφέν, 1.28.8).

[5] For more on metalepsis and ekphrasis see Trimble in this volume.

[6] On the narrativity of ancient vase-painting, see, for example, Giuliani (2013).

but it is certainly true to the spirit of metalepsis as discussed in this volume.

Firmly established in narrative theory and at last also increasingly widely discussed in Classics, the concept of metalepsis has also come to attract the attention of scholars investigating visual culture.[7] It has even been applied to ancient vase-painting. In two papers, one from 2007, the other from 2013, Lorenz conducts an inquiry into what she calls 'the anatomy of metalepsis', especially on late fifth-century vases.[8] Lorenz's analysis is laudable and thought-provoking, especially in its careful attention to the shape of vessels and the impact it has on the viewing of their pictures, but labelling the phenomena she discusses metalepsis is not unproblematic: Lorenz discusses as metaleptic correspondences and interactions between figures. While these figures belong to different pictorial frames and in some cases are part of narrative versus descriptive representation, they are all on a single vase and therefore form part of the *same level* of representation.

Lorenz's misleading use of the label of metalepsis alerts us to an important prerequisite of the term's application to cross-medial discussions. In Lorenz's notion of the concept, metalepsis is seen as hinging on the existence of 'narrative agents'.[9] Since narrators are hard to identify in visual art, she feels free to redefine the concept of 'narrative level' and assigns different levels to characters who figure on the same vase and, as she acknowledges, would belong to the same level if they were part of a textual narrative.[10] Metalepsis is in fact often defined as the transgression of distinct narrative levels. Most prominently, Genette explains metalepsis as 'le passage d'un niveau narratif à l'autre', but he wisely speaks of 'métalepse narrative'.[11] More broadly understood and not confined to narrative, metalepsis is the crossing of the boundaries between different levels of *representation*. As Wolf notes, metalepsis is not bound to texts and does not even hinge on narrativity; all it requires is the representation of a world. Metalepsis can feature in texts that are not or are only qualifiedly

---

[7] For surveys of work on metalepsis in narrative studies, see Pier (2016); Klimek (2010: 31–72); in Classics, see De Jong (2009); Eisen and von Möllendorff (2013b); Whitmarsh (2013b). On metalepsis in visual art, see some of the contributions in Pier and Schaeffer (2005b), Kukkonen and Klimek (2011), as well as Baetens (1988; 2001). Stoichiță's classic investigation of the 'self-aware image' in the late Renaissance and Baroque (1993) describes metaleptic elements, albeit without reference to the concept. See also his essay on 'l'effet Don Quichotte' (2013).

[8] Lorenz (2007); Lorenz (2013) rehashes some of the material and then applies the concept to relief, namely the friezes of the Pergamon Altar.

[9] Lorenz (2007: 118; 2013: 120).   [10] Lorenz (2007: 127).

[11] Genette (1972: 243–4).

narrative, such as descriptions and drama, and in non-textual media that may but need not be narrative, for example films and pictures that represent something.[12] If we look for pictorial metalepsis, we will find it in transgressions of the line between the world of the picture, that is, the world of the painter and the viewers, and the pictured world, that is, the world inhabited by the characters and objects in the image, and, potentially, worlds embedded in the pictured world, as in pictures in the picture. The parallel to the crossing of narrative levels, I would argue, is not the complex interactions of figures in the pictorial frame so well analysed by Lorenz, but their traffic with the world of the painter and viewer or with worlds represented within the world of the picture.

Various typologies of metalepsis have proliferated in scholarship. Here, I will adopt a typology that, while sufficiently abstract to apply to various media, captures the central aspect of metalepsis, concentrating on the direction of the transgression.[13] There are inward metalepses when the world of the producer and recipient meets with the represented world or when elements of the represented world enter embedded worlds.[14] Inversely, when characters and elements inhabiting the represented world cross the boundary to the world of the representation or when entities of the embedded worlds surface in the represented world, I shall speak of outward metalepses. External metalepses concern the delimitation of what is represented from the representation, internal metalepses the delimitation of embedded worlds from the represented world.[15]

It is worth classifying the elements that are brought into contact through metalepsis. The producer, the recipient, and other elements of the world of the representation, most notably the representation itself, can be brought

[12] Wolf (2005; 2009: 50–6). Adopting this perspective also removes the need to worry about the narrativity of texts that feature metalepsis, as De Jong does in her discussion of epinician poetry (see De Jong 2013: 99 n. 8).

[13] The following model is indebted to Wagner (2002: 244), adopted for example by Klimek (2010: 70–2). I leave aside the horizontal metalepses discussed by Wagner, which discard the hierarchical aspect of metalepsis and make it ultimately encompass the large field of intertextuality, as well as the 'Komplexitätsformen' introduced by Klimek, which do not feature in my ancient examples.

[14] I use the dichotomy 'inward'–'outward' instead of the common pair 'descending'–'ascending', since its signification of the direction is less ambiguous. It is possible to imagine the world of the representation as the ground on which the represented world is grafted or to envisage the represented world as one that lies below the world of the representation. Whereas most anglophone scholars visualize the world of the representation (the extradiegetic world) as above the represented world (the diegetic world), and the latter as above embedded worlds (meta- or hypodiegetic worlds), Genette and other francophone authors take the opposite view. Cf. Kennedy and Trimble in this volume.

[15] Cf. Cohn (2005).

to the same level as the characters or other entities of the represented world. Furthermore, it is important to distinguish the form and intensity of the trespassing. There is not only the strong or 'ontological' metalepsis that has a character or element fully enter a higher- or lower-ranking world, but also weaker forms that merely gesture towards a transgression, for example when Balzac writes: 'While the venerable churchman climbs the ramps of Angoulême, it is not useless to explain...' ('Pendant que le vénérable ecclésiastique monte les rampes d'Angoulême, il n'est pas inutile d'expliquer...').[16] Labelling such tentative transgressions 'rhetorical', Ryan notes: 'Rhetorical metalepsis opens a small window that allows a quick glance across levels, but the window closes after a few sentences, and the operation ends up reasserting the existence of boundaries.'[17] Since the term 'rhetorical' may misleadingly evoke the notion of metalepsis in ancient rhetoric,[18] I prefer the alternative term that Ryan uses: 'discursive metalepsis'.

My initial example can serve to illustrate this typology: the pictorial metalepsis in Philostratus' *Hunters* is inward and internal: it involves a character in the text, who plunges into the painted world. The metalepsis is, if only momentarily, ontological as the rhetor hears sounds and addresses the figures. The textual metalepsis encapsulated in the ambiguous use of γραφή is also inward, but external: it is the reader who appears to see what Philostratus verbally describes. Since this transgression is only intimated, one would call it discursive to distinguish it from the stronger metalepsis that the rhetor incurs within the ekphrasis.

A wealth of ancient anecdotes bespeaks the capacity of texts and artifacts to enthrall their recipient. The kind of inward metalepsis illustrated in Philostratus' *Hunters* has been amply discussed under various labels such as mimesis, epiphany, and *enargeia*.[19] Since there is no need to discuss well-known phenomena under a new label, this chapter will focus on outward metalepses. First, however, another kind of inward metalepsis deserves mentioning as it alerts us to differences between texts and pictures whether they are narrative or not. Not only the recipient but also the narrator can step into the represented world. In fact, one of the most

---

[16]   For a discussion of this sentence, see Genette (1972: 244); Fludernik (2003b: 386–7).

[17]   Ryan (2006: 207); see already Ryan (2005) for 'métalepse ontologique' and 'métalepse rhétorique/discursive'. For other labels and concepts, see Cohn (2005: 121), who speaks of 'métalepse au niveau du discours' and 'métalepse au niveau de l'histoire', and Fludernik (2003b: 384), who distinguishes 'literal metalepsis' from 'metaphorical metalepsis'.

[18]   On this topic see Matzner in this volume.

[19]   Halliwell (2002) on mimesis; Platt (2011); Steinhart (forthcoming) on epiphany; Zanker (1981); Webb (2009: 87–130) on *enargeia*. For further perspectives, see Porter (2010); Halliwell (2011); Peponi (2012); Grethlein (2015; 2017).

striking cases of metalepsis in literature is apostrophe: the narrator directly addresses one of the characters as if that character shared the same place with the narrator.[20] Apostrophes in ancient epic in particular have attracted scholarly attention. While it is difficult to find an explanation that fits all cases, it is obvious that apostrophes bring narrator and audience close to the world of the characters and thereby render the narration particularly vivid.[21]

Now the narrator, defined as 'the inner-textual (textually encoded) highest-level speech position from which the current narrative discourse as a whole originates and from which references to the entities, actions and events that this discourse is about are being made',[22] is an essential feature of narrative in a strict definition, but is absent from visual presentation. Hence, there is no iconic metalepsis that parallels apostrophe in textual narrative. The case of inward metalepsis thus sensitizes us to the differences that balance the similarities between pictorial and textual metalepsis. Ancient anecdotes illustrate that both modes of representation are able to pull, or at least almost to pull, the recipient into their worlds; at the same time one of the most flagrant forms of metalepsis in literature, namely apostrophe, has no equivalent in pictures.

The outward metalepses to be discussed in this chapter will reveal further similarities and differences between pictorial and textual metalepsis. I will first focus on how characters in texts and figures in painting address the recipients ('Addressing the Reader, Looking at the Beholder'). Then I shall consider cases in which characters and figures seem to reflect on the representation of which they form a part ('The Presence of the Representation in the Represented World'). In the course of the enquiry, we will see the impact that the form of the representation has on metalepsis: neither are all textual metalepses paralleled in pictures nor can we find equivalents to all pictorial metalepses in literature. That being said, literature and vase-painting share traits that reveal a distinct tendency of ancient metalepsis. I will finally try to identify this tendency without undue generalization and propose an explanation that resides in an understanding

[20] On metaleptic apostrophe in general see Budelmann, De Jong, and Trimble in this volume.

[21] While Matthews (1980) contends that Homeric apostrophes are used *metri causa*, Parry (1972) argues that they evoke sympathy with characters, and Mackay (2001) makes a case that they highlight pivotal moments. More recently, see De Jong (2009: 93–7); Klooster (2013); Budelmann, De Jong, and Lovatt in this volume.

[22] Margolin (2014). There are, however, linguists and narratologists who challenge the assumption that all narratives have narrators. See Banfield (1982); Spearing (2005: 17–31); Patron (2009).

of art different from our modern concept ('Context Matters: Metalepsis in Antiquity').

Addressing the Reader, Looking at the Beholder

Metalepses can be outward as well as inward. Not only can the narrator or recipient step into the represented world, but the represented world may also merge with the world of the representation. In this section, I shall discuss texts and images in which characters make the leap and address, directly or obliquely, audiences or viewers. De Jong has identified epinician poetry as 'the Greek metaleptic genre par excellence'.[23] Pindar and Bacchylides not only evoke myths as a foil to the victory of the *laudandus*, but repeatedly obliterate the boundaries between the two. When the voice of the chorus performing the epinician blends together with the voice of a heroic character, their song gains in authority.[24] Likewise, when the speech of mythical heroes has double significance and applies to the present victor as well as to the mythical foil, a continuum emerges that aggrandizes the athletic feat.

To give an example discussed by De Jong: in *Olympian* 1, Pelops asks his former lover Poseidon for help, closing his prayer with the following words (1.81–5, trans. Race): 'Great risk does not take hold of a cowardly man. But since men must die, why should anyone sit in darkness and coddle away a nameless old age to no use, deprived of all noble deeds? No! That contest shall be mine to undertake; you grant the success I desire.' Pelops' implicit self-characterization fits Hieron, the *laudandus*, well. He is 'expert in noble deeds' (104) and has put forth the 'boldly laboured feats of strength' (95–6). Moreover, Pelops' victory over Oenomaus in the chariot race not only prefigures his own present-day victory in the horse race, but also gestures towards a future success in the even more prestigious chariot race towards which Pindar's final prayer seems to be directed (106–11). Working for Hieron as well as for Pelops, the prayer by Pelops fuses together the mythical world with the world of the epinician's performance. The metalepsis is admittedly not ontological; even for a discursive metalepsis it is weak: Pelops' words make good sense in the mythical realm and bring it together with the world of the performance only by *additionally* applying *also* to the victor.

---

[23] De Jong (2013: 116). See further De Jong in this volume on metalepsis in Pindar.
[24] Cf. Matzner and Trimble in this volume on pseudo-diegesis or 'pseudo-metalepsis'.

To be more precise than the dichotomy of weak and strong, discursive and ontological metalepsis allows, I suggest labelling such cases as 'elastic metalepses'. Elastic metalepses are weak in that they do not involve an actual encounter of elements from different realms; more specifically, however, they signify utterances of characters that, while firmly embedded in the represented or embedded world, have an additional meaning unintended by the speaker that refers to the embedding world. Elastic metalepsis works, to take up Matzner's compelling analysis of metalepsis in rhetorical terms, as a figure rather than as a trope.[25] Elastic metalepses powerfully drive home the point that ancient metalepsis need not have the abrasive quality that modern scholars tend to ascribe to metalepsis.[26] Metalepsis may also lay bare and reinforce the communicative situation to which the text belongs. In the case of *Olympian* 1, Pelops' prayer opens the mythical narrative to the celebration of the victory, for which the song is primarily destined.[27]

Epinician is not the only genre in which the levels of representation become permeable. In fact, parallel to De Jong, if critical of her approach, Whitmarsh has made a case that classical Greek drama is particularly metaleptic. Whitmarsh argues that the phenomena analysed by De Jong do not actually imply a penetration of separate realms. They are merely 'a non-intrusive stylistic feature, whereby narrators temporarily affect a convergence between their act of narration and the events described' and should be labelled 'weak' metalepses.[28] Strong metalepsis, 'the hidden motor of all fictional creativity', is something different that comes to the fore in drama: 'Individuals onstage are simultaneously actors and characters, space is at once the physical architecture of the theatre and the imagined world of the "fiction", dramatic time is at once concurrent with the spectators' and the represented world of the past (or, conceivably, future).'[29]

Whitmarsh is certainly right to note that De Jong fails to differentiate between degrees of intensity in metalepses. It makes sense to distinguish between weak and strong metalepsis, but as the last quote illustrates, Whitmarsh's argument does not map onto the dichotomy established in

[25] Matzner in this volume, pp. 10–22, esp. p. 21. What I call 'elastic metalepsis' is related to a comparable phenomenon labelled 'metonymic association' by Matzner (2016b: 140–7): words that can be read literally, but their context strongly suggests further significance along the lines of metonymy. One could thus also speak of 'metaleptic association'.

[26] See, for example, Wolf (2005: 90–1; 2009: 52).

[27] On the issue of original performance and later recitations especially in the symposium, see, e.g., Currie (2004); Hubbard (2004); Agócs, Carey, and Rawles (2012).

[28] Whitmarsh (2013b: 5–6).   [29] Whitmarsh (2013b: 7).

scholarship on metalepsis to which he refers. For Whitmarsh, 'strong' metalepsis is *equal* to representation: actors represent characters, the stage the fictional world. This equation of metalepsis with representation, however, is highly questionable.[30] Representation of course yokes together a representing object with a represented object—yet this happens not only in theatre where an actor embodies a character in the play, but also in pictures in which a carrier represents something, or in poetry through words that signify something. Calling this metalepsis, however, would render the concept useless. If metalepsis means representation *tout court*, then it loses its power to signify transgressions, violent or smooth, of the boundaries between different levels of representation. Highlighting the links between the represented world and the world of the representation is different from simply representing something.

These conceptual issues notwithstanding, Whitmarsh nicely teases out some metaleptic features of tragedy, most of which however would count as weak metalepses. The chorus is a case in point: their very position in the orchestra mediates between stage and spectators, and their songs, highly indebted to the lyric tradition and saturated with gnomic wisdom, create a horizon that connects the world of the play with the spectators' world.[31] Let me give a striking example that Whitmarsh does not discuss, but that helps us trace some of the special dynamics of metalepsis in tragedy. As Henrichs has shown, rituals performed or commented on by the tragic chorus tend to be self-referential, as the chorus is itself involved in a ritual, the ritual of the Great Dionysia.[32] Most often, the perversions of ritual in the tragic action contrast with the proper celebration of the tragic contest. In the *Eumenides*, however, the rituals performed in the tragic world and the tragic performance of ritual converge.[33] Self-reference thus morphs into metalepsis: with the move from Delphi to Athens at the beginning of the *Eumenides*, the space of the dramatic action becomes identical with the space of the performance. Deictic pronouns referring to 'this city' work now both in the internal and external communication systems. There is also a temporal opening of the action towards the present in three charter myths: the newly founded court is introduced as the Areopagus;

---

[30] See also Matzner in this volume, pp. 20–1, against making the concept of metalepsis too broad and thereby gambling away its critical value.

[31] It is surprising that Whitmarsh does not refer to Calame's fine model of the tragic chorus as a multiple mediation (esp. Calame (1999) which has found a strong echo also in anglophone scholarship, see most recently Gagné and Hopman (2013)).

[32] Henrichs (1994/5; 1996).

[33] For this and the following interpretation, see Grethlein (2013a: 96–8).

the military help promised by Argos evokes the contemporaneous alliance with Argos; the Semnai Theai, as which the Erinyes are integrated, have a cave sanctuary close to the Areopagus.

When the appeased Erinyes sing their benedictions in an *amoibaion* with Athena (916–1020), it is thus hard to confine their wishes to the Athens of the dramatic action. Based on the spatial and temporal merging of the world of the play with the world of the performance, a ritual metalepsis takes place. Simultaneously Erinyes and performing citizens, the chorus blesses the Athens of the Great Dionysia as well as the Athens in the play. The metalepsis would have had a further twist if the audience and not actors on stage represented the Athenian people in the final procession of the play.[34] With the presence of the audience becoming an act of representation in the play, the performed world and the world of the performance would have fully merged.

Whether or not the play completely absorbed the audience, the metalepsis in the *Eumenides* is not abrupt. There is no violation of the boundaries of the representation that highlights its artificiality. Instead, the action is gradually opened to and finally engulfs the world of the audience without losing its integrity and plausibility. It would be tempting to trace elastic metalepses in other genres, also in prose, perhaps even in factual literature, but it is now time to turn to vase-painting and to see whether it features outward metalepses that can be compared with those in literature. The closest equivalent is to be found on vases that combine painting with writing.[35] After the middle of the sixth century, Attic painters started using letters to render unambiguously utterances of the figures in their pictures.[36] Sometimes emanating directly from the mouths, sometimes placed elsewhere for ornamental purposes, this representation of speech was particularly popular with the Pioneers, but also occurs on vases of other vase-painters. On the B side of a red-figured cup by Oltos, for example, we see two naked women lounging on cushions, one playing the flute, the other handing the first a cup (Figure 1).[37] Following and reinforcing the

---

[34] Already Wilamowitz-Moellendorff (1914: 185) suggested that the audience joined in the *ololygmos*.

[35] On inscriptions on vases, see, above all, the publications by Lissarrague (1985; 1987; 1992; 1999). See also Kretschmer (1894); Immerwahr (1990); Wachter (2001); Steiner (2007: 74–93); Catoni (2010: 154–215); Gerleigner (2014).

[36] Cf. Walter-Karydi (2014). There may be earlier instances: see Ferrari (2008: 14–15) on a protoattic stand.

[37] Madrid, Museo Arqueológico Nacional 11 267; Beazley, ARV² 58/53 (Beazley Archive Database 200443); CVA, Madrid, Museo Arqueológico Nacional 2, IIIIC.3, pls. (58, 59, 61, 62) 1.3A–B, 2.2, 4.1, 5.1. The A side shows Theseus pursuing the bull.

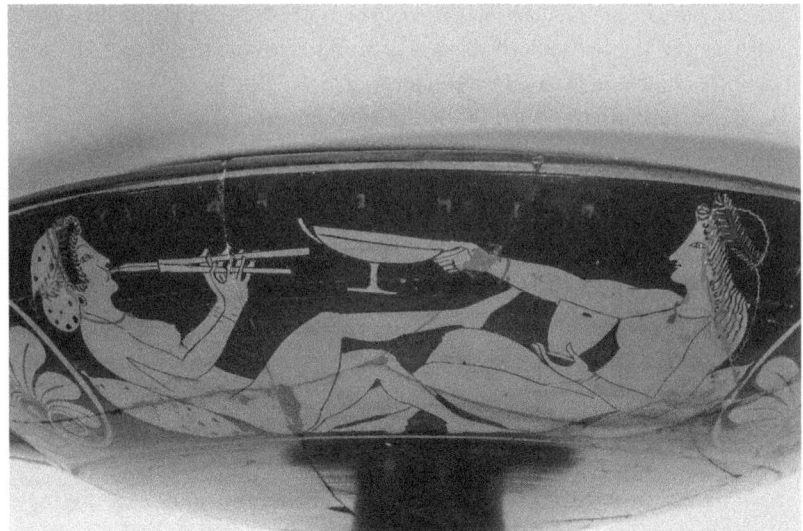

Figure 1 Attic red-figured cup by Oltos, two naked women lounging on cushions, c.525–475 BCE. Madrid, Museo Arqueológico Nacional 11 267.
© Museo Arqueológico Nacional. Foto Ángel Martínez Levas.

movement of her arm, an inscription reads: πῖνε καὶ σύ—'you drink too!' The inscription obviously renders the words with which the woman passes on the cup to her fellow. That being said, what is first an appeal within the represented scene also reaches out to the viewer and especially the user of the cup. When the symposiast drinks from the cup, he follows the request of the figure in the picture.

There is a fair number of cups, especially the Little Master cups, that feature inscriptions which directly address the user. The second-person singular imperative 'drink' can be found on several of them.[38] The cup just mentioned takes up this message to the beholder and gives it a metaleptic spin by embedding it in the represented scene. As in literature, the second person easily crosses from the represented world to the world of the representation. Like the literary metalepses mentioned, this metalepsis does not undercut or interrupt the representation; the inscription works simultaneously as part of the pictorial plane and as part of the vase, thus qualifying as an elastic metalepsis. Another parallel that can be noted is the importance of the reception context with which the represented scene needs to be

---

[38] Lissarrague (1987: 61–4). See also Catoni (2010: 196–200).

aligned to secure a smooth transition. Just as Pelops' race parallels Hieron's past and future races and the ritual song of the Erinyes fuses with the ritual context of the tragic performance, the two nude females appear in the very symposiastic situation in which the cup itself circulates. While the serious tone of the two former examples matches their solemn occasions, the play with the vase as carrier of a picture and as a drinking vessel is in tune with the ludic nature of the symposium.[39]

Writing obviously eased the interaction between the pictured world and the world of its beholders. Discussing the 'x is handsome' inscriptions popular in Athens in the second half of the sixth and the first half of the fifth century, Lissarrague notes: 'Because the formula *ho pais kalos* applies to two different fields of references, it can serve as the interface between the real world and the world represented; it reinforces the links between the two fields, the real and the representation, through the reading that the user performs.'[40] That being said, vase-painting does not require writing in order to proliferate outward metalepses. In the remainder of this section, I wish to argue that there is an iconic equivalent to speech as a means of transition from the represented world to the recipient: the gaze.

The figures on Greek vases are in general presented in profile. There are, however, noteworthy exceptions to this convention. Gorgons nearly always look out of the picture. Dying and sleeping characters are also often depicted frontally, even if in many cases their eyes are closed. Other figures that appear regularly *en face* are symposiasts and komasts as well as satyrs. This list is by no means exhaustive—one could also mention panthers, Dionysus, etc.—but it suffices to indicate how variegated the frontal presentation is in vase-painting. This is not the place to rehash the numerous explanations that have been advanced.[41] Two pivotal points, however, are important for my argument here. Characters that are presented *en face* while the other figures are shown in profile are to a certain extent unhinged from the represented world. The frontal representation thus lends itself to representing drunk and maniac as well as dead and sleeping figures. What is more, instead of looking at the represented action, these figures fix the beholder of the representation. Crossing with the eyes of the viewer, their

---

[39] The literature on the symposium is vast: see, e.g., Lissarrague (1987); Schmitt Pantel (1992); Murray (1990); Vetta (1995); Slater (1991); Catoni (2010).

[40] Lissarrague (1999: 367).

[41] For a survey of earlier scholarship see Korshak (1987). See also Frontisi-Ducroux (1995); Mackay (2001); Hedreen (2017). On the motif of the eye in Greek images, see Steinhart (1995). For some general reflections on the 'Bildblick', consult Bredekamp (2010: 233–49).

gaze forges a link between the world in the picture and the world of the picture.

The frontal face in vase-painting has been compared with the apostrophe in Homeric epic.[42] This is an apt comparison in so far as both unambiguously transgress the boundaries of representation. In this regard, the *en face* presentation differs from the elastic metalepses in literature and vase-painting discussed above. The speeches or, in the case of vases, brief utterances of the characters extend to the recipient, but are nevertheless fully integrated in the represented world. The frontal face, on the other hand, stares out of the picture and, deviating from the conventional depiction in profile, breaks out of its world. However, while sharing this rupture with apostrophes, its metalepsis takes the inverse direction. It is not the viewer who steps into the represented world as the narrator in apostrophe, but the character who turns to the recipient, here with visual means.

This metalepsis is independent of a specific reception context; no matter where or by whom it is seen, the gaze out of the vase breaks the boundary of representation. And yet the metalepsis is particularly powerful in representations that chime with the context of their perusal. The similarity endows the erasure of the separating line with special force; two worlds that are alike anyway merge more easily. The numerous symposiastic scenes on pottery made for the symposium are a case in point. Mirroring the context of its use, the represented scene can seamlessly blend into the external world if the eyes of an internal symposiast establish contact with the eyes of an external fellow drinker. Then the reflection of the context in the picture that has been examined by Lissarrague and Frontisi-Ducroux approaches a fusion of the two.

To give an example: a red-figured cup potted by Hieron and painted by Macron features six symposiasts, three on each side (Figures 2.1, 2.2).[43] The two figures on both sides of one of the handles look out of the picture. The face of one of them is not visible any more due to abrasion, but the presentation of the flute makes the frontal presentation a safe assumption. It has been noted that the placing of the two figures on both sides of the handle is a way of bridging the interruption of the pictorial field caused by the handle.[44] Arguably more incisive, however, is the bridge to the

---

[42]   Frontisi-Ducroux (1995: 90–3); Mackay (2001).

[43]   The cup was part of the Borowski Collection, Toronto: Beazley, ARV² 467/120 (Beazley Archive Database 2573); Kunisch (1997: 47, T 21). For its interpretation, see especially Frontisi-Ducroux (1995: 99).

[44]   Kunisch (1997: 82).

Figures 2.1, 2.2 Attic red-figured cup by Hieron (potter) and Macron (painter), six symposiasts, c.500–450 BCE. Toronto, Borowski Collection/ Florence PD 317.
© Phoenix Ancient Art SA.

viewer that the look out of the picture builds. Turned away from the represented world, the eyes of the figures establish a contact with the beholder of the vase.

The fully visible figure in particular merits our attention. Sporting a long beard, he holds two cups, one in each hand. While the left arm is propped on the cushions so that the cup is in front of his chest, the right arm is put forth, obviously to pass on the other cup. In the picture, however, there is nobody to whom the cup could be passed on. The slave boy, crouching under the handle, is asleep, and the symposiast on the other side of the handle also faces, as we have seen, the beholder and is busy playing the flute. It seems that the hand holding the cup is extended to the viewer of the vase, that the painted cup is about to join the paths in which the cup featuring the painting circulates. The visual contact across the divide between pictured scene and outside world is reinforced by an at least potential haptic contact. Reaching out to the beholder, the eye and hand of the figure intimate a fusion of the symposium seen on the cup and the symposium in which the cup is passed around.

The playful interaction between vase-painting and the outside world in the symposium is particularly prominent in eye-cups. There are many cups, mostly Athenian and Chalcidian and dating from around 540 to 480 B C E, that feature two large eyes on the exterior between their two handles, sometimes also on both sides (Figure 3).[45]

When a symposiast lifts such a cup and drinks from it, then it covers his face and shows the face painted on the exterior to fellow symposiasts—the cup becomes a mask.[46] The faces of many eye-cups seem not to be generic, but to represent specific individuals, notably Silens and nymphs, but also Dionysus himself or a panther.[47] As argued by Hedreen, they may even have invited the spectator to identify himself with the kind of creature that was most likely to face these creatures, namely another member of this Dionysiac circle.[48] On eye-cups, it is not the eyes of a figure on the cup, but the eyes of the cup itself that interact with the outside world. Becoming the face of a drinking symposiast, the cup and its painting are fully integrated into the world of their beholders.

---

[45] E.g. Ferrari (1986); Kunisch (1990). Beazley, ARV² 161/1 (Beazley Archive Database 275075); CVA, Cambridge Fitzwilliam Museum 2, III.H, I, pls. (514, 517, 518) 5.1 A–B, 8.3, 9.2.

[46] See especially Kunisch (1990: 23–6). More broadly on anthropomorphization in Greek vases, see Martens (1992: 284–363).

[47] Hedreen (2007: 228–32) gives a convenient survey of these identifications.

[48] Hedreen (2007: 232–4).

Figure 3 Attic red-figured eye-cup (Type A) by Hischylus (potter), between eyes a nose, *c.*525 BCE. Cambridge, Fitzwilliam Museum 37.14.
© The Fitzwilliam Museum, Cambridge.

While turning the eye-cup's face to the others, the drinking symposiast himself will have seen his own reflection in the wine and emerging beneath it the picture in the tondo. In many cases, this picture will have been a Gorgon, a popular motif, which yields an uncanny confrontation of the self with the other for the drinker (Figure 4).[49]

Found not only in tondi, but also as ornament and as part of narrative scenes, the motif of the Gorgon adds an important point to my analysis of the metaleptic quality of frontal faces.[50] So far we have seen that the gaze at the beholder permeates the wall between the world in the picture and the world of the picture. While sharing this quality, the *en face* presentation of the Gorgon also highlights the gap that separates the two worlds.[51] Since the lethal gaze is the most characteristic feature of the Gorgon, it is natural to depict her frontally. At the same time, the gaze straight at the beholder calls attention to the fact that he is *only* looking at a *picture*. The Gorgon in a tondo or on the exterior of a cup does not petrify the viewer.

[49] Beazley, ABV 257/23; CVA, Cambridge Fitzwilliam Museum 2, III.H, I, pls. (513, 517, 518) 4.1, 8.1, 9.4.

[50] On the Gorgon in ancient art, see besides Mack (2002) also Howe (1954); Vernant (1990: 115–17); Frontisi-Ducroux (1995: 71–4); Grethlein (2016; 2017). Further literature can be found in Neer (2002: 43 n. 56).

[51] For this argument, see Grethlein (2016: 96–105; 2017: 222–48).

Figure 4 Attic black-figured eye-cup by the Lysippides Painter, Gorgoneion, *c.*550–500 BCE. Cambridge, Fitzwilliam Museum GR.12.1937.
© The Fitzwilliam Museum, Cambridge.

One could even argue for an inversion: not the beholder, but the Gorgon has been turned into stone, or rather into clay. The safety of the beholder bespeaks the status of the Gorgon as a mere representation.

Since the frontal presentation of the Gorgon is a firm iconographic convention, her stare out of the picture will have struck ancient viewers far less than the frontal presentation of individual symposiasts deviating from the norm.[52] That being said, the ubiquity of the motif of the Gorgon on vases highlights the salience of the reflection it encapsulates, namely that pictures are only representations. While reaching out of the picture to the recipient, the gaze of the Gorgon throws into relief the ontological gap separating the world in the picture from the outside world. It interlaces a strong metalepsis, the violent transgression of the boundary between the viewer and the represented through the gaze out of the picture, with a

---

[52] Cf. Mackay (2001: 26).

reminder of the different levels of representation inherent in the harmlessness of an otherwise lethal stare.

The Presence of the Representation in the Represented World

Cases of outward metalepsis are not confined to the characters' addressing the audience, be it through speech or gaze. Another type of outward metalepsis occurs in poetry when the characters refer to the text in which they figure. This phenomenon has been much discussed under the label of metapoetry.[53] Most often, such references are oblique and constitute elastic metalepses. Firmly embedded in the represented world, the utterances bear additional significance that is not intended by the speaker but easy to pick up for the reader. References to *kleos* in epic poetry, for example, can be metapoetically charged, as *kleos*, besides meaning glory and 'what is heard' in general, often signifies specifically the glory purveyed by epic poetry.[54] When it is epic heroes who invoke *kleos*, the self-reference becomes a metalepsis, as the self-reference is embedded in the world of the narrative. Take for example Odysseus' proud proclamation of his identity at the court of the Phaeaceans (*Od.* 9.19–20, trans. Lattimore): 'I am Odysseus son of Laertes, known before all men | for the study of crafty designs, and my fame goes up to the heavens.' Of course, Odysseus is still in the midst of his adventures and a significant part of the ordeals that Homer reports lies ahead of him. That being said, the idea of Odysseus' glory is not unlikely to evoke the *Odyssey*, which is the medium of the glory; the boast that the glory reaches the heaven reflects the pride of Homer as well as that of Odysseus.

Comparable cases occur in ancient historiography, corroborating the need not to confine the investigation of metalepsis to fictional texts.[55] As in epic, the pivot that connects the narrated world with the world of the narrative is glory, or, more neutrally, memory, being simultaneously something which historiography tries to establish and something to which historical agents aspire. When agents meditate on memory, especially their

---

[53] Literature on metapoetics is vast, as the concept has become a staple in literary scholarship. Among recent contributions see, e.g., Torrance (2013); Heerink (2015).

[54] E.g. *Od.* 1.337, 8.73–4; Hes. *Th.* 99–101; *h.Hom.* 32.18. See, for example, Ford (1992: 59–67).

[55] Pier (2016) is representative of a general consensus when he asserts (2): 'On the whole, discussions support the idea that metalepsis appears only in fictional contexts.'

own future memory, these comments are potentially metaleptic. Herodotus, for instance, writes that the Spartan Leonidas sent away the allies from Thermopylae in order to secure *kleos* only for the Spartans (7.220.2–4). Given the salience of *kleos* in the Greek world, this motivation is entirely plausible, and yet it is difficult to ignore the nod towards the *Histories* in which we read about Leonidas' feat.[56] In having a character invoke his glory, Herodotus slyly corroborates his proem's claim to preserve the *kleos* of great deeds.

The *Anabasis* provides another intriguing example. In one of his exhortatory speeches to the Cyreans, Xenophon asserts (6.5.24, trans. Waterfield): 'It is sweet that whoever says or does something manly and beautiful creates a memory of himself in the things he wants to.' Again, this statement is well integrated in the action; at the same time, it also has a metaleptic quality: after all, it is the *Anabasis* that preserves the memory of the Ten Thousand. This metalepsis forms part of a complex traffic between Xenophon the narrator and Xenophon the character on which I have commented elsewhere.[57] Choosing a heterodiegetic stance, Xenophon separates his narratorial persona from the character in the narration. Clandestinely, however, the character arrogates important narratorial functions. Not only does his focalization pervade the narrative, he also reports, comments, and judges while the narrator nearly fully recedes from the narrative. The adoption of narratorial privileges endows the character with authority; it effects that the positive presentation of Xenophon appears to stem not from the narrator but to emerge from history itself.[58]

In vase-painting, figures that identify themselves to the viewer are similar to literary characters that evoke the text in which they figure. In both cases, members of the represented world acknowledge, implicitly or explicitly, their representation and thereby cross the boundaries of their world. A black-figured amphora in Berlin shows the birth of Athena, emerging from the head of Zeus, who is in the middle of two female deities (Figure 5).[59]

---

[56] Pelling (2006: 93), who notes that the phrase 'Spartan prosperity would not be wiped out' (οὐκ ἐξηλείφετο) in particular evokes the proem in which Herodotus claims that thanks to his *Histories* great deeds would not become 'faint'/'erased' (ἐξίτηλος), that is unknown.

[57] Grethlein (2012), with p. 36 on 6.5.24.

[58] For a similar metalepsis in Tacitus' *Annals* that is key to the author's self-fashioning, see Grethlein (2013b: 173–4).

[59] Berlin F 1704; Beazley, ABV 96/14 (Beazley Archive Database 310014); CVA, Berlin, Antikenmuseum 5, 23–5, Beilage C1, pls. (2157, 2159, 2161) 12.1–2, 14.1–2, 16.1–3. On this vase, see Lissarrague (1985: 82–4).

Figure 5 Attic black-figured amphora, birth of Athena, *c.*575–525 BCE. Berlin F1704.

© bpk / Antikensammlung, SMB / Ingrid Geske.

There are two further groups of three gods, one to the left of this scene, the other on its right. While the scene on the left has suffered badly from abrasion, the one on the right is fully preserved. It shows Hermes, Hephaestus, and Dionysus. The gods are all identified by inscriptions, the inscription for Hermes standing out for at least three reasons. It is not the only vertical inscription on the vase, but the only one that reaches from the top to the bottom of the picture and thereby separates the scene from the birth of Athena. Further, Hermes' identity is specified by an *epiklesis* as Hermes Cyllenius, that is, Hermes of the famous sanctuary in Arcadian Cyllene. Finally, the inscription is formulated in the first person, rendering the words of the god himself: 'I am Hermes Cyllenius.' The self-designation, rare in itself, is the more remarkable as it contrasts with the other, conventional ascriptions of names to the other figures. Phrased in the first person, the identification of Hermes belongs to the pictured world. It is, however, not his fellow gods to whom Hermes reveals his identity, but the viewers of the vase. Whereas the literary metalepses discussed above derive from the ambiguity of the words of characters, this metalepsis unambiguously violates the boundary between picture and world.

Figure 6 Attic red-figured cup by the Antiphon Painter, young man holding a lyre and a cup, *c*.500–450 BCE. Erlangen 454.
© Antikensammlung der Friedrich-Alexander-Universität Erlangen-Nürnberg, Georg Pöhlein.

Another vase provides an example that is closer to the parallel in literature. In the tondo of a fragmentary red-figured cup in Erlangen, we see a young man, who holds a lyre and a cup (Figure 6).[60] From his open mouth spout words which yield a semi-circle around him reaching down to his feet: κω[μά]ζων ὑπ' αὐ[λοῦ/λῶν ('I am on a *komos* under the spell of flute/s'). The words scan metrically and are very similar to drinking songs; they seem to render the beginning of a song which the young man, obviously a komast, sings.[61] The inscription thus fully matches the situation. At the same time, however, it can be read as addressing the beholder of the vase. Then the figure informs the viewer about whom the figure represents:

---

[60] Erlangen 454; Beazley, ARV² 339/49 (Beazley Archive Database 203407). Cf. Frontisi-Ducroux and Lissarrague (1983); Lissarrague (1985: 85–6); Lissarrague (1990: 199–200). Further fragments of the vase are in Göttingen: ARV² 343/41; CVA 92/4: T 39.1–6.

[61] See Wilamowitz-Moellendorff (1926: 282). For the inscription of drinking songs on vases, see Csapo and Miller (1991).

someone on a *komos*, enchanted by flutes. Just as the comments on *kleos* by characters in epic and historiography make sense in the world of the action and simultaneously reference the text, the line sung by the young man, while fully integrated in the context, also refers to himself as a representation.[62]

I have again first turned to vases that feature inscriptions in order to find parallels to a type of textual metalepsis. Here, too, metalepses can be added that work without the help of writing and rely solely on iconic means. For this, we have to consider briefly how pictorial representation works. All sorts of pictures have carriers that represent something. There are thus two levels involved in pictorial representation: on the one hand, the representing material, the strokes and colours applied to a canvas or another carrier, and, on the other, the represented objects.[63] Both levels are inextricably linked, the former representing the latter. Our understanding of pictures is decisively shaped by the modern tableau, which tries to be transparent. The carrier tries to disappear behind what it represents. As Alberti famously put it, pictures are windows through which we see. Now the representational logic of ancient vase-painting is markedly different. Here, the carrier, that is the pot, does not negate its own existence, but the represented figures and entities interact with it.[64] On the famous Eleusis amphora, for example, Polyphemus, whom the Greeks are blinding, is propped against the handle of the vase (Figure 7). The handle has no iconographic value, it does not represent something, and yet it is present in the pictured world.

To give a later example that is no less famous: in the tondo of a cup by the Sosias Painter in Berlin, we see Achilles bandage the arm of Patroclus (Figure 8).[65] Patroclus, pain-stricken, braces his left foot against the circle

[62] Characters in narratives saying 'I am x' are not necessarily analogous to the inscription on this vase. Whereas the young man singing is what the painting represents, the character is part of the narrative representation, but may not be its core: the *Odyssey* represents not so much Odysseus as his adventures. The narrative analogy to this iconic metalepsis would be rather a reference to the *kleos* which the narrative creates. In other words, Odysseus' words in *Od.* 9.19–20 offer an analogy not so much through their first part—'I am Odysseus son of Laertes'—as through their second part—'and my fame goes up to the heavens'. Note that this analogy is not an exact parallel, as the young man implicitly refers to his representation whereas Odysseus gestures to the fame proliferating from Homer's narrative. Nonetheless, in both cases represented characters implicitly reach out to the level of the representation.

[63] Phenomenological picture theory tends to add a third level, besides the representing carrier and the represented object also the real object that the represented object signifies, in the terminology of Husserl 'Bildträger', 'Bildsujet', and 'Bildobjekt'. Cf. Wiesing (2005: 30–3).

[64] Cf. Dietrich (2010: 107–230).

[65] Berlin F2278; Beazley, ARV² 21/1, 1620 (Beazley Archive Database 200108); CVA, Berlin, Antiquarium 2, 7–9, pls. (978–80, 991) 49.1–2, 50.1–4, 51.1–4, 62.3.

Figure 7 Proto-attic black-figured amphora by the Polyphemus Painter, neck: blinding of Polyphemus; body: Gorgons chasing Perseus, *c*.670–660 BCE. Eleusis, Archaeological Museum 2630.
© Carole Raddato, Wikimedia Commons, CC BY-SA 2.0.

that frames the representation. The circle has no representative value, it merely reinforces the limits of the picture, but nonetheless the character interacts with it. Not only figures but also objects can be in direct contact with what is without iconographic significance. On the Vatican amphora by Exekias showing Ajax and Achilles playing dice, the shields of the heroes lean against the lines that limit the picture (Figure 9).[66]

Perhaps even more confusing for our eyes are the dagger, quiver, and further objects that hang from the rim of a red-figured cup in Athens while Heracles is attacking Procrustes on one side and Antaeus on the other (Figure 10).[67] Here, as on the Eleusis amphora, objects relate directly not to the frame, but to the vase itself.

Examples could be effortlessly multiplied, but the point, irritating as it is for our perception, should be clear by now: the representing medium

[66] Museo Gregoriano Etrusco 16757 (344); Beazley, ABV 145/13, 672/3, 686 (Beazley Archive Database 310395).
[67] Athens National Museum 1666; Beazley, ARV² 1567/13 (Beazley Archive Database 350911); CVA, Athens National Museum 1, III.I.c, pls. (26, 27) 4.1–4, 5.1–2.

Figure 8 Attic red-figured cup by the Sosias Painter, Achilles bandaging the arm of Patroclus, c.550–500 BCE. Berlin F2278.
© Bibi Saint-Pol 2008, Wikimedia Commons, public domain.

not only depicts something, but is also itself present in the represented world. Without representing something, handles and frames are part of the pictured scene. This peculiarity of vase-painting is thrown into relief by modern paintings that are similar only at first sight.

In Rembrandt's *Hendrickje at the Window* (Figure 11), for example,[68] the left arm of Hendrickje is propped on the lower margin of the painting. Simultaneously, the right arm seems to push against the left border of the picture. Here, however, the figure does not directly interact with the space of representation, but with the frame of a represented window that coincides with the margins of the painting. There may be a weak metalepsis as the portrayed figure seems to touch the frame of the picture, but, unlike the frame on the Exekias amphora in the Vatican, this frame still has iconographic value as a window.

---

[68] See, e.g., Stoichiță (2013: 190–2).

Figure 9 Attic black-figured amphora by Exekias, Ajax and Achilles playing dice, c.575–525 BCE. Vatican, Museo Gregoriano Etrusco 16757 (344).
© bpk | Scala.

Figure 10 Attic red-figured cup, Theseus attacking Procrustes, c.525–475 BCE. Athens, National Museum 1666.
© DAI Athen, D-DAI-ATH-NM 1549.

Figure 11 Rembrandt, *Hendrickje at the Window*, 1656–7. Berlin, Gemäldegalerie.
© bpk / Gemäldegalerie, SMB / Christoph Schmidt.

The metalepsis in vase-painting is also different from the metalepsis at play in Murillo's self-portrait (Figure 12).[69] Murillo's hand reaches out of the picture and grips the frame. The metalepsis is thus far stronger than in Rembrandt's Hendrickje painting: it is ontological. Whereas, however, the figures and objects in vase-painting interact with the carrier of the picture, this metalepsis is embedded in the pictured world; it concerns a picture in the picture. A further difference is also noteworthy and alerts us to the significance of conventions for the study of metalepsis:[70] Murillo's hand is paradoxical and consciously breaches the conventions of the modern tableau. The interaction between vases and their pictures, on the other hand, strikes us as bewildering, but will not have raised eyebrows with ancient users. It is part of the distinct representational logic of vase-painting. There are even vases that use the shape of the pot to enhance their mimesis.

---

[69] Cf. Stoichiță (2013: 204–16) for an interpretation of this painting.
[70] On the importance of conventions see also Matzner in this volume.

Figure 12 Bartolomé Esteban Murillo, self-portrait, 1668–70. London,
National Gallery 6153.
© The National Gallery, London.

To give just one example, the interior of a much-discussed Exekias cup
shows Dionysus in a sailing boat from which a vine sprouts forth. The
concave shape of the vase mimics the form of the sails filled by the wind.[71]
What is peculiar in our eyes is the conventional way of representing
space, which Dietrich has elucidated in an important monograph. Stones,
trees, and walls, Dietrich shows, are used to depict settings, but do not
yield a full-blown pictorial space: 'Although places can play an important
role in a picture, they are without impact on the spatiality of the image.
Places in Attic vase-painting lack spatial quality: their relevance is con-
fined to characterizing actions and figures (which, however, can be crucial
to the understanding of the image).'[72] As much as Greek vase-painters

[71] On this phenomenon see Martens (1992: 67–148) and Grethlein (2018b).
[72] Dietrich (2010: 98): 'Doch auch wenn Orte gelegentlich eine wichtige Rolle in einem
Bild einnehmen können, haben sie keinerlei Auswirkungen auf die Räumlichkeit des Bildes.

were interested in mimetic depictions, they showed little interest in making the pictorial field a window into a specific spatial setting. The figures appear as moving on the vase and thus directly interact with it. What is a transgression for the conventions of the modern tableau is hence itself a convention in vase-painting. This convention lays bare the link between the representing material and the represented material. The modern tableau tries to make the carrier of the picture disappear behind the represented scene, and yet its representation, just like that of vase-painting, is sustained by this link, namely that we are made to see something in a carrier.[73]

While pictorial figures referring to their own representation resemble literary characters referencing their text, the interaction of figures with frames and vases is without a close equivalent in literature. This is due to the different means of representation. Language is a semiotic system in which signs signify according to the rules of convention. Attempts to comprehend pictorial representation as a semiotic system have failed no matter the degree of their nuance. The marks, colours, and lines of pictures do not signify, they show.[74] While it is possible to hear a text, to read it, visually or haptically as Braille, and even to reproduce it in various languages,[75] pictures depend on their unique representation. The represented object is bound in an essential way to the representing carrier. It is this special relation between the levels of the represented and the representing that is unveiled when figures are propped against handles and shields lean against frames.

Die Orte in der attischen Vasenmalerei haben keinerlei räumliche Qualität: Damit liegt ihre Bedeutung bloß mehr in der (freilich manchmal für das Verständnis des Bildes entscheidenden) Charakterisierung von Handlungen und Figuren.'

[73] Such pictorial transgressions between the represented and the representing are not confined to antiquity. We can find similar cases in medieval book illustrations where figures crouch in letters and are attached to their ligatures. As in ancient vase-painting, the objects represented are envisaged less in their own space than as part of the representing medium. For an analysis of the interaction between text and illustration in medieval manuscripts, see, for example, Camille (1992: 11–55).

[74] E.g. Wiesing (2005: 17–36). Unlike other phenomenologists, Wiesing admits that there is a semiotic aspect in pictorial seeing. However, it is not the seeing of something in a picture but the relating of the represented object to something in the real world that is semiotic. On the 'showing' of pictures, see, e.g., Boehm (2007).

[75] This is not to deny that the form in which a text is conveyed is important: especially in poetry the visual arrangement of letters may matter, and, as we all know, the process of translation changes texts, sometimes considerably. That being said, the relation between the representing medium and the represented object is more essential in pictures.

Context Matters: Metalepsis in Antiquity

The idea that not only texts but also pictures can feature metalepses has proven fruitful. Understood as the transgression of different levels of representation, metalepsis can be traced in ancient vase-painting as well as literature. Attic vase-painting employs inscriptions for metaleptic purposes, but it also features specifically iconic metalepses. Due to the different modes of presentation, the pictorial and textual metalepses discussed in the course of this chapter do not always map onto each other. For instance, apostrophe is one of the most glaring cases of metalepsis in ancient literature, but it cannot be found in vase-painting, which represents without a narrator. Inversely, the interaction between figures and other entities of the represented world with the carrier of the picture, namely the vase, is not easily paralleled in literature, where the medium of representation is far less salient.[76]

The spatial logic of vase-painting is also a forceful reminder of the importance of conventions mentioned by Matzner in his introductory chapter to this volume:[77] what is disruptive for the modern understanding of painting as a window appears as natural for a mode of representation that envisages figures on the carrier itself, not in a full-blown space represented on it. The medial differences notwithstanding, metalepses in ancient literature and in vase-painting feature common traits that reveal a specifically ancient treatment of metalepsis. To close this chapter, I will try to pinpoint at least one key aspect of ancient metalepsis and tentatively suggest an explanation. Due to its structuralist heritage, narratology considers its taxonomies ahistorical, but there are more and more voices that demand a historical narratology.[78] Metalepsis is, I think, a case in point; it illustrates that concepts derived from modern texts are often insufficient to do justice to ancient material, that narrative devices and narratological categories change their shapes and functions in the course of time.[79]

---

[76] See, however, references to the blots on the paper which stem from the writer's tears in Ov. *Her.* 3.3 and *Tr.* 1.1.13–14. These and similar references establish a bridge between the world of the writing character to the world of the reader, if through contrast: unlike the 'original' letter, the reader's copy will not be tearstained. I thank the editors for pointing me to this parallel.

[77] Matzner in this volume, pp. 21–3.   [78] E.g. Fludernik (2003a); von Contzen (2014).

[79] For the argument that narratological categories, which are doubtless very useful tools, also tend to limit our sensitivity to distinct features of ancient narrative, see Grethlein (2018a).

We have seen that not only modern but also ancient metalepsis may be abrupt and paradoxical. Metalepsis as a trope, as a textual or pictorial dynamic 'that causes a deviation from what is considered coherent narrative',[80] or, more broadly, coherent representation, is not alien to antiquity. The immersion of the recipient in the narrated world is a case in point. Ancient writers love to embellish stories that blur the boundaries between art and reality. And yet such anecdotes not only highlight the paradox that persons can feel the desire of the flesh for a statue or see a scene about which they only hear, they often also undercut, if only implicitly, the idea of a complete absorption. *Enargeia*, for instance, is sometimes defined as the capacity of speech to make the audience *almost* see what they hear.[81] A specifically iconic metalepsis that is abrasive is constituted by *en face* representations on vases. The frontal depiction jolts the figure out of the pictured world and establishes a direct contact with the beholder. In the case of the most frequent frontal depiction, though, the Gorgon, this violent transgression of the line between the represented world and its external viewer simultaneously underscores that they are viewing only a representation.

While abrasiveness is not unknown in ancient metalepsis, our material abounds in metalepses that cannot be classified as 'paradoxical' and a violent transgression of a 'sacred' boundary. Both ancient texts and pictures feature utterances of characters that fully work in the represented world and unintentionally also address the recipient or refer to the representation. To capture fully this unintrusive kind of metalepsis that seems to range widely in ancient material, I have suggested the term of elastic metalepsis. When the recipients notice this additional significance, they will not feel a jerk that draws their attention to the mediation. On the contrary, they will feel that the represented scene also pertains to them. While reaching out to them, the metalepsis does not destroy the internal plausibility of what is represented. Instead of constituting a rupture, this kind of metalepsis rather creates a continuum between the representation and the represented and brings the recipients closer to the narrated or pictured world.[82]

---

[80] Matzner in this volume, p. 19.

[81] E.g. Theon, *Progymnasmata*, 11 [= *Rhetores Graeci*, ed. Spengel, vol. ii, pp. 118–19]. For more on the balance between immersion and reflection, as explored in ancient material, see Grethlein (2015; 2017).

[82] In Grethlein (forthcoming), I further explore ancient concepts of the relationship between author and characters. I argue that interactions which we describe as metaleptically

There is one point that, while not singlehandedly explaining this tendency of ancient metalepsis, identifies a salient aspect, not least because it occurs in both picture and text. This is the rootedness of the representation in a specific context. Archaic and classical poetry for one is firmly embedded in a performative setting. As we have seen, it is this specific context with which the represented is aligned, thereby becoming metaleptic. The speeches of characters in epinician poetry are metaleptic because the myths narrated mirror the victory that is being celebrated. Tragedy is part of a highly ritualized civic festival, another context with which the world of the text can fuse through the representation of rituals. Historiography is admittedly different, as it is not bound to a specific context, but, in the case of Thucydides and his successors, prides itself on its universality. The transcendence of time, the idea of memory is in fact the hinge on which the metalepsis observed in the works of ancient historians is based. While not capitalizing on a fixed context, indeed making the overcoming of such a context its point, this metalepsis is predicated on a specific function, namely the preservation of memory. Since historiography is closely bound up with memory, references to memory in the world of the action easily index the historian's work.

What I have said about archaic and classical poetry also applies to vase-painting. Most pottery is destined for specific purposes. Metalepses are intensified by depictions that mirror the context in which the vessels are used. I have focused on symposiastic vessels featuring symposiastic scenes that can easily merge with this environment. The eye-cups nicely illustrate how vase-painting comes alive in its use, but the inscriptional rendering of such appeals as 'drink' also unfold their metaleptic quality only in the context of the symposium. As in literature, metalepsis lays bare the communicative situation for which the painting is produced.

The firm embedding in a context distinguishes vase-painting and many ancient texts from most modern literature and art. Modern novels, for example, on which the investigations of literary metalepsis have concentrated, are read in all kinds of setting, in bed or at a desk, individually or as part of a reading group, before going to sleep or on the train to work. We also seclude art pictures from the traffic of the everyday world. Whereas some vase-paintings only reveal their full meaning when held or moved, pictures in galleries and museums are positioned beyond touch. It is wrong to claim, as scholars have done under the influence of Kristeller,

---

transgressing narrative boundaries appear as rather natural in a logic for which the notion of impersonation is central.

that aesthetics emerged only around 1800, but it is equally misleading to ignore differences between the aesthetic autonomy that, albeit not unchallenged, defines modern art, and the pragmatic dimension of much of ancient art: texts that do not bespeak a genius but have a clear function and pictorial carriers that are commodity goods.[83]

This discrepancy is, I think, crucial to why ancient metalepsis often fails to conform to the modern concept that puts a premium on its paradoxical nature. The modern (artificial) seclusion of art including literature, culminating in the idea of *l'art pour l'art*, fosters an understanding of metalepsis as rupture. When texts and pictures are produced to be autonomous, bridges between the represented world and the world of the recipient are seen to violate a sacred border. By the same token, embedded worlds are envisaged as categorically separated from the represented world. In art and literature, however, that is created for a specific setting and with a pragmatic function, metalepsis can be marshalled to reinforce the links between the represented and its use on this occasion. On the one hand, content that directly relates to the context in which a text or a picture circulates helps their representations to fulfil their functions. On the other, the performance of a text aims at pulling the audience into its world, and commodity goods such as vessels invite a bodily engagement that modern galleries deny their guests. The prominence of metalepsis as a means of reinforcing the communicative situation, instead of dismantling the wall around an autonomous narrative or picture, is keyed in to a pragmatic view of art, an understanding of literature and images as acts of communication.

---

[83] For a powerful argument against Kristeller's thesis (1951; 1952), see recently Porter (2009a and 2009b, the latter a response to Shiner 2009). For further positions on ancient notions of art and aesthetics, see the contributions to Platt and Squire (2010). See also Gadamer's classical critique of the modern notion of the autonomy of art in the first part of *Wahrheit und Methode* (1990: 9–174) and, from an anthropological perspective, Gell (1998) as well as Bourdieu (1979) in sociology.

3

Metalepsis and Readerly Investment in Fictional Characters

Reflections on Apostrophic Reading

Felix Budelmann

'Sometimes', so the Irish novelist Colum McCann tells an interviewer, 'I want to run away and just spend an afternoon in the pub with my characters, or walk through the Bronx with them.'[1] Viewers of *Coronation Street* express how they feel when a car crash injures certain characters: 'You feel as if they had been in a real road accident and you'd like to do something for them,' and 'My wife was very upset. So was I. I hope they'll be all right.'[2] A *Harry Potter* fan writes, 'I love Molly. The more I start to think about and analyse the depth of her mothering for her own children and for Harry, the more overwhelmed with emotion I become.'[3] With rather different levels of ontological and emotional commitment, ranging from mere turns of phrase to psychological disorders, readers and viewers sometimes imagine their relationship with a fictional character as one of not just observation but also interaction. This, we might say, is a metaleptic phenomenon, a crossing of the boundary between narrative and reality. Readers (including, as with McCann, authors as readers of their own fictions) let the character into their own world, or enter the character's world.

* I am grateful to the editors and to Tom Phillips for their acute comments on an earlier draft, and to Barbara Graziosi, Tim Whitmarsh, and Evert van Emde Boas for helpful replies to my queries.

[1] Lennon (2012: 165).   [2] McQuail et al. (1972: 157).
[3] From a *Harry Potter* discussion forum, cited by Giles (2010: 442), in the context of studying 'parasocial relationships' with fictional characters.

Felix Budelmann, *Metalepsis and Readerly Investment in Fictional Characters: Reflections on Apostrophic Reading* In: *Metalepsis: Ancient Texts, New Perspectives.* Edited by: Sebastian Matzner and Gail Trimble, Oxford University Press (2020). © The editors and Oxford University Press.
DOI: 10.1093/oso/9780198846987.003.0003

In pursuing such ideas in relation to apostrophe in ancient Greek narrative texts, this chapter takes its inspiration not from narratological discussions of metalepsis—at least not classical structuralist narratology which, with its 'implied' authors and readers, tends to shun questions of reality—but from a different strand of work on metalepsis, in which metalepsis serves as a prompt to think about fictionality and the relationship of the reader with the fictional world.[4] Metalepsis, even though a text-internal trope, opens out vistas beyond the text.[5] By 'breaking the frame' that surrounds the fictional world, it suggests that the fictional world is not hermetically sealed.

Authorial apostrophe in narrative, my topic here, is one of the most common modes of metalepsis in ancient texts, and has a prominent place in studies of metalepsis in Classics, including indeed this volume.[6] Fundamentally, apostrophe has two aspects, the turning away that gives it its name, as well as a turning toward. The former is crucial for the metaleptic effect, as the narrator turns away from the business of narrating. This is why apostrophe often does not feel metaleptic in certain non-narrative contexts (e.g. an address in the opening line of a poem, where there is nothing to turn away from yet). The latter, the turning toward, has been examined especially by theorists of lyric, and can shade into prosopopoeia: 'O Rose, thou art sick'.[7] By adopting a second-person voice, whether or not turning away from anything, the speaker accords to an absent lover, an imaginary friend, or an inert object a presence, a sentience, and indeed an existence that they do not necessarily have. In both its aspects—and in narrative texts both are present at the same time—apostrophe manipulates the boundary between the fictional and the real, addressing a fictional character or thing as though he, she, or it could hear the address. The difference is one of markedness: the more clearly apostrophe interrupts a narrative, the more emphatic is its metaleptic effect.[8]

---

[4] For the two traditions of thinking about metalepsis, see the concise statement at the beginning of Baron (2005); cf. Pier (2016: §3). For examples of the latter tradition, see below, pp. 75–6.

[5] The ambivalence of metalepsis as both trope and figure is discussed by Matzner, this volume, pp. 10–22, esp. p. 21.

[6] Apostrophe is the topic of the first section in De Jong (2009), the foundational article for the study of metalepsis in ancient literature, and is discussed in six of the sixteen articles in Eisen and von Möllendorff (2013b). In this volume, it is at the centre of the chapters of De Jong and Trimble, and is discussed also by Grethlein, Lovatt, and Kennedy; see the index.

[7] See esp. Kneale (1991), who argues for the distinction between apostrophe proper (viz. turning away) and address, and suggests that Culler's influential analysis of apostrophe is really an analysis of prosopopoeia.

[8] The question of apostrophe in lyric, as well as the distinction between apostrophe and address, are discussed more fully in Trimble's chapter in this volume.

My project in this chapter is as follows. I will explore the act of addressing fictional, and in several cases long-dead, characters (and in my final example a long-dead author) as an expression of the kind of relationship with fiction illustrated in my opening paragraph. This is not, therefore, an attempt to provide a general discussion of apostrophe. Rather, I want to ask, by way of taking the author as the first reader, what model of engagement with fiction we find ourselves presented with if we experimentally take the gesture of speaking to a fictional character literally, reading it not merely as a rhetorical trope but a meaningful speech act. Central to such a model, I suggest, is the idea of the *availability* of the character. To address a character is to suggest that the character can, somehow, still be accessed and interacted with. Apostrophe, in this mode of reading (the 'apostrophic reading' of my title), serves as an invitation to form relationships with characters—to admire them, love them, hate them, argue with them, mourn for them. Importantly, and this is my second overarching point in this chapter, the kind of relationship enacted by apostrophe varies from text to text. It is for this reason that I will look at four rather different texts, Homeric epic, Sapphic lyric, a bucolic poem by Theocritus, and a progymnasma by Musonius Rufus, and will consciously be stretching the remit of metalepsis. The aim of the chapter is to suggest not only that apostrophe repays reading as a model of how readers engage with fiction, but that each text models its own version of this engagement.

Homer

Nineteen times in the *Iliad* and fifteen times in the *Odyssey*, Homer interrupts his third-person narrative to address one of his characters: Eumaeus, Patroclus, Menelaus, Apollo, Achilles, Melanippus (in descending order of frequency).[9] My example here will be the address to Patroclus immediately before he is stunned by Apollo.

> ἔνθ' ἄρα τοι, Πάτροκλε, φάνη βιότοιο τελευτή
> There, Patroclus, appeared for you the end of life.   (*Il.* 16.787)

Attempts to interpret this and other instances of Homeric apostrophe go back to the ancient scholiasts, who suggest that apostrophe is an indication

---

[9] The passages are listed, e.g., by Richardson (1990: 237–8 nn. 5 and 6).

of sympathy.[10] Modern scholarship has added a range of further approaches. For my concerns here, the best starting point is a statement by Clay:[11] 'The speaker momentarily turns his back on his audience, as it were, and is absorbed into the story world, directly addressing a Patroclus or a Menelaus as if they were standing here and now in the very space of performance. The real world seems to recede as the past becomes almost palpably present. But in apostrophizing his characters, the poet uses the past tense, which in itself indicates the non-presence of the addressee.' In concise form, Clay brings out several characteristics of Homeric apostrophe. She starts with the idea that Homer, in an act of true ἀποστροφή, 'turns his back on his audience' and takes himself to the world of his characters, yet in the same sentence there is also the notion that it is the characters, rather than the poet, who have done the travelling and are now present 'in the very space of performance'. Indeed, Homer does not make it clear how the barrier between poet/audience and fiction is broken, or who does the breaking; what matters is that an undefined space emerges in which the poet, and at one remove the audience, can interact with the characters.[12]

A temporal fusion corresponds to the spatial one. To address Patroclus, Homer needs, somehow, to occupy the same temporal plane, but Clay makes the important observation that he nevertheless uses the past tense: the end of life 'appeared'. Here as elsewhere, Homeric apostrophe creates mixed temporalities, staging an interaction without denying the categorical distance of the world of heroes from the world of the audience that the *Iliad* consistently asserts. In so far as it is now that we are reading or listening to the narrative, the act of metaleptic transgression takes place in the present, and yet no attempt is made to deny that Patroclus lived, and died, a long time ago. (In fact, quite apart from the use of the past tense, Patroclus is told something—the imminence of his death—that the poet clearly did not tell him back then, and in the lines that follow we learn that he did not even notice Apollo approach (789–90).)

[10] Yamagata (1989: 91 n. 1) gathers some of the relevant scholia; one of them is quoted below, p. 64. For modern treatments of apostrophe along broadly similar lines, see e.g. Block (1982: 15–17) and Richardson (1990: 170–4).

[11] Clay (2011: 20). Related points, also relevant to my discussion here, are made by Graziosi (2013: 17–24). For an overview of the different views on apostrophe taken in Homeric scholarship on apostrophe, see De Jong (2009: 94).

[12] De Jong in this volume discusses briefly the two potential directions of travel (poet to character, character to poet) for Homer (p. 80) and Pindar (p. 94), and, more than I do here, considers ways of choosing between them.

Homeric apostrophe, then, is a self-conscious poetic gesture that con-
veys a temporally and spatially complex form of availability. The poet lays
claim to a relationship with the characters, and in doing so enacts a model
that audiences can adopt, modify, or reject. The fictional world as enacted
by apostrophe is not wholly closed off, and, despite its ontological distance,
is there for us to engage with. Metalepsis in this sense does not just lay
bare the fictionality of the narrative, as it is widely acknowledged to do,[13]
but also portrays the author as doing what readers often do—creating rela-
tionships with characters that in certain ways resemble relationships with
real people.

Significantly, the nature of these relationships is left open. Most scholars
agree that emotional and ethical readings along the lines of the ancient
scholiasts—the poet sympathizing with, or pitying, the character—are
indeed possible in certain instances, but that they cannot be extended
across the board: attractive for Patroclus, Eumaeus, and Menelaus, they
work less well for the other characters. Homeric apostrophe provides a
model that allows readers to mould their own relationships with the char-
acters. It prefigures the possibility that there can be a relationship, but it
does not prescribe the particular form such a relationship might take. It is
semantically open.

Neither, for that matter, does Homeric apostrophe limit relationships to
particular types of character. The characters the poet addresses are a mixed
group: a god (Apollo), three Greek heroes (Achilles, Menelaus, Patroclus),
a little-known Trojan hero (Melanippus), and a swineherd (Eumaeus).
This assortment of major and minor, human and divine, Greek and Trojan,
sympathetic and less so has, negatively, made it impossible to produce a
one-fits-all interpretation of Homeric apostrophe, but, positively and in
the terms of my discussion here, the absence of an obvious pattern goes
some way towards presenting Homer as a poet who is catholic in his vision
and does not neglect any of his characters, small or large. Indeed, the his-
tory of Homeric reception shows that readers, in one way or other, have
allowed themselves to be affected by all manner of characters. Homer, one
might be tempted to say, has no favourites. Such an interpretation has
much to recommend it, but has important limitations. There is one prom-
inent group of characters that is notably absent from the list of Homeric

---

[13] I take the formulation from De Jong (2009: 91), who is referring to McHale (1987) ch. 8:
'McHale suggests that metalepsis lays bare the fictionality of fiction.' De Jong herself argues
that Homeric apostrophe creates *enargeia*. My own position here tries to find a way of
acknowledging both effects, but with a different conceptual framework.

addressees: none of them are women, even though some of the most engaging characters in both epics are female. Why does Homer not speak to any of them? Pursuing this question could take us in a number of different directions (women subordinate, women inward, women replaced by the Muse, and so on), but in any case we have to admit that where female characters are concerned there is a marked discrepancy between the author, who does not address them, and his modern and indeed ancient readers, who again and again have been drawn towards them.[14]

The scholium on the address to Patroclus cited above will round off this section. In one of the fullest ancient treatments of Homeric apostrophe, the scholiast puts forward the following interpretation:

ἡ ἀποστροφὴ σημαίνει τὸν συναχθόμενον· σοὶ γάρ, ὦ Πάτροκλε, τῷ οὕτως ὑπ' Ἀχιλλέως ἀγαπωμένῳ, τῷ πᾶν εἰς σωτηρίαν τῶν Ἑλλήνων πραγματευσαμένῳ, τῷ Νέστορος φιλοπόνως ἀνασχομένῳ, τῷ Εὐρύπυλον φιλοστόργως ἰασαμένῳ, τῷ ὑπὲρ τῶν Ἑλλήνων δακρύσαντι καὶ τὸν σκληρῶς διακείμενον Ἀχιλλέα πείσαντι, τῷ κατὰ τῆς ἑαυτοῦ ψυχῆς τὴν ἔξοδον κατορθώσαντι. ταῦτα πάντα ἔνεστιν ἐπαναφέροντας ἐπὶ τὴν ἀποστροφὴν ὁρᾶν τὸ ἐν αὐτῇ περιπαθές.

The apostrophe signals (the poet's) empathy: with you, Patroclus, who was so loved by Achilles, who did everything to save the Greeks, who put up with Nestor strenuously, who looked after Eurypylos tenderly, who cried for the Greeks and persuaded Achilles when he was not disposed to yield, who created a way out at the expense of your own life. If one relates all this to the apostrophe one can see its very great emotional charge.   (bT schol. ad *Il.* 16.787, my translation)

The apostrophe prompts the scholiast to interpret both the poet's attitude and the character. He goes far beyond the immediate context, and sees the apostrophe as a response to Patroclus' life as a whole. Strikingly, he does not just impute a sympathetic attitude to the poet but himself chooses to address Patroclus. The tone is difficult to make out: is this a primarily playful imitation of Homer's literary gesture or is the scholiast for his own part expressing the sympathy that he diagnoses for Homer? The

---

[14] Regarding ancient readers: in general terms, a particularly obvious example is the extensive Helen tradition (cf. n. 17 below). A specific example is Hermesianax fr. 7.27–34 Powell, who goes so far as to depict Homer as in love with Penelope. It is notable that Socrates, in his vision of meeting some of the characters of epic in the underworld (cited p. 77–8 below), names only male characters, adding, however, that there are 'countless others, men and women'.

latter is perhaps more likely, but either way, at least verbally the scholiast enters into, and imaginatively extends, the relationship with Patroclus that Homer models.

Sappho

Lyric, as noted, is a more problematic form in which to discuss the metaleptic effects of narrative apostrophe, both because apostrophe is a signature trope of the genre and because lyric, certainly the relatively short lyric poems of Sappho, which I will be looking at here, is not on the whole a narrative form. Apostrophe does not here stand out in the same way as in epic, and does not usually constitute a marked shift in ontological level. Accordingly, my aim in this section is not to argue the merits or demerits of the case for classifying lyric apostrophe as a variety of metalepsis, but to discuss ways in which one particular poem, Sappho 1, allows one to interpret lyric apostrophe, properly metaleptic or not, as modelling a reading experience that is characteristic of the genre. Here is Sappho's poem in full:

ποικιλόθρον᾽ ἀθανάτ᾽ Ἀφρόδιτα,
παῖ Δίος δολόπλοκε, λίσσομαί σε,
μή μ᾽ ἄσαισι μηδ᾽ ὀνίαισι δάμνα,
πότνια, θῦμον·

ἀλλὰ τυίδ᾽ ἔλθ᾽, αἴ ποτα κἀτέρωτα   5
τὰς ἔμας αὔδας ἀίοισα πήλοι
ἔκλυες, πάτρος δὲ δόμον λίποισα
χρύσιον ἦλθες

ἄρμ᾽ ὑπασδεύξαισα. κάλοι δέ σ᾽ ἆγον
ὤκεες στροῦθοι περὶ γᾶς μελαίνας   10
πύκνα δίννηντες πτέρ᾽ ἀπ᾽ ὠράνω αἴθε-
ρος διὰ μέσσω·

αἶψα δ᾽ ἐξίκοντο. σὺ δ᾽, ὦ μάκαιρα,
μειδιαίσαισ᾽ ἀθανάτῳ προσώπῳ,
ἤρε᾽ ὄττι δηὖτε πέπονθα κὤττι   15
δηὖτε κάλημι

κὤττι μοι μάλιστα θέλω γένεσθαι
μαινόλᾳ θύμῳ · "τίνα δηὖτε πείθω
] †σαγην ἐς σὰν† φιλότατα; τίς σ᾽, ὦ
Ψάπφ᾽, ἀδικήει;   20

καὶ γὰρ αἰ φεύγει, ταχέως διώξει·
αἰ δὲ δῶρα μὴ δέκετ᾽, ἀλλὰ δώσει·
αἰ δὲ μὴ φίλει, ταχέως φιλήσει
κωὐκ ἐθέλοισα."

ἔλθε μοι καὶ νῦν, χαλέπαν δὲ λῦσον   25
ἐκ μερίμναν, ὄσσα δέ μοι τέλεσσαι
θῦμος ἰμέρρει τέλεσον, σὺ δ᾽ αὔτα
σύμμαχος ἔσσο.

Ornate-throned immortal Aphrodite, wile-weaving daughter of Zeus, I entreat you: do not overpower my heart, mistress, with ache and anguish, but come here, if ever in the past you heard my voice from afar and acquiesced and came, leaving your father's golden house, with chariot yoked: beautiful swift sparrows whirring fast-beating wings brought you above the dark earth down from heaven through the mid-air, and soon they arrived; and you, blessed one, with a smile on your immortal face asked what was the matter with me this time and why I was calling this time and what in my maddened heart I most wished to happen for myself: 'Whom am I to persuade this time †to bring you back to your† love? Who wrongs you, Sappho? If she runs away, soon she shall pursue; if she does not accept gifts, why, she shall give them instead; and if she does not love, soon she shall love even against her will.' Come to me now again and deliver me from oppressive anxieties; fulfil all that my heart longs to fulfil, and you yourself be my fellow-fighter.   (Sappho 1, trans. Campbell, adapted)

Like many Greek lyric poems, Sappho 1 draws on the traditional tripartite prayer form. An address to Aphrodite, culminating in the cletic appeal 'come here!' (1–5), is followed by an extended account of Aphrodite's past benevolence (5–24), before the final section makes a full request for support (25–8).[15] If the poem is treated as a sung prayer—a hymn, in later terminology—the address to Aphrodite can hardly be called metaleptic. What nevertheless creates related effects is the mixing of address, dialogue, and narrative in the account of Sappho's earlier encounters with the goddess. At line 18, in an instance of De Jong's third category of ancient metalepsis ('blending of narrative voices'), Sappho slips from indirect into

---

[15] For Sappho's use of this form see Burzacchini (2005). For secondary literature on Sappho 1 in general see Budelmann (2018: 116).

direct speech and begins to enact the goddess's voice.[16] When the direct speech ends, at line 25, the return to second-person address (ἔλθε μοι καὶ νῦν) produces a more noticeable jolt than the earlier down-shift. The direct speech, despite its past-tense framing ('you asked', 15), creates the sense that Aphrodite has listened to Sappho's first call (5) and is speaking to her right now, and it is only when Sappho evidently feels the need to repeat the request to come that we are reminded that Aphrodite's speech was embedded in a past-tense narrative. Even though, strictly speaking, no narrative boundaries are crossed, an appearance of metaleptic apostrophe is nevertheless generated, and as a result the smooth shift from indirect to direct speech seems with hindsight less smooth. Sappho 1 never categorically jumps from narrating a character's action to addressing the character, yet by the time the final stanza is reached the shifts between speaking-about, speaking-as, and speaking-to have become more and more noticeable.

Where Homer grants his long-dead characters a form of availability and presence despite awareness of temporal boundaries, Sappho stages an encounter with a goddess who is not a figure of the past but who is shaped, perhaps even created, by Sappho's own mind. Sappho's meeting with Aphrodite has a degree of intimacy and intensity that is absent from Homer's interactions with his characters, and the weakness of the metalepsis is an indication of the permeability of the boundaries that separate poet and goddess, narrative and address. In fact, it is more than that: it is also an indication of the all-important role Sappho accords to her imagination. The immediate presence of Aphrodite, so immediate that the past-tense framing is almost forgotten until the 'come now too!' in the final stanza jolts the reader back to the scenario of a prayer to an absent deity, is generated by Sappho's rehearsal of her memory. As in Homer, temporalities here are mixed, but the present, as often in lyric, exerts a centripetal force, as encounters of the past become present in Sappho's memory. The interaction with Aphrodite is taking place—now—in her head. Aphrodite is Sappho's Aphrodite.

The ode to Aphrodite, placed first in the Alexandrian edition of Sappho, has often been read as programmatic, announcing as it does love, poetry, and intimacy with Aphrodite as pervasive themes of Sappho's poetry. From the viewpoint of this chapter, the poem may be seen as typical of Sappho, and indeed of personal lyric more widely, also in the kind of

---

[16]   De Jong (2009: 99–106), expanded on in De Jong (2013).

relationships it models through its metaleptic shifts between address, dialogue, and report. Lyric holds out the promise of close encounters with another person, much closer both temporally and epistemically than those enabled by epic, yet the person we meet exists only in the imagination. The power Aphrodite has to affect Sappho's life[17] may be read as an expression of the transformative capacity of lyric, its promise to affect us deeply, both emotionally and cognitively, yet this promise is entirely dependent on our willingness to invest. More radically than in the case of Patroclus, whose existence is given solidity by his participation in an extensive narrative, the lyric encounter is personal—individual experiences, affinities, and memories fill the gaps left by the lack of plot. Even though Sappho 1, then, is one of only a small handful of Greek lyric poems that enact a dialogue between 'I' and other, creating metaleptic effects in the process, the characteristics of this dialogue mirror the experience of reading lyric more generally.

Theocritus

Hellenistic poets used apostrophe widely, variously, and virtuosically.[18] Often it is poets and singers of the past that are addressed, as part of a programme of poetic self-definition, and this is the case also in the passage that I shall discuss here. Theocritus' seventh Idyll may well be his most difficult, and is certainly the most discussed.[19] As Hunter puts it, 'perhaps the only thing about Idyll 7 upon which most critics agree is that it is "programmatic" in the broad sense that it both displays and reflects upon important aspects of Theocritus' poetic art as we find it in the rest of the corpus'.[20] The great majority of the many problems posed by this intriguing poem will be set aside here as I focus specifically on the address to Comatas and explore it as a model of reading Theocritus' bucolic poetry.

---

[17] In even more pronounced form, this dynamic may have been encapsulated in Helen's effect on Stesichorus in the *Palinode*, even though it is uncertain whether all the detail in the testimonia, especially the blinding, goes back to the poem itself. (As with Sappho's address to Aphrodite, the effect will have been metaleptic only in a weak sense: see Bing, this volume, pp. 102–3.)

[18] On apostrophe in Apollonius and Callimachus see Klooster (2013: 158–71), with earlier literature. Several examples in the discussion of 'the poet's link with the literary past' discussed by Bing (1988: 50–90) involve apostrophe.

[19] Specifically on the passage discussed here (*Id.* 7.83–9) see, apart from the commentaries: Goldhill (1991: 234–6), Stanzel (1995: 274–5), Krevans (2006: 133–4), Payne (2007: 124–8).

[20] Hunter (1996: 22).

The apostrophe is placed emphatically at the very end of Lycidas' song. Twenty lines into his performance, Lycidas describes how another singer, Tityrus, will sing about Daphnis as he was fed by bees while shut away in a box. Then, possibly continuing Tityrus' song, possibly speaking in his own voice, Lycidas shifts the focus to yet another herdsman poet, Comatas, and with this shift abruptly switches from third- to second-person phrasing:

> ὦ μακαριστὲ Κομᾶτα, τύ θην τάδε τερπνὰ πεπόνθεις·
> καὶ τὺ κατεκλάσθης ἐς λάρνακα, καὶ τὺ μελισσᾶν
> κηρία φερβόμενος ἔτος ὥριον ἐξεπόνασας.
> αἴθ' ἐπ' ἐμεῦ ζωοῖς ἐναρίθμιος ὤφελες ἦμεν,
> ὥς τοι ἐγὼν ἐνόμευον ἀν' ὤρεα τὰς καλὰς αἶγας
> φωνᾶς εἰσαΐων, τὺ δ' ὑπὸ δρυσὶν ἢ ὑπὸ πεύκαις
> ἁδὺ μελισδόμενος κατεκέκλισο, θεῖε Κομᾶτα.

Blessed Comatas, you have experienced these pleasures; you too were shut in a chest; you too were fed on honeycomb and laboured hard in the year's springtime. If only you had been counted among the living in my day, so that I could have herded your fine goats in the hills and listened to your voice as you sat making sweet music under the oaks or pines, divine Comatas.   (Theoc. 7.83–9, trans. Hopkinson)

Comparison with the address to Patroclus in *Iliad* 16 suggests itself. Both passages are couched in historical tenses, and like Patroclus, Comatas is explicitly dead, a legendary figure of the past, and yet, again like Patroclus, he can still be addressed. Conceivably, the ambiguity of the tense of πεπόνθεις attempts to encapsulate this paradox: if we take it as an (unaugmented) pluperfect Comatas' pleasurable fate is a matter of the past, but if we read it as a perfect his sweet suffering persists.[21] Hymnic overtones (θεῖε Κομᾶτα) may provide a further connection.[22]

Despite such similarities, the framing lends Theocritus' apostrophe a level of complexity that is absent from Homer and even Sappho. The issue is first of all one of voice. It is unclear whether Comatas is addressed by Tityrus

---

[21] The majority of commentators, including most recently Hunter (1999) *ad loc.*, opt for pluperfect; perfect is advocated by Gow (1952) *ad loc.*

[22] Hymnic address to deities and cult heroes as a background to epic apostrophe is discussed by De Jong in her 2009 article (pp. 95–6) and in this volume, as well as by Klooster (2013: 154–8). On divine address in Catullus, see Trimble in this volume, pp. 129–33.

(as reported by Lycidas), by Lycidas himself, or indeed by 'Theocritus'.[23] As Tityrus', Lycidas', and 'Theocritus" voices fuse, so do the temporalities they inhabit. Tityrus will sing in the future (ᾀσεῖ, 72), Lycidas' speech and song are narrated in the past (χὠ μὲν τόσσ᾽ εἰπὼν ἀπεπαύσατο, 90), and 'Theocritus', as the narrator, inhabits the reader's present. This extravagant blending of temporalities, considerably more elaborate than what we have seen so far, adds to the sense of Comatas' timeless availability and at the same time lends the apostrophe an elusive quality.

To the layered and elusive speaker corresponds a, certainly to us, barely individualized addressee. No historical or mythical poet Comatas has left any trace, and it is at least possible that none was known to ancient readers either.[24] Even if Comatas was a well-known figure, Theocritus makes a point of presenting him as something like a copy: 'you too (καὶ τύ, 84)...'. There is Daphnis, there is (probably) the unnamed goatherd of 78–82,[25] and there is Comatas, who therefore is third (or certainly second) in a sequence of comparable poetic founding figures. If mimesis is a constituting trope of bucolic poetry, characters do not come more bucolic than Comatas.[26]

Unlike Homer's and Sappho's apostrophes, then, the address to Comatas flaunts a sense of repeatability and exchangeability on part of both speaker and addressee, and this absence of individuality is felt also in the nature of the address itself. Where Homer's apostrophes have been read as expressions of sympathy and pity, and Sappho calls upon Aphrodite for help, no such ethical interpretations are invited here, and where Lycidas' desire for Ageanax in the lines before (52–70) is an erotic or romantic longing for another person, the yearning for Comatas is considerably more restrained—to live at the same time and have the opportunity to listen. There is admiration, certainly, and a wish to experience his art, but the passage does not enact a meeting of selves. The speaker, whoever he is, does not open himself up to Comatas, nor does he expect Comatas to open himself up to him.

Theocritus' metaleptic apostrophe, then, is characterized by a tension. The nostalgic wish to inhabit the same world as Comatas is both ardently

[23] See Goldhill (1991: 235–6), Hunter (1999: ad 72–89).
[24] Comatas is a goatherd in Idyll 5.
[25] See Hunter (1999: ad 78–89) on whether the unnamed goatherd is the same as Comatas or a separate figure.
[26] There are also close similarities between Comatas and Lycidas; see e.g. Segal (1981 (1974): 125).

expressed and hedged by a sense of replicability and mediation. The kind of reading modelled here is not one of reaching out to the characters that inhabit the text but one of longing for a whole fictional universe, a reading that is oneiric and nostalgic rather than ethical. In the context of investigating what he calls Theocritus' 'fully fictional' worlds, Payne puts it like this: 'Lycidas suggests that the effect of such songs is to create a yearning in their audience to belong to the world that they portray.'[27] The passage, in other words, models fascination with a fictional world qua fictional world. On this paradigm, we as readers, taking our lead from the author, do not bridge the gap and enter the fictional word but remain acutely conscious of its distance and artificiality, and it is this consciousness that stands in the way of encounters charged with personal meaning and in their stead generates a stance of nostalgia.

Musonius Rufus

My final case study takes variation yet further: prose rather than poetry, philosophical argument rather than narrative, and an address to a dead author rather than to a fictional character.[28] The Stoic Musonius Rufus (first century CE), a native of Etruria but teaching in Greek, did not apparently publish any writings, but we have a number of his discourses as recorded by his students.[29] (For my purposes it does not matter how much the students shaped the text, and for convenience I shall refer simply to 'Musonius'.)

Discourse 9 is entitled 'That exile is not an evil'. Among those who suggest otherwise, and with whom Musonius takes issue, is Euripides or, as we would put it, Euripides' character Jocasta:

νὴ Δί᾽ ἀλλ᾽ Εὐριπίδης φησὶν ἐλευθερίας στέρεσθαι τοὺς φυγάδας, ἐπεὶ καὶ παρρησίας. πεποίηκε γὰρ τὴν μὲν Ἰοκάστην πυνθανομένην Πολυνείκους τοῦ υἱέος, τίνα δυσχερῆ τῷ φεύγοντί ἐστιν· ὁ δ᾽ ἀποκρίνεται ὅτι

---

[27] Payne (2007: 125).

[28] See Kearey in this volume for discussion of a much more sustained and developed dialogue with a dead author, Fulgentius' conversation with the shade of Virgil.

[29] For Musonius' philosophy see Laurenti (1989), Belliotti (2009: 197–203), and Thorsteinsson (2010: 40–54).

ἓν μὲν μέγιστον, οὐκ ἔχει παρρησίαν,
ἡ δ' αὖ πρὸς αὐτὸν
δούλου τόδ' εἶπας, μὴ λέγειν ἅ τις φρονεῖ.

ἐγὼ δὲ φαίην ἂν πρὸς τὸν Εὐριπίδην ὅτι, ὦ Εὐριπίδη, τοῦτο μὲν ὀρθῶς
ὑπολαμβάνεις, ὡς δούλου ἐστίν, ἃ φρονεῖ μὴ λέγειν, ὅταν γε δέῃ λέγειν· οὐ
γὰρ ἀεὶ καὶ πανταχοῦ καὶ πρὸς ὀντινοῦν λεκτέον ἃ φρονοῦμεν. ἐκεῖνο δὲ οὔ
μοι δοκεῖς εὖ εἰρηκέναι, τὸ μὴ μετεῖναι τοῖς φεύγουσι παρρησίας, εἴπερ
παρρησία σοι δοκεῖ τὸ μὴ σιγᾶν ἃ φρονῶν τυγχάνει τις. οὐ γὰρ οἱ φεύγοντες
ὀκνοῦσι λέγειν ἃ φρονοῦσιν, ἀλλ' οἱ δεδιότες μὴ ἐκ τοῦ εἰπεῖν γένηται αὐτοῖς
πόνος ἢ θάνατος ἢ ζημία ἤ τι τοιοῦτον ἕτερον. τοῦτο δὲ τὸ δέος μὰ Δία οὐχ ἡ
φυγὴ ποιεῖ. πολλοῖς γὰρ ὑπάρχει καὶ τῶν ἐν τῇ πατρίδι ὄντων, μᾶλλον δὲ τοῖς
πλείστοις, τὰ δοκοῦντα δεινὰ δεδιέναι. ὁ δὲ ἀνδρεῖος οὐδὲν ἧττον φυγὰς ὢν
ἤπερ οἴκοι θαρρεῖ πρὸς ἅπαντα τὰ τοιαῦτα, διὸ καὶ λέγει ἃ φρονεῖ θαρρῶν
οὐδὲν μᾶλλον ἢ ὅταν ᾖ μὴ φυγάς, ὅταν φεύγων τύχῃ. ταῦτα μὲν πρὸς
Εὐριπίδην εἴποι τις ἄν.

But, by Zeus, Euripides says that exiles lose their freedom when they are deprived of freedom of speech. For he represents Jocasta asking Polyneices, her son, what misfortunes an exile has to bear, and he answers,

'One is greatest of all, that he does not have freedom of speech.' [Eur. *Ph.* 391]

She replies,

'You name the condition of a slave, not to be able to say what one thinks.' [*Ph.* 392]

But I should say to Euripides: 'You are right, Euripides, when you say that it is the condition of a slave not to say what one thinks (whenever one *ought* to do so, that is, for it is not always, nor everywhere, nor before everyone that we should say what we think). But one point, it seems to me, you have not made well, namely that exiles do not have freedom of speech (if to you freedom of speech means not to be silent about whatever one happens to think). For it is not exiles who shrink from saying what they think, but men afraid lest from speaking pain or death or punishment or some other such thing befall them. Fear is the cause of this, and not, by Zeus, exile! For to many people, indeed to most, even though dwelling in their native city, fear of what seem to them dire consequences of free speech is present. The courageous man, in exile no less than at home, is dauntless in the face of all such fears; for that reason also he is not being more courageous if he says

what he thinks when he happens to be in exile than when he is at home.'
Those are the things that one might say in reply to Euripides.
(Muson. 9, pp. 48–9 Hense, trans. Whitmarsh (2001b), adapted[30])

The passage quotes Euripides to introduce the claim that exiles do not possess freedom of speech, and then presents Musonius' retort, addressed directly to Euripides. In so far as the retort is couched in counterfactual terms ('I should say to Euripides') it is only borderline metaleptic, but the shift of narrative levels is nevertheless marked, even more so since Musonius has quoted Euripides already twice before in this speech, both times maintaining third-person discourse (pp. 42 and 45 Hense), and since the rhetorical figure he employs here, 'refutation' (*anaskeuē*) of a putative objection, is normally couched in the third person.[31] Hypothetical though it is, the address to Euripides stands out from the discursive context.

As in Homer, Sappho, and Theocritus, the apostrophe conveys availability. Euripides, although doubtless understood to be a poet of the past, is somebody with whom Musonius can converse as with a contemporary. If one wanted to press the text, one might point out that the formulation 'one point, *it seems to me* (δοκεῖς), you have not made well' opens the door for Euripides to argue back—an appropriate expression of respect for somebody whose views are endorsed earlier in the speech. The temporal distance is at best hinted at (does 'I would say' imply 'if he were still alive and present here'?). What Musonius is doing here is to develop the implications of the conventional present tense 'Euripides says' at the beginning of the passage. Euripides was often thought of as a philosopher,[32] and these particular lines from *Phoenician Women* may well have been staples of intellectual debate.[33] Musonius is staging a literalized version of the intuitive metaphorical notion that philosophers are in dialogue with one another through their texts and across the barriers of time.

---

[30] I deviate above all, and with considerable hesitation, in the penultimate sentence (ὁ δὲ ἀνδρεῖος ... τύχῃ), where Whitmarsh accepts the emendation ἧττον for μᾶλλον, and translates 'However, one who is manly, in exile no less than at home, is dauntless in the face of all such fears; for that reason also he has the courage to say what he thinks no less when he happens to be in exile than when not.' The sentence is difficult, but the uncertainty does not affect my discussion of apostrophe.

[31] Cf. Aphthonius' *Progymnasmata* §5, whose example includes a refutation of 'the poets', as ever in the third person.

[32] For references, see Wright (2005: 226 n. 2).

[33] Plu. *De Exilio* 605f–606f (cf. 599d–e) cites a slightly longer extract, introducing it 'because many are stirred by the words of Euripides'; D.Chr. 51.1 quotes part of *Ph.* 392, approvingly. Both Plutarch and Dio were younger contemporaries of Musonius.

This literalized metaphor is part and parcel of Musonius' broader programme. The whole of *Discourse* 9, like several of his other discourses, is framed as a dialogue; it begins, 'When an exiled person was lamenting that he was living in exile, Musonius consoled him along the following lines' (p. 41 Hense). Second-person phrasing, including rhetorical questions, appears throughout, and there are instances beyond this passage in which Musonius responds to an imaginary objection. Not for nothing has Musonius been termed 'the Roman Socrates'.[34] The address to Euripides emblematizes this pervasive dialogical stance by extending it from the anonymous exiled interlocutor to a named, long-dead, addressee. The choice, moreover, to adopt the marked apostrophe at this particular point and on this particular issue may not be accidental. Musonius was himself an exile, banished first by Nero and again under the Flavians, and it is above all in the final section of the speech, straight after the address to Euripides, that he appeals to his own experience. Like Diogenes, he there suggests, he is an example of an exile who maintains the power to say what he wishes to say: 'Do you not know that I am an exile myself? Have I been deprived of free speech?' The immediately preceding argument with Euripides, it turns out, is one in which Musonius maintains a particular investment.[35] One way of interpreting the apostrophe, therefore, is as an expression of strong feeling at a climactic point in the argument. It is because he really means it (or purports to mean it), that he does not just refute Euripides' position but imagines himself as arguing with him.

Musonius models intellectual argument as ethically invested engagement in which both persons can learn. In part this is, as Whitmarsh has demonstrated, a sophisticated act of self-positioning vis-à-vis the classical past by a Greek-speaking intellectual active in a Roman environment,[36] but it is also, it seems to me, a dramatization of Musonius' philosophical argumentation: engagement with a text is conceived as a conversation with a person. The notion that authors can be conjured from their texts is very familiar and has found memorable expression throughout Greek literary history, from Aeschylus' and Euripides' altercation in Aristophanes' *Frogs*, to the speaking tombs of Hellenistic epigram, and Lucian's

---

[34] The term seems to have been coined by Hirzel (1895: ii.239), and has established itself since. It is based on the juxtaposition of Socrates and Musonius in a number of ancient texts; see Lutz (1947: 3–4).

[35] On self-exemplification in Musonius more widely see Dillon (2004: 86–8). The relevance of the political context for Musonius' position on free speech is drawn out by Whitmarsh (see next note).

[36] Whitmarsh (2001a: 276–85 and 2001b: 41–55).

conversation with Homer in the *True History*. What interests me in the way this notion surfaces in Musonius is that the conceit of speaking to the author expresses a particularly active form of reading, so active that Musonius' engagement with Euripides' lines is barely distinguished from real-life interaction. Notably, it is with only the slightest of markers ('I would say to Euripides') that Musonius shifts from talking to the plaintive exile to talking to Euripides. Euripides, so Musonius' apostrophe implies, is sufficiently part of his life, perhaps because he has read him so often (four quotations in this discourse), perhaps because he has pondered his thoughts on this particular topic so intensely, that he feels he is able to converse with him.[37] There is more than a hint of rhetorical display to this pretence of easy familiarity—self-consciousness runs deep in this as in all apostrophe—and Musonius does not claim that he could *really* speak with Euripides, but the conceit of easy availability is nevertheless suggestive, as well as integral to how Musonius thinks about himself.

Conclusion

'Le récit de fiction est toujours métaleptique.'[38] This programmatic subtitle of an article by Bessière encapsulates in pregnant form an idea shared by other critics who approach metalepsis with an interest in fictionality rather than narrative. Metalepsis is a useful metaphor for thinking about the way readers engage with fiction and about the negotiation of temporal, spatial, and ontological boundaries that is involved in all such engagement.[39] For McHale and Majola-Leblond it is specifically the emotional investment in the fiction, and above all the fictional characters, that is metaleptic.[40] 'Love as a principle of fiction', McHale suggests, 'is, in at least two of its senses, metaleptic. If authors love their characters, and if texts seduce their readers, then these relations involve violations of ontological boundaries.' Focusing on empathy rather than love, Majola-Leblond makes much the same point: 'Ultimately, empathy must therefore be seen as an intrinsically

---

[37] This model of dialogue with past thinkers is particularly at home in philosophy; e.g. the critical yet respectful address to Homer at Pl. *Rep.* 10.599d–e, and cf. *Ap.* 41a–c quoted pp. 77–8 below. But see also the repeated address to Lucian, often hostile, sometimes appreciative, in the (Byzantine) scholia on Lucian.

[38] 'Fictional narrative is always metaleptic': Bessière (2005). The notion that metalepsis is integral to fiction is expounded also by Genette; see Matzner in this volume, pp. 6–10, 21.

[39] In addition to the critics cited in this paragraph, see also Fludernik (2003b: 392–7) and Baron (2005).

[40] McHale (1987), Majola-Leblond (2015). Quotations from p. 222 and p. 314, respectively.

metaleptic process, a perpetual stepping over the threshold between the diegetic world and the extradiegetic level of "reality".

Perhaps no metaleptic trope encapsulates and enacts such invested relationships with fictional characters more vividly than apostrophe. In my four case studies I have tried to trace some of the different ways in which different texts and different genres employ the trope. The overall claim here is that apostrophe, even though it breaks with standard narrative protocols, brings out modalities characteristic of the text in question. Homeric apostrophe says something about the modes of engagement readers are offered by Homeric narrative in general, Theocritean apostrophe says something about the modes of engagement offered by Theocritus' narrative in general, and so on. As a form of metalepsis, apostrophe is never a default, or even a common, narrative mode, and yet it is exactly its metaleptic force that enables apostrophe to serve as a *mise en abyme* of a particular form of readerly engagement invited by a particular narrative.

In the remaining paragraphs, I shall take this text-specific variation for granted and elaborate more generally on the type of reading modelled by apostrophe—what I have called apostrophic reading. A welcome trend in recent literary theory has been the renewed attempt to do justice to the whole gamut of ways in which books affect their readers and play a role in their readers' lives. Critics are widening their remit, and think of readers not only as interpreting and making sense of books, but also as loving or hating them, getting bored or letting themselves be guided by them, learning them by heart or putting them aside half-read.[41] Apostrophe has the potential to contribute to this project by prompting us to think about the author's and thus, at one remove, the reader's engagement with a text in terms of a relationship. Rather than just foregrounding questions of narrative or fictionality, apostrophe also enacts relationships with characters. For the apostrophic reader what matters is not whether a character is real or unreal, or something in between, but the offer of a relationship that the character extends.

Such a relationship may be momentary, a glimpse of an interaction as we feel a sharp pang of sorrow for Patroclus, or it may be long-lasting, as a character becomes important to us as we compulsively reread a favourite text many times over and (like the *Harry Potter* fan at the outset) have the sense that we really get to know a character, beyond the words of the text. Strong forms of such long-lasting intimate relationships include the

---

[41] E.g. Felski (2008), Keen (2014), Moi (2017).

creation of fan fiction and the grief felt by readers when the hero or heroine of a favourite series is killed off. Most apostrophe in classical texts does not go so far, but it certainly sits on the same spectrum. It encourages us to reach out to the character and let the character affect us.

As I have emphasized throughout, apostrophe is a self-conscious gesture. The quality of appeal, willing an address to be possible where really it is not, is more or less strongly felt in all my examples. Homer, Sappho, Theocritus, and Musonius both highlight the gap and perform the act of crossing it. What is more, apostrophe in narrative is never sustained, and indeed will only ever model one form of reading among several. At different times, we may read for the story, wanting to know what happens without necessarily involving ourselves, may read reflectively, may read against the grain—or may read apostrophically, such as to form relationships with one or more characters.

Yet while apostrophe will always stand out, ancient narrative texts on the whole do not treat it as strange. As De Jong and others have pointed out, it is rare that ancient metalepsis, apostrophe included, is truly transgressive.[42] The texts glide into and out of apostrophe without a marked sense that impermeable walls are broken. Eisen and von Möllendorff speak of a 'metaleptische Grundbefindlichkeit', which they explain as a product of (among other things) specifically ancient regimes of historicity and fictionality.[43] In my terms here, the predominantly non-transgressive use of apostrophe is indicative of a pervasive understanding that the channels between the textual and the real world are open, and that the emotional, ethical, and intellectual relationships with characters that texts offer do not require the breaching of impervious barriers. With his characteristic light touch, hovering elusively between self-conscious irony and serious argument, Plato's Socrates performs this attitude in the *Apology*:

> If death is a kind of migration from here to another place, and what they say is true, that indeed all the dead are there, what greater good could there be than this, members of the jury? ... [T]o meet up with Orpheus and Musaeus and Hesiod and Homer, what price would any of you pay for that? You see I'm willing to die many times over if this is the truth, since for myself spending time there would be wonderful, when I could meet Palamedes and Aias, Telamon's son, and any others of olden times who died as a result of an unjust judgment, and compare

[42] De Jong (2009).
[43] An 'underlying metaleptic sensibility': Eisen and von Möllendorff (2013a: 4).

my experiences with theirs—in my view it would not be unpleasant—and what's more, the most important thing, I could go round, examine and inquire, just as I did here, who is wise and who thinks he is, but isn't. What price, members of the jury, would one pay to examine the leader of the great army against Troy, or Odysseus, or Sisyphus, or the countless others one could mention, men and women, to converse with whom there, and meet and examine them would be utmost happiness?

(Pl. *Ap*. 40e–41c, trans. Emlyn-Jones[44])

Like some of the apostrophic interactions that I have discussed, and like Colum McCann's trip to the pub with his characters, Socrates' ethical interrogation of the poets and their characters is a counterfactual fantasy. We reach for imaginary conceits to say something that is difficult to explain, but no less important for it. Literature, and especially literary characters, have a reality irrespective of their fictionality. They affect us, and mean something to us, sometimes in lasting ways. This paradox is very old—Plato's worry about the effect of tragedy is an early example in a negative key—but it is one that has lost none of its power, and that concepts such as willing suspension of disbelief, double vision, or immersion do not wholly capture. It has not been the aim of this chapter to make progress with understanding analytically the work our imagination does when we engage with fiction. What apostrophe offers is something much less ambitious, but, I hope, useful nevertheless: it gives us, immanent in the texts, the model of the invested relationship, and prompts us to think, for each text, about the specific exigencies of such invested relationships.

---

[44] The passage is discussed in relation to apostrophe by Klooster (2013: 157–8).

4
Metalepsis and the Apostrophe of Heroes in Pindar

Irene J. F. de Jong

'O mysterious apostrophe, teach us to understand your workings! Show us your varied talents here!'

(Culler 1981: 135)

Introduction

A clear case of metalepsis with a long and distinguished history in classical literature is the apostrophe in a narrative: when a narrator turns away from their default addressee, the narratee, and addresses one of the characters.[1] Narrator and characters in principle inhabit different universes since the narrator (qua narrator) belongs to a later moment in time and often to a different space, but when a narrator addresses a character the boundaries between these universes are blurred and the narrator 'enters' the world of the character.

Richardson in *The Homeric Narrator* was the first to analyse the apostrophes in Homer in terms of metalepsis and he defines the effect as follows:

The sympathy for the apostrophized characters in Homer comes not from the attitude expressed by the narrator but from the intimacy

---

[1] The definition is adapted from Quintilian *Inst.* 4.1.69, 9.2.38–9 (when an orator turns away from the judge and addresses a secondary addressee, which may consist of his opponent, an absent person, either dead or alive, or things, including personifications). For a definition of apostrophe in modern lyric texts, see Culler (1981: 138) ('invocations which turn away from empirical listeners by addressing natural objects, artefacts, or abstractions'). See further Trimble in this volume, pp. 126–7.

Irene J. F. de Jong, *Metalepsis and the Apostrophe of Heroes in Pindar* In: *Metalepsis: Ancient Texts, New Perspectives.* Edited by: Sebastian Matzner and Gail Trimble, Oxford University Press (2020). © The editors and Oxford University Press.
DOI: 10.1093/oso/9780198846987.003.0004

effected by the metalepsis…By getting the narratee to cross the bridge that separates them into the second narrative level, the narrator engages the narratee's sympathy by establishing a close alliance between the narratee and the character who inspires the transgression.[2]

In my study on 'Metalepsis in Ancient Greek Literature' I suggested that:

the sum effect of the apostrophe is to add to that vital characteristic of Homeric epic, *enargeia*: the events are presented in such a way that they seem to take place before the eyes of the narratees. Addressing characters directly is as 'enargetic' as the many speeches, when the narratees seem to actually hear the characters, impersonated by the narrator.[3]

Connecting apostrophe with *enargeia* means that I take the movement to be from the narrator (and the external narratees) into the world of the characters. *Enargeia* is a form of what nowadays is known as 'immersion': the hearers/readers of a narrative are so strongly absorbed by a narrative that they feel as if they are present themselves at the events told. They are mentally transported into the narrative world and become spectators of the events from the past.[4] Exactly the opposite movement, of character into the world of narrator, has been argued for by Bakker: Patroclus has an epiphany and 'literally *is* there, and the poet's addressing him creates, as well as presupposes, a maximum of presence in the epic performance'.[5] However we analyse it (as a form of immersion or of epiphany), apostrophe is a marked way of presentation and hence often (though not always) is used at a crucial point of the narrative, the clearest example being the apostrophes of Patroclus that mark the (advent of) his death (*Iliad* 16.692–3 and 787):

[2] Richardson (1990: 170–4, quotation from 173–4). For a summary of the debate on the interpretation of the Homeric apostrophe (is it merely used to fit in metrically difficult names or does it (also) have an expressive function?) and bibliography, see e.g. De Jong (2009: 94), to which should be added Dubel 2011. See also Grethlein, Budelmann, and Trimble in this volume.

[3] De Jong (2009: 93–7, quotation from 95). A similar analysis (without using the concept of metalepsis) in Asso (2008: 163, 167).

[4] For *enargeia* and immersion in Homer, see Allan, De Jong, and De Jonge (2017) and Grethlein and Huitink (2017). For more on *enargeia* see also Grethlein in this volume.

[5] Bakker (1993: 22–3). Cf. Fulkerson in this volume on metaleptic epiphany.

ἔνθα τίνα πρῶτον, τίνα δ' ὕστατον ἐξενάριξας,
Πατρόκλεις, ὅτε δή σε θεοὶ θάνατονδε κάλεσσαν;

Then who was the first, who the last that you killed, Patroclus, when the gods called you to your death?

ἔνθ' ἄρα τοι, Πάτροκλε, φάνη βιότοιο τελευτή·

then the end of your life manifested itself to you, Patroclus.[6]

The Homeric narrator arguably was inspired to use apostrophes by the genre of the hymn and its 'Du-Stil' (he apostrophizes Apollo in *Il.* 15.365–6 and 20.152),[7] and applying them not only to gods but also to the characters, who are after all 'semi-divine' heroes (cf. ἡμιθέων γένος ἀνδρῶν, 12.23), he set a trend: all later Greek and Roman epic narrators to a greater or lesser degree address their characters, with a multitude of effects.[8]

Apostrophe is also regularly found outside epic: in hymns, the choral lyrics of tragedy, bucolic poetry, didactic poetry, and Latin lyric.[9] Prose narrative texts on the contrary, both ancient and modern, feature apostrophes more rarely. Two effective examples are: *tu uero felix, Agricola, non uitae tantum claritate, sed etiam opportunitate mortis,* 'You truly are fortunate, Agricola, not only in the lustre of your life, but also in the timeliness of your death' (Tacitus *Agricola* 45.3)[10] and 'Arme Effi, du hattest zu den Himmelwundern zu lange hinaufgesehen und hatte darüber nachgedacht, und das Ende war, dass die Nachtluft und die Nebel, die vom Teich her aufstiegen, sie wieder aufs Krankenbett warfen...', 'Poor Effi, you spent too long looking up at the wonders of the heavens and thinking about them, and the result was that the night air and the mist rising from the pond brought on a recurrence of her illness...' (Theodor Fontane *Effi Briest*, chapter 36, trans. Mitchell).[11]

---

[6] More on Homer's apostrophe of Patroclus in the contribution of Budelmann in this volume. Where no translator is indicated, translations in this chapter are my own.

[7] De Jong (2009: 95–6). This suggestion is taken up and expanded by Klooster (2013). More on the hymnic Du-Stil in the next section on 'The Pindaric 'You' from a Literary Historical Perspective'.

[8] See e.g. Endt (1905), Effe (2004), Georgacopoulou (2005), D'Alessandro Behr (2005), Asso (2008), and Cadau (2015: 234–45). I have not been able to consult Zyroff (1971).

[9] For examples see Hampel (1908), Tränkle (1960: 147), Morrison (2007a (see index)), De Jong (2009: 97), and Klooster (2013).

[10] Some other examples are Livy 9.1.7, Velleius Paterculus 2.66.3–5.

[11] I thus concur with Richardson (1990: 18) ('narratorial apostrophe of a character rarely occurs in modern narrative') rather than Fludernik (1994b: 474 n. 26) ('emphatic apostrophe to the character has been a fairly common device even in realist narrative', but she gives no examples). Narratologists hardly discuss apostrophe as such but focus on second-person

In this chapter I will discuss the apostrophe of heroes in Pindaric epinician odes. Before being able to do so, however, I need to clear the ground since the Pindaric 'I' actually addresses many 'you's.[12] If apostrophe means the 'turning away' by a speaker from their default addressee to address someone or something else, we will first have to establish who that default addressee is in a Pindaric ode. While there is a massive bibliography on the Pindaric 'I',[13] the Pindaric 'you' has been much less explored.[14]

The Pindaric 'You' from a Literary Historical Perspective

The basic structure of the Pindaric victory ode consists of a combination of a *lyric frame in the present*, which contains praise of the victor, his family and home city, references to the games in which the victory was won and the celebration of that victory, and prayers or other forms of divine address, and a *(mythical or historical) narrative from the past*, which functions as a positive or negative paradigm for the victor, while the different elements of the ode are 'glued together' with the help of *omnitemporal gnomes*.

The voice that presents the odes is an 'I' (or 'we'), who for the sake of simplicity I take to be (in the majority of cases) a carefully stylized persona of the poet. The 'I' addresses a multitude of 'you's: the victor or members of his family, gods, Muses, geographical locations, heroes, and himself. I will shortly go into these 'you's in more detail, but first I want to establish a kind of hierarchy and decide who is the epinician speaker's default

---

fiction, which they explicitly (Kacandes 1994) or fleetingly (Fludernik 1994a: 288, 302) relate to apostrophe. For another study of modern second-person narration see e.g. the second chapter in Richardson (2006).

[12] On underdetermined personal pronouns and metalepsis see also Matzner and Grethlein in this volume.

[13] For a recent overview of the discussion with full bibliography, see Currie (2013). He argues that references to the Pindaric 'I' can fluctuate from 'generic, rhetorical poses—a laudator, an *aoidos* in the rhapsodic tradition…an Everyman…—to strongly individualized figures: the Theban poet Pindar, the chorus, the victor' (243). Schmid (1998) is also a highly commendable discussion of the many voices in the Pindaric ode.

[14] There are Kambylis (1964) on Pindaric vocatives and the unpublished dissertation of Colwell (1993), both of which I have not been able to consult, and Griffith (1991). I am talking about the 'you' *inside* the text; for Pindar's *historical* audience(s), see e.g. Kurke (1991) and Morrison (2007b).

addressee, the receiver who corresponds to him as sender.[15] In order to do so it may be instructive to look back briefly to two genres that arguably influenced the epinician genre: epic and the hymn.[16]

In the Homeric epics the main form of communication is that of an external narrator who addresses external narratees. Both are highly covert, the Homeric 'I' only surfacing in the proems and a handful of passages in the course of the narrative, the Homeric 'you' in a limited set of passages of the type 'there you would have seen'.[17] The narrator also occasionally addresses the Muses or, as we already saw, apostrophizes his heroes. What is crucial here is that even though the narrator at such moments briefly turns away from his default addressee, the narratees, and addresses some-one else, the narratees *remain his receiver*.[18] The Muse-invocations and apostrophes are inserted to have a certain effect on the narratees, who are supposed to respond to them cognitively and emotionally: the Muse-invocations should ensure them of the narrator's professional status and authority, while the apostrophes, as we have already seen, should trigger their sympathy for certain heroes.

When we turn from epic to cultic hymn the situation is different: here we find 'I' and 'you' forms throughout, and the 'you' almost invariably is the god hymned. The hymnic speaker starts by invoking the god (mentioning his or her name, attributes, genealogy), then praises him/her (through lists of his/her powers, reminders of earlier benefits, descriptions of his/her person, haunts or actions, and narratives), and at the end prays to him/her.[19] Although the typical 'Du-Stil'[20] is usually not maintained through-out the entire hymn, the hymned god from beginning to end clearly is the default addressee (receiver) of the hymnic speaker (sender).

---

[15] I am using here the well-established terminology of Jakobson, who distinguishes six factors that are involved in communication: (1) context, (2) sender, (3) receiver, (4) contact, (5) common code, and (6) message. See Jakobson (1960).

[16] For epic elements in the epinician genre, see e.g. Braswell (1988: *ad* 1–3), for hymnic elements, e.g. Bremer (2008).

[17] See e.g. De Jong (2004: 45–60).

[18] Cf. Kacandes (1994: 330) ('the apostrophe bears two "addresses". Overtly, a speaker sends a message to someone or something as if that being or thing could respond but will not. Covertly, an apostrophe is meant to provoke response through its reception in a second(ary) communicative circuit, received by the readers of a poem in the cases of lyric or the audience in the case of oratory') and Klooster (2013: 152).

[19] For the typical structure of cultic hymns, see Furley and Bremer (2001: 50–63).

[20] The instances of the 'Du-Stil' are regularly referred to as apostrophes, whereby it should be noted that apostrophe is here used in its more general sense of 'invocation' or 'address' rather than the more restricted sense of the turning away from a default addressee to another addressee (which is the sense adopted in this chapter).

Hymnic speakers also occasionally address the Muses and—a difference vis-à-vis the epic narrator—the geographical location where the hymn is performed or the chorus that performs it.[21] The 'you' that is conspicuously lacking is that of the human addressees, the text-internal counterparts of the flesh-and-blood persons who attend the performance of the hymns. They may be briefly referred to,[22] but are never addressed as 'you'. Clearly, the religious nature of the hymn prescribed an exclusive focus on the god as its recipient.[23]

Returning to the Pindaric epinician ode, we can now observe that the epinician speaker follows the example of epic speakers in addressing Muses and heroes, that of hymnic speakers in addressing gods and geographical locations, and adds as new categories of addressees the victor (and his family) and himself. Who of these many 'you's is the default addressee, the receiver corresponding to the epinician sender? The question has been hardly discussed, probably since most scholars simply assume that default addressee to be the victor.[24] This is also the position of one of the few scholars who does express an explicit opinion on the matter: 'When the poets of victory odes use a second person in order to address an audience for their songs, this second person nearly always refers to an individual, most often the victor himself' (Pfeijffer 2004: 219).[25] To take the victor as the main addressee is a priori plausible in view of the overriding encomiastic goal of victory odes. If we accept this analysis, as I am inclined to do, we may observe that the very fact that the victor occupies the honorific position of the default 'you' that in hymns is taken by the god adds to his elevation.[26] It also means that the victor hears all other

---

[21] For Muses, see e.g. Pindar, *Paean* 6.54–8 (Furley and Bremer number 2.2), Limenius' *Paean to Apollo* 1–6 (Furley and Bremer 2.6); for geographical locations, e.g. Pindar, *Paean* 6.1–11 (Furley and Bremer 2.2); for the chorus, e.g. *Paean to Asclepius* 1–2 (Furley and Bremer 6.1).

[22] E.g. in Pindar, *Paean* 6.64: 'the sacrifice is on behalf of all Greece, inaugurated *by the Delphic people* [for deliverance] from famine' (Furley and Bremer 2.2).

[23] The situation is more or less the same in the subgenre of the *Homeric Hymns*: cf. Nünlist (2004: 36): 'the narratee of the hymn is the god to whom the hymn is dedicated...(Needless to say, the ultimate narratees of the hymns are, of course, the human audience, who, however, cannot be addressed, lest the *phthonos theōn* [envy of the gods] be roused.)'

[24] Or because they assume Pindar to simply switch between addressees without there being one default addressee; for this analysis, see e.g. Obbink (1993: 70–1), who speaks of a 'progression of addressees' in lyric.

[25] A different position is taken by Bremer (2008), who argues that 'victory songs were addressed to the god who presides over the festival' (Bremer 2008: 6).

[26] It is a matter of debate how far we should go in this alignment of mortal victor and god. Did (some of the) victors receive hero cult? For a positive answer, see Currie (2005), for a negative answer Bremer (2008: 12–17).

addresses by the epinician speaker, notably the prayers to the gods for his benefit. I will now take a closer look at the many identities of the Pindaric 'you'.[27]

The Many Identities of the Pindaric 'You'

The epinician speaker's main or default addressee is the *victor*, including members of his family, his trainer, and his charioteer or mule driver, e.g. *O.* 11.11–15:

> ἴσθι νῦν, Ἀρχεστράτου
> παῖ, τεᾶς, Ἁγησίδαμε, πυγμαχίας ἕνεκεν
> κόσμον ἐπὶ στεφάνῳ χρυσέας ἐλαίας
> ἁδυμελῆ κελαδήσω...

Be assured now, *son of Archestratos*, that because of *your* boxing, *Hagesidamos*, I shall adorn your crown of golden olive with my sweet song of celebration...[28]

After the victor, *gods*, including personifications such as Fortune, are most frequently addressed, especially at the beginning or end of odes, e.g. *O.* 13.115–16:

> Ζεῦ τέλει', αἰδῶ δίδοι
> καὶ τύχαν τερπνῶν γλυκεῖαν.

Zeus accomplisher, grant them respect and sweet attainment of success.[29]

---

[27] The 'you' can take the form of a vocative and/or a second-person indicative and/or an imperative and/or a second-person pronoun. See the list in Griffith (1991: 32), which is not completely identical with my categories and lists.

[28] Throughout this chapter, I quote for Pindar the text and translation of Race (1997), with occasional adaptations. See *O.* 1.106–8, 114–15; 5.21–3; 6.12, 22–3, 77–9, 80–1; 8.15–16; 10.91–6; 11.16; 12.13–19; 13.43–5; *P.* 1.85–92; 2.18–20, 57–72; 3.80–4; 4.250, 255, 259–62, 263, 270–8, 298; 5.5–11, 14–31, 45–53; 6.14–20; 7.17–18; 8.32–8, 71–2, 78–82; 9.90–2 (if Hermann's εὐκλέιξας is read), 97–103; *N.* 1.29–30; 2.14–15; 3.76–80, 83–4; 4.13–14, 77–81, 89–90; 5.41–3, 48–9; 6.60–3; 7.58–60, 70, 75; 8.44–8; 10.37–8; *I.* 2.1, 12, 30–2; 4.2–5; 5.17–18; 7.31–6.

[29] See *O.* 2.12–15; 4.1–10; 5.9–11, 17–21; 6.103–5; 7.87–94; 12.1–5; 13.24–30; 14.1–7, 13–17, 20–4; *P.* 1.29–30, 39–40, 67–71; 5.78–81, 118–21; 6.50–1; 7.9–11; 8.1–13, 61–9; 10.10–11; 11.1–13, 62–4; *N.* 3.65–6; 7.1–8; 8.1–3, 35–7; 9.28–32, 53–5; 10.29–30; 11.1–7; *I.* 3.4–5; 5.1–6; 6.3–4; 7.49–51.

The address of *geographical locations* can be considered a subtype of the address of gods, since they are mainly represented by their eponymous nymphs, e.g. *N.* 1.1–5:

> ἄμπνευμα σεμνὸν Ἀλφεοῦ,
> κλεινᾶν Συρακοσσᾶν θάλος Ὀρτυγία,
> δέμνιον Ἀρτέμιδος,
> Δάλου κασιγνήτα, σέθεν ἁδυεπής
> ὕμνος ὁρμᾶται...

Hallowed spout of Alpheos, Ortygia, offspring of famous Syracuse, couch of Artemis, and sister of Delos, from *you* a sweetly worded hymn issues forth...[30]

With the invocations of the *Muses* we are moving from the sphere of the victor to that of the epinician speaker, since they bear upon his poetic art, e.g. *N.* 6.27–8:

> εὔ-
> θυν' ἐπὶ τοῦτον, ἄγε, Μοῖσα,
> οὖρον ἐπέων
> εὐκλέα·

Come, Muse, direct to that house a glorious wind of verses.[31]

Finally there is the *self-address*, when the epinician speaker, talking about his task as a poet, addresses his heart, lyre, song, or himself, e.g. *N.* 4.44–6:

> ἐξύφαινε, γλυκεῖα, καὶ τόδ' αὐτίκα, φόρμιγξ,
> Λυδίᾳ σὺν ἁρμονίᾳ μέλος πεφιλημένον
> Οἰνώνᾳ τε καὶ Κύπρῳ, ἔνθα...

Quickly now, *sweet lyre, weave out* this song too in Lydian harmony, one beloved by Oenona and Cyprus, where...[32]

---

[30] See *O.* 5.1–8; 9.16–18; *P.* 8.98–100; 12.1–8; *N.* 1.1–6; 7.50–3; *I.* 1.1–3; 7.1–15. Even when a real physical place is addressed, it usually still has a numinous aspect in that it is pictured as a living being: *P.* 2.1–4; *O.* 8.1–10. Here lies the origin of the modern definition of apostrophe (quoted in n. 1), which concerns the invocation of natural objects.
[31] See *O.* 10.1–6; 11.16–19; *P.* 1.58–9; 4.1–3; 11.41–5; *N.* 3.1–17; 9.1–3; 10.1–2 (Graces); *I.* 5.38–42; 6.57–8. For discussion, see Morrison (2007a: 76–7, 84–9) and Kantzios (2003).
[32] See *O.* 1.3–6, 17–19; 2.1–2, 89; 9.1–16, 35–42, 47–9; *P.* 1.1–12, 81–4; 3.61–2; 10.51–2; *N.* 3.26–8, 31–2; 4.36–7, 69–70; 5.2–3, 50–4; 7.77, 80–2 (or the chorus leader); 9.1–2; *I.* 5.24, 51; 7.20; 8.7. For discussion, see Sullivan (2002) and Morrison (2007a: 151).

Such self-addresses are a novelty in comparison to the more covert style of epic and hymnic narrators and well suit the explicit self-promotion of lyric poets.[33] Taken together, second-person forms are all over the place in Pindaric odes, some being particularly full of them (e.g. *Pythian* 2) and few entirely lacking them (e.g. *Olympian* 3). A cluster of addresses at a particular point of an ode may serve a special purpose: thus the many references to Arcesilas at the end of *Pythian* 4 (263, 270, 275, 276, 278, 298) underscore the appealing nature of this section, in which Pindar urges him to allow his exiled compatriot Damophilus to come back.

All of the persons or entities addressed in 'you' form can also be referred to in the third person. The epinician speaker may, for instance, pray to a god in the traditional second-person form but he may also vary the pattern[34] and refer to that god in the third person, as he does e.g. in *O.* 8.84–5:

$$\dot{\epsilon}\sigma\lambda\grave{\alpha} \; \delta' \; \dot{\epsilon}\pi' \; \dot{\epsilon}\sigma\lambda o\hat{\iota}s$$
$$\ddot{\epsilon}\rho\gamma\alpha \; \boldsymbol{\theta\acute{\epsilon}\lambda o\iota \; \delta\acute{o}\mu\epsilon\nu}, \; \dot{o}\xi\epsilon\acute{\iota}\alpha s \; \delta\grave{\epsilon} \; \nu\acute{o}\sigma o\nu s \; \dot{\alpha}\pi\alpha\lambda\acute{\alpha}\lambda\kappa o\iota.$$

May *he* [Zeus] *be willing to provide* success upon success and ward off painful diseases.

Likewise he will commonly address the victor as 'you' at the moment he speaks about his victory but he may also refer to him, though present in his audience, in the third person, e.g. *O.* 3.1–3:

$$T\upsilon\nu\delta\alpha\rho\acute{\iota}\delta\alpha\iota s \; \tau\epsilon \; \varphi\iota\lambda o\xi\epsilon\acute{\iota}\nu o\iota s \; \dot{\alpha}\delta\epsilon\hat{\iota}\nu$$
$$\kappa\alpha\lambda\lambda\iota\pi\lambda o\kappa\acute{\alpha}\mu\varphi \; \theta' \; \acute{E}\lambda\acute{\epsilon}\nu\alpha$$
$$\kappa\lambda\epsilon\iota\nu\grave{\alpha}\nu \; \dot{A}\kappa\rho\acute{\alpha}\gamma\alpha\nu\tau\alpha \; \gamma\epsilon\rho\alpha\acute{\iota}\rho\omega\nu \; \epsilon\ddot{\upsilon}\chi o\mu\alpha\iota,$$
$$\boldsymbol{\Theta\acute{\eta}\rho\omega\nu o s} \; \dot{O}\lambda\upsilon\mu\pi\iota o\nu\acute{\iota}\kappa\alpha\nu$$
$$\ddot{\upsilon}\mu\nu o\nu \; \dot{o}\rho\theta\acute{\omega}\sigma\alpha\iota s \ldots$$

---

[33] Some remaining minor categories of 'you's are: generic 'you' (*P.* 10.29–30; *O.* 13.112–14; *N.* 9.34–7), citizens (*O.* 13.14–17; *N.* 2.24–5; *I.* 3.15–17b; 4.35–6b), the chorus (*O.* 6.87–92; *I.* 8.1–3, and perhaps *N.* 7.80–2), and the unique case of a named person who is ordered by the epinician speaker to bring his poem to the victor (*I.* 2.47–8). Some debated passages are *N.* 1.13 σπεῖρε (if we read this imperative with Beck and the scholia) and *I.* 5.62–3 λάμβανε, φέρε: Muse-invocations or self-addresses?; *P.* 6.1 ἀκούσατε: the victor and his family or Akragan citizens?; *P.* 11.38 ὦ φίλοι: Theban citizens or the victor and his family?; *I.* 8.63 γεραίρετ' (if we read this imperative with Bothe and most editors): the chorus or the Muses?

[34] I use the word 'vary' on purpose here, since I think what is at play is indeed variation, Pindar's celebrated *poikilia*. For discussions of second-person and third-person deixis in Pindar, see Athanassaki (2004) and Bonifazi (2004: 395–407).

I pray that I may please the hospitable Tyndaridai and Helen of the beautiful locks, as I honour famous Akragas, when, *for Theron*, I raise up an Olympic victory hymn…

The effect of this use of the third person to someone who is present is 'to make that individual stand out'.[35]

An interesting in-between form of reference, less direct than 'you' but more direct than a third person, consists in the proximal deictic pronoun ὅδε,[36] e.g. *N*. 2.1–5:

> ὅθεν περ καὶ Ὁμηρίδαι
> ῥαπτῶν ἐπέων τὰ πόλλ᾽ ἀοιδοί
> ἄρχονται, Διὸς ἐκ προοιμίου, καὶ ὅδ᾽ ἀνήρ
> καταβολὰν ἱερῶν ἀγώ-
>   νων νικαφορίας δέδεκται πρῶτον Νεμεαίου
> ἐν πολυυμνήτῳ Διὸς ἄλσει.

Just as the sons of Homer, those singers of verses stitched together, most often begin with a prelude to Zeus, so has *this man* received his first instalment of victory in the sacred games at the much-hymned sanctuary of Nemean Zeus.[37]

The *first-time* listeners to the ode will have easily understood who 'this man' was, because they were present at the celebration of the victory of Timodemos of Acharnae (and would see him in their midst, probably sitting in one of the front-row seats). We may even hypothesize that the chorus in their performance somehow would have directed attention at Timodemus, reinforcing the zooming effect of ὅδ᾽ ἀνήρ through their body language. As for the *later* listeners and readers, the ode quickly goes on to record the name of the *laudandus* so as to allow them to identify 'the man' too: 'but you, O Timodemos, the stout-hearted strength of the pancratium exalts' (14–15).

I wrap up the first part of my argument. The Pindaric ode features a multitude of 'you's, of which the victor and his family are the epinician speaker's default addressee, and the Muses, the gods, geographical locations,

---

[35] Athanassaki (2004: 320).   [36] On deictics cf. Matzner in this volume, p. 23.
[37] Cf. further *O*. 2.36; 9.110; *I*. 1.34; 4.70. For discussions of deixis in Pindar, see Felson (1999) and the special issue of *Arethusa* 37.3 (2004).

and the poet himself various kinds of secondary addressees. I now turn to the last 'you', which I have so far left out of the discussion: heroes.

The (Metaleptic) Apostrophe of Heroes

The 'you'-references discussed in the previous section all stem from the lyric frame of Pindaric odes. The narrative parts are almost completely devoid of them: Pindaric narratives are regularly interrupted by passages featuring the 'I', but the 'you's (victor, gods, Muses) disappear out of sight when the epinician speaker turns narrator.[38] What we do find, albeit only rarely (three times), is an apostrophe of one of the characters of the narrative. *O.* 1.36–51:

> **υἱὲ Ταντάλου,** σὲ δ' ἀντία προτέρων φθέγξομαι,
> ὁπότ' ἐκάλεσε πατὴρ τὸν εὐνομώτατον
> ἐς ἔρανον φίλαν τε Σίπυλον,
> ἀμοιβαῖα θεοῖσι δεῖπνα παρέχων,
> τότ' Ἀγλαοτρίαιναν ἁρπάσαι,
>
> δαμέντα φρένας ἱμέρῳ, χρυσέαισί τ' ἀν' ἵπποις
> ὕπατον εὐρυτίμου ποτὶ δῶμα Διὸς μεταβᾶσαι·
> ...
> ὡς δ' ἄφαντος **ἔπελες,** οὐδὲ ματρὶ πολ-
> λὰ μαιόμενοι φῶτες ἄγαγον,
> ἔννεπε κρυφᾷ τις αὐτίκα φθονερῶν γειτόνων,
> ὕδατος ὅτι τε πυρὶ ζέοισαν εἰς ἀκμάν
> μαχαίρᾳ τάμον κατὰ μέλη,
> τραπέζαισί τ' ἀμφὶ δεύτατα κρεῶν
> **σέθεν** διεδάσαντο καὶ φάγον.

Son of Tantalus, of you I shall say, contrary to my predecessors, that when your father invited the gods to his most orderly feast and to his friendly Sipylos giving them a banquet in return for theirs, then it was

---

[38] The one exception is the three references to the victor Arcesilas and his family in one of the narrative parts of *Pythian* 4 (250, 255, 259), arguably because at this point the narrative touches the genealogy of the Euphemid Arcesilas (I owe this suggestion to Bruno Currie). An additional reason might be the exceptional length of this narrative, which would lead Pindar to bring back in focus his main addressee Arcesilas before the return to the lyric frame, where, as we have already seen (in the section on 'The Many Identities of the Pindaric "You"'), he is addressed very frequently and urgently.

that the Lord of the Splendid Trident seized you, his mind overcome by desire, and with golden steeds conveyed you to the highest home of widely honored Zeus...But when *you* disappeared, and despite much searching no men returned you to your mother, one of the envious neighbours immediately said in secret that into water boiling rapidly on the fire they [the gods] cut up your limbs with a knife, and for the final course distributed *your* flesh around the table and ate it.

P. 4.59–63:

> ὦ μάκαρ υἱὲ **Πολυμνάστου**, σὲ δ' ἐν τούτῳ λόγῳ
> χρησμὸς ὤρθωσεν μελίσσας
>   Δελφίδος αὐτομάτῳ κελάδῳ·
> ἅ **σε** χαίρειν ἐστρὶς αὐδάσαισα πεπρωμένον
> βασιλέ' ἄμφανεν Κυράνᾳ,
> δυσθρόου φωνᾶς ἀνακρινόμενον ποι-
>   νὰ τίς ἔσται πρὸς θεῶν.

O blessed son of Polymnastus [Battus], it was *you* whom the oracle, in accordance with that speech, exalted through the spontaneous cry of the Delphic Bee, who thrice bade *you* hail and revealed you to be the destined king of Cyrene, when you were asking what requital would come from the gods for your stammering voice.

P. 4.172–5:

> ...δοιοὶ δ' ὑψιχαῖται
> ἀνέρες, Ἐννοσίδα γένος, αἰδεσθέντες ἀλκάν,
> ἔκ τε Πύλου καὶ ἀπ' ἄκρας Ταινάρου· τῶν μὲν κλέος
> ἐσλὸν Εὐφάμου τ' ἐκράνθη
> **σόν** τε, **Περικλύμεν**' εὐρυβία.

[*Swiftly came*] *the two men with hair piled on high, offspring of Earthshaker, out of respect for their valor, from Pylos and the headland of Taenarus, whose glory was fulfilled, that of Euphemus and yours, mighty Periclymenus.*

What is the effect of these apostrophes? I do not think it can be upheld, with Braswell (1988: *ad* 59a), that the apostrophe's 'main function in epinikia is doubtless that of emphasis'.[39] For one thing, I do not see why

---

[39] His corpus consists of *N.* 8.44 (the address of the deceased Megas, which I include in my category of 'addresses of the victor and his family'; see above, n. 33); *P.* 4.89 and 11.61–2 (see next note).

Periclymenus in *P.* 4.175 would be in need of more emphasis than Euphemus. And what exactly does Braswell mean by 'emphasis' in the first place? More reflection clearly is asked for.

Where the apostrophe of Periclymenus is concerned, I contend that we are dealing with stylistic variation. Pindar regularly alternates between direct address and third-person reference when dealing with a pair of persons or places, cf. e.g. *O.* 9.16–18:

$$\theta\acute{a}\lambda\lambda\epsilon\iota\ \delta'\ \mathring{a}\rho\epsilon\tau\alpha\hat{\iota}\sigma\iota\nu$$
$$\sigma\acute{o}\nu\ \tau\epsilon,\ \mathbf{Ka\sigma\tau a\lambda\acute{\iota}a},\ \pi\acute{a}\rho a$$
$$\mathring{A}\lambda\varphi\epsilon o\hat{v}\ \tau\epsilon\ \mathring{\rho}\acute{\epsilon}\epsilon\theta\rho o\nu\cdot$$

It [the city of Opous] flourishes with achievements by *your* stream, *Castalia*, and that of Alpheus.[40]

The apostrophes of Pelops in *O.* 1 and Battus in *P.* 4 are more intriguing and in demand of a longer argument.

Let us start with Pelops.[41] The passage 36–51 forms part of one of three mythical sections which together tell the story of how young Pelops was abducted by Poseidon to Olympus, rather than, as earlier poets sang, cooked by his father Tantalus (26–51), how Tantalus lost his divine favour and was punished by the gods (54–64), and how Pelops, sharing in his father's fall from grace, had to return to mortal life and defeated Oenomaus in the first Olympic chariot race with the help of his former lover Poseidon (65–93). The whole story is carefully tailored by Pindar to mirror Hieron's Olympic victory. Why does he address his character Pelops in the second person?

First, second-person narration instead of the default third-person narration is, as we have already seen in connection with the apostrophes of Patroclus in the *Iliad*, a marked form of presentation[42] that directs extra attention to what is recounted. The you-narration underscores the force of the Pindaric narrator's emotional claim: Pelops was *never* boiled by his father and the gods *never* ate him (cf. his ensuing remark, 'But for my part,

---

[40] Cf. Gerber (2002: *ad* 17–18), who lists as parallels (in a speech embedded in the narrative) *P.* 4.89; (in the lyric frame) 11.61–2; *N.* 7.84–6; and *I.* 1.52–7.

[41] The myth of *O.* 1 has been the subject of many studies (Segal 1974, Köhnken 1974, 1983, Krischer 1981, Gerber 1982, Sicking 1983, Howie 1983, Hubbard 1987, Morrison 2007b: 57–65), but without discussion of the second-person forms. For the second-person (and third-person) forms in the entire ode, see Athanassaki (2004).

[42] I think 'marked form of presentation' is probably what Braswell means by 'emphasis', and taken this way I agree that this is one of the effects of the apostrophe. See also below on the jolting effect of the apostrophe of Battus.

I cannot call any of the gods a glutton', 52). Second, the you-narration flags Pindar's innovation of myth since it is found exactly at the point where he departs from the version of his predecessors.[43] One could fruitfully compare here Stesichorus fr. 192 = 91a Davies and Finglass (trans. Campbell):

> οὐκ ἔστ' ἔτυμος λόγος οὗτος,
> οὐδ' ἔβας ἐν ναυσὶν ἐυσσέλμοις
> οὐδ' ἵκεο πέργαμα Τροίας...

That story is not true, and *you* [Helen] did not go on the well-benched ships and *you* did not reach the citadel of Troy...

Here too the poet turns to second-person forms, engaging in some kind of dialogue with a mythical character, at the very moment when he changes the literary tradition about that character.

But I think more is involved in the use of the apostrophe of Pelops, and here its analysis in terms of metalepsis, a blurring of the temporal or spatial differences between the world of the characters and the world of the narrator and the narratees, becomes relevant. My suggestion is that the apostrophe also hints at the character Pelops' *future* status as a *hērōs* with a cult,[44] a status which he has in the time of the narrator Pindar and his narratee Hieron, as becomes explicitly clear at the end of the poem, *O.* 1.90–3:

> νῦν δ' ἐν αἱμακουρίαις
> ἀγλααῖσι μέμικται,
> Ἀλφεοῦ πόρῳ κλιθείς,
> τύμβον ἀμφίπολον ἔχων πολυξενω-
> τάτῳ παρὰ βωμῷ·

And now he [Pelops] partakes of splendid blood sacrifices as he reclines by the course of the Alpheus, having his much-attended tomb beside the altar thronged by visiting strangers.[45]

---

[43] Pindar's corrections of myth have been much discussed; for a recent discussion, see e.g. Vöhler (2005).

[44] For the different uses of the word *hērōs* in Pindar, see Currie (2005: 60–1).

[45] See Currie (2005: 57, 75, 301). Pindar again refers to the tomb of Pelops in *O.* 4.24–5 and its existence is confirmed by Pausanias 5.13.1 and excavations.

This interpretation can be backed up by comparing places *in the lyric frame* of odes where the epinician speaker apostrophizes heroes with a hero cult, e.g. *O.* 9.112:

> ...Αἶαν, τεόν τ᾽ ἐν δαιτί, Ἰλιάδα,
> νικῶν ἐπεστεφάνωσε βωμόν.

...and at *your* feast, *Ajax, son of Ileus,* the victor has placed a crown upon *your* altar.

or *I.* 6.19–28:

> ὔμμε τ᾽, ὦ χρυσάρματοι Αἰακίδαι,
> τέθμιόν μοι φαμὶ σαφέστατον ἔμμεν
> τάνδ᾽ ἐπιστείχοντα νᾶσον ῥαινέμεν εὐλογίαις.
> ...
> οὐδ᾽ ἔστιν οὕτω βάρβαρος
> οὔτε παλίγγλωσσος πόλις,
> ἅτις οὐ Πηλέος ἀΐει κλέος ἥ-
> ρωος, εὐδαίμονος γαμβροῦ θεῶν,
> οὐδ᾽ ἅτις Αἴαντος Τελαμωνιάδα
> καὶ πατρός·

And as for *you, O Aeacidae with your golden chariots,* I declare that I have the clearest mandate, when coming to this island, to shower *you* with praises... and there is no city so alien or of such backward speech that it does not hear tell of the fame of the hero Peleus, the blessed son-in-law of the gods, or of Telamonian Ajax, or of his father.[46]

In passages such as these the lyric speaker employs the hymnic 'Du-Stil' for (semi-divine) heroes with a cult. An interesting parallel is offered by Simonides' Plataea elegy, where Achilles is apostrophized in the

---

[46] For hero cult of the Aeacidae on Aegina, cf. *I.* 5.34–5. See Bonifazi (2004: 400): 'the poet chooses a "you"-deixis, presumably pointing to a physical presence, but it is not clear which kind of physical presence. At least three possibilities are to be considered: an *am Phantasma* reference to the Aeginetan ancestors, an ocular reference to some artistic representation of the Aeacids, or an ocular reference to the Aeginetan clan, metaphorically indicated by the address to their ancestors.' Other examples: *N.* 7.86 (Heracles; for his divine status, see *I.* 4.55–60); *I.*1.32 (hymnic farewell to the heroes Castor and Iolaus; for the hero status of Castor, cf. *O.* 3.39–41; of Iolaus: *I.* 5.32), 55–6 (Heracles and Iolaus), 58–9 (Protesilaus, who, as Pindar himself tells, has a precinct at Phylaka and is honoured with athletic contests).

hymnic proem (κούρης εἰν]αλίης ἀγλαόφη[με πάϊ, 'glorious [son] of the sea-dwelling [girl]', fr. 10.5; ἀλλὰ σὺ μὲ]ν νῦν χαῖρε, θεας ἐρικυ[δέος υἱέ κούρης εἰν]αλίου Νηρέος, '[but] fare you well now, famous [son] of the goddess [daughter] of sea-dwelling Nereus', fr. 11.19–20). The apostrophes are generally taken by commentators as suggesting his status as a cultic *hērōs*;[47] one may note especially the presence of hymnic χαῖρε.

Returning to Pindar apostrophizing Pelops in *O.* 1.36–51, I suggest that he blends the epic use of the apostrophe of a character in a narrative with the hymnic 'Du-Stil' that suits a *hērōs*. The effect is that Pelops' future heroic status is as it were adumbrated at the very start of his life story. Addressing him as hero the narrator marks the vital moment when Poseidon becomes his lover and the basis for Pelops' future success in the race with Oenomaus and hence future hero cult is laid.[48]

As in the case of Homer's apostrophe of his heroes, we may ask our-selves what the direction of the metalepsis is: does the epinician narrator (and his narratee) mentally enter the world of the past and become a kind of eyewitness of the mythical events recounted (immersion) or is Pelops qua (present-day) hero somehow present at the performance of the ode (epiphany)? The second position is defended by Athanassaki: 'the effect of the speaker's speech to Pelops…is to draw the past gradually into the present and to foreground the "sacred presence" of the heroic founder of the Olympic games'. Pelops, thus, would be present in a kind of epiphany, an experience which the re-enactment of the story by the chorus performing the ode of course greatly facilitated.[49] Here I am more inclined than in the case of the Homeric apostrophe to accept a movement of past character into present world of narrator and narratee, and thus to concur with Athanassaki in opting for the second interpretation.[50]

---

[47] See different scholars in Boedeker and Sider (2001: 93, 156–7, 164–81).

[48] A rather 'odd' interpretation of the apostrophe is given by Griffith (1991: 33): he starts by claiming that the second person in general indicates a 'wished-for presence' and then continues 'Since the infant Pelops…was not actually present when the ode was performed, Pindar's second-person narration must denote wished-for presence. The object par excellence of wished-for presence is the beloved. Does the narrator love Pelops?…it would be odd that he should love a character in a story in which…he was not himself also a character. Odd though it is, we are driven to this conclusion.'

[49] Athanassaki (2004: 329, 334). She is not entirely consistent in her analysis, however, for on p. 341 she writes: 'The speaker creates the illusion of stepping for a while into a mythical time and setting in order to play the role of an eyewitness', which is the exact opposite of her earlier analysis.

[50] For another interpretation, see Pavlou (2012: 103), who suggests that here and at *N.* 4.46–53 (no apostrophe) and *I.* 6.19 'Pindar invokes mythical heroes as if they were still alive'. See also Budelmann in this volume, pp. 61–5.

I now turn to the apostrophe of Battus in *Pythian* 4. Its presence can be explained in the first place in connection with the very conscious epic colouring of this exceptionally long ode; see, for example, its Muse-invocation (1–3) and the question starting off the (second) narrative ('what beginning took them on their voyage, and what danger bound them with strong nails of adamant?', 70–1). Apostrophes of characters are a traditional element of epic, and as such the apostrophe is likely to have been inserted by Pindar to add to the epic hue of this ode. But again more seems to be at play, and for this we must take a closer look at the apostrophe's position and context.

The two narrative parts of the ode (4–63 and 70–262) together recount the story of the Argonauts and their quest for the Golden Fleece. The epinician narrator starts with an incident on the way back (Medea predicts to the Argonauts that a descendant of Euphemus, one of the Argonauts, will one day found Cyrene), while recounting in the second narrative the story from beginning (the oracle given to Pelias concerning the man with one sandal) to end (the recovery of the fleece and the return via Lemnos) and even beyond that end (the founding of Cyrene by the descendants of Euphemus).

The apostrophe of Battus occurs in the first narrative. In a riddling prophetic speech Medea predicts that Euphemus 'will find in the beds of foreign women a chosen race, who will…beget a man to be ruler of the plains with dark clouds. And when, at a later time, he enters the temple of Pytho…Phoebus will admonish him through oracles to convey many people in ships to the fertile domain of Kronos' son on the Nile' (50–6). Explaining this prophecy, the narrator says that 'it was you, Battus', who was this man who received the oracle and was thereby divinely appointed to found Cyrene. He thus repeats in 'you' form what he had earlier recounted in 'he'-form: 'Pytho, where long ago the priestess…prophesied…that *Battus* would be the colonizer of fruit-bearing Libya' (4–6).

The apostrophe of Battus has a rather jolting effect and draws attention to the narrator making a leap in time (skipping seventeen generations, 10) and shifting briefly from the (main) Argonaut story to the 'Battus and his stammer' story, only alluded to in the well-known elliptic manner of lyric narrative.[51] Apart from this structural function, the apostrophe has an extra significance similar to that of the apostrophe of Pelops in *O*. 1.

---

[51] For a fuller version, see Hdt. 4.155.

Through it the epinician narrator hints at the future status of Battus as a *hērōs* with a hero cult, about which we hear in another ode, *P.* 5.93–5:

> ...ἔνθα πρυ-
> μνοῖς ἀγορᾶς ἔπι δίχα κεῖται θανών.
> μάκαρ μὲν ἀνδρῶν μέτα
> ἔναιεν, ἥρως δ' ἔπειτα λαοσεβής.

And there, at the end of the agora, he [Battus] has lain apart since his death. He was blessed while he lived, and afterwards a *hērōs* worshipped by his people.[52]

Battus' future status as hero is advertised in *P.* 4 even more explicitly than in the case of Pelops in *O.* 1, since the narrator calls him μάκαρ and the Pythia says χαίρειν to him, two words with cultic associations.[53] As Currie writes, 'Applied by Pindar to the living Battos, the word μάκαρ may *approximate* him *already* to the heroes' (my italics). The metaleptic apostrophe thus may have been chosen by Pindar again both for its epic and its hymnic associations.[54]

There is in this particular case an additional reason for Pindar's apostrophe of Battus. At the time he composed this ode for Arcesilas, king of Cyrene, the latter's political position was threatened.[55] One of the purposes of the ode was therefore to emphasize Arcesilas' divinely authorized right to the throne. The apostrophe of Battus, the founder of the city, 'emphasizes his importance as a link between Euphemus, the argonaut, and Arcesilas, the reigning (Euphemid-Battid) king of Cyrene',[56] and, I would add, capitalizes on Battus' status as the main cult hero of Cyrene.

---

[52] His tomb has been found by archaeologists, see Currie (2005: 229 n. 20).
[53] Cf. Braswell (1988: *ad* 59 (b)): 'Battus receives the epithet by virtue of being the founder of Cyrene. (The oecist of a successful Greek colony was normally regarded, like Battus, as a ἥρως who deserved special honours after his death)' and Currie (2005: 231).
[54] Two other interpretations of the apostrophe have been given. (1) Segal (1982: 147–8) sees a parallel between Battus being freed from his stammer and addressing the Pythia (in 63) and the poet, who 'breaks free of the "dense craft" of Medea's embedded prophecy when he moves from this complicated speech-in-the-speech to a direct second-person address to Battus' and suggests that this 'paradigmatically lifts Pindar's own poetry closer to the penetrating communication of divine speech'. I am not sure I understand what Segal wants to say. (2) Felson (1999: 18–19) suggests that 'in his sudden intimacy with Battus the speaker impersonates the priestess even as he interprets her message for' Battus and that in fact the whole passage 6–58 was spoken by the priestess, i.e. is the content of χρῆσεν (6). Though Pindar is well capable of such merging of voices, I am not convinced of it here.
[55] For particulars, see Braswell (1988: 1–6).　　[56] Braswell (1988: *ad* 59–63).

Conclusion

The two metaleptic apostrophes of heroes in Pindaric narratives are an effective blend of the epic and hymnic uses of the apostrophe. As a marked way of narration they draw attention to important points in the narrative (the epic use) and as an echo of the hymnic 'Du-Stil' they anticipate a (mythical or historical) character's status as a *hērōs* enjoying hero cult (the hymnic use). The worlds of the past and of the present for a moment merge, not only in the sense that the epinician narrator addressing characters from his narrative 'enters' their world (or vice versa, those characters are imagined to be present at the performance), but also in that the characters are looked at both in their past and in their future (from the point of view of the narrator and his narratee: present) status. We are thus, quintessentially, dealing with metalepsis, and this use of the metaleptic apostrophe, rare though it is, can be added to the other metaleptic devices employed in the epinician ode (fade out at the end of narrative parts; the merging of the voice of the epinician speaker and of a character quoted; and the double relevance of words spoken by mythical characters, for addressees both in the past and in the present), which makes it 'the metaleptic genre par excellence'.[57]

---

[57] The other forms of metalepsis in Pindar are discussed in De Jong (2009 and 2013); the quotation is found in (2013: 118). See also Currie (2013: 269–74), who speaks of 'leaps' or 'zooms'. Cognitive psychologists refer to more or less the same phenomenon as 'blending'; for an application to Pindar, see Kirchenko (2016). One could also connect metalepsis with the concept of the eternal return of sacred time of Mircea Eliade (1967). In general on the collapsing of past and present in Pindar, see Pavlou (2012).

5

Anachronism as a Form of Metalepsis in Ancient Greek Literature

Peter Bing

'Un effet de bizarrerie' ('an effect of strangeness'). That is the sensation, according to Genette, produced by metalepsis,[1] a transgression across the fixed narrative boundary constituting the 'shifting but sacred frontier between two worlds, the world in which one tells, the world of which one tells' (Genette 1972 = 1980: 236).[2] Genette illustrates the metaleptic 'effect of strangeness' through various examples, among them Cortázar's story 'Continuity of Parks'. Here, seated in an armchair covered with green velvet, his back to the door, 'which would otherwise have bothered him as an irritating possibility for intrusions', a man spends a pleasant evening engrossed in a novel about an unfaithful wife and her lover, who conspire to kill her husband; the lover sets out on his deadly mission, penetrating the house, advancing stealthily from room to room, until finally emerging, knife in hand, behind his target as he sits in an armchair covered in green velvet, reading a novel... The story breaks off provocatively at this very moment of metaleptic transgression—or rather, at precisely the moment when the reader feels that 'effect of strangeness' as the boundary dissolves between the different narrative planes.

A character's bold intrusion across narrative levels, while certainly more typical in works of the modern era, may occur in ancient literature as well. To cite just one prominent example, Stesichorus' *Palinode* offers a case that

---

[1] See Genette (1972: 244 = 1980: 234–5) for the definition of metalepsis and this description of its effect. For further discussion, see especially Matzner in this volume, pp. 3–6.

[2] Thus the translation of Genette (1972: 245), 'frontière mouvante mais sacrée entre deux mondes: celui où l'on raconte, celui que l'on raconte'.

Peter Bing, *Anachronism as a Form of Metalepsis in Ancient Greek Literature* In: *Metalepsis: Ancient Texts, New Perspectives*. Edited by: Sebastian Matzner and Gail Trimble, Oxford University Press (2020).
© The editors and Oxford University Press.
DOI: 10.1093/oso/9780198846987.003.0005

both suggestively resembles Genette's paradigm in the Cortázar story, yet also exposes the different mentality at work in ancient literature, which renders comparison problematic.[3] In this poem, according to Isocrates (*Enc. Hel.* 10.64 = 91c Davies and Finglass, likely our earliest source), 'Stesichorus'—the poet-speaker as persona in the work—'at the start of his song said something slanderous about her' [*scil.* about his heroine, Helen] (ἀρχόμενος τῆς ᾠδῆς ἐβλασφήμησέ τι περὶ αὐτῆς);[4] in response, 'she demonstrated her power to the poet Stesichorus' (ἐνεδείξατο δὲ καὶ Στησιχόρῳ τῷ ποιητῇ τὴν αὐτῆς δύναμιν): 'he stood up bereft of his sight' (ἀνέστη τῶν ὀφθαλμῶν ἐστερημένος) and, on realizing the cause of his calamity, produced his so-called *Palinode* (addressing his character directly, as it seems),[5] whereupon 'she restored him to his old state' (πάλιν αὐτὸν εἰς τὴν αὐτὴν φύσιν κατέστησεν). Here, the character in the poem appears precisely to cross that 'sacred boundary' between 'the world in which one tells' and 'the world of which one tells', with the alarming purpose of doing injury to her author.

The same basic scenario appears also in Plato's discussion of Stesichorus' *Palinode* in the *Phaedrus* (243a–b = 91a Davies and Finglass),[6] the wording

---

[3] For discussion of some of the differences and the problems of applying Genette's term to ancient texts, see Eisen and von Möllendorff (2013a) and Matzner in this volume, pp. 21–4.

[4] Unless otherwise indicated, all translations are my own.

[5] 'You did not go on the well-benched ships, nor did you reach the citadel of Troy', οὐδ' ἔβας ἐν νηυσὶν εὐσέλμοις, | οὐδ' ἵκεο Πέργαμα Τροίας· (Pl. *Phdr.* 243b = 91a Davies and Finglass). For an external (extradiegetic) narrator's direct address to a character in the poem as itself a form of metalepsis, see De Jong (2009: 93–9) on 'apostrophe in narrative texts'. Cf. also the discussions of De Jong, Trimble, and Lovatt in this volume.

[6] 'So I need to purify myself, my friend. And for those who have erred regarding a mythical narrative there is an ancient purification, that Homer did not know, but Stesichorus did. For having been deprived of his sight on account of slandering Helen, he did not fail to understand as Homer had, but being skilled in music he knew the cause, and at once composed the words,

> This tale is not true.
> You did not journey in the well-benched ships,
> You did not reach the towers of Troy.

And on having composed the whole so-called Palinode, he saw again at once. Now I will be wiser than them in this point at least, for before suffering something on account of slandering Eros, I will try make up to him by giving him my Palinode.'

ἐμοὶ μὲν οὖν, ὦ φίλε, καθήρασθαι ἀνάγκη· ἔστιν δὲ τοῖς ἁμαρτάνουσι περὶ μυθολογίαν καθαρμὸς ἀρχαῖος, ὃν Ὅμηρος μὲν οὐκ ᾔσθετο, Στησίχορος δέ. τῶν γὰρ ὀμμάτων στερηθεὶς διὰ τὴν Ἑλένης κακηγορίαν οὐκ ἠγνόησεν ὥσπερ Ὅμηρος, ἀλλ' ἅτε μουσικὸς ὢν ἔγνω τὴν αἰτίαν, καὶ ποιεῖ εὐθύς—

> οὐκ ἔστ' ἔτυμος λόγος οὗτος,
> οὐδ' ἔβας ἐν νηυσὶν εὐσέλμοις,
> οὐδ' ἵκεο Πέργαμα Τροίας·

καὶ ποιήσας δὴ πᾶσαν τὴν καλουμένην Παλινῳδίαν παραχρῆμα ἀνέβλεψεν. ἐγὼ οὖν σοφώτερος ἐκείνων γενήσομαι κατ' αὐτό γε τοῦτο· πρὶν γάρ τι παθεῖν διὰ τὴν τοῦ Ἔρωτος κακηγορίαν πειράσομαι αὐτῷ ἀποδοῦναι τὴν παλινῳδίαν.'

of which indeed hews so closely to that of Isocrates that numerous scholars have suggested they share a common source,[7] quite possibly the *Palinode* itself. As in Isocrates, Plato's 'Stesichorus' is struck blind 'on account of his slandering Helen', διὰ τὴν Ἑλένης κακηγορίαν, an offence which evidently happened in the context of 'poetic narrative', περὶ μυθολογίαν (recall Isocrates' 'at the start of his song', ἀρχόμενος τῆς ᾠδῆς). Plato's familiarity with the poem, not just with a secondary tradition, is signalled by the fact that Socrates quotes the three verses from it here.[8] These show that 'Stesichorus' slandered Helen in this same poem by initially following the traditional Homeric tale.[9] But after doing so, he bluntly claimed in polemical contrast to his model, 'this tale is not true' (οὐκ ἔστ' ἔτυμος λόγος οὗτος). Indeed, 'Stesichorus' then addressed Helen directly, suggesting that she was in some sense present and listening: 'you did not journey in the well-benched ships; you did not reach the towers of Troy'. In a further indication that Plato knew the poem, Socrates comments in the *Republic* (9.586c = 91b Davies and Finglass), 'Stesichorus said it was a phantom of

Thereafter see the commentary on lyric poets in P. Oxy. 2506 fr. 26 col.1 = 90 Davies and Finglass, which cites Chamaileon as its authority.

[7] I cite Isocrates first in each instance: τῶν ὀφθαλμῶν ἐστερημένος, 'deprived of his eyes'; τῶν γὰρ ὀμμάτων στερηθείς, 'for deprived of his sight'; γνοὺς τὴν αἰτίαν, 'recognizing the cause'; ἔγνω τὴν αἰτίαν, 'he recognized the cause'; τὴν καλουμένην Παλινωιδίαν, 'the so-called Paliode'; πᾶσαν τὴν καλουμένην Παλινωιδίαν, 'the whole so-called Palinode'.

[8] Ercoles (2013: 306) is misleading when he suggests that the three verses quoted by Socrates 'resounded like a sort of "refrain" at Athenian symposia and became proverbial as τὰ τρία τῶν Στησιχόρου [the three by Stesichorus], verses of which no educated citizen could be ignorant' ('risuonavano come una sorta di *refrain* nei simposî ateniesi e divennero, proverbialmente, τὰ τρία τῶν Στησιχόρου, versi che nessun cittadino dotato di istruzione poteva ignorare' (cf. Hesych. τ 1343 C. = Tb9 (c)). Nothing in Hesychius, nor in the two other attestations to τὰ τρία τῶν Στησιχόρου in Zenobius and the Suda (Ercoles' Tb9 (a–b)) suggest that this expression refers to the verses cited in the *Phaedrus*. Indeed, in Zenobius and the Suda it refers explicitly to strophe, antistrophe, and epode.

[9] The demonstrative οὗτος, 'this', in οὐκ ἔστ' ἔτυμος λόγος οὗτος, 'this tale is not true', refers to something that was just spoken (like Isocrates' ἀρχόμενος τῆς ᾠδῆς ἐβλασφήμησέν, 'at the start of his song he said something slanderous about her'), *not* to a song delivered on an altogether different occasion. With more detail, see similarly Beecroft (2006: 51): 'The logos of Helen is not identified anaphorically by *ho* ["the"]—it is not a story to which the narrator has made brief reference earlier, and of whose previous mention is now reminding his audience. It is not identified by the speaker-oriented *hode* ["this here"], which would indicate that the story that is the referent of the demonstrative, while known to the narrator, has yet not been identified for his audience; the use of *hode* ["this here"] would imply that the narration of a logos, perhaps one unfamiliar to the audience, was yet to come. Finally, it is not identified by the demonstrative of more remote deixis, *ekeinos* ["that"], which would establish the logos as known to the speaker and audience, but beyond, or at least at the edges of, their current sphere of interest. *Houtos* ["this"] is none of these things. The use of *houtos* ["this"] in this line indicates that the logos it describes is vividly present before the audience, that it has just been narrated for them.'

Helen that was the focus of strife for those at Troy, in ignorance of the truth'. Helen herself remained in safekeeping with Proteus in Egypt.

To compare this narrative with that of Cortázar's story is certainly tempting, yet one cannot do so unproblematically. For instance, given the state of our evidence we cannot say with absolute certainty whether the narrative of Helen blinding Stesichorus was even present in his poem or belongs merely to the biographical tradition reflecting its reception. Yet it is not unreasonable to assume that it did indeed have its place in the poem.[10] As Kelly has shown (2007: 5), there are in Greek literature numerous scenes of 'encounter in which the poet-narrator appears as a character' who meets and converses with the subject of their own narrative, for example 'Sappho' and Aphrodite in Sappho 1.[11] It is perfectly conceivable, then, that Helen here breached the confines of the story in which she was a character, so as to blind her narrator. The incident's subsequent renown— caused by that 'effect of strangeness'?—suggests that it worked its magic on Stesichorus' public quite powerfully. At the same time, the account of the blinding points up the problem in taking Helen's action as a form of metalepsis. For Helen is not just a creature of fiction present within the narrated work; she is a goddess thought to exist outside the text.[12] The epic heroine was also a deity, worshipped in Sparta, southern Italy, and Sicily.[13] In other words there is a 'Helen' in the poem and a Helen outside it, just as there is a 'Stesichorus' in the narrative and a Stesichorus outside it. Helen, therefore, has status and power independent of the poem, functioning ambiguously within it as both narratee ('you did not journey in the

---

[10] Similarly Dornseiff (1933: 34–5), Sider (1989), Bowie (1993), Graziosi (2002: 148–9), Kelly (2007: 1–11), and Grossardt (2012: 50). An alternative approach is to suppose that Stesichorus spoke in his poem only metaphorically of being blind and that the biographical tradition seized on this nucleus, so as to elaborate it into a narrative, thus e.g. Bowra (1961: 108), Fränkel (1962: 322 n. 7), Woodbury (1967: 174), Kannicht (1969: I 29). To illustrate the type of metaphor that could have given rise to the story, the latter two scholars cite Pindar's *Paean* 7b.18–20 Snell and Maehler, τυφλαὶ γὰρ ἀνδρῶν φρένες, | ὅστις ἄνευθ᾽ Ἑλικωνιάδων | βαθεῖαν ἐ.. [..] . ων ἐρευνᾷ σοφίας ὁδόν, which—significantly—comes just after the speaker has rejected the well-worn path of Homer, κελαδήσαθ᾽ ὕμνους, | Ὁμήρου [δὲ μὴ τρι]πτὸν κατ᾽ ἀμαξιτόν | ἰόντες, ἀ[λλ᾽ ἀλ]λοτρίαις ἀν᾽ἵπποις (lines 10–12).
[11] On this poem see further Budelmann in this volume, pp. 65–8.
[12] Whether and how an audience of Sappho's or Stesichorus' time (indeed even of later eras) would have distinguished between fiction and reality in myth is a notoriously difficult question. See Fowler (2011) and Hunter (2016).
[13] See the brief overview in Kannicht (1969: 38), who sees the two parts of Stesichorus' poem as reflecting precisely the ambivalence between Helen as mortal epic heroine and the divine goddess: 'Der Sinn dieser Anlage des Gedichts wäre dann...also in der dialektischen Beziehung zwischen sogenannter Schmähung und sogenannter Palinodie wie in einem Diptychon die Ambivalenz Helenas als der Göttin und als der Heroine sinnenfällig zur Erscheinung zu bringen' (1969: 41).

well-benched ships...') and external audience. Indeed, one could say that qua goddess she belongs to a higher order of reality than the poet, existing on a divine plane.[14] From that perspective, both narrator and author are subject to *her* authority, and she can enact a sort of ferocious reader-response criticism by seizing authorial power and dictating the terms of the narrative: she can blind the poet if she does not like what she hears, or restore his sight if she does. The 'sacred frontier' between levels of narrative that Genette evokes (see n. 2 above) may in this instance be more than a metaphor: human narrative may quite literally have run up against the sacred.[15]

A world of difference, then, separates the conceptual universe of Stesichorus' *Palinode* and Cortázar's 'Continuity of Parks', not to speak of ancient and modern literature more generally, so that we may wonder if it is helpful or even legitimate to appeal to the modern Genettian notion of 'metalepsis' when discussing an ancient text—even one that seems at first to fit the metaleptic pattern to a T. Perhaps it is, but if we are going to bring the term into play, then, best to do so with due caution.[16] That said, the concept of metalepsis can, I think, prove fruitful in dealing with other types of transgression across fixed narrative boundaries in Greek literature.

In what follows, I therefore want to focus on another manifestation of metalepsis, namely anachronism, which has to do with a different but no less fundamental line separating that 'world in which one tells' from 'the world of which one tells', that is, their temporal or chronological disjunction. As De Jong reminds us (2009: 88),[17] 'the narrator and his act of narration belong to a different time and place, a different universe than the characters in the story and fabula. Even a first-person or internal narrator tells about his former self at a different (later) time.' Anachronism[18] comes about when narrators cross that line, retrojecting a feature of their

---

[14] On metalepsis and the divine see especially Trimble, Fulkerson, and Lovatt in this volume.

[15] See also the contribution by Kennedy in this volume.

[16] Matzner suggests similar caution in his introductory chapter to this volume.

[17] See also De Jong's chapter in this volume. De Jong's 'story' and 'fabula' are terms derived from Bal (1997: 5), who distinguishes between *text* ('a finite, structured whole composed of language signs'), *story* ('a fabula that is presented in a certain manner'), and *fabula* ('a series of logically and chronologically related events'). The latter two correspond to Genette's *récit* ('narrative') and *histoire* ('story').

[18] The term must be distinguished from what Genette (1972: 78–89, here 79 = 1980: 35–47, here 36) calls 'anachronie' (usually translated into English as 'anachrony'), in speaking of 'anachronies narratives (comme j'appellerai ici les différentes formes de discordance entre l'ordre de l'histoire et celui de récit)', 'narrative anachronies (as I will call the various types of discordance between the two orderings of story [*histoire*] and narrative [*récit*])'. For Genette, the narrative [*récit*] is the account of events as ordered by the narrator; the story [*histoire*] is the purely chronological order of events reconstructable from the narrator's narrative.

present-day world onto the earlier time of the story (noticeable particu-
larly when that story—like so many ancient narratives—takes place in a
remote heroic past),[19] or inversely, projecting an archaic element onto a
later period. Either way, anachronism renders synchronous things that
from a historical/chronological perspective do not belong together. The
degree to which the temporal anomaly within the narrated universe is per-
ceived varies greatly. Some anachronisms are blatant and easily discerned;
some are subtler and escape notice.[20] In any case, anachronism has its
impact in the eye of the beholder,[21] dependent on what an audience brings
with it to the experience, its prior knowledge, its engagement with the nar-
rative, its attentiveness to detail.[22]

Anachronism can take many forms. But let us start with a modern
instance that highlights its transgressive potential, an anachronism so
blatant and in-your-face as to be impossible to overlook; instead, it provokes
an audience to think about the work that it does in its context. My example
comes from Brian Helgeland's 2001 movie, *A Knight's Tale*, a romantic
adventure set in medieval Europe of the 1370s, peopled by historical figures
such as Edward the Black Prince of Wales and Geoffrey Chaucer. The story
follows William (played by Heath Ledger), a squire of Sir Ector, who, when
his master suddenly dies in the midst of a jousting match, just one pass
away from victory, decides to don Sir Ector's armour and vie for the prize.
He wins, of course, and with the support of Chaucer, among others, con-
tinues to compete in further tournaments, ultimately proving himself
worthy of knighthood in his own right. Following a brief prelude announc-
ing William's decision to impersonate his lord, the movie strikes the first
of its many anachronistic chords while still in the opening credits.

That anachronism here consists in how Brian May's famous 1977 song
for Queen, 'We Will Rock You', is overlaid onto the historically quite
meticulous, and certainly convincing, visual evocation of a medieval

---

[19] See Kroll's 'Exkurs: Anachronismen' (1924: 178–84) for a helpful discussion of
anachronism, mainly in the *Aeneid*. On Latin literature he cites further Jacob (1839: 188–91),
Ebert (1888), and Miedel (1892). In Greek literature, see Easterling (1985).

[20] This should not be taken as corresponding to the distinction drawn by Whitmarsh
(2013b) between 'strong' and 'weak' metalepsis. Subtler, hidden metalepses can be very
strong indeed, as I hope to show through the different instances of metaleptic anachronism
treated below.

[21] The differences among critics about what phenomena should be characterized as meta-
lepsis are symptomatic. Cf. Matzner in this volume. Thus, with regard to epic apostrophe of
Patroclus by the narrator of the *Iliad*, studied by De Jong (2009) and Klooster (2013) as
instances of metalepsis, Whitmarsh (2013b: 5) says that 'to my eyes…the apostrophe is,
rather, the vehicle for a stylized rhetorical question'.

[22] On metalepsis and the expectations of the audience see Matzner in this volume.

jousting tournament. Overlaid, however, is the wrong word, since the song does not merely accompany the action as a background soundtrack; it is fully integrated into the scene. The tournament spectators themselves punch out the beat, thumping on the railings of the stands with their fists, clapping their hands, pounding the ground with a spear, and chanting the words of this *a cappella* anthem. A young woman dances to the beat. The knights, too, clank their armour in rhythm. Even the snooty nobles cannot help tapping along, ultimately clapping and mouthing the words, as they look on from their box, powerless against the rhythmic wave. And speaking of wave, the spectators even perform The Wave like fans at a modern-day sports event. The mostly *a cappella* song ends with an electric guitar solo, an embellishment that underlines the scene's time-fusing effect, for it is made to coincide visually with the appearance of trumpeters, who look as though they are actually playing Queen: their fanfare ends precisely on the guitar's final note.

In his commentary on the movie in the DVD, writer-director Brian Helgeland talks about the anachronism of this scene and its sometimes hostile critical reception (2001: 5 mins, 32 secs): 'someone came up to me and said "You know, they didn't have Queen in medieval times," and I felt quite foolish when I found that out: Stupid, stupid, stupid!' In fact throughout his commentary Helgeland impishly envisions nit-picking audience members, people who want 'to split historical hairs' (2001: 1 hour, 32 mins), helpfully informing him of his anachronisms after the fact, to which the director responds with a shammed smack to the forehead and a quip like, 'You know what, an entire crew read the script, they saw the allusions to 70s rock, and no one had the decency to come up to me and say they didn't have that music back then' (2001: 1 hour, 3 mins, 25 secs). At the same time, Helgeland hints at what he may truly have been up to in brandishing his anachronism. That early scene, he says, marks the point in the film when you realize that 'it's not your father's Oldsmobile' (2001: 3 mins, 55 secs). Later in the commentary he adds a witty explanation, one that also reveals something essential (2001: 27 mins, 38 secs): 'It's important', he says, 'to point out that this is the 1370s, and the 70s never really change: the 70s are always the 70s, so 1370, 1470, 1570 ... That's why the 70s music. Maybe not such a crazy idea after all.'[23] The 70s music, in other words, exposes affinities and thus brings us closer to another world. Through it,

---

[23] At another point, Helgeland suggests, 'It's really movie convention that we're fighting, also with the music. The instruments of an orchestra not having existed for three hundred years until after the date this film was made [*scil.* set]. And certain people have insisted that it

we can see how a medieval crowd's experience of a tournament, its excitement and high spirits, the sheer pleasure of the joust, mirrors our own at the countless modern-day events, where spectators shake the rafters with the raucous chant of 'We will, we will rock you'. The anachronism collapses the distance between our present and the Middle Ages, allowing us to connect with that historically distant time and appreciate the similarities—without totally effacing the difference. At the end of the movie, Helgeland puts it this way (2001: 2 hours, 7 mins, 56 secs): 'I've taken some flack…People keep saying how can you have the modern and the old? And I remember that old Reese's Peanut Butter Cup commercial where You've got chocolate on my peanut butter, No you've got peanut butter on my chocolate. And to me, what this movie is all about is You've got Chaucer on my Queen, No way, you've got Queen on my Chaucer. And I think…somewhere in the continuum of time and space worlds collide, and this just happens to be where this world collided with the other world.'

The idea that anachronism lets connections emerge by collapsing the distance between disparate worlds—letting them collide—provides us with a potent image we can usefully add to the stock of metaphors habitually applied to metalepsis: *incursion, invasion* across a fixed line, *transgressing* boundaries or *blurring* them. It is something we will come back to.[24] But first I want to spend more time with the nit-pickers and 'historical hair-splitters', who view anachronisms as lamentable mistakes to be corrected. I dwell on these not least because their classical counterparts form by far the largest (and loudest) contingent when it comes to discussing anachronism in the ancient sources. Their assumption is mostly that anachronism is inadvertent, resulting merely from ignorance or (if not ignorance) carelessness, while their job is to set the record straight.

By characterizing them as nit-pickers, I do not mean that their critical fussiness is without use. The ability to expose an inadvertent anachronism can be a serious business, a potent instrument in a reader's toolkit, and not mere pedantry. That is the case, for instance, when a corrector recognizes a chronological anomaly and so unmasks a forgery. Grafton cites how the fourth-century BC historian Theopompus (*FGrHist* 115 F 154) questioned the authenticity of the mid-fifth-century Peace of Callias because, as he

---

should be orchestral…I think it's the nay-sayers that we've really drawn the line against and that we've really been fighting against our whole lives' (2001: 1 hour, 32 mins, 50 secs).

[24] Such a view of anachronism as metalepsis dovetails intriguingly with Matzner's exploration (2016a) of the 'New Queer Unhistoricism' through the novels *Este latente mundo* by José Luis de Juan and *Boy Caesar* by Jeremy Reed.

noted, its Athenian inscription used the Ionic alphabet, only adopted in Attica decades later in 403/2 BC. This is the bright side of nit-picking. An observation like that of Theopompus reveals, as Grafton puts it (1990: 10), 'an aptitude essential to anyone trying either to create a plausible document or to expose one', since 'any forger, however deft, imprints the pattern and texture of his own period's life, thought, and language on the past he hopes to make seem real and vivid'; attentive readers will later 'recognize the forger's period superimposed on the forgery's' (1990: 67).

Yet ancient discussion of anachronism tends to be, as Easterling puts it (1985: 9), 'at a tedious level of triviality'. The longest such discussion known to me concerns precisely the inadvertent variety. It comes in a passage of Athenaeus (216c–217c) in which one of the *deipnosophistai*, Masurius, denigrates philosophers, who 'fail to realize that much of what they write is full of anachronisms' (πολλὰ παρὰ τοὺς χρόνους γράφοντες οὐκ αἰσθάνονται; trans. Olson, here and below). For instance, 'the noble Xenophon is unaware of this…in his *Symposium* (1.2), where he…represents himself as present along with the other dinner-guests, although he may well not even have been born yet or was only a boy' (καθάπερ οὐδ᾽ ὁ καλὸς Ξενοφῶν, ὃς ἐν τῷ Συμποσίῳ ὑποτίθεται…καὶ σὺν τοῖς ἄλλοις δαιτυμόσι παρόντα <αὐτὸν> τὸν ἴσως μηδὲ γεννηθέντα ἢ περὶ τὴν παιδικὴν ἡλικίαν ὑπάρχοντα). Ouch! Xenophon, what *could* you have been thinking? The learned Masurius, who typically supports his arguments with detailed reference to the sequence of Athenian archons, calls him out on another anachronism as well: in Xenophon's *Symposium*, whose dramatic date is 422, Socrates criticizes Pausanias *in absentia* for having once argued that an army of *erastai* and their *eromenoi* would be the most effective military force (8.32–3), while in Plato's *Symposium* (178e), whose dramatic date is six years later in 416, that argument is put into the mouth of Phaedrus (in the presence of that same Pausanias) as though it were something new. 'It is therefore remarkable and strange', says Masurius, 'if, when Socrates is having dinner at Callias' house, he censures as inappropriate remarks that have not yet been made' (θαυμαστὸν οὖν καὶ τερατῶδες, εἰ τὰ μήπω ῥηθέντα…Σωκράτης παρὰ Καλλίᾳ δειπνῶν εὐθύνει <ὡς> οὐ δεόντως ῥηθέντα). This whole discussion in Athenaeus, which continues at great length, resembles a game of historical 'Gotcha!' through which the critic performs his erudition. Academics are all familiar with the performance of erudition; we recognize its features, we have probably engaged in it ourselves. When Masurius finally concludes, he leaves his listeners dumbstruck διὰ σοφίαν (on account of his learning).

Similar critiques of anachronism abound in the scholia to Greek tragedy. To take just one famous example, when Sophocles depicts Orestes participating in the chariot race at the Pythian games in his *Electra*, the scholia point out that those games were founded well after the time of Orestes (*ad* 49, τοῖς χρόνοις ἀνῆκται· νεώτερος γὰρ Ὀρέστου ἐστὶν ὁ Πυθικὸς ἀγών, *ad* 682, οὔπω ἦν ἐπὶ Ὀρέστου ὁ Πυθικὸς ἀγών). Indeed, already Aristotle seems to refer to this particular anachronism when he highlights 'those who report about the Pythian Games in *Electra*' as an example of the ἄλογα, 'irrational components', which are best to avoid in a tragedy (*Poetics* 1460a31).

If such is the tenor of most ancient discussion of anachronism, is that all there was to it? Was inadvertent anachronism the only kind recognized? And was 'Condemn and Correct' the only conceivable or sanctioned response? Or to the contrary, did ancient audiences allow that anachronism could also be used pointedly to accomplish a variety of ends? Our experience with the *Knight's Tale* certainly disposes us to think that it could be deliberate, a useful and eye-opening transgression—a metalepsis— across that 'sacred frontier' Genette described between 'the world in which one tells' and 'the world of which one tells' (as we saw at the start of this chapter). And modern literature certainly treats anachronism as a given, both necessary and useful. In a famous passage from his 'Teilnahme Goethes an Manzoni', Goethe (1950: 806) contends that anachronism is an *indispensible* part of any work of literature dealing with the past. Here, he defends the Italian poet-novelist Manzoni against the nit-pickers, praising him both for his meticulous accuracy in dealing with the past and for endowing historical characters with more modern sensibilities ('something that others [the historical hair-splitters] had condemned', 'was man anderwärts wohl zu tadeln gefunden hat'): 'In his [Manzoni's] defence, we make a perhaps paradoxical-seeming assertion, namely that all poetry actually deals in anachronisms... The *Iliad* and *Odyssey*, all the tragedians and whatever true poetry has survived lives and breathes only from anachronisms. We confer the new upon all situations so as to make them clear and even bearable.'[25] Using anachronism, then, may be necessary to serve a particular end ('so as to make [the content] clear and even bearable'), and 'a poet may reconcile himself to this in his conscience', according

---

[25] 'Wir sprechen zu seiner [Manzonis] Rechtfertigung das vielleicht paradox scheinende Wort aus: dass alle Poesie eigentlich in Anachronismen verkehre... Die Ilias wie die Odyssee, die sämtlichen Tragiker und was uns von wahrer Poesie übrig geblieben ist, lebt und atmet nur in Anachronismen. Allen Zuständen borgt man das Neuere, um sie anschaulich, ja nur erträglich zu machen...'

to Goethe ('der Poet mag hierüber mit seinem Gewissen übereinkommen'). He advocates, further, for an attitude of tolerance among readers regarding anachronism: they should look 'through their fingers', he says ('der Leser aber muss gefällig durch die Finger blicken'), i.e. with sightlines partially blocked, rather than examining the matter too closely. That is, he counsels readers to accept, if not embrace, anachronism as a means for understanding a text.

Coming back now to Sophocles, in her helpful discussion Easterling acknowledges the dreary discourse of the scholia, but tries to look beyond its 'strictures' to understand the function of anachronism in tragedy. She argues that in the example from Sophocles' *Electra* and elsewhere we may not be dealing with inadvertent or 'thoughtless anachronism' at all (1985: 5), but rather with its purposeful use. The tragedian, she says, takes pains to 'naturalise' such temporal anomalies by 'setting them in a familiar heroic context which prevents our feeling any jarring incongruity' (1985: 2). Coming before Aristotle's researches into the victor lists of the Pythian Games, Sophocles may (she suggests) not even have realized that he was engaging in anachronism. But in any case, chariot-racing heroes were familiar from the funeral games in the *Iliad*, and indeed Sophocles clearly drew on the description of Antilochus from *Iliad* 23 (1985: 8). Orestes' participation in the chariot races at Delphi would thus have seemed plausible, a familiar component of heroic action. Anachronism may thus serve to render a distant world accessible to its audience. This would be a kind of metalepsis in keeping with many of De Jong's observations (2009: 92, 95, etc.) about the phenomenon in ancient literature, namely that it often serves to reinforce the realism and illusionistic artifice of the text, rather than to undermine it.

Easterling would, however, go further when it comes to Euripides. In her view, this tragedian deploys anachronism in 'novel and subversive' ways. His 'startling and ironic [anachronistic] effects', condemned by the scholia,[26] are part of his 'dramatic strategy'. When, for instance, Tyndareus rebukes his matricide-grandson in the *Orestes* for not using the law to prosecute Clytemnestra for Agamemnon's murder, 'as if the whole story of Orestes and the first murder trial were not still to come', we can see this, according to Easterling, 'as offering the audience different perspectives on the heroic action, to "shock them out of their complacency"...inviting

---

[26] E.g. *ad Hec.* 254: 'that's how Euripides is, combining his own period with that of the heroes and mixing up the times' (καί ἐστι τοιοῦτος ὁ Εὐριπίδης, περιάπτων τὰ καθ' ἑαυτὸν τοῖς ἥρωσι καὶ τοὺς χρόνους συγχέων; trans. adapted from Easterling).

them to think critically' (1985: 9).[27] As in *A Knight's Tale*, then, the work of anachronism—when conscious and pointed—may be both to render distant worlds accessible, but also to suggest new ways to consider them.

This makes a lot of sense. Yet these conclusions about the effect of anachronism in tragedy—perceptive and reasonable though they may be—remain speculative. So far as I can see, we simply do not *know* how audiences reacted to anachronism in tragedy, apart, that is, from those niggling responses in the scholia. Is there an ancient discourse about anachronism that allows us to get beyond this? One place that might be worth looking at is works that themselves depict the use of anachronism and dramatize a response to it. What do I mean by this? Perhaps a modern instance can clarify. The passage I have in mind comes from William Faulkner's *Absalom, Absalom!* (1990: 179) As in Athenaeus, this example has to do with an inadvertent anachronism. Here, however, two responses to it are modelled in the narrative: one of these is by a historical hair-splitter who performs his erudition by correcting the anachronism (though he does so a bit more playfully than in Athenaeus); the other is the response this provokes in the narrator/source of the anachronism. In addition, Faulkner stages the discussion in such a way as to invite us, his readers, to implicate ourselves in one or the other response. In a scene set at Harvard in 1910, the young Southerner, Quentin Compson, and his Canadian roommate, Shreve, talk about Thomas Sutpen, the Mississippi plantation owner whose story forms the chief focus of the novel:

> [Thomas Sutpen] 'was born in West Virginia, in the mountains where—' ('Not in West Virginia,' Shreve said. '—What?' Quentin said. 'Not in West Virginia,' Shreve said. 'Because if he was twenty-five years old in Mississippi in 1833, he was born in 1808. And there wasn't any West Virginia in 1808 because—' 'All right,' Quentin said. '—West Virginia wasn't admitted—' 'All right all right,' Quentin said. '—into the United States until—' 'All right all right all right,' Quentin said.) '—where that few other people he knew lived in log cabins boiling with children like the one he was born in.'

---

[27] Whitmarsh (2013b) sees this more unsettling aspect of metaleptic anachronism as especially characteristic of fifth-century comedy, while arguing that the metalepsis of Greek tragedy is mostly less transgressive, a function of the fact that it operates with one foot in the heroic past (the normal locus of its plots) and one foot in the here and now (with its actors and audience, scenery, architecture, etc.).

Here Quentin acts as narrator (one of four in Faulkner's novel), while Shreve injects comments. That commentary—or better, correction— characterizes Shreve. Though impressively quick with his mental arithmetic, he appears pedantic and fussy, a fastidious person determined to set the record straight, though to do so is beside the point. The irrelevance of his correction appears in his interlocutor's sputtering irritation, expressed in his escalating 'All right…All right all right…All right all right all right'. Quentin clearly considers the nit-picking stupid (and so models a possible audience response). Ignoring this entirely, Shreve persists, comically so inasmuch as he is the outsider—a Canadian—who nevertheless knows more about American history than Quentin, true son of the South. And how do we, the readers, respond to Shreve's correction? The text teases us by cutting Shreve off ('West Virginia wasn't admitted…into the United States until—') before he has the chance to tell us precisely *when* the state entered the union.[28] That silence invites readerly intervention, potentially making us part of how the response to anachronism is enacted in the text: for it invites us either to align ourselves with Shreve by filling in the blank with what we know about West Virginia history (or take the trouble to look up); alternatively, it allows us align ourselves more with Quentin by not troubling to supplement the text, since we might consider the infor- mation irrelevant to the narrative's larger point. Taken purely on its own terms, Shreve's commentary erodes the positive work of the anachronism, namely in making information accessible to a contemporary audience by drawing its attention more precisely to the geographic locality in present- day terms (though in the narrative context, Faulkner's dialogue still wittily accomplishes that end).

Can we find a comparable ancient text that dramatizes the use of anachronism, and models an audience's response? The one that occurs to me is from Plato's *Symposium*. Here, in his great speech on *erōs*, Socrates recounts 'the discussion of love that I once heard from Diotima, a woman from Mantinea' (τὸν δὲ λόγον τὸν περὶ τοῦ Ἔρωτος, ὅν ποτ᾽ ἤκουσα γυναικὸς Μαντινικῆς Διοτίμας, 201d). Until then, he asserts, he had been just as clueless about love as the youthful Agathon, whose idea of Eros he just demolished using the very same arguments Diotima had once deployed to shred his own (201e). Plato takes pains to locate this prior occasion in a fairly remote past. For although Socrates here assigns it to an indefinite

---

[28] I am grateful to Jenny Clay for noting to me that the text pointedly leaves this informa- tion unstated so as to invite the audience's involvement.

earlier time ('which I once heard', ὅν ποτ' ἤκουσα), it becomes clear in the course of Diotima's speech and the rest of the dialogue that his encounter with her occurred quite long ago. In her speech, for instance, Diotima characterizes the Socrates of that moment as one whose only thought is for beautiful boys and youths, 'who, if you see them now (νῦν ὁρῶν), strike you out of your senses, and make you, you and many others, eager to be with the boys you love and look at them forever, if there were any way to do that, forgetting food and drink, everything but looking at them and being with them' (211d–e, trans. Nehamas and Woodruff; τοὺς καλοὺς παῖδάς τε καὶ νεανίσκους δόξει σοι εἶναι, οὓς νῦν ὁρῶν ἐκπέπληξαι καὶ ἕτοιμος εἶ καὶ σὺ καὶ ἄλλοι πολλοί, ὁρῶντες τὰ παιδικὰ καὶ συνόντες ἀεὶ αὐτοῖς, εἴ πως οἷόν τ' ἦν, μήτε ἐσθίειν μήτε πίνειν, ἀλλὰ θεᾶσθαι μόνον καὶ συνεῖναι). This is a Socrates who only dimly resembles his current self. As Hunter (2004: 83) wittily puts it, the fact 'that Socrates (incredibly, if with the admirable politeness of a guest) presents himself as once upon a time as ignorant about *erōs* as Agathon is now, as emotionally but unreasoningly attached to "boyfriends" as any Athenian (211d5–8), and as entirely "unironic" and un-Socratic (as we are familiar with that mode from Plato's dialogues) reinforces the distancing effect of Diotima's intervention'. Socrates has changed a lot in the meantime. That much is clear from Alcibiades' account of the philosopher's heroic resistance to his charms (an account, one should stress, that itself is set already quite some time before), and from his disdain for the younger man's proposal of an unfair swap, 'you are trying to acquire genuine beauty in exchange for the appearance thereof' (ἀλλ' ἀντὶ δόξης ἀλήθειαν καλῶν κτᾶσθαι ἐπιχειρεῖς, 218e). We see then that a wealth of detail situates Diotima's encounter with Socrates fairly long ago in his lifetime.

All the more surprising, then, when Socrates has Diotima mention that 'there is indeed a story told according to which lovers are those who seek their other halves, though by my account love is neither of the half nor of the whole, unless of course, my friend, it also happens to be good' (καὶ λέγεται μέν γέ τις … λόγος, ὡς οἳ ἂν τὸ ἥμισυ ἑαυτῶν ζητῶσιν, οὗτοι ἐρῶσιν· ὁ δ' ἐμὸς λόγος οὔθ' ἡμίσεός φησιν εἶναι τὸν ἔρωτα οὔθ' ὅλου, ἐὰν μὴ τυγχάνῃ γέ που, ὦ ἑταῖρε, ἀγαθὸν ὄν, 205e). This is a pointed and brazenly transgressive anachronism. For although Socrates carefully sets his encounter with Diotima at a remote time, her allusion to 'a certain story' obviously (if with a teasing coyness) refers to Aristophanes' fantastical account of the origins of love, which guests at the symposium had heard only shortly before. Comically, Diotima—or rather, Socrates in the role of

Diotima—attacks the comic poet's narrative *ante factum*.[29] To be sure, one can at any number of points see Diotima's discourse as building on and answering themes sounded in the dialogue's previous speeches (for instance, at 208d she takes up Phaedrus' examples from 179b–180a of the mythic characters Alcestis and Achilles, who were willing to die for their lovers, or at 209a she builds on Pausanias' tale of the two kinds of *eros* to distinguish the sort of immortality sought by those who beget physical offspring from the higher kind of those who procreate in their soul). But in pointing to 'a certain story' (τις...λόγος) that explains *eros* as a search for our other halves, Diotima makes an allusion of far greater specificity than any of these, and her critique of that story yanks us out of the narrated encounter between Socrates and Diotima in the past, back into the narrator's present at the symposium—from the 'world of which one tells' to the 'world in which one tells' (cf. Genette's description of metalepsis cited at the start). Aristophanes, sitting in the audience, clearly recognizes the attack on his speech. That's what we learn when Socrates finishes his oration: 'everyone applauded him, but Aristophanes tried to speak up in response, because Socrates had made mention of his speech in the midst of his own' (τοὺς μὲν ἐπαινεῖν, τὸν δὲ Ἀριστοφάνη λέγειν τι ἐπιχειρεῖν, ὅτι ἐμνήσθη αὐτοῦ λέγων ὁ Σωκράτης περὶ τοῦ λόγου·, 212c). And by the way, the ὅτι-clause here need not suggest that only Aristophanes 'got' the allusion; rather it is consistent with the others present at the party getting it as well.[30] Perhaps their reaction to the speech, which is one of appreciation (τοὺς μὲν ἐπαινεῖν), indicates their strong approval for (among many other things) that anachronistic teasing that Aristophanes came in for. In any case, the words demonstrate beyond a doubt that, unlike Athenaeus' Masurius, Aristophanes does not consider the anachronism inadvertent

---

[29] One could regard this anachronism as a kind of (retrospective) foreshadowing—what ancient sources call *proanaphonesis* or *prolepsis*. In Genettian terms it is simultaneously 'extradiegetic' from the perspective of Diotima's past discourse inasmuch as it points beyond its own confines, and 'intradiegetic' from the standpoint of Socrates' speech at Agathon's symposium, inasmuch as it playfully 'foreshadows' Aristophanes' speech within the same event. On *prolepsis* as a device in ancient Greek literature, see Nünlist (2009: 34–42). See also n. 38 below for an instance in Homer. *Prolepsis* has also been fruitfully studied in Latin literature, e.g. by Fowler (1997: 77) and Harrison (2001) and (2010) with regard to foreshadowing in ecphrasis.

[30] Aristodemus, on whom the narrator Apollodorus relies (though he also checked the details with Socrates himself), clearly understands that Aristophanes tried to speak up because Socrates had referred to his speech in his own: where does he come by this knowledge? Had Aristophanes already blurted out, 'Hey! You were referring to my speech!', or was that self-evident to all assembled?

(Socrates is here the hands-on agent recalling Aristophanes' speech). Nor is it likely that Aristophanes—the creator of a comic myth about the source of our sexual urges—would have reacted with historical hair-splitting. We never find out what he would have said because at precisely that moment Alcibiades arrives with his drunken *komos*. Yet the ludic setting of the symposium itself suggests that the anachronism would have seemed as pointed and mischievous to Aristophanes (and to the rest of the partiers) as it does to us. After all, in having Diotima make this time-bending reference, Socrates answers Aristophanes' own *hysteron-proteron* inversion in the temporal sequence at the party, his hiccup-induced request to change places with Eryximachus in the normal order of the speeches ἐπὶ δεξιά.[31] Can we see Diotima's anachronism as a temporal hiccup in turn?[32] Be that as it may, her chronological anomaly certainly creates that 'effect of strangeness' Genette suggested. But more, by playfully collapsing the space between present and past, it brings those disparate times to bear on each other in a productive and meaningful way—a function of ancient metalepsis that we will see illustrated again shortly in our final case study.

The example from the *Symposium* leads to the unavoidable—if hardly surprising—conclusion that anachronism could be deployed as pointedly in ancient literature as it is today, and that audiences could perceive it not merely as a flaw to be corrected, but as a deliberate if humorous provocation to ponder a text's significance. Not all anachronisms are, of course, as flamboyant and self-dramatizing as that in the *Symposium*. In Hellenistic poetry, for instance, they could—as we might expect—be cunningly veiled, imperceptible except to those learned enough to uncover them. An example displaying all the intricate erudition we expect from poets of that age, and at the same time suggesting circumstances of reception quite different from that experienced by Agathon's guests in Plato's *Symposium*, appears in Theocritus' *Idyll* 24, the *Herakliskos*. I myself would never have found this anachronism—not in a million years—though its imprint on the text is cosmic. The keen-sighted Gow (1942) discovered it, and it is thus well-known to those who use his great commentary (1952).

As we learn from the fragmentary scholium at the end of the poem (*ad* 171), the *Herakliskos* was composed for a musical *agon* and closed with a prayer to Herakles for victory in the contest. Though we don't know

---

[31] On the standard order in which participants at a symposium took turns ἐπὶ δεξιά, i.e. from left to right around the room, see Wecowski (2002).

[32] I owe this thought to Regina Höschele.

exactly when, where, or for what particular festival that competition was,[33] a Ptolemaic context seems plausible, as Herakles has special significance to the Ptolemies as the presumed ancestor of their dynasty (something Theocritus highlighted in his *Encomium to Ptolemy*, 17.26–7).[34] At the start of *Idyll* 24, the poet describes a moment of blissful domesticity in the life of the mythic family: Alcmene, having washed and nursed her sons, Herakles and Iphikles, lays them in their cradle—a bronze shield Amphitryon once took as plunder from the Taphian king Pterelaos—and sings them a lullaby. She rocks them gently in the shield and the babies fall asleep (lines 1–10). Yet the heart-warming serenity of the moment quickly shatters, as Hera sends two monstrous serpents to kill the boys. Before that, however, Theocritus pauses to set their arrival against the backdrop of the night-time sky:

> ἆμος δὲ στρέφεται μεσονύκτιον ἐς δύσιν Ἄρκτος
> Ὠρίωνα κατ᾽ αὐτόν, ὃ δ᾽ ἀμφαίνει μέγαν ὦμον,
> τᾶμος ἄρ᾽ αἰνὰ πέλωρα δύω πολυμήχανος Ἥρα
> [*scil.* ὦρσεν]

> But when the Bear at midnight swings down
> over against Orion himself, who shows his mighty
>   shoulder,
> then it was that crafty Hera [sent] two dread
>   monsters
>   **(Theoc. 24.11–13; trans. adapted from Gow)**

What Gow realized was that these indications about the position of the constellations Ursa Major (Ἄρκτος) and Orion at midnight (μεσονύκτιον), in particular the appearance of the star Betelgeuse, Orion's 'mighty shoulder', visible above the horizon, did not merely adorn the mention of the hour. Rather, they could be used, together with a particular latitude and year appropriate to the period, to work out the precise day and month for the scene described.

To help him, Gow enlisted astronomer Sir Arthur Eddington, who found that, around 300 BC at 35° N, Betelgeuse would set at midnight on 26 February. Now as Theocritus specified in line 1 that Herakles 'was ten

---

[33] For the plausible suggestion that it was for the Ptolemaic *Basileia* and *Genethlia* of Ptolemy Philadelphus, see especially Koenen (1977: 29–32).

[34] For the political importance of Heraklean ancestry more generally among kings, see Huttner (1997) along with Hunter (2003: 12–13, 116–17, 120–1).

months old' at the time (δεκάμηνον ἐόντα), Gow thought that the poet was deliberately pointing to a birthdate for the hero in the preceding April. In addition, he observed how Herakles' victory over the serpents had long been used 'to convey a political significance' on coins of other states (1952: 418), and that the poet's depiction of the hero's education later in the poem 'is consistent with the view that Heracles symbolizes a Hellenistic prince'. Most importantly, he noted that Ptolemy Philadelphus ascended to the throne as co-regent on the 25th of the Macedonian month Dystros in 285 BC, a date that was—as with Herakles—probably also his birthday, and which fell precisely in April (thus Gow 1942: 107). As Gow put it, 'it seems possible that Theocritus is making some point connected with Philadelphus' (1952: 418). In other words, Theocritus appears to have projected onto the heavens of a mythical scene from the remote past the coordinates of a night-time sky of his own era, ones that point to a date of epochal significance, the birthday of Ptolemy Philadelphus and his ascension to the throne. Worlds in collision indeed: an anachronism of cosmic proportions.

Recently, Murray (2014: 256–8) has modified Gow's conclusions somewhat, arguing that 'the best evidence' suggests that Philadelphus became co-regent with his father Ptolemy Soter only a year later, in 284, and that the 25th of Dystros for that year fell in late February (Murray 2014: 257).[35] She therefore sets aside the mention of Herakles being ten months old as pointing to 'an event that happened outside the temporal bounds of the poem' (Murray 2014: 257). The emphasis, rather, is on the narrative present, where the hero first demonstrates his divine patrimony. That, according to Murray, and not ten months before, is the moment that Theocritus makes correspond with Philadelphus' rise to power—thereby bringing those disparate times into meaningful relation. Her basic conclusion, therefore, remains the same as Gow's.[36]

What sort of audience would have seen and appreciated an anachronism such as this—one encoded in the heavens? One must acknowledge, of course, that astronomy was a standard means of timekeeping in antiquity

---

[35] The data are, however, complex and debatable. For discussion, see Bennett (2001–13).

[36] Murray adds an observation about the starscape that Theocritus had left unspoken: at precisely 'the same time that Orion is setting and Ursa Major is turning west, the constellation rising in the east is Ophiuchus (the serpent strangler)', a further, tacit allusion to Herakles (Murray 2014: 257). Prioux challenges this suggestion in an as yet unpublished paper (2016), arguing that 'a figure holding a serpent...can by no means be identified with Heracles'. In this paper, Prioux suggests that the date Theocritus points to ten months prior to the scene in his poem may be 'the symbolic birthday of the pharaoh' on the 1st of Thot according to the Egyptian calendar, which coincides with the start of Philadelphus' reign in November 285 BC.

and would have been far more familiar to an ancient audience than it is to one today. As Gow put it (1942: 105), 'We cannot guess how much astronomy his audience knew…Still, they were more star-conscious than most moderns, and though perhaps not many could have said offhand that the date fixed by T. was in February, not one can have been unaware that the midnight sky is not uniform in appearance throughout the year.'[37] It seems to me that Gow's concessive clause ('though perhaps not many could have said offhand that the date fixed by T. was in February') is the crucial one here in assessing how an audience could have perceived the anachronism: it takes sophistication, some special knowledge, and the time to stop and contemplate a text while reading, to discover that precise date and its political significance. This is not what an audience experiencing the *Herakliskos* at a festival would have tumbled to—unlike *our* experience when watching the *Knight's Tale* and noticing the anachronistic use of Queen. This is a *Night's Tale* (with*out* the 'k'!) of an altogether different kind. Theocritus' poem thus points to different audiences in divergent circumstances of reception—one a learned readership considering a text at leisure, the other experiencing the poem linearly in performance at a festival and without the benefit of pauses.[38] The two audiences perhaps let us

---

[37] Murray is even more optimistic in what she expects from the audience (2014: 256): 'In general, ordinary ancients had a far better understanding of the relationship between the heavens and time-keeping than we do today. Meanwhile, poets and playwrights, for their part, could not only rely on their audience to catch the temporal meaning of astronomical references without too much ado, but they could also easily avail themselves of astronomical records, parapegmata, and, if need be, consult astronomers or astrologers or their works.' Her last sentence, however, suggests that if poets themselves might feel the need to consult astronomers, one should—as Gow suggests—not imagine audiences making calculations in their heads on hearing a poem such as the *Herakliskos* performed at a festival.

[38] It is worth mentioning an instance of metaleptic anachronism in Homer, which suggests an audience like the first I mentioned here, one well-versed in the tradition (though reflecting circumstances of reception appropriate to early epic) and perhaps already familiar with the *Iliad* as we have it. This anachronism, if/when detected (it is carefully hidden), generates that Genettian 'effect of strangeness' produced by a transgression across narrative boundaries. One may also view it as a kind of *prolepsis*, cf. n. 29 above. I am referring to the tale of Phoenix in *Iliad* 9.

Here, in pleading with Achilles to set aside his anger and help his comrades by returning to combat, Phoenix recounts the story of Meleager. As has often been noted, he carefully shapes his narrative to Achilles' situation, first by focusing on Meleager's anger as the cause for his withdrawal from the fight against the Kouretes, then by giving a leading role to the hero's companions in entreating his return. But Phoenix' tale looks ahead to things he cannot possibly know: not only do his comrades fail to persuade Meleager (as will happen with Achilles as well), but the hero will return to the fray only once the enemy breaches the walls and sets fire to what lies within (as Hector later penetrates the Achaean camp and sets fire to the ship, *Iliad* 16.112–29); most importantly, Meleager will be moved to act only through the pleas of his closest companion, his wife Cleopatra, whose name seems deliberately to recall that of Patroclus by inverting its parts (an exceptionally veiled reference: what sort of audience would have spotted this inversion? No evidence suggests that anyone did until the Middle

chart the upper and lower limits of reception for an anachronism of this kind, one cunningly hidden in plain sight. But we can plot another point in the range of ancient metaleptic anachronism and its reception if we set the Theocritean instance beside the one we examined in the *Symposium*—one certainly not so recondite as that in the *Herakliskos*, but whose reception (envisioned in the written text as being performed 'live' within the setting of the party) required an audience of considerable poetic-philosophical sophistication, which deliberately stayed sober so as to have their wits about them. In these examples, where different times are deliberately made to collide, we may begin to discern the parameters of the phenomenon of metaleptic anachronism.

Ages: possibly Eustathius vol. 2 p. 808 line 27 Van der Valk; in modern times first Howald 1924: 411; for subsequent discussion see Alden 2000: 239–41 with n. 152; Burgess 2006: 175–6). In other words, Phoenix anachronistically anticipates both the firing of the ships (not previously an explicit part of Zeus' plan, 8.470–7) and the role of Patroclus in moving Achilles to act (Patroclus' part in the epic remains marginal until *Iliad* 11.601).

What makes this foreshadowing feel transgressive and anachronistic is that neither Phoenix, despite being the speaker, nor his internal audience grasp the *prolepsis*. He is, moreover, *not* singled out as a figure endowed with the gift of foresight—for instance, a god, a seer, a dying man—as would typically be the case in Homer (Nünlist 2009: 242). Rather, the *prolepsis* occurs strictly at the level of extradiegetic narrator and narratee (De Jong 2004: 85), put into the mouth of Phoenix by the poet, as a ventriloquist throws their voice.

6

Narrative and Lyric Levels in Catullus

Gail Trimble

Metalepsis is most straightforwardly understood as a feature of narrative literature. The foundational definition given by Genette in *Figures* III assumes the existence of a narrator and a narratee, existing in an extradiegetic universe within which an act of narrating is taking place, and of characters, existing in a diegetic universe governed by that act of narrating.[1] This chapter takes as its starting point the Catullan poem which might be expected to show the clearest potential for metaleptic readings: Catullus 64, the (short) epic story of the wedding of Peleus and Thetis which is the most obviously narrative poem in the corpus.[2] Catullus, however, is not normally seen as a primarily narrative poet. He has often been claimed as an important figure in the history of lyric poetry, and although this claim has usually been made by critics who have more or less explicitly had his short 'personal' poems in mind, certain aspects of his 'long poems' too can be fruitfully analysed by making use of concepts conventionally associated with lyric, whether they draw more on ancient or modern understandings of that difficult term.

This leads to an interesting problem for the reader interested in metalepsis. If narrative typically creates distinct narrative levels across which a narrator, narratee, or character might make a metaleptic leap, lyric may be

---

* The conference paper behind this chapter was supported by an AHRC Research Fellowship (Early Career), grant reference AH/K008145/1. Many thanks to the participants in the 'Breaking and Entering' conference, and to those who attended seminars at Royal Holloway, University of London in May 2015 and at the University of Cambridge in February 2010, where some of the chapter's ideas were first tried out. For essential discussion at an early stage, thanks also to Matt Hosty.

[1] Genette (1972: 243–6 = 1980: 234–7).
[2] For my reasons for avoiding where possible the term 'epyllion' see Trimble (2012).

Gail Trimble, *Narrative and Lyric Levels in Catullus* In: *Metalepsis: Ancient Texts, New Perspectives*. Edited by: Sebastian Matzner and Gail Trimble, Oxford University Press (2020). © The editors and Oxford University Press. DOI: 10.1093/oso/9780198846987.003.0006

understood, on the contrary, as tending to establish some kind of unified poetic moment in which the lyric speaker, addressee(s), and perhaps other people and objects all come to exist on the *same* level.[3] In such a situation metalepsis might seem unlikely or impossible. Lyric, however, is like a highly reactive chemical element: it is rarely found in its pure form, and then not for very long. When reading poems in which a lyric mode seems dominant, readers may find themselves identifying narratives, however brief, which establish narrative levels, however subtly suggested: and with narrative levels comes the potential for metaleptic transgressions from one level to another. At this stage, we may reasonably begin to ask who exactly it is that might have the potential to make such transgressions. This question becomes particularly interesting if we look at the diverse corpus of a single author who wrote both narrative and lyric, and the case of Catullus may offer some challenging answers.

Narrative Levels: Catullus 64

The opening of Catullus 64 creates a basic boundary between two narrative levels: the diegetic world in which the events of the narrative take place, and the extradiegetic world in which its narrator is telling his story. The first two lines are framed by the words *quondam...dicuntur* (64.1–2)[4] as the pine trees cut down to build the Argo 'are said' to have swum as a ship in the sea 'once', long ago. Whatever else an expression of this kind may imply about this highly allusive text,[5] it establishes the poem as a story told, *dicuntur*, known from an existing and possibly even oral tradition, and puts its events in the past, *quondam*, at a considerable temporal distance from its anonymous epic narrator. Then, as the indirect speech construction *dicuntur...nasse*, 'are said to have swum' (64.1–2), is soon succeeded by finite verbs,[6] we might already observe an instance of mild metalepsis. The slippage is normal epic convention, but it is also, in Genette's terms, pseudo-diegesis, and in De Jong's, the 'blending of narrative voices':[7]

---

[3] See further below, pp. 126–7.

[4] Unless otherwise specified all references are to Catullus. The text of Catullus is taken from Goold (1989), except in the case of poem 64, where I use my own working text for my forthcoming edition with commentary (Cambridge University Press); translations are my own unless otherwise indicated.

[5] For such formulae as 'Alexandrian footnotes' marking literary allusion see Hinds (1998: 1–3).

[6] *ausi sunt*, 'dared' of the Argonauts (64.6), *fecit*, 'made' of Minerva (64.9), and following.

[7] Genette (1972 = 1980: 236–7); De Jong (2009: 99–106).

the main narrator starts to speak on behalf of his equally anonymous, traditional informants, blurring the boundary between them.

We should remember this effect as we look at the way in which a second boundary between narrative levels is soon established in Catullus 64: the boundary between the two stories told in the poem, one nested inside the other, which is actually cited by Genette in his discussion of narrative levels just before he first introduces the concept of metalepsis.[8] As the primary narrative continues from the opening discussed above, we learn that the immediate result of the launching of the Argo is that the Nereids rise to the surface of the sea to wonder at it. One of the Argonauts, Peleus, falls in love with one of the Nereids, Thetis, and we are soon hearing about the setting of their wedding celebrations (64.43–9). Among the furniture in Peleus' luxurious palace is the couple's marriage bed, which is covered with a dyed purple cloth. Here begins the transition onto a new narrative level: and like many, following Bal, I find it more helpful to conceptualize this level as 'inside' or 'beneath' the primary one and therefore to call it 'hypodiegetic' rather than Genette's 'metadiegetic'.[9] The coverlet is 'decorated with ancient figures of people' (*priscis hominum uariata figuris*, 64.50). Assuming that the epithet is transferred, we understand 'figures of people from former times'—and one can debate whether *priscis* is focalized through the narrator, again emphasizing that the characters and events soon to appear in the hypodiegetic narrative are in the far past from his point of view, or through Peleus and Thetis and their wedding guests, indicating a significant temporal gap between the two levels about to be established, even though that causes serious problems for mythical chronology.[10] But even without such a temporal gap, there is an ontological gap: the coverlet that those present at the wedding can see has representational content. It signifies (*indicat*, 'gives information about') the brave deeds or virtues (*uirtutes*) of the heroes (64.51).

---

[8] Genette (1972 = 1980: 231): 'the second narrative can be handled as a nonverbal representation...which the narrator converts into a narrative by describing it himself (the print representing the desertion of Ariadne, in *The Nuptial Song of Peleus and Thetis*...)'. 'Print' translates 'toile peinte', 'painted canvas' (Genette 1972: 241), which is itself misleading: the text of Catullus 64 gives no information about whether the coverlet is a painting, embroidery, tapestry, or some other kind of artwork.

[9] Bal (1977: 35); Genette (1972 = 1980: 228), keeping the terms from Genette (1969: 202). Cf. Grethlein in this volume, p. 29 n. 14.

[10] In the standard chronology of Greek myth the voyage of the Argo predates the adventures of Theseus. Catullus' apparent reversal of this order follows Apollonius' *Argonautica*, in which Jason tells the story of Theseus and Ariadne as something that has already happened (A.R. 3.997–1004); but Catullus makes the 'problem' worse by presenting the Argo as the first ship in history (64.11), which Apollonius avoids doing. See O'Hara (2007: 34–41), Weber (1983).

This statement is then explained with the word *namque* 'for' (64.52)—and in the rest of that line, the transition onto the hypodiegetic level is complete.

> *namque fluentisono prospectans litore Diae*
> *Thesea cedentem celeri cum classe tuetur*
> *indomitos in corde gerens Ariadna furores...*

For, looking out from the wave-sounding shore of Dia, Ariadne sees Theseus departing with his swift ship, bearing in her heart uncontrollable fury...   (64.52–4, trans. adapted from Goold)

The narrator is now telling us about Ariadne, who finds herself abandoned by Theseus on the island of Dia. Although, following that *namque*, we assume that this is a description of a picture that appears on the purple cloth—an epic ecphrasis—for the next two hundred lines there are no explicit reminders of this. Even the initial twenty lines or so are presented as a description of Ariadne on the beach, not, in fact, as a description of a picture of Ariadne on the beach. In the terms of Becker's useful analysis of the levels on which a piece of ecphrastic text can represent a work of visual art that itself represents something, Catullus' text has moved completely from the level of the *opus ipsum*, the artwork itself, onto the level of the *res ipsae*, whatever it is that the artwork depicts.[11] This makes it easier for the text to move from the descriptive to the narrative mode. The narrator soon begins to characterize the single moment in time depicted on the coverlet by referring to its immediate past—Ariadne *has just* woken up (64.56)—and its immediate future—she therefore *does not yet* believe what she is seeing (64.55). Before long, deciding to explain in more detail why Ariadne is experiencing the emotional turmoil in which he is so interested, he leaves behind the present and imperfect tenses in which the description has been couched so far, and moves into the finite aorist-perfect of narrative with the word *externauit* (64.70)—Venus 'afflicted' Ariadne with grief... some time earlier, at the point when Theseus first came to Crete.[12] The next sentence, explaining Theseus'

---

[11]   Becker (1995: 42–3). Cf. also Grethlein in this volume on the levels involved in pictorial representation.

[12]   In 64.73 I read *illa tempestate... quo tempore*, 'at that time, at the time when', following a reading found in some humanistic manuscripts, rather than either of the usually printed possibilities *illa tempestate... quo ex tempore* (Lachmann), 'at that time, ever since the time when' or *illa ex tempestate... quo tempore* (Baehrens), 'ever since that time, the time when'—largely because this makes better sense of the tense of *externauit*. For a full *apparatus criticus* see Kiss (2013) *ad loc.*

quest, is framed by the words *perhibent olim*, 'they say that once' (64.76), equivalent to *quondam…dicuntur* at the beginning of the poem. The narrator is no longer telling us about what the coverlet depicts, but is now drawing again on some sort of inherited, verbal narrative tradition.

Therefore, although we may still reasonably choose to refer to the central part of the poem, its inner story of Ariadne, as 'the ecphrasis', we should acknowledge that strictly speaking only this very first section and the very last are formally ecphrastic, describing scenes on the coverlet. Everything in between—the whole story of Ariadne's relationship with Theseus, her revenge on him, and the unintended death of his father Aegeus, told with the help of direct speech, epic simile, divine machinery, and a very free approach to narrative order—is introduced either by that initial *perhibent olim* or by another formula of verbal authority.[13] We may conclude that it stands in the same relation to the extradiegetic narrator as do the events of the poem's opening—irrespective of the ontological hierarchy between the two stories that was established by the presence of a picture on Peleus' and Thetis' bed. Only at the end of 'the ecphrasis' does the narrator remind his readers that this long section of the text has supposedly been his response to a visual stimulus. At 64.251, the descriptive mode returns with *at parte ex alia*: 'in another part' of the picture, Bacchus was arriving, inflamed with love for Ariadne. After a brief description of the god's maenadic followers, the text leaves the hypodiegetic level behind to return to the wedding (64.265–8). By describing the reaction of the couple's local Thessalian guests to what they see, the narrator reminds us that Ariadne and Bacchus exist within an artistic representation that can be enjoyed as such by characters in the poem's primary narrative universe: the Thessalians gaze 'eagerly', *cupide* (64.265). This remains the case even though those characters see a picture that contains less than the narrator's ecphrasis (only, we may assume, the scenes described in the two formally ecphrastic panels) and emphasizes rather different aspects of the story (essentially, Ariadne's future with Bacchus rather than her past with Theseus). Yet, simultaneously, by turning most of this ecphrasis into a narrative governed by *perhibent, ferunt*, and so on, the narrator has largely removed any formal distinction between the hypodiegesis and the diegesis in which it is embedded. Moreover, he has strongly implied that *his* position with respect to all parts of the inner story is exactly the same as it is

---

[13] *sed quid ego…commemorem?* 'but why should I relate?' (64.116–17); *perhibent*, 'they say' (64.124); *ferunt olim*, 'they say that once' (64.212).

for the outer one. That, perhaps, is hardly surprising, since even the visual content of the coverlet is presumably something he heard about from the same verbal tradition that gave him the rest of the details of Peleus' and Thetis' wedding.

Later in this chapter I will discuss the complexities created for some possible instances of metalepsis in Catullus 64 by the nature of the poem's narrative levels. In order to discuss these alongside certain dynamics in other poems, however, I will first explore some ways of approaching literary mode and level across the Catullan corpus.

Catullus, Lyric, and the Second Person

In the history of Catullan criticism the literary mode that has played the largest part is lyric.[14] Specifically, the Catullan corpus—or at least those parts of it in which Catullus himself seems to speak of his own experiences—has been seen as a place where the kind of first-person perspective often thought to be a defining feature of lyric poetry emerges in a particularly important way and perhaps for the first time. This theme is important from the early twentieth-century Romanticism of Havelock in *The Lyric Genius of Catullus* to Johnson's history of *The Idea of Lyric* in the early 1980s and through to Miller's *Lyric Texts and Lyric Consciousness* in 1994, which calls Catullus' poetry 'the first extant example of a true lyric collection'.[15] With Miller's book, however, this strand of criticism in terms of 'lyric' actually comes to give an important place to narrative, although not so much to the clearly narrative poems like 64. Rather, Miller describes how narrative emerges in Catullus from a collection of individual lyric moments. For him (however counterintuitively for classicists thinking of the performed lyric of archaic and classical Greece), Catullus' collection is significant because lyric only becomes lyric when it is written, collected, and ready to encourage the reader to attempt to use it in the construction of narratives, albeit always plural narratives rather than a single, decidable one. It is Miller who likens Catullus' work to a 'Garden of Forking Paths', the image from Jorge Luis Borges that characterizes a work of literature which seems to contain no plot, but 'in fact possesses a plurality of them'.[16]

---

[14] Wray (2001: 1–35). Note the telling chapter title: 'Catullan criticism and the problem of lyric'.

[15] Havelock (1939); Johnson (1982); Miller (1994) (quotation at 52).

[16] Miller (1994: 75). For a recent discussion of narrativization and Catullus see Lewis (2013).

Such an account of lyric and narrative in Catullus raises a dizzying question, especially from this volume's perspective: could narratives constructed in this way ever establish narrative levels across which metalepsis might take place? I will return to this question in a rather different way at the end of the chapter.[17] I think it is best approached by sidestepping for the moment the possibility of giving a narratological analysis of any narratives that may emerge from the corpus as a whole, in order to make room for looking instead at literary mode on the small scale, in specific poems— and for doing so in as open-minded a way as possible. However exactly it got into that state, Catullus' poetry as we read it today is a uniquely diverse and unpredictably ordered collection.[18] This means that the genre (in ancient or modern terms), mode, and entire *mise en scène* of any individual poem are always underdetermined by external factors and renegotiated with us as readers every time we turn from one poem to another—and frequently within a poem too. In spite of the critical history just summarized, then, Catullus' work may be said to invite a reading strategy which does not immediately seek to categorize each poem as 'lyric', 'narrative', or something else, but remains willing to respond to elements that impel a poem towards either the 'narrative' or the 'lyric' end of a spectrum.[19] Pushing in the direction of narrative might be the presence of third-person actors or the passage of time in the past, while lyric might be suggested by a sense of first-person involvement in a present moment or the appearance of certain kinds of second-person address.[20] In fact, the second person, just as much as the first, is a speciality of lyric criticism, and my discussion will make particular use of some different ways of thinking about the second person drawn from such sources, while

---

[17] See below, pp. 142–5.

[18] Skinner (2007a) gives a useful account of the perennial debate over what role Catullus himself might have played in the arrangement of the corpus as it survived to its Renaissance rediscovery. I am sympathetic to the idea advanced by Butrica (2007: 23–4) that 'what we have is simply "one man's Catullus"' compiled during the technological transition from papyrus roll to codex in late antiquity.

[19] Of the traditional threefold categorization of literary form going back ultimately to Pl. *Rep.* 3.394c, drama plays a less important role in Catullus: only poems 62 and 67 are primarily dramatic.

[20] The rest of this chapter largely uses this kind of minimal approach, paying attention to person and tense or time. It would be a larger project, and a fascinating one, to explore the application to ancient poetry of some of the categories suggested by recent scholarship asking what narratology can say about modern lyric or more generally poetic texts. These categories include 'sequentiality', 'mediacy', and 'articulation' (Hühn 2004, 2005), 'ambivalence' between fictionality and factuality (Hühn 2014), 'progression' and 'judgment' (Phelan 2007), 'segmentivity' and 'countermeasurement' (McHale 2009, following Rachel Blau DuPlessis and John Shoptaw). I am grateful to one of OUP's anonymous readers for drawing my attention to this.

not forgetting that appearances of the second person in narrative texts—
that is, apostrophes—now also draw significant interest from classicists
looking for ancient metalepsis.[21]

The first approach to the second person comes from an account of lyric
which seeks to emphasize the first-person lyric 'I' to the virtual exclusion
of the 'you'. This might make sense to a critic who believes that what
matters in lyric poetry is meditative introspection. In the case of Catullus
this line is taken by Quinn in the last chapter of *The Catullan Revolution*,
which is called 'The beginnings of modern lyric'.[22] Quinn's Catullus is
working his way towards being a properly introspective 'modern' lyric
poet, who can speak simply in the first person without needing to address
anyone. Therefore, where a second person does appear in Catullus it is,
according to Quinn, just 'a device', an unfortunate 'formal survival' of
earlier poetry in which the poet's self-analytical interior monologue was
hampered by having to consider an audience.

In contrast to this, Culler in *The Pursuit of Signs*, and then even more
explicitly in *Theory of the Lyric*, sees the second person as essential to
lyric.[23] Culler's preferred term is 'apostrophe'; and while, as just suggested,
a classicist might more typically understand apostrophe as an occasional
effect within a narrative text,[24] Culler, writing about modern and particu-
larly Romantic poetry, uses it to articulate the distinction between the lyric
and narrative modes. For Culler, this distinction is predicated on the dif-
ference between second-person address and third-person narrative, but it
also involves will and time—or, perhaps, level. To apostrophize, he argues,
is to establish a relation between the speaking subject and something else,
'to will a state of affairs, to attempt to call it into being'. Moreover, whereas
narrative depends on the passage of time, apostrophe draws what is apos-
trophized into a different kind of temporal space shared by the lyric first
person: 'what might be called a timeless present but is better seen as a
temporality of writing', or 'a time of discourse rather than story'.[25] One
could, despite Culler, repurpose this as a description of the metaleptic
effect of apostrophe in a narrative text and say that a narratorial apostro-
phe pulls a character in the diegesis onto the extradiegetic level on which

---

[21] See De Jong (2009: 93–7), Nauta (2013b: 234–43), and De Jong in this volume, with
further references.
[22] Quinn (1959: 85–100).
[23] Culler (1981: 149–71; 2015: 186–243). See also Budelmann in this volume, p. 60.
[24] As suggested by its etymology, 'turning aside', and by ancient definitions, e.g. Quint.
Inst. 9.2.38–9.
[25] Culler (1981: 165; 2015: 226).

the first-person narrator speaks; this already seems to me a useful account to keep available next to the alternative explanation that in apostrophe it is the narrator who moves onto the diegetic level.[26] But Culler is actually saying something more radical: that lyric dissolves all boundaries between the lyric speaker and other subjects by bringing everyone and everything that is addressed into the same world—perhaps into the same 'temporality'—as the poet. Either this is a sort of universal metalepsis operating throughout a text, all the time, or it is an effect that precludes metalepsis across narrative boundaries by putting everything involved, or at least everything addressed, in a text onto a single, lyric level.

Culler's discussion, however, is largely concerned with apostrophes to inanimate things: 'O wild West Wind'. Drawing on Northrop Frye (who was drawing on John Stuart Mill), he writes that the lyric poet 'turns his back on his listeners' to address 'himself or someone else', and does not always seem to mind whether it is himself or someone else.[27] If we begin to suspect that Culler is really concerned with a Romantic interiority not too different from Quinn's modernist meditative introspection, we might wonder whether a different sort of approach would be more helpful if we prefer to understand the second person in ancient poetry as fundamentally rhetorical. In the first chapter of her book on narrative in Horace's lyric poetry, Lowrie refers to Culler's argument and then distinguishes between address, which expects or allows for the possibility of receipt by the person addressed, and apostrophe, which does not.[28] This is a potentially useful distinction, more precise than one based on the reality versus unreality, or the presence versus absence, of the addressee, although those too *may* be relevant. Insisting too strongly on it, however, could lead to our ignoring or accommodating too easily the very aspect of second-person address whose strangeness Culler wanted to highlight: that is, the idea of bringing into existence a state of affairs in which whatever is addressed in the second person has the potential to be—a person. As we examine potentially metaleptic uses of 'you' in Catullus, we may sometimes want to speculate, with Culler, that any apostrophe, or any address, might create the possibility that the 'you' might be a subject who could potentially listen, speak back, or take action, on the level of the one who addresses it—even if we do not actually see it doing so.

---

[26] On these alternatives cf. De Jong in this volume, pp. 80, 94.

[27] Culler (1981: 151–2; 2015: 186), quoting Frye (1957: 249–50).

[28] Lowrie (1997: 20–6). Lowrie goes on to explore the differences between lyric and narrative in much more rigorous detail than I am able to do here.

I would like to keep an open mind, too, about the best way of conceptualizing whoever or whatever appears in this poetry in the first, second, or third person. I have so far used terms such as 'actor', 'speaker', and 'subject' that aim to be reasonably neutral, as well as others such as 'narrator' and 'character' that imply more about the nature of the text concerned and the relation in which their referents stand to the levels it establishes. The notion of a 'subject' seems particularly helpful for two reasons. On the one hand, it suggests subjectivity. In literature we may meet subjects that can perceive things; that can respond subjectively to what they perceive, by feeling emotions or making judgements; that can speak, often to communicate these responses; that have the will or the power to take actions in the world around them; and that perhaps exist in one 'place', in terms of space and time and literary level, but may be able to do any of these subjective things metaleptically across those boundaries. On the other hand, this kind of 'subject' interacts with grammatical subject. This point is interestingly emphasized in the work of Janan on Catullus, although this chapter is far from adopting her fairly thoroughgoing Lacanian approach.[29] When looking microscopically at the poetry of Catullus and paying attention to the dimension of grammatical subject, we will be primed to notice grammatical person, and, in particular, a very simple formal effect that Ellis, the nineteenth-century commentator, noted alongside such features as diminutives and prosaic expressions among 'peculiarities in the language of Catullus':[30] frequent, obtrusive, interesting *changes* of grammatical person. It is, as we have seen, well established that interesting effects may occur when second-person address appears as an unexpected interruption to a narrative in the third person; but it may be just as interesting when the basically I–you scenario of a lyric poem is conversely interrupted by third-person statements that push towards narrative—cases where, as Évrard-Gillis tantalizingly observes in her brief study of poems in which Catullus himself appears in a combination of first, second, and third person, it might be the case that 'the [lyric] speaker becomes a character in a represented [narrative] universe'.[31] As we consider these and other effects in Catullus' poetry, and particularly as we observe potential instances of metalepsis that

---

[29] Janan (1994: x): 'The model is the grammatical subject, governed from outside itself by rules of grammar and syntax making up a linguistic structure—rules that grant the "I" its meaning.'

[30] Ellis (1889: xxix): 'Catullus passes rapidly from speaking in one person to speaking in another.'

[31] Évrard-Gillis (1977: 116): 'le locuteur s'éloigne et devient personnage d'un univers représenté'.

seem connected with them, we may want to leave open the possibility of using still other terms for the subjects we encounter, and perhaps even of moving from speaking of *person* to speaking of *people*.[32]

Divine Address and Metalepsis in the Long Poems

I turn now to three cases of an unexpected second person in Catullus' 'long poems',[33] beginning with Catullus' second most obviously narrative poem, poem 63. After ninety lines of mythological narrative about Attis' religious madness and self-castration—and, fortuitously, in Mynors' Oxford Classical Text, just after a page turn[34]—the reader is confronted with what is clearly a hymnic close. The speaker turns to address Attis' goddess in an apotropaic prayer:

> *dea, magna dea, Cybebe, dea domina Dindymi,*
> *procul a mea tuos sit furor omnis, era, domo:*
> *alios age incitatos, alios age rabidos.*

Goddess, great goddess, Cybele, goddess, lady of Dindymus, far from my house be all your fury, queen: drive others to that frenzy, drive others to that madness!   (63.91–3, trans. adapted from Goold)

These lines contain an unexpected second *and* an unexpected first person. Other than the galliambic metre, there has been no clear internal clue to prepare the reader for a hymnic ending.[35] In particular, the narrator's voice has been straightforwardly third-person. Or—has it? In fact, the narrator has used the second person before, at 63.9, *tympanum tuum, Cybebe, tua, mater, initia*, as Attis picks up 'the light tambourine, your tambourine, Cybele, your mystic instrument, Mother' (trans. Goold). On a first reading, this line probably strikes the reader as a 'formal' poetic apostrophe, a passing

---

[32] See also Malina (2002) on metalepsis and subject construction. Malina is particularly interested in how metalepsis may construct the *reader*'s subjectivity: cf. below, pp. 142–5.

[33] The conventional designation for poems 61–8. Although these poems range in length from 24 lines (65) to 408 lines (64), it is fair to say that they are all 'long' for Catullus, and it may well have been their length that led them to be grouped together in the copy of the collection from which the surviving manuscripts descend.

[34] Mynors (1958: 58).

[35] Harrison (2005: 18–22) gives a balanced analysis of the poem's multiple generic affinities.

second person in the middle of third-person narrative, something familiar since Homer.[36] However, if the same reader remembers 63.9 after reading the end of the poem, the effect is disconcerting. In Lowrie's terms, the ending looks like true address, intended for receipt by the goddess: so does that mean that the earlier line was address too, and not 'mere' apostrophe? Was the goddess somehow 'there' or 'listening' on the narrator's level throughout? The poem began with no indication of the circumstances in which we were to imagine it as being uttered: in fact, it began like an epic, *in medias res*.[37] But if it always was a lyric hymn, perhaps Cybele is not at such a safe distance, on the level of narrated myth, as we thought. This appears to be an *anti*-hymnic close, not summoning the goddess but pushing her away: and while Nauta has sensibly argued that 'apostrophe may be construed as a sign of the narrator's own immersion in his story',[38] here I would argue not only that such immersion has become dangerous to this narrator—or more generally the speaking subject who suddenly emerges in the first person in these lines, possessed of a home (*domo*) and a mind susceptible to fury (*furor*)—but that it may be the goddess as much as the speaker who is breaking down the barrier between the world in which Attis' sufferings take place and the world in which that speaker lives.[39]

There is a syntactical difference between the two addresses to the goddess in 63. In 63.9, the vocative nouns and second-person pronominal adjectives simply cluster around the words for an object appearing in the ongoing narrative (the tambourine), whereas 63.91–3 focus on verbs, a jussive subjunctive and a repeated imperative. It is this difference of syntax that makes the former address look so innocuous on first reading, and marks the latter so clearly as a prayer. This may be contrasted with two other divine addresses in Catullus' long poems which are specifically *not* prayers just where we might expect them to be, and which therefore invite us to consider quite how Catullus' narrative levels might be meeting at moments of potential metalepsis. The first takes us back to near the beginning of poem 64: it is the invocation of the heroes at 64.22–30, immediately after Peleus has fallen in love and Thetis—in contradiction of the usual mythical tradition—has been said not to be unwilling to marry a mortal.[40] This is the first appearance of a second-person address—and also

---

[36] See references under n. 21 above.

[37] Attis' story simply starts: *super alta uectus Attis celeri rate maria*, 'Attis carried in a speedy vessel on the crest of deep seas…' (63.1, trans. adapted from Goold).

[38] Nauta (2013b: 235).

[39] Cf. below, p. 137, on Troy in Catullus 68, and Bing in this volume on Stesichorus' Helen.

[40] 64.20 *humanos non despexit hymenaeos*, 'did not disdain a human marriage'; contrast e.g. *Il.* 18.434.

of a first person of any kind—in this third-person narrative poem, and, like the end of 63, it is marked as hymnic. The heroes are praised for their ancestry (64.23–23b) and Peleus for his good fortune (64.25–7); there is a hymnic anaphora of *te*, 'you', and the repeated *saluete*, 'hail', is equivalent to the Greek hymnic χαίρετε. However, something is missing. In both lyric and hexameter traditions, Greek and Roman hymns usually combine praise and prayer;[41] and where a hymnic invocation appears, as here, near the beginning of an otherwise non-hymnic text, it usually turns into a prayer for inspiration.[42] Here there is no prayer, only the first-person promise of future song offered by this narrator in 64.24, his imitation of the 'rhapsodic farewell' of the Homeric hymns: *uos ego saepe meo uos carmine compellabo*, 'You, you I will often invoke in my song'.[43] *saluete* is the only imperative.[44] Hymnic convention is similarly subverted as the narrator goes on at 64.28–30 to ask Peleus a series of apparently enthusiastic questions: did Thetis really become his wife? did her divine family really consent? Questions can certainly be a hymnic feature; but then, however rhetorical, formally they will still ask for unknown information: 'who' or 'which'.[45] The questions here, in contrast, require only a 'yes' or 'no' answer. Applying Culler's approach, it might be that by apostrophizing the heroes, and Peleus in particular, the narrating voice of Catullus' poem draws the characters of his primary narrative onto the level that he occupies as he tells their story. Yet not only do these characters leave Catullus' questions unanswered—the opportunity for a moment of very strong metalepsis is *not* taken, as Peleus himself does not speak—but even the questions themselves are not of a form that invites the contribution of new information. Despite the pious enthusiasm for the heroic age that seems to characterize the Catullan narrator at this point, it appears that he does not want to relinquish his own control over the content of his mythical narrative.

[41] Furley and Bremer (2001: 50–64).

[42] This is particularly characteristic of didactic: e.g. Hes. *Th.* 104–15, Arat. *Phaen.* 17–18, and even a version at Lucr. 1.24–8.

[43] The formulaic final line of many of the Homeric hymns is αὐτὰρ ἐγὼ καὶ σεῖο καὶ ἄλλης μνήσομ᾽ ἀοιδῆς, 'but I will remember you and another song too'. This probably referred originally to the epic recitation that immediately followed, perhaps also to singing of the deity again on a future occasion: see Richardson on *h.Hom.* 2.495.

[44] Contrast even the Apollonian narrator's farewell to the Argonauts at A.R. 4.1773–5, also in the background for Catullus here. There the request for the heroes' favour, ἵλατε, 'be gracious', though initially seeming unspecific, is still a request; moreover, it soon comes to imply that the Argonauts may also be being asked to fulfil the immediately following wish that 'these songs' may be 'sweeter' in the future (αἵδε δ᾽ ἀοιδαὶ | εἰς ἔτος ἐξ ἔτεος γλυκερώτεραι εἶεν ἀείδειν).

[45] Fedeli (1983: 49), citing parallels for Catullus' repeated *quis*, 'who…?' questions to Hymen at 61.46ff.

A still stranger absence of prayer occurs at the beginning of poem 68b. One of the features suggesting that what is printed in most texts of Catullus as 68.41 should actually be understood as the opening of a new poem is the address to the Muses.[46] But instead of asking the Muses to tell him a story of the distant, mythical past which he can then tell in the poem that follows,[47] Catullus announces that he will tell *them* what his friend Allius did for him (a story of the recent, personal past), so that they will be able to speak to 'many thousands' of others, and will also be able to make the paper on which he writes loquacious too (68.41–6). There is one possible parallel for this reversal of what would usually happen when the first-person poet and second-person Muses confront one another. In the proem to the first book of his *Argonautica*, Apollonius asks that the Muses should be the ὑποφήτορες of his song (A.R. 1.22); Morrison makes a careful argument for understanding this word as 'interpreters' rather than 'inspirers', so that Apollonius is asking for the Muses to pass on to others the story about the Argonauts that he tells on his own narrative authority.[48] But even if this is right, Apollonius is less explicit than Catullus, and also less intimate, less oddly chatty: his reference to the Muses is not even in the second person.[49] The opening of 68b is more generally reminiscent of Callimachus' conversation with the Muses in *Aetia* books 1 and 2, where Callimachus calls the Muses θεαί, 'goddesses' (Call. fr. 7c.1 Harder), in the same sort of way as Catullus uses *deae* here, while Catullus' opening address *non possum reticere, deae*, 'I cannot keep silent, goddesses', would be an accurate encapsulation of the typical stance of the garrulous Callimachean persona throughout the first two books of the *Aetia*. In the extant fragments, however, Callimachus never goes as far as Catullus does here. At one point he tells his readers how an earlier writer, Xenomedes of Ceos, wrote down the μῦθος, 'story', of Acontius and Cydippe, from which source it reached ἡμετέρην ... Καλλιόπην, 'my Calliope' (Call. fr. 75.76–7 Harder). But even there, and assuming that Calliope is more than just a metonym for poetry,

---

[46] The question whether Catullus 68 is one poem or two (or three, with 68c starting at 68.149) is very old and very vexed. For an introduction to the bibliography see Lowrie (2006: 116 n. 7), and for a cogent new argument Leigh (2016). I agree with Leigh that 'Catullus 68 is so conspicuously built out of recurrent terms, motifs, themes and preoccupations that any attempt to divide it into two entirely separate poems must fail' (223), but would add a strong emphasis to the word 'entirely'.

[47] As paradigmatically at *Od.* 1.1, ἄνδρα μοι ἔννεπε, Μοῦσα, 'tell me, Muse, about the man...'.

[48] Morrison (2007a: 286–93).

[49] A.R. 1.22, Μοῦσαι δ' ὑποφήτορες εἶεν ἀοιδῆς, 'may the Muses be the interpreters/inspirers of the song'; note the third-person εἶεν.

we have the 'well-read Muse'[50] informing the current writer, not vice versa. In Catullus 68b, as in Catullus 64, the speaking voice again subverts the reader's expectations of divine address in order to assert his own authority over the story he will tell: and since the speaker of 68b is also the protagonist of that story, this use of the first and second persons is one way in which the poem raises what we might call Catullus' own experiences to the status of myth. This looks like a complex negotiation between poet and gods about what are going to count as the relevant narrative worlds in the first place.

Lyric Subjects and Narrative Metalepsis: Catullus 68

The extraordinarily rich and confusing Catullus 68 can be partially tamed by an analysis in terms of multiple ring composition.[51] 68a, the letter to Manlius, begins and ends with Catullus' depression and inability to write, and centres (68.19–26) on the death of his brother. 68b opens, as we have just seen, with Allius' house and Catullus' love, proceeds via several similes to the story of the love and marriage of the mythical heroine Laodamia, then to the Trojan War, and in the centre, again, the death of Catullus' brother (68.91–100); the return journey is via the Trojan War, Laodamia (with a simile), another series of similes (with further reference to Laodamia), to Catullus' love and Allius' house. But this account in terms of two nested series of topics becomes considerably destabilized if attention is paid both to narrative level and to second-person address.

In 68a things are not too difficult. The situation in both outer sections (68.1–19, 27–40) is a present tense I–you address, in a letter, from Catullus to Manlius, complicated only temporarily and comprehensibly by the accounts scattered throughout the poem of the content of the letter from Manlius that Catullus is answering (a sort of recurrent embedded narrative); by Catullus' references to both of them as drowning or shipwrecked sailors in 68.3–4 and 13 (a hint at a metaphorical world); and by the statement in 68.15–17 that 'when' Catullus was first grown up he 'played often enough', *multa satis lusi* (a brief narrative of his past). The central section is clearly

---

[50] See Bing (1988), especially 27–8.

[51] See e.g. Courtney (1985: 92–9). Goold (1989) indicates one possible scheme for 68b with subheadings in his translation.

marked by the change in the reference of the second person from Manlius to Catullus' brother.

In 68b, however, the constantly renewed topics of the poem are introduced unpredictably, often with a new second-person address and/or with an indication of a new narrative level, but not in a way that clearly marks each of the concentric rings as an utterance existing on one defined level and directed at a distinct addressee. In the very centre, the section on the dead brother at 68.91–100 is again a second-person invocation of him. But Laodamia, the mythical figure who is such an important part of the nested structure, is only addressed during her second appearance (68.105, 117, 129); her first in fact contains another apotropaic prayer, as Catullus briefly addresses Nemesis (68.77–8). 68b opens, as we have seen, as an address to the Muses *about* Allius (40ff.); it closes as an address *to* Allius (68.149ff.), preceded, probably, by Catullus' address to himself (68.142).[52] Catullus' apparent attempts to begin a narrative about his love and Allius' service, with the shifts to a third-person, past-tense narrative mode at 68.51 and 68.67, are soon interrupted by similes. This happens first with similes in the present tense (a stream 'gushes', *prosilit*, from a rock and runs down a valley to a road, 68.57–62; a favourable wind 'comes', *uenit*, to sailors in a storm, 68.63–5), then with one clearly defined as belonging to a narrated past (Laodamia 'once arrived', *quondam... aduenit*, at her husband's house, 68.73). If Laodamia's embedded narrative level is fairly well established by that *quondam*, then on what level or levels do the actions narrated in the present-tense similes exist—either in 68.57–65 or when new worlds open up as we hear in 68.119–28 about a daughter who 'nurses', *alit*, a longed-for grandson for her father, and a dove who, with a confusing further indication of other potential storytellers, '*is said* to snatch kisses', *dicitur... oscula... decerpere*? Within one of the sections on Laodamia is a further simile whose content is attributed to others (*ferunt Grai*, 'the Greeks say', 68.109); her love is compared to an abyss which Hercules 'is said to have once dug', *quondam... fodisse... audit* (68.111–12), but it is not simply the case that everything narrated in this simile exists in a deeper past than that of Laodamia, since 'the Greeks say' in Catullus' time that this abyss still drains its marsh in the present (68.109–10). And in any case, the second pair of present-tense similes in 68.119–28 turn out to apply first to Laodamia (68.129–30), if also to Catullus' beloved (68.131).

---

[52] Catullus seems the most likely addressee of the imperative in this line (*tolle*, here probably 'take away' or 'cease'). A lacuna should be printed after 68.141.

There are, it seems to me, two main ways of understanding the effect of all this, along the lines I have suggested earlier in this chapter.[53] On the one hand, it is possible to see the multiplicity and confusion of addressees and narrative levels in Catullus 68 as tending to create, overall, a single level, world, or poetic 'moment' on or in which everything in the poem exists. This can be analysed in terms of 'lyric', and in more than one way. One could argue that the repeated use of the second person with different referents eventually frees 68, or at least 68b, from a strong sense of being addressed to anyone at all, especially in the longer sections in between explicit addresses: it is easy to see Quinn's 'meditative lyric introspection' in Catullus' words on his own love at 68.130–48, for instance, and possibly throughout. Or one could make the case that all the subjects in the poem come to exist in Culler's 'temporality of writing', in which 'the lyric can displace a time of narrative, of past events recorded, and place us in the continuing present of apostrophic address, the "now" '.[54] Feeney has noted that on what is perhaps the primary narrative level of 68b, in which Catullus' beloved 'goddess' (*diua*, 68.70) comes to meet him at Allius' house, very little 'actually *happens*'; '[a] man provides a house, a woman arrives—the rest is analogy and reflection'.[55] The rest, perhaps, 'displacing' the narrative of the woman's arrival, is lyric. The arrival of the beloved in 68 is, or is a parody of, the arrival of a bride,[56] and this effect of the 'displacement' of narrative by lyric may be compared not only to Catullus 61, a formally lyric wedding song in which the present-tense 'narration' of what is going on at the bride's arrival blends constantly with second-person address in which she and everyone else involved are encouraged to get on with it all, but also with the primary narrative of Catullus 64: one of the very strangest things about the treatment of narrative there is that while, as I have shown, the ecphrasis develops into a narrative in which a great deal happens, the outer story of Peleus and Thetis, at least after its fast-moving opening, very soon slows down into a highly descriptive account of their wedding in which, again, very little actually happens, except for a series of arrivals at

---

[53] See above, pp. 120, 126–7.

[54] Culler (2015: 226). Culler associates the effect particularly with 'poems that multiply apostrophes to different figures' (225).

[55] Feeney (1992: 35).

[56] She arrives on the threshold, though unluckily stepping on it (68.70–2); this moment prompts the first comparison, to Laodamia's arrival as a bride (68.73–4); she is accompanied by Cupid, dressed and behaving rather like Hymen (68.133–4, cf. 61.1–35, esp. 8–10); however, she is not given away by her father, but rather steals away from her husband (68.143–6).

the palace in which the wedding takes place.[57] It is well known that the narrator of Catullus 64 seems determined to present a bright, happy version of this wedding in which Peleus is supremely blessed, Thetis is willing to marry him, their future separation is not envisaged and the moment at which Eris arrives with the apple that will trigger the Trojan War is never actually reached; it is in Greek lyric poetry, in Alcaeus and Pindar, that other references to this wedding as an example of mortal good fortune tend to appear,[58] and perhaps there is something 'lyrical' about the rather anti-narrative nature of Catullus 64's outer frame, as if it has caught the lyric spirit of the apostrophe to the heroes at 64.22–30.[59]

Such 'lyric' readings, however, are not the only way of responding to the complicated use of narrative and address in Catullus 68. If, as we read, we are more inclined to accept the text's frequent invitations to register a shift onto a new narrative level, then, even if these levels are not always completely coherent, we will still see multiple boundaries in the text: more of the cases of second-person address may strike us as instances of metaleptic apostrophe, gaining their power from a transgression of these boundaries, and raising the question we have already encountered of which subject is to be identified as transgressing them;[60] and we may find other metalepses besides those effected by apostrophe, too. As we have seen, it is at the moment when the presumed primary narrative level of 68b adopts the narrative mode most obviously, as the *diua* arrives on Allius' threshold (68.70–2), that this narrative is interrupted by a new narrative about Laodamia. In the words *ut quondam*, 'as once' (68.73), the hypodiegetic level of Laodamia's world is doubly established: its role in the poem is the subordinate one of simile, and its action took place in the distant past.[61] When Catullus returns to Laodamia and apostrophizes her (68.105), the second-person *tibi*, 'you', is juxtaposed with *tum*, 'then', re-emphasizing the second of these differences. Laodamia seems safely on her level, and so in this apostrophe, it looks as if it is Catullus who briefly crosses over to that level in order to address Laodamia, and the metaleptic effect is mild.[62] What happens in between these two passages, however, complicates

[57] The Argo sails and Peleus and Thetis come together in the first thirty lines; then the human guests arrive (31–49) and depart (267–77), the divine guests arrive (278–302), and the Fates' spinning is described (303–22).
[58] Alc. 42 Voigt, Pi. *N.* 5.22–37, *I.* 6.25, 8.26–46, *P.* 3.86–96.   [59] See above, pp. 130–1.
[60] See above, pp. 126–7, 129–30.
[61] Cf. the double move onto a new level of representation and (almost certainly) into the deeper past at the start of the ecphrasis in poem 64 (above, p. 121).
[62] Cf. 63.9 (above, pp. 129–30).

matters considerably. Telling the story of Laodamia's marriage, the poem begins to explain the context of her husband Protesilaus' death by opening another past-tense narrative, *nam tum*, 'for then' (68.87), that for a moment threatens to begin at the beginning and tell the story of the entire Trojan War. But that potential narrative is derailed, not by a new simile, but by the mention of Troy itself, not quite addressed, but repeatedly named as if in invocation, exclaimed at with the parenthetical *nefas*, 'horror!' (68.89), immediately presented as a subjective agent, rousing the Greeks against itself (68.87–8), and then acting subjectively not in the deep narrative world of simile and mythical past, but in the recent and personal past in which it has killed Catullus' brother (68.91–2). Here, as at the end of poem 63,[63] the subject which crosses over from one narrative level to another seems to make a move upwards and outwards onto the level of the poem's main speaker, and a move full of threat: and it even seems possible for this subject not to be a person at all, but merely a personified place. Seeing Troy itself as the subject of the metaleptic movement here allows us to appreciate more keenly the contrast with the immediately following apostrophe to Catullus' brother himself: a person, but a dead one. Buried at Troy, he is geographically distant from Catullus (68.97–100 contain *tam longe*, 'so far away', *nec prope cognatos cineres*, 'not near kindred ashes', *extremo…solo*, 'distant soil', *terra aliena*, 'foreign land', trans. adapted from Goold); killed by Troy, he seems to have been instantly dragged back onto the deep narrative level from which Troy metaleptically rose to snatch him. Catullus attempts to bridge the gap by addressing him (68.92–6); but whereas Culler is relatively optimistic about what poetic apostrophes to the dead can achieve, saying that they 'displace' the 'irreversible sequence' of linear, 'empirical time' by a move into the 'discursive time' of poetry,[64] Catullus, here and every time he addresses his brother—and throughout the corpus he seems unable to mention him without addressing him[65]—emphasizes separation in the very apostrophe itself, *misero frater adempte mihi*, 'brother stolen from me to my misery' (68.92, trans. Goold). It is difficult to see either Catullus or his brother as successfully crossing narrative levels here; this looks like a failed attempt at metalepsis.[66]

---

[63] See above, pp. 129–30.   [64] Culler (1981: 166).

[65] 65.10–12, 68.20–4; poem 101.

[66] This account in terms of metalepsis takes its place alongside other discussions which investigate the tension between presence and absence, distance and closeness in Catullus 68 and especially in these lines: see in particular Miller (2004: 52–4), Lowrie (2006), esp. 127–8. Meanwhile, Feldherr (2000) discusses the related dynamics of poem 101 as informed by Roman funerary practices, epitaphs, and monuments: cf. esp. 216–17 on whether Catullus, in

In my discussion above of the apostrophes to Peleus at 64.25–30 and the Muses at 68.41ff. I argued that the Catullan narrator seemed determined not to give up control over what happens in his narrative.[67] In this apostrophe, meanwhile, it looks as if the power exercised by Troy and death make it impossible for Catullus to give any agency to his brother, even if he would like to. But there is a final subject in poem 68 whose agency is very much at stake, and who is almost the only person involved in the poem who is never addressed: Catullus' beloved. Insofar as the poem is a many-layered narrative, she remains on its primary level only, arriving at Allius' house, giving Catullus 'stolen joys', *furtiua…munuscula* (68.145, trans. Goold), yet unfaithful to him (68.135). Insofar as it is a meditative lyric, while Manlius, Allius, Laodamia, and the brother all appear in the second person on the same lyric level as companions in Catullus' meditation, the *diua* remains in the third person, at a distance, even at the very end in which a wish for her future happiness still seems to be addressed to Allius and not to her (68.155–60). By not addressing her Catullus tries to avoid raising questions about the scope of her power over what happens to him and his poetry.

The Narrator and His Characters

With this focus on subjective power in mind, we can return to three potential cases of metalepsis within the ecphrasis of Catullus 64.[68] The first shows a subject crossing, or almost crossing, both of the boundaries that I identified between narrative levels in this poem—the boundary between the ecphrasis and the outer story, and the boundary between the world of all the poem's mythical events and the world of the narrator—and doing so very nearly simultaneously. That subject is not, on this occasion, the narrator, who (we might think) would be the most likely to possess the ability to do such a thing, but one of the characters, Ariadne.[69]

Ariadne is a very strong subjective presence in the ecphrasis, especially as she makes the extended speech that dominates the longest of its narrative sections (64.124–211). While in some ways she is in an extremely weak

---

apostrophizing or addressing his brother, is actually 'recovering his ability to address a living audience' or 'has indeed entered the world of the dead'.

[67] See above, p. 131.

[68] I mean by 'ecphrasis' here the whole of the inner story, 64.50–266: see p. 123 above.

[69] Cf. Nauta (2013b: 243–8) on some other mythical characters in Latin poetry who seem to have similar power.

position—not only objectified by her position as an artistic representation under the gaze of eager viewers, but quite simply abandoned on a desert island, and, as she believes, about to die—through her speech she gains strength, as her eventual curse on Theseus is implemented by Jupiter, allowing her to get her revenge (64.188–248). Earlier in the speech, however, she is still addressing Theseus. Her words so far have been full of excoriation, but she now concludes this section with a surprisingly tender image:

> *at tamen in uestras potuisti ducere sedes,*
> *quae tibi iucundo famularer serua labore,*
> *candida permulcens liquidis uestigia lymphis,*
> *purpureaue tuum consternens ueste cubile.*

Yet at least you could have brought me to your house to be your slave and serve you as a labour of love, bathing your bright feet with flowing water or spreading your bed with a purple coverlet.

(64.160–3, trans. adapted from Goold)

We can call this *mise en abyme*, since the purple coverlet Ariadne imagines is a double of the purple coverlet on which she is herself depicted (*purpura, uestis*, 64.49–50). But if we admit the possibility that Ariadne herself, as well as the reader, might remember or notice at this point that she is a picture on a purple coverlet, we can also call it metalepsis, as Ariadne seems to catch sight of her depicted self, thus crossing the boundary between the world of the ecphrasis and the world of Peleus' and Thetis' wedding. Such a reading is supported by the way in which, in the very next line, Ariadne perhaps crosses the more fundamental boundary between the world in which both stories of the poem are set and the world in which its narrator speaks:

> *sed quid ego ignaris nequiquam conqueror auris,*
> *externata malo, quae nullis sensibus auctae*
> *nec missas audire queunt nec reddere uoces?*

But why do I complain in vain to the unfeeling breezes (beside myself with unhappiness), which, unendowed with sense, can neither hear words uttered nor give them in reply?

(64.164–6, trans. adapted from Goold)

Here it suddenly seems that as well as having seen the picture of herself, she might have heard the narrator telling her story. Her self-questioning words *sed quid ego?*, 'but why do I…?', exactly repeat those of the narrator some fifty lines earlier, as he asked himself why he should narrate various different moments in Ariadne's myth (64.116). There are many layers to the irony of what Ariadne says here, but one of them resides in this echo of the narrator. Like him, despite questioning the usefulness of speech, she goes on speaking; and although she claims that it is useless to speak to the breezes, she stops speaking to Theseus at this point to address, for the central section of her speech, no one in particular. It seems that her metaleptic self-consciousness has opened up a space where she can simply talk without a defined addressee, making her more like—perhaps *not* a narrator, but an introspective lyric poet that Quinn would be proud of.

Ariadne, then, like Troy in poem 68, makes a metaleptic leap all the way out to the extradiegetic level of the poem's main speaker from a deeply embedded level within the text—in her case, an explanatory narrative within an ecphrasis within the main narrative, itself told at second hand. But there are other moments in which the narrator seems to enter the world of his characters, rather than vice versa: they are, again, apostrophes. The narrator has one to Theseus (64.69) and one to Ariadne (64.253). The usual comment on Catullus' apostrophes in this poem is that they are markers of a subjective 'sympathy' characteristic of neoteric epic,[70] and in fact it is easy to see such 'sympathy' in the case of the apostrophe to Theseus—not, however, because the narrator sympathizes with Theseus, but because he sympathizes with Ariadne. He therefore addresses Theseus reproachfully, at the end of a line, *Theseu*, just as she does later (64.132). In neither case can Theseus literally, logically hear this, so perhaps it is equally true in both cases that (following Lowrie's distinction) he is apostrophized rather than addressed. But if the gap between him and Ariadne is simply one of physical distance, what kind of gap exists between him and the narrator? Both the narrator's apostrophes occur not in the parts of the ecphrasis that are actually marked off as epic narration, but in the properly ecphrastic, descriptive panels, one at the beginning and one at the end. Ariadne and Theseus are therefore at three removes from the narrator: depicted in a picture which exists in a mythical setting about which the narrator has heard from the anonymous traditional sources referred to with *dicuntur*, 'are said', in the poem's opening lines.[71] The apostrophes

---

[70] E.g. Fordyce on 64.69. Fernandelli (2012: 140–4) uses the terminology of metalepsis to discuss the apostrophe at Virg. *Ecl.* 6.47 as an example of 'neoteric narration' influenced by Catullus 64, but without specific discussion of the narrator's apostrophes in Catullus 64 itself.

[71] See above, pp. 120, 123.

metaleptically collapse at least two of these distinctions, producing the illusion, so typical of ecphrasis, that the narrator is standing in front of the coverlet depicting Ariadne and Theseus, so that they are in a sense *there* to be addressed, paradoxically closer to him than the mythical characters of epic narration normally would be.

Closer, but still distinct. If in the vocative *Theseu* the narrator's voice sympathetically merges with that of Ariadne, and in the question *sed quid ego?* hers with his, then the final apostrophe at 253 shows the narrator distinguishing himself from his heroine, and emphasizing that his knowledge is superior to hers. He apparently tries to tell her that she is not alone on the island, but that the picture also depicts Bacchus, 'seeking you, Ariadne, and inflamed with love of you', *te quaerens, Ariadna, tuoque incensus amore* (trans. Goold). Like the apostrophe to the brother in 68b, this might be another moment of failed metalepsis, the attempted interaction between the narrator and one of his characters finally underlining the fact that they exist in different narrative worlds. The narrator tries to communicate with Ariadne at this point because except through metalepsis she will never see or hear Bacchus approaching—despite the fact that his maenads are producing raucous music that the text vividly evokes (64.261–4)—since Bacchus exists 'in another part' of the picture (*parte ex alia*, 64.251), and since the picture, being a picture, depicts only one moment of time, and, being a picture, is literally silent. The narrator, existing outside the picture— on whatever level exactly that is—is not restricted in the same way.

At the end of Catullus 64, the narrator's self-positioning turns out to be crucial. The poem has a formal conclusion or epilogue (64.382–408). Whereas in all the different sections up to this point the narrator seems to have had the power to choose what to narrate, describe, or address from a body of myth that appeared to be simultaneously available, spread out before him in all its colourful, emotional luxuriance like the picture on the coverlet, in these final lines he suddenly asserts that he stands in quite a different sort of relation to all of these events and characters. He is, he now says, on the same level as the mythical content of the poem after all, because it is in fact simply the past: *quondam*, 'once', appears again at 64.382 as it did at 64.1, but with no *dicuntur* to underline the distinction of narrative level. This is his past, and, he wants to tell us, also our, the readers', past as well. Mingling between gods and humans will never happen now as it did when Peleus married Thetis in the heroic age, the narrator says, because humans have now become so wicked that the gods have turned their attention away from 'us', *nobis* (64.406). That first-person plural reaches out to the poem's readers, as the narrator tells us that we, like him, are stuck in the terrible present—a present that the poem never actually specifies as Rome in the first century BC, and which could just as well be here and now. But we can, finally, ask ourselves whether we feel that we have to accept the narrator's assertion. Are we really on the same level as he is? Or, just as he tried to tell Ariadne that he could see a part of the picture that she could not, will we feel able to assume a more powerful position, deciding that we can, in some sense, see another part of the picture? We may even decide that our experience is more like that of the Thessalian guests who enjoyed looking at the picture on the coverlet (64.265–8): on finishing the poem, we may have the option of walking away and leaving the narrator inside it, on the level in which he performs his act of narrating, a level that is still not the same as real life. It is probable that metalepsis is important in Catullus 64 because this poem is all about the tension between immersion in and alienation from the mythical world.[72] In the epilogue, alienation finally wins out; but paradoxically it does so in the narrator's assertion that the mythical world is 'our' world at an earlier period in time. It is not, after all, a world that is accessible to and controllable by a poet because it exists on a different, possibly fictional, narrative level.

Catullus and His Readers

Considering the different narrative and lyric levels in these poems, and the subjects who make (or fail to make) metaleptic moves from one to another, therefore raises an extremely important and difficult question: what role is played in Catullus' poetry by real life, and on what level does Catullus himself exist? Catullus appears in a variety of subject-positions throughout his corpus: as the second-person addressee of others (10.25) or, much more frequently, of himself (8.1, 19, 46.4, 51.13, 52.1, 4, 76.5, 79.2); as a third-person character in statements which he either makes about himself (6.1, 7.10, 8.12, 11.1, 13.7, 14.13, 38.1, 44.3, 49.4, 56.3, 58.2, 68.135, 79.3, 82.1) or reports others making about him (68.27, 72.1);[73] and, obviously (but implicitly), as a first-person narrator or lyric speaker—his name never

---

[72] For approaches emphasizing this theme see e.g. Fitzgerald (1995: 140–68), Dufallo (2013: 39–73).

[73] The conventions of reported speech mean that we cannot tell whether Manlius' letter and Lesbia's utterance are to be imagined as having addressed Catullus in the second person or named him in the third.

appears straightforwardly in the first person, 'I, Catullus', but in poems in which it appears in the second or third person, it does so in such a way as to invite the reader to call that poem's speaker Catullus, and probably to do the same for other poems too. Catullus is also a Roman author in whose real past existence we believe.[74] As we have seen, his longer, more clearly narrative poems use metaleptic effects to explore exactly where their narrator—implicitly or presumably, Catullus—stands with respect to their various narrative levels, and what control he or other subjects may have over what happens on any of them. Poem 68 does so in a particularly suggestive way because it contains both mythical narratives and narratives of Catullus' own life—but the same is true, after all, of the corpus as a whole. Many of the shorter and more 'lyric' poems also contain brief narratives, and we may turn to them with the same question: how much of what happens on the various levels created in this poetry, and perhaps on a level outside it, in his life or in reality, can Catullus control?

In poem 58, for instance, Catullus tells Caelius that Lesbia, whom Catullus once loved overwhelmingly (58.1–3), now performs sex acts at crossroads and in back alleys (58.4–5). Genette suggests that we can say 'Virgil has Dido die';[75] we can presumably say 'Catullus has Ariadne get her revenge on Theseus'; but should we also say 'Catullus has Lesbia set herself up as a street prostitute'? In poem 72, Catullus reminds Lesbia of past promises of fidelity:

> *dicebas quondam solum te nosse Catullum,*
> *Lesbia, nec prae me uelle tenere Iouem.*

You once used to say, Lesbia, that you knew [*or*: wished to know] Catullus alone, and did not wish to possess even Jupiter in preference to me.

(72.1–2, trans. adapted from Goold)

dicebas quondam sounds like Ariadne addressing Theseus at 64.139–40, *at non haec quondam blanda promissa dedisti | uoce mihi*, lamenting that Theseus has not kept the promises he 'once' gave her in a 'winning voice'; *quondam* is not part of Lesbia's speech here, and is an example of the regretful use of 'once' to refer to a happier time in one's own personal past,

---

[75] Genette (1972 = 1980: 234). On the ambivalence of the expression in the French original, see Matzner in this volume, p. 3 n. 6. For further discussion of the complexities of this statement see Kearey and Lovatt in this volume.

employed by Catullus elsewhere.[76] And yet, in juxtaposing a verb of speech with an adverb of past time, *dicebas quondam* also evokes the traditional way of opening a mythical narrative which we saw at the opening of 64, *quondam... dicuntur*—and at least one mythical character, Jupiter in his capacity as a potential sexual partner, duly appears in what Lesbia says.[77] Are Lesbia and Catullus, who also appear in the report of Lesbia's speech here, mythical characters too? If so, then while the pines on the peak of Pelion at the beginning of 64 'are said' to have fallen in the stable, generalized impersonal passive of mythical tradition, in 72 Jupiter, Lesbia, and Catullus himself are all characters on a level dependent on what Lesbia, briefly a mythical narrator, once used to say. Unlike in poem 68, Catullus does now address his beloved—but he does so in order to lament his lack of control over the contrast between what happens on the level she once created, *dicebas*, and what is now happening in the world he describes in the second half of the poem, in which her promises have not been kept (72.5–8).[78]

Genette refers to Borges to make the point that metalepsis may be perturbing because it can suggest that there might be another level above and outside what we might think of as the outermost, topmost one on which the act of narrating takes place: 'that the extradiegetic is perhaps always diegetic, and that the narrator and his narratees—you and I—perhaps belong to some narrative.'[79] We know that Catullus does indeed belong to such a narrative, in at least two ways: he belongs to the narratives about his life that readers inevitably construct out of his poetry,[80] and he belongs to the narratives of Roman literary history written by critics and—long before them—by other poets. Being poets, these first few writers in the extant record to mention Catullus may do so in either a narrative or a lyric mode. Though already dead, Catullus can easily be addressed: Propertius, boasting about the power of his own books to make Cynthia famous, nods an apology to him (Prop. 2.25.3–4, *pace, Catulle, tua*, 'by your leave, Catullus'). Elsewhere, Propertius is more careful to give Catullus his due,

---

[76] 8.3 *fulsere quondam candidi tibi soles*, 'once the sun shone bright for you' (trans. Goold; Catullus addresses himself), contrasted with 8.9 *nunc*, 'now'.

[77] See above, p. 120; reading the opening words of 72, Kubiak (1986) begins to move in this direction.

[78] For his attempts to exert control over that world and his reader's response to it, see Pedrick (1986: 201–7), Janan (1994: 88–92).

[79] Genette (1972 = 1980: 236). Borges (1964: 46): 'if the characters in a story can be readers or spectators, then we, their readers or spectators, can be fictitious'. Cf. Kennedy in this volume.

[80] See above, p. 124.

stating that his poetry has put Lesbia onto the same level as famous mythical heroines, making her 'better known than Helen herself' (Prop. 2.34.87–8, *scripta Catulli | Lesbia quis ipsa notior est Helena*). Lygdamus mentions that Catullus has sung about Ariadne—and suddenly Ariadne is on a level where Lygdamus seems to feel comfortable addressing her ([Tib.] 3.6.41, *sic cecinit pro te doctus, Minoi, Catullus*, 'so, daughter of Minos, did learned Catullus sing for you'). Yet in Horace's *Satires*, Catullus appears as the *object* of a verb of singing (Hor. *S.* 1.10.18–19, *simius iste | nil praeter Caluum et doctus cantare Catullum*, 'that ape, learned only in singing Calvus and Catullus'), a metonym for his poetry, as in the title of this chapter. And for Ovid, imagining the fate of the dead Tibullus, he has become a mythical character, crowned with ivy in a mythical underworld (Ov. *Am.* 3.9.61–2)—but again, one who can be addressed, *docte Catulle*, 'learned Catullus' in the vocative. These poets have started to explore the levels on which Catullus—and two of his most powerful characters, Lesbia and Ariadne—can exist. But most of them, too, will soon join Catullus as characters in the writings of their successors, both poets and, later, critics. Looking at Catullus and metalepsis, then, ultimately leads us to ask who may be in control not only of narratives and lyrics about Catullus, but also narratives (if rarely lyrics) about his readers—us.

7

Close Encounters

Divine Epiphanies on the Fringes of Latin Love Elegy

Laurel Fulkerson

'Many of the most interesting problems associated with divinity are to be found at moments when the divine crashes through the barrier between its own medium and ours, in epiphany' (Feeney 1998: 104).[1] Feeney refers to epic, but elegiac epiphany too poses 'interesting problems' in its breaches of frame and poetic decorum, and also in the ways it can overturn the relative positions of god and mortal. This chapter explores the disruptive narrative potential caused by the metaleptic appearance of a god into an elegiac poem ([Tib.] 3.4) in which, arguably, he has no business. Along the way, it suggests that elegy, because it is a genre in which author and narrator usually share a name but fulfil multiple narrative functions, is especially liable to a form of metalepsis which, following Whitmarsh, we might call 'strong',[2] and that the literary epiphany which features in the elegy under discussion (as well as some companion texts) represents a medley of authorial and narrator metalepsis in ways that prove destabilizing for both subject positions,[3] but also for the internal and external narratees, who are left wondering who really says what, and with what authority.

* Many thanks to Gail Trimble and Sebastian Matzner for the impetus to think through the issues presented here, to the original audience for a number of stimulating comments, and to Joel Christensen for help with Homeric bibliography.

[1] On epiphany and metalepsis see also De Jong in this volume.
[2] Whitmarsh (2013b: 5–6) on the distinction; for him, 'strong' metalepsis involves the extrafictional world.
[3] See Matzner and Kearey in this volume.

Laurel Fulkerson, *Close Encounters: Divine Epiphanies on the Fringes of Latin Love Elegy* In: *Metalepsis: Ancient Texts, New Perspectives*. Edited by: Sebastian Matzner and Gail Trimble, Oxford University Press (2020).
© The editors and Oxford University Press.
DOI: 10.1093/oso/9780198846987.003.0007

My starting point is to notice that a literary epiphany inevitably creates a tension between parts of the narrative: the gods are by definition powerful, but gods who appear in poetry are also 'scripted', and so, like other characters in the story, have no choice but to mouth the words of their authors.[4] In the case of elegy, those authors are also characters, who are thus able to control events through what they tell and do not tell, but also through the power of fiction, while representing themselves as being 'merely' victims of the *puella*. For, however we want to understand the complex *persona* of the elegist, whether his poetry represents reality in some broadly (or narrowly) autobiographical sense, or whether it is simply a series of scenarios through which to explore other issues, the *auctor* simultaneously is and is not the same as the *amator*, and the tension which ensues is a fruitful one. After a brief summary of some important Greek and Roman predecessors, my main text will be a lengthy section of [Tib.] 3.4, a poem by the obscure Lygdamus telling of a dream, or perhaps a vision, in which Apollo has appeared to him and given him certain advice about his personal life. I then touch briefly upon one of its main parallels, Ovid's *Ex Ponto* 3.3, and suggest that both epiphanies point to at least one earlier poetic scene.

In Greco-Roman poetry, the divine and human spheres have been distinct yet mutually interpenetrating from the time of Homer on, and there has been an enormous amount of scholarship on what this juxtaposition-cum-separation might tell us about ancient mythology, religion, politics, poetics, and even categories of thought.[5] However special and striking such literary moments are, they are also relatively frequent, and they perform, narratively speaking, a wide variety of functions. For Homer, they provide a sophisticated means of motivating action (how and how much are notoriously complex subjects),[6] but they also allow for sophisticated expression of different points of view. For instance, when Athena

---

[4] See, conveniently, Wyke (1987).

[5] I make no attempt in what follows to engage with the complex issues of Greco-Roman religious beliefs and practices. Rather, I am concerned only with the first of Varro's three categories of gods (mythic/poetic, philosophical/natural, civic; August. *C. D.* 6.5): the Apollo/Cupid of the poems under treatment are their usual textual incarnations (though note that Apollo in [Tib.] 3.4 may be designed to evoke the Apollo of the (recently built?) Palatine; see below, n. 18, on dating). The poetic depiction of gods combines with the 'autobiographical' nature of elegy to provide a situation in which 'authors' come face to face, in some sense, with their own 'creations' (see Rabau 2005 for this conjunction, and its implications, in both ancient and modern literature).

[6] Bibliography on Homer's portrayal of the gods and their effects on human decision-making is immense; starting points are Snell (1960) and Lesky (1961), both heavily refined by later authors; see e.g. Gaskin (1990, discussing Achilles and Athena at 154–5), Williams (1993: 21–7), Pelliccia (1995: 15–27), and especially Gill (1996); useful summary in Russo (2012).

appears to Achilles in *Iliad* 1.193–222, she asks him to refrain from killing Agamemnon.[7] He complies with her wishes, although she observes that he has the option not to. It is possible to all but erase the goddess in this scene, assuming that she 'really' represents an externalization of Achilles' conscience or rational self as against his more primitive impulses.[8] Homer has structured the narrative to allow for both of those options (Athena-as-personification and Athena-as-agent), and also to provide more context than an internal monologue might do: we see that Achilles really does want to attack Agamemnon, but also that there are good reasons for him not to.

Moreover, on the extradiegetic level, Homer's ability to detail something that would have been opaque even to eyewitnesses augments his authority. Although all authors have a degree of omniscience simply because they are in charge of the plot, detailing a divine intrusion unnoticed by anyone else allows the poet to become a kind of super-character located between the human plane and the divine, able to discern the connections between the two and provide explanations to ordinary people.[9] The use of divine epiphany, then, can simultaneously elevate authors and distance them from taking responsibility for what they describe, since, to the extent that we 'buy into' the fiction presented to us, we see gods as separate from human characters. I focus closely in what follows on this nexus between the differing narrative levels of characters, gods, and authors, because it is this feature of literary descriptions of divine epiphany that makes them so compelling a subject from a theoretical perspective.

Further, the concept of narrative metalepsis, one form of which involves an authorial intrusion into the story, allows us to focus more precisely on what occurs when such an intrusion disguises itself as *part of* the story.

---

[7] There is a difference between poetic divine interventions that clearly manifest themselves as gods and those that do so in more ambiguous fashion; I reserve for another occasion allegorical or impersonational epiphanies, gems such as Nestor's appearance to Agamemnon, Penelope's geese, and the friend of Nausicaa. Such instances are part of the same phenomenon, but a god in the flesh, even when mediated by a dream, has a distinctly more impressive feel than a dream or vision involving a figure seen in everyday life. So too, the gods seem less likely to intervene in deceptive ways when they appear as themselves than when they work through intermediaries. On the topic of epiphanic dreams, see Harris (2009: 23–90, with characteristics described at 36–7). Harris (2003) discusses the veracity of dreams, and Versnel (1987: 49–50) notes that divine epiphanies are liable to occur in or near sleep. See too Harrisson (2013) on the Roman understanding of what dreams can mean/do. Cic. *Div.* 1.39–70 and 2.120–50 offer two radically different views of prophetic dreams and their truth-value.

[8] E.g. Sharples (1983); although he does not mention divine examples, his rationalistic interpretation entails understanding them metaphorically.

[9] For the 'miraculous' nature of ordinary authorial intrusion into narrative, see Fludernik (2003b: 383–5), building upon Genette (1972 = 1980: 234–5).

Three discrete but intertwined things happen when a god intervenes in narrative, which is essentially what a divine epiphany is. First, a change of subject is introduced by the divine visitor, who has his or her own agenda; such a change can also be accomplished through much more mundane means (like a human entrant into the conversation, or a transitional device such as 'meanwhile elsewhere on the battlefield…'). Second, an elevation in both tone and authoritativeness are inevitably felt once a god takes the stage—even if no marked difference in language signals this change: gods are Big News whatever they say and do. And finally, I want to argue that we can discern the author hiding behind the god, taking advantage of the fact that gods are both 'real' and 'fictional'; nobody can gainsay what is reported in a work of fiction, or in a dream, and a god's authoritativeness can thus 'bleed over' even into realms where the god is not actually present.[10]

Now to categories of literary epiphany. Two primary categories of divine/mortal interaction will prove relevant to the present discussion.[11] The first is the *Dichterweihe*, in which a divine being concerned with literary composition (most often the Muses or Apollo) gives advice about the writing of poetry. There are any number of such scenes; after the originary Hesiodic moment (*Theogony* 22–34), Callimachus' *Aetia* prologue frr. 1.21–8 and 2 are probably of greatest import for Latin poets. In the first, Apollo tells the poet to feed his sacrificial victims fat but keep his poetry thin and to avoid the well-travelled path, and in the second (less well-known, so cited here) Callimachus seems to retell the story of the Muses' appearance to Hesiod (*Aetia* fr. 2):

> Ποιμένι μῆλα νέμοντι παρ᾽ἴχνιον ὀξέος ἵππου
> Ἡσιόδῳ Μουσέων ἑσμὸς ὅτ᾽ἠντίασεν
> μ]έν οἱ Χάεος γενεσ[
>] ἐπὶ πτέρνης ὑδα[
> τεύχων ὡς ἑτέρῳ τις ἑῷ κακὸν ἥπατι τεύχει.

---

[10] Note, for instance, the ways that divine visitors tend to look like statues of themselves; as Platt (2011) notes, this makes them easy to recognize (within the epiphany itself) but also easy to narrate to others (e.g. 16, 78, 290).

[11] I have already blurred what are to us two very discrete categories, 'dream' and 'vision'; this fuzziness reflects the tendency of ancient epiphanic texts, which sometimes, but not always, specify whether they are waking or sleeping events; the modern preconception that a divine epiphany that occurs in a dream is less authentic or valuable, less 'real', than one which happens in the waking hours does not seem to hold true for ancient visitations: both are perceived as external rather than internal events. If anything, sleep seems to be a more congenial medium—especially in poetry—for gods to manifest themselves, perhaps because it elides the boundary between reality and unreality. See, e.g., Prop. 4.1(b), which suggests that the distinction is not essential.

...when the gathering of Muses met the shepherd Hesiod tending his sheep by the footprint of the dazzling horse...the birth of Chaos...at water of the hoof...how someone causing evil to another man causes evil to his own heart.[12]

It is not clear to what end Callimachus tells this story; a good guess, given subsequent poetic practice, would be that he inserts himself into the lineage (e.g. the same Muses which appeared to Hesiod also appeared to me, or, perhaps, the Muses appeared to Hesiod and Hesiod appeared to me).[13]

Ennius' *Annales* 3 is our first such moment in Latin literature, and it complicates the very category of a divine epiphany: Homer appears to Ennius, possibly in a dream (*uisus Homerus adesse poeta*, 'The poet Homer seemed to appear...', fr. 3 Skutsch; cf. Cic. *Acad.* 2.51). Presumably the context is one in which Homer either tells Ennius how he should write, or encourages him to keep up the good work. But Homer is not a god, although we might, at a stretch, see him as a divinized avatar who personifies the writing of epic poetry. Alternatively, we might decide that Ennius has compressed the Callimachean scenario (divine apparition to famous poetic progenitor, with some [details unknown] implication for contemporary poet, is rewritten as quasi-divine progenitor appearing directly to contemporary poet).[14] Other relevant and more traditional examples are Vergil, *Ecl.* 6, where Apollo offers advice about what kind of poetry to write, Horace, *Odes* 4.15, where Apollo slaps the poet back into submission, and even Horace, *Satires* 1.10.31–5, where Quirinus offers poetic advice.

The second relevant category of divine–human interaction is the prophetic dream or vision, in which an authority figure, sometimes but not always a god, delivers some piece of hitherto unknown information, sometimes about the present, sometimes about the future. Such interventions regularly happen to heroes about to found cities or do great deeds; the topos is familiar enough, especially in epic and in certain kinds of history, that I resist providing examples.[15]

Ontologically, these are two distinct events: the gods of poets provide information, advice, and commands relevant to poetry. Heroes, by contrast, need and receive reminders and encouragement as they go off into

---

[12] All translations are my own.

[13] See below, pp. 163–5, for the suggestion of another referent.

[14] Or perhaps Ennius already combined the divine poetic epiphany with the prophetic apparition (see below, n. 37).

[15] Among the more obscure is the otherwise unknown work by Istros, *Apollonos Epiphaneai, FGrHist* 334 FF 50–2, which seems to have detailed the god Apollo's appearances in military contexts.

the world. So too, prophetic epiphanies are located wholly within the narrative, while scenes of poetic inspiration jump out of the poem to have real-world (textual) implications: they are a poet's way of justifying to external narratees his poetic choices within the narrative frame. Yet we have already seen hints that the two might be combined; the author of an epic poem can be conceived of as an epic hero in his own right, and elegists occasionally apply this to themselves by analogy. So too, famous poets can seemingly take on the role of poetic gods of inspiration.

I suggested above that a complex tension is inevitable in literary depictions of divine epiphany, because of the sleight of hand involved in attributing agency to the god when it is really the author's. But ordinarily—if there is any such concept in this extraordinary event—this tension is only implicit, since gods usually concern themselves with grand historical events or with inspiring poets. In elegy, however, where the elegist is both the hero of his own story and simultaneously the omniscient extradiegetic narrator (again, sharing a single name), divine epiphanies tend to be more personal, and an author might conceivably use them to affect the world 'outside' of the poetry.

Still, most elegiac scenes of divine visitation tend to fall into one category or the other, and to prove relatively unproblematic. A few examples: Prop. 3.3.15–24 narrates a dream in which Apollo warns the poet in no uncertain terms away from the *carminis heroi* (16) he has been planning to write about early Roman history and guides him instead toward soft, small poetry (*mollia, paruis*, 18; *libellus*, 19). Apollo leads him from Helicon with its gushing epic rivers to a small grotto, where he visits with the Muses, one of whom reiterates the message and offers him a little water from a small stream. This poem provides a double consecration, one negative and one positive, and two gods, but it is wholly about poetry, and the god's advice is economically followed right within the compass of the poem.

The Muses also appear at Prop. 3.10.1–4, but are not given direct speech; they remind the poet that it is Cynthia's birthday and then disappear. The writing of a poem about a visitation that announces Cynthia's birthday is itself a poetic commemoration of that birthday, and so Propertius has, again, both identified a desideratum and fulfilled it. Despite Propertius' regular fashioning of his relationship with Cynthia as epic in stature, there is nothing in this poem to suggest a heroic quest. So too, in Propertius 4.6.25–57, Apollo reappears to prophesy the Actian victory. This is unambiguously the second sort of epiphany: he tells of future events—which have already happened—and has no special message for Propertius-the-poet.

The divine epiphany is a favourite device of Ovid's; in addition to *Pont.* 3.3, discussed extensively below, Amor appears right at the start, in *Am.* 1.1.1–4, and steals a foot, thus dooming Ovid to write elegiac couplets instead of the epic he had planned:

> *arma graui numero uiolentaque bella parabam*
> *edere, materia conueniente modis.*
> *par erat inferior uersus; risisse Cupido*
> *dicitur atque unum surripuisse pedem.*

I was planning to publish arms and violent wars in a heavy strain, with the subject suiting its metre. The second verse was equal—but Cupid is said to have laughed and to have stolen one foot.

This epiphany is stealthy; *dicitur* suggests that this is Ovid's best guess about what has happened: Cupid, it seems, has not simply offered advice, but has taken decisive steps to ensure that Ovid writes the sort of poetry the god wants him to write.[16] Here too, the world of the poem is complete: we hear about a sort of poetry that might have been written but are only permitted to read the divinely sanctioned final product. At *Ars* 2.493–510, Apollo appears to Ovid and explains that would-be lovers must know themselves; specifically, they ought to show themselves to best advantage. In *Rem.* 549–75, Cupid appears in a dream (maybe: *puto somnus erat*, 'I *think* it was a dream', 556) and reminds Ovid that focusing on other problems is a good way to fall out of love.[17] These latter two Ovidian instances are fairly banal, insofar as the advice given is common knowledge and does not need a divine pedigree. But they also show Ovid's interest in the blurring of the two categories I have identified, in which a god of poetry offers direction to the poet about his (heroic) love life-cum-poetic output. (I suggest below yet another poetic scene that combines the two

---

[16] McKeown observes *ad loc.* '*dicitur* is problematic'. Narratively speaking, this is an epiphany which seems to occur 'above' the narrative level where Ovid-the-author exists, since he represents himself as passing along information for which he cannot vouch. (This might, of course, be another of the elegists' ways of avoiding responsibility: not an epiphany but a reported epiphany.)

[17] Armstrong (2004) offers useful discussion of these Ovidian scenes from another angle, as does Miller (2009: 324–6). See too McKeown *ad Ov. Am.* 1.1 for further epiphanies of Cupid in Euripides and Bion.

kinds of epiphany, and argue that it helps our understanding of the poems under discussion here.)[18]

Let us turn now to [Tib.] 3.4, which is a curious blend of the two kinds of epiphany I have identified.[19] Apollo visits the poet, but makes no mention of Lygdamus' poetry. On the one hand, the information Apollo brings to Lygdamus is unwelcome: he informs the poet that his beloved Neaera is unfaithful (*alterius mauult esse puella uiri*, 'she prefers to be the *puella* of another man', 3.4.58). On the other, the god *also* compliments Lygdamus and encourages him in his vocation. The already extant tension between Lygdamus the author of the poem and Lygdamus the character within it is exacerbated by 'Apollo's' conflation between the two sorts of epiphany; this tension persists throughout the poem and provides a first indication that this is not your ordinary Apollo. Rather, 3.4 systematically undermines the god as it elevates the poet.

The epiphany further breaks the narrative frame because Apollo's message is neither that Lygdamus should write the kind of poetry he was already going to write, nor is it a prediction of events which have already happened. Rather the god interferes in what is presented as an ongoing romantic relationship in the 'real' world. Apollo starts off in customary fashion, even if he soon takes a sharp turn toward the unexpected (43–50):

> '*salue, cura deum: casto nam rite poetae*
> *Phoebusque et Bacchus Pieridesque fauent;*
> *sed proles Semelae Bacchus doctaeque sorores*   45
> *dicere non norunt quid ferat hora sequens;*

---

[18] See below, pp. 161–3, on Ov. *Pont.* 3.3. On the other hand, recombination of previously disparate material is quintessentially Ovidian, such that we might see the full integration of poetic inspiration and heroic prophecy as originating with *Pont.* 3.3 and from there making its way into [Tib.] 3.4. The relative dating of our two poems remains hotly debated, despite the decisive tone of most of the scholarship on the topic. See now Martelli (2013) and Thorsen (2014) for discussion of the manifold difficulties with Ovidian chronology. Lygdamus' dating is even more confused, in part because it is not clear whether he borrowed lines from Ovid or vice versa. The most notorious of these is [Tib.] 3.5.18 ~ Ov. *Tr.* 4.10.6; the question is complicated by the putative 'first edition' of the *Amores*, which may or may not have included lines eliminated by the 'second' edition but in the meantime used by Lygdamus. The question reached an equilibrium in the early 1960s with the publication of Lee (1958–9) and Axelson (1960), each of whom proposed a 'method' for determining priority of texts. Their opinion, that Ovid predates Lygdamus, continues to hold the field, although the method has been criticized as overly subjective by any number of scholars. For entrée into the bibliography, see too Hagen (1954) and the relevant sections of Tränkle (1990) and Navarro Antolín (1996), all of whom date Lygdamus substantially later than Ovid; see too Somerville (forthcoming) for the opposite argument.

[19] See Fulkerson (2017) for more extensive discussion of this poem.

> *at mihi fatorum leges aeuisque futuri*
> *euentura pater posse uidere dedit;*
> *quare ego quae dico non fallax accipe uates*
> *quodque deus uero Cynthius ore feram.'*   50

'Greetings, favourite of the gods: for it is proper that Phoebus and Bacchus and the Pierides favour a chaste poet; but Bacchus, son of Semele, and the learned sisters do not know how to say what the coming hour will bring: to me, my father has given the power to see the laws of fate and what will be the events of future time. Wherefore listen to what I, a truthful bard, say and how I, Cynthian god, am considered to have a true mouth.'

The god greets Lygdamus and confirms him in his poetic vocation (note *cura deum*, 43). Apollo then establishes his own prophetic credentials, referring to his father and badmouthing the competition. His tactics are better suited to a mortal: his status as the god of prophecy ought to need no defence.[20] Even the allusion to Jupiter raises suspicions: like Homeric heroes on the battlefield and unknown visitors, he seems to sense a need to situate himself by means of his relatives. *Non fallax* and *uero* of 49 and 50 provide further unnecessary detail.[21]

Despite this somewhat unconventional behaviour on the part of Apollo, we might expect a grand prophecy—some new poetic enterprise for Lygdamus, perhaps. But, as noted above, the god's message for Lygdamus is banal: it turns out that Neaera is behaving just like every other elegiac *puella*. Apollo continues with name-calling and a personal anecdote (3.4.61–80):

> '*a crudele genus nec fidum femina nomen!*
> *a pereat, didicit fallere si qua uirum!*
> *sed flecti poterit: mens est mutabilis illis;*
> *tu modo cum multa bracchia tende prece.*
> *saeuus Amor docuit ualidos temptare labores,*   65
> *saeuus Amor docuit uerbera posse pati.*
> *me quondam Admeti niueas pauisse iuuencas*
> *non est in uanum fabula ficta iocum;*

---

[20] Note, as a single counter-example, the way the Apollo of Prop. 3.3 launches immediately into attacking Propertius, rather than explaining himself.

[21] Note, in this context, Propertius' description of elegy as *fallax opus* (4.1.135), and see Kennedy in this volume on the metaphysical questions raised by this blurring of narrative, fiction, and dream.

> *tunc ego nec cithara poteram gaudere sonora*
> *nec similes chordis reddere uoce sonos,*   70
> *sed perlucenti cantum meditabar auena*
> *ille ego Latonae filius atque Iouis.*
> *nescis quid sit amor, iuuenis, si ferre recusas*
> *immitem dominam coniugiumque ferum.*
> *ergo ne dubita blandas adhibere querellas:*   75
> *uincuntur molli pectora dura prece.*
> *quod si uera canunt sacris oracula templis,*
> *haec illi nostro nomine dicta refer:*
> *hoc tibi conigium promittit Delius ipse;*
> *felix hoc, alium desine uelle uirum.'*   80

'A cruel race, woman without trustworthy name! May she perish, if any woman has learned to cheat her man! But she can be changed: the mind is fickle in them: you just stretch your arms forth with many a prayer. Savage Love has taught us to undergo harsh labours, savage Love has taught us to suffer beatings. I too, once fed the snowy heifers of Admetus—the common tale was not made up to be an empty joke— then I was not able to glory in the sounding cithara nor to return back sounds like unto its chords with my voice, but instead I practised my song on the transparent reed I, son of Latona and Jupiter. You do not know what love is, young man, if you refuse to bear a harsh mistress and savage partnership. Wherefore do not hesitate to make use of the blandishing complaint: hard hearts are won over by a soft prayer. But if oracles in holy temples sing the truth, bring these words to her in my name: this is the mate that the Delian himself promised to you: lucky in him, stop wishing for another man.'

Apollo has gone to all the trouble of appearing to Lygdamus in order to inform him of something he already knows. While divine confirmation of your worst fears might add a further layer of wretchedness, the care with which Apollo speaks suggests that he is anxious about Lygdamus' reaction, which in turn hints at the god's peculiarly human concerns. Depending upon our viewpoint, this might seem either alarming or reassuring: it is nice to know that sometimes the gods take such a personal interest in mortals, but it is also worrying that Apollo does not have more important things to do.

But that is only the start of what goes so comically awry in this poem: after offering confirmation that Neaera really is an elegiac *puella*, rather than doing something to re-establish himself as a powerful character, Apollo first attacks women in general, in a way that is extremely familiar in the poetic tradition[22]—although, interestingly, Lygdamus never uses such language of Neaera—and then alludes to Mercury's statement in the *Aeneid* about the changeableness of women (*mens est mutabilis illis*, 'their minds are changeable': cf. *Aen.* 4.569–70). Only Apollo misses the point of Mercury's speech by taking it out of context; here he means to encourage Lygdamus to keep trying, because Neaera may eventually take him back, rather than to warn him of a Dido-like revenge.

Apollo's misprision of mythology and undermining of his own authority continue, as he goes on to tell the story of his unsuccessful affair with Admetus. As the implicit contrast with Mercury's role in Vergil hints, Apollo's tale depicts the god less as a knowledgeable and powerful prophet than as a fellow-sufferer, and thus puts him in the same boat as Lygdamus himself. Gods do not usually feel the need to share sob stories with mortals, and Apollo's comment at 3.4.68 ('not funny!') only underlines the point. There is no need for Apollo to tell any story at all, let alone one that makes him look so foolish: autobiographical anecdotes serve to provide corroborating evidence, to convince, but divine visitors ought not to have to bother.[23]

Moreover, the story has (probably)[24] already been told in elegy, in Tibullus 2.3.11–28—but there it authenticates Tibullus' willingness to engage in degrading labour if that is what Delia wants.[25] It fits much more appropriately in that poem, despite the fact that here it is a first-person narrative. And in fact, the transferral of a story from the third person to the first almost inevitably involves a deflation: the sorts of things that you can say to praise someone else rarely fit comfortably into the personal voice (cf. e.g. Apollo's hymn to himself as a wooing technique in Ov. *Met.*

---

[22] See e.g. Prop. 2.9.31–2, which attributes to all women the (putative) vices of the *puella*, with Enk *ad loc.*, briefly, on the Greek poetic tradition of invective against women.

[23] Mortal visitants (usually ghosts, but sometimes dreams) more characteristically feel the need to explain themselves; see e.g. 'Nestor' in *Iliad* 2, who justifies his nocturnal visit to Agamemnon both in practical terms (generals should not sleep, 2.23–5) and in divine ones (Zeus has sent him with a message, 25–34).

[24] See above, n. 18, for the difficulties of Lygdaman chronology; in the oral presentation of this paper, Evert van Emde Boas noted that *o quotiens* of Tib 2.3.17 and 19 might hint at that poet's belatedness, and could suggest that Lygdamus' work circulated among the canonical elegists.

[25] On the 'particularly transumptive' or metaleptic properties of mythological narrative, see especially Hollander (1981) and Barkan (1991).

1.504–24). Further, far from marking out the story as recondite and sophisticated, Tibullus himself had already noted that it was a trite story, and had drawn attention to the fact that despite his shameless behaviour, Apollo both became a subject for gossip and wound up alone (*fabula nunc ille est: sed cui sua cura puella est,* | *fabula sit mauult quam sine amore deus,* 'that is now a common tale; but he for whom his own girl is a concern, would rather be a common tale than a god without love', Tib. 2.3.31–2). Tibullus has learned from Apollo's misfortunes that no behaviour is excessive, so long as you get the girl, but Apollo has not—although of course this is precisely the advice he passes along to Lygdamus, parroting without comprehending.

Finally, and perhaps most significantly, this story, as a story, is more or less irrelevant to its narrative frame, as it has only the most minimal point of overlap with Lygdamus' own situation. Both man and god love unhappily, in common with more or less everyone in Latin elegy; Apollo's story is not even about a *puella*, though his lack of success with women is notorious (at least in the *Metamorphoses*; see Coronis, for instance, in *Met.* 2, who likes 'somebody else' better than Apollo). The generalizing plural *illis* of line 63, adapted from the Vergilian Mercury's singular *femina*, becomes wildly general, applying in Apollo's understanding even to men. The tale of Apollo and Admetus appears to have originally had no erotic component;[26] rather, Apollo was in servitude to him as punishment for killing the Cyclopes. But by the time the elegists get to it, it has become a tale of suffering for the sake of love. Here, however, it undermines the point Apollo is trying to make: for the outcome of the Admetus tale is unclear, but it does not seem to result in a permanent or even semi-permanent relationship between god and beloved mortal. I have suggested that there was never a need for Apollo to tell any story at all—but if he thought one was necessary, he ought to have found one in which someone wins over a girl through his persistence.[27] One lesson Lygdamus might learn from Apollo's inset tale is that Amor is savage (line 66)—although everyone already knows that, or that love is sometimes fruitless in addition to being painful and degrading—although everyone in elegy already knows that too. Perhaps it is a comfort to Lygdamus to know that these rules apply to the

---

[26] Apollo and Admetus: Eur. *Alc.* 1–14 (punishment); Call. *Hymn Ap.* 2.47–54 with Williams (1978: *ad loc.*), Rhianus fr. 10 Powell, schol. Eur. *Alc.* 1, Tib. 2.3.11–28, Ov. *Met.* 2.679–83, Plu. *Num.* 4.8 (love story); Ov. *Her.* 5.151–2, *Ars* 2.239–41, Sen. *Phaed.* 296–8, and Stat. *Silv.* 3.3.58 leave the matter unclear.

[27] Perhaps the exempla of Milanion or Acontius; see below, p. 164 n. 38.

gods as well as mortals, but his ultimate reaction does not suggest that he has found the apparition's visit to be a soothing one.[28]

Apollo finishes up by offering Lygdamus the advice to keep suffering and to try pleading too (3.4.73–6), and ends with an official-sounding pronouncement, which Lygdamus is instructed to pass along to Neaera. The *si* of line 77, *quod si uera canunt* ('but if oracles in holy temples sing the truth') doesn't necessarily express a conditional, but it is nonetheless a puzzling statement for a god of prophecy to utter: if anybody knows whether prophecies are true it ought to be the divinity in charge of them! Still, Apollo's final words are, at long last, impressive, just the sort of thing to encourage the poet and finish off the poem properly.

Or rather, they would be, if Lygdamus did not immediately work his hardest to undermine them (3.4.81–96). In these lines, Lygdamus first wishes the dream away and expresses his shock at Neaera's betrayal, a betrayal all the more shocking because she is not one of the dread monsters of mythology. The poem finishes by praying to some god (why not Apollo?) to make the winds blow the whole dream away. Commentators are usually puzzled by this section of the poem: given that the god of prophecy has come out so strongly on Lygdamus' side, uttering a dire warning to Neaera if she continues her unfaithfulness, why is Lygdamus so keen to pretend the incident never happened?[29]

I suggest that the poem is designed to persuade Neaera without implicating Lygdamus. Employment of a divine epiphany enables Lygdamus to have his say without taking responsibility for it: you can't blame someone for what a god tells him, let alone for what happens in his sleep. It is not Lygdamus but Apollo who accuses Neaera of cheating, who chastises her and draws all sorts of insulting parallels. And how much more innocent must we find Lygdamus because he has already expressed the explicit hope, before and after this disturbing narrative, that it isn't true? It's up to Neaera what she wants to make of it; Lygdamus isn't the sort to believe in dreams. But—just in case—he's prayed to avert all of the consequences, especially from the guilty and heartless Neaera.[30]

---

[28] See below, this page.

[29] They usually suggest either that the poem has been poorly put together, or, more charitably, that the poet is representing himself as having awoken with disordered thoughts.

[30] I noted that Apollo is more or less the only character in Lygdamus' poetry who attacks Neaera; [Tib.] 3.1.8 has a textual crux which does not allow us to know whether it is the poet or the Muses who describe Neaera as *auara*, greedy. The latter, which I prefer for a variety of other reasons (see Fulkerson (2017) *ad loc.*), gives us another denigration of Neaera displaced from Lygdamus to a divine source.

This point is especially interesting in light of the usual understanding of narrative metalepsis, which holds it to be an intrusion into 'normal' narrative which has the ultimate effect of collapsing, or at least destabilizing, boundaries. Here, on the contrary, the incursion is carefully orchestrated to fit into the poem, and works to distance the intrafictional poet's persona from views which he nonetheless wishes to have 'on the record', and from the mouth of one who is an authority figure because of his divine status, but whose authority has been called into question by the peculiarities of his self-presentation. The poet manages to have it all ways, voicing a statement by a disreputable but powerful other who is simultaneously linked to him and carefully separated.

This poem, in fact, contains precisely the message Lygdamus would wish Neaera to hear but cannot himself tell her. By putting the words in the mouth of the god, Lygdamus can maintain the pose of a wronged lover who cannot bring himself to say anything negative about his beloved, but also give vent to his feelings of frustration. If Neaera happens to take any of the poem seriously, she will surely pay especial attention to the end of Apollo's speech, in which he delivers a vague threat and orders her to stick to Lygdamus. But at the very least, Lygdamus has given Neaera fair warning that her behaviour upsets the divine order of things, and Apollo has had to make a special trip to mention it.

Further, Apollo's tale may offer a Lygdaman parody of elegy's habit of using myth inappropriately, both in terms of the selfishness of its aims and of the inapplicability of the mythic paradigms often brought to bear; his Apollo is reminiscent of the narrator of the *Ars Amatoria*, who gives advice he cannot follow and who is not fully in control of the mythic tales he attempts to deploy. And Apollo is obviously on Lygdamus' side. But perhaps too much so, or for the wrong reasons: his diatribe against women is partisan, and suggests closer attention to his overblown self-justification; the best time to insist that you are telling the truth is when you are not.

Through a leap which is metaleptic in its dizzying confusion of who really thinks and says what, and also in its overturning of the delicate but key boundaries between what happens in poetry and what happens out of it, this poem has harnessed a god into coercing an author's *puella* and threatened her with divine retribution if she does not fall in with the author's wishes.[31] Lygdamus-the-author scripts the narrative which Apollo the god delivers to Lygdamus-the-lover to pass along to Neaera the *puella*.

---

[31] There is a similar scenario in the tale of Acontius and Cydippe, known to us from Callimachus and Ovid (*Her.* 20–1), in which, even more cleverly than Lygdamus, Acontius

(And the message is delivered in a dream, so Neaera will simply have to take Lygdamus' word for the whole thing.) Of course, this is how both narrative and literary depictions of divine epiphany tend to work; we are normally forgetful of authors' control over their material until they remind us by inserting an extradiegetic comment. But in this poem the intrusion works rather differently, and to a different end: divine epiphanies tend to authenticate themselves automatically, insofar as they either use the future tense to depict events of the past, or suggest that poets do the very things they are in the process of doing. Here, by contrast, the conceit ruptures yet another narrative frame, breaking entirely out of the world of the poem to intrude into 'real life'.

Ovid's *Pont.* 3.3 contains a similar scene, in which Amor appears to the exiled Ovid, to bring the latest news (*Pont.* 3.3.21–32):

> *hunc simul agnoui—neque enim mihi notior alter—*
> *talibus adfata est libera lingua sonis:*
> *'o puer, exilii decepto causa magistro,*
> *quem fuit utilius non docuisse mihi,*
> *huc quoque uenisti, pax est ubi tempore nullo*   25
> *et coit adstrictis barbarus Hister aquis?*
> *quae tibi causa uiae, nisi uti mala nostra uideres,*
> *quae sunt, si nescis, inuidiosa tibi?*
> *tu mihi dictasti iuuenalia carmina primus,*
> *adposui senis te duce quinque pedes.*   30
> *nec me Maeonio consurgere carmine nec me*
> *dicere magnorum passus es acta ducum...'*

I recognized him straightaway—for no other was better known to me—and my free tongue spoke to him in such words: 'O, boy, cause of the exile of your deceived teacher, whom it would have been more useful for me not to have taught, have you also come here, where there is peace at no time, and the barbarian Hister flows with narrowed waters? What is the reason for your trip, unless so that you could see my troubles, which are, in case you didn't know, your fault? You used to dictate to me my first youthful poems, and I put five feet next to six at your command. And you did not allow me to rise up in Homeric poetry, nor to say the deeds of great heroes...'

---

had dragged Artemis into his affairs by writing an oath, which Cydippe read out loud, and in which she swore by Artemis to marry him.

These lines come immediately after a physical description of the god which, scholars note, shares numerous points of contact with Lygdamus' description of Apollo. But here, in a way that I believe is unparalleled in ancient literature, mortal addresses god *first*:[32] Ovid recognizes Amor and attacks him, blaming him for his exile and for giving the poet bad advice. This moment of misadvising is nowhere else described in Ovid's poetry, unless we are to understand the start of *Amores* 1.1 as alluding to it.[33] If that is the referent, then Amor is wholly to blame: once he had stolen the all-important twelfth foot, Ovid had to make do with what was left. As we have already noted, that earlier theft of Ovid's epic pretensions is—by far—the most direct divine intervention in Latin elegy: Amor didn't merely tell Ovid what kind of poetry he ought to write; he prevented him from writing any other kind. Responsibility for the results, Ovid argues from exile, ought at least to be shared, if not wholly displaced onto the god. And Amor agrees, at least in part (*Pont.* 3.3.67–76):

> 'per mea tela, faces, et per mea tela, sagittas,
>   per matrem iuro Caesareumque caput
> nil nisi concessum nos te didicisse magistro
>   artibus et nullum crimen inesse tuis.   70
> utque hoc, sic utinam defendere cetera possem!
>   scis aliud quod te laeserit esse magis.
> quidquid id est,—neque enim debet dolor ipse referri,
>   nec potes a culpa dicere abesse tua—
> tu licet erroris sub imagine crimen obumbres,   75
>   non grauior merito iudicis ira fuit…'

'By torches, my weapons of choice, and by arrows, also my weapons, and by my mother I swear and by the head of Caesar: I learned nothing under your tutelage except what was allowed, and there is no crime in your Ars. But would that I were able to defend you thus against the remaining charges! You know that there is something greater which harms you. Whatever it is—for the pain itself ought not to be talked about—however much you cover over your crime with the pretence of an error, the anger of the judge is not greater than deserved…'

---

[32] The fact that Amor is (seemingly) physically present makes Ovid's speech noticeably different both from the 'tragic' apostrophe and from normal human habits of internal monologue addressed to a god.

[33] See above, p. 153.

In response to Ovid's plea that he to try to mitigate the anger of Augustus, Amor agrees that he has *not* learned anything illegal from Ovid, then brings up the touchy subject of Ovid's *error* first mentioned in *Tristia* 2 (and there opposed to the offending *carmen*). Amor finishes by asserting that Augustus will forgive Ovid, probably shortly after the triumph.[34] And then the god departs; Ovid claims that Maximus, the poem's addressee, will certainly believe the story (unlike Lygdamus, who disavows belief in his own narrative).

Both Lygdamus' poem and Ovid's are deeply metapoetic, raising implicit questions about whether the divine visitations actually happened, but also more explicit questions about whether the content of those dreams were truthful in precisely the sense we have identified above, i.e. whether they will, or should, have effects in the extra-poetic world. They also revisit standard poetic questions about who is allowed to say what to whom, allowing poets to convey messages which they need not vouch for. Similarities between the two poems are sustained and noteworthy, and it is generally agreed that they bear some intrinsic relationship of dependence to one another.[35]

But, by way of conclusion, I'd like to revive the suggestion that the Augustan poet Gallus serves as a model for these two poems in particular and perhaps even for all divine appearances of Apollo in Latin elegiac poetry in general.[36] More particularly, I want to suggest that Gallus might be the first to have combined the two categories of literary epiphany I have separated out for the purposes of this chapter.[37] Compare, for instance, 3.4.57–8, where Apollo tells Lygdamus of Neaera's infidelity, to Vergil, *Ecl.* 10.21–3:

> *uenit Apollo:*
> *'Galle, quid insanis?' inquit; 'tua cura Lycoris*
> *perque nives alium perque horrida castra secuta est…'*

---

[34] The god refers to the triumph of Tiberius, celebrated in January 13 CE, which brought no change for Ovid, despite the optimism expressed in this poem.

[35] As always with Lygdamus, chronological questions remain unclear. For bibliography on the general question of Ovidian vs. Lygdaman priority, see above, n. 18; on this poem see Fulkerson (2017: *ad* 3.4).

[36] The idea of a Gallan source for Lygdamus seems to be first in Marx (1893: col. 1326), and was picked up on by Bürger (1903: 23). The latter suggested that Gallus too related an Apolline dream-vision in his poetry, and expressed the wish (as he does in *Eclogue* 10) that the unfaithful Lycoris come to no harm. Neither Marx nor Bürger makes a connection to the Ovidian poem.

[37] See n. 14 above for the suggestion that this conflation originates with Ennius. There is, of course, no way of knowing for certain.

Apollo came, and said, 'Gallus, are you mad? Your beloved Lycoris follows another through the snows and through the rugged camps...'

Gallus, of course, exists for us only in/as eleven lines, which have raised more questions than they answer. I would like to add to the lengthy list of things that might have been in Gallus' poetry[38] a divine epiphany of the god Apollo, saying something close to what he says to Gallus in Vergil's version of that moment. Servius *ad Ecl.* 10.26 mentions Apollo's own biography (*nam Apollo amauit Daphnen, Pan Syringa, Syluanus Cupressum*, 'for Apollo loved Daphne, Pan Syrinx, Sylvanus Cypressus'), so it might even be possible that Gallus' Apollo told some story of his own peccadillos, either the tale of Admetus or some other story.[39] So too, the informality with which Apollo addresses Gallus in *Eclogue* 10 has parallels in both of my two main texts, and may help to explain the more puzzling aspects of their tone.[40]

Vergil's Apollo tells Gallus that his girlfriend Lycoris follows another. That is, Apollo gives Gallus more or less the same message he will give Lygdamus, adding the motif of a journey. In addition to other points of contact with Lygdamus' poem,[41] the Gallus of Vergil speaks, wishing he

---

[38] See Anderson, Parsons, and Nisbet (1979) on the 'New Gallus' papyrus discoveries. Scholarly consensus seems to have come around again to the notion that portions of Vergil's *Eclogues*, *Georgic* 4, and some bits of Propertius, especially book 1, might well contain allusion to or even actual quotations from Gallus. More specifically, Gallus' poetry may have told, in some form, the stories of Milanion and Acontius (Ross 1975: 63, 73–4, 91; Conte 1986: 100–12; Rosen and Farrell 1986 date the motif to Callimachus). Our clearest testimony, Servius *ad Ecl.* 10.46, does not help as much as it might: the phrase *hi autem omnes versus Galli sunt, de ipsius translati carminibus*, 'but all these verses are Gallus'/Gallan, taken from his poetry', might mean either direct translation, with the necessary metrical changes, or simply that the themes are recognizably Gallan.

[39] Note too that at *Ecl.* 6.61–73 Gallus is connected to Apollo in a moment of poetic epiphany (he is given the reeds the Muses gave to Hesiod).

[40] The notion of love as madness is also thought by some to be a Gallan touch, appearing in elegy especially in the word *demens* and variants. Note the Propertian examples, which feature questions, the idea that travel provides no relief, and the appearance of Apollo: Prop. 1.5.1, 2.30.1–2, 3.3.13–16, *'quid tibi uis, insane?'* 'What do you want, madman?'; *'quo fugis a demens? nulla est fuga: tu licet usque | ad Tanain fugias, usque sequetur Amor'*, 'Where do you flee, crazy one? There is no escape: though you head all the way to Tanais, Amor will follow you all the way there'; *cum me Castalia speculans ex arbore Phoebus | sic ait aurata nixus ad antra lyra: | 'quid tibi cum tali, demens, est flumine? quis te | carminis heroi tangere iussit opus?'* Then Phoebus, espying me from his Castalian grove, leaned on his golden lyre, near a cave, and said, 'what do you want with such a stream, crazy one? Who told you to touch the work of heroic song?' Propertius 3.3 in particular is often recognized as a poem likely to owe much to Gallus (e.g. by Ross 1975: 121).

[41] Büchner (1965: 76–7) notes other potential Gallan allusions in 3.4, such as the phrase *blandas...querellas* (75); see too *tanta mala* of 82, which could well be a Gallan tag, and *crudelis* of *Ecl.* 10.29 with 3.4.61 and 95.

had been a pastoral poet instead of an elegiac one (31–43), expresses the hope that the story he has just heard might not be true, *nec sit mihi credere tantum* ('would that it were not for me to believe such a thing', 46), and addresses Lycoris directly, wishing her well, *a te ne frigora laedant! | a, tibi ne teneras glacies secet aspera plantas!* ('O, may the chill not harm you! O, may the harsh frost not cut your tender feet', 48–9). Like Lygdamus, then, Gallus may have taken no responsibility for his dire prediction-cum-curse of the abandoning *puella*. Lygdamus, however, seems to have innovated in using the metaleptic device of a literary divine epiphany as a way of manipulating events outside of his poem.[42] Ovid, as is typical for him, seems to have worked further changes on the theme, altering the identity of the god, the topic of the discussion, and the audacity of the disruption of planes.[43] For while Neaera might or might not exist outside of Lygdamus' poetry, though she is known to us only within it, Ovid's much bolder divine assertion describes the actions of an emperor who has his own reality, and predicts/hopes to provoke a decision which will have had much greater effects on his own life.[44]

---

[42] To me, the Ovidian changes seem to presuppose the Lygdaman ones, but, again, it is unclear which poem predates the other (see above, n. 18).

[43] See Armstrong (2004) on the characteristic Apollo-to-Amor shift. It is typical too of the exilic Ovid to offer a reversal of elegiac norms; compare the un-polishing of the book of poems at *Tristia* 1.1, and the pose throughout of Augustus as forcing Ovid to engage in long-distance *paraclausithura*.

[44] This presumes, of course, that Ovid's relegation to Tomis has an extra-poetic reality. Interestingly, we have no way of determining this, as Ovid is our only contemporary evidence (see Fitton Brown 1985 for the case against, Williams 1994 for sustained argument that it doesn't much matter): 'Tomitian exile' might be as real, or as fictional, as 'Neaera' is. But Augustus *does* have extra-fictional existence, such that Ovid's incorporation of him as a character into the poetry makes *Pont.* 3.3 an ontologically different sort of exercise from either Lygdamus' or Gallus' poem.

8
Metalepsis, Grief, and Narrative in *Aeneid* 2

Helen Lovatt

Aeneid 2 is a book of intense emotion. It is also a book of great narrative complexity: the first-person narrative of Aeneas slips in and out of focus, and Sinon tells his own story within it.[1] With so many narrative levels, the potential for metalepsis (fundamentally understood as breaking through narrative levels, as outlined by Genette) is high.[2] Further, epic as a genre, with its typical focus on the objective distance of the narrator, perhaps tends towards metaleptic moments in negotiating extended first-person narratives.[3] I am interested in the interactions between metalepsis and emotional responses to reading: for me, metalepsis is a phenomenon which requires and is open to interpretation.[4] Readers must decide what

* Many thanks to Gail Trimble and Sebastian Matzner for organizing the conference, including me in the volume, giving extremely constructive comments, and being patient in waiting for this contribution.

[1] The figure of Aeneas as narrator has received a certain amount of attention, but the concept of metalepsis has not yet been used to explore narrative in *Aeneid* 2, nor has the relationship between metalepsis and emotional response been much examined. On Aeneas as narrator see Casali (2003), Bowie (2008), Powell (2011). Bowie (2008) and Horsfall (2008) recognize many of the same moments as jarring, but neither discuss the connection between intense emotion and narratorial inconsistency. On inconsistency and reading Latin epic, see also O'Hara (2007). There is as ever much secondary literature on every aspect of Virgil. I will only skim the surface here and mention the pieces I have found most useful.

[2] 'Any intrusion by the extradiegetic narrator or narratee into the diegetic universe (or by diegetic characters into a metadiegetic universe) or the inverse' (Genette 1972 = 1980: 234–5).

[3] Perhaps generic expectations are as important for ancient readers as ontological expectations are for modern readers?

[4] Bell and Alber (2012) discuss the importance of interpretation in construing metalepsis; they are more interested in ontological metalepses, in which authors or characters are represented as not just looking or intruding into other narrative levels, but actually moving between them. So even Le Guin's *Lavinia* (2008) in which Virgil communicates with his character Lavinia through dreams and visions would not properly constitute metalepsis. The

Helen Lovatt, *Metalepsis, Grief, and Narrative in* Aeneid 2 In: *Metalepsis: Ancient Texts, New Perspectives*. Edited by: Sebastian Matzner and Gail Trimble, Oxford University Press (2020). © The editors and Oxford University Press. DOI: 10.1093/oso/9780198846987.003.0008

constitutes a break between narrative levels and what effects these jarring moments can have.[5] Virgil's *Aeneid* is a good text in which to explore these phenomena, because of its rich and varied tradition of readers and reading, and *Aeneid* 2 is one of the most frequently read and famous books.[6] This chapter addresses the question of the emotional functions of metalepsis: does narrative complexity intensify emotional engagement or make it bearable through moments of withdrawal?[7] How does metalepsis contribute to the representation of grief? Is there something metaleptic about intense emotion, especially grief, which can create a numbness or shock that separates the sufferer from a sense of reality?

The chapter begins with an examination of narrators and narrating in *Aeneid* 2. Both Aeneas and Sinon are fascinatingly complex narrators, who use their grief to establish authority and create a positive reception. This complexity encourages constant interplay between narrative levels, which creates dissonances for readers, but ultimately intensifies the emotional response of the various levels of audience. If Dido models the ideal response as created by the *Aeneid*, this text never intended to turn us off. The narrator's constant presence, in counterfactuals that remind us we are in the predetermined world of myth, the operation of hindsight which activates lament, and the irony more often associated with tragedy, do not alienate but draw us in.

The second section tackles narrative transition: ends of scenes and sequences and changes of setting are often characterized by emotional intensity and lack of narrative realism. Metalepsis often occurs at the edges of narrative, including problematization of the narrator's knowledge of

question of what counts as jarring is difficult, and culturally constructed: gods intervening in the action would appear metaleptic in a modern realist novel, but not at all in ancient epic. Similarly, transfictional metalepsis (a character from one story appearing in another) does not work in the ancient world, where story worlds are not securely separated off from each other or from historical 'reality'. Yet Diomedes' appearance in the *Aeneid* does feel to a certain extent transfictional, in that he is marked as the *Iliadic* Diomedes. For a discussion of yet another metaleptic constellation with bearings on literary interpretation, namely instances where it is not a character but an author that appears in another's fiction, see Kearey in this volume on 'secondary metalepsis'.

[5] It is likely that different readers will respond differently to features that have the potential to be metaleptic (on this question of reader response cf. Matzner in this volume). As a reader, I have changed a great deal: I remember with nostalgia childhood experiences of extreme immersion, in which not just the act of turning pages but the entire world disappeared around me as I read. Now, perhaps through training as an academic, or through a visual impairment which has radically slowed my reading speed, I get into a narrative with difficulty and remain constantly aware of its artificiality. Everything is metaleptic for me. It would be useful to have reading experience studies that focused on metalepsis.

[6] I will only be able to touch on these histories of reading, via the commentary tradition, due to lack of space.

[7] Cf. Fulkerson in this volume on metalepsis and emotion in elegiac contexts.

events, anachronism, and focus on the narrator's physical location. The chapter then examines the epic voice of Aeneas, beginning with similes, which also often feature at the ends of sections both as emotional high points and moments of self-conscious reflection for narrator and narratees. In many ways, Aeneas as narrator takes on the epic voice of the primary narrator, and Aeneas' narrative as well as that of the primary narrator shows through the other narrative levels.[8] When Polites dies *ante ora parentum* ('before the faces of his parents'), he is an image of the universality of epic death, and connects to Aeneas' own desire to die in the storm of book 1. This tendency of epic to speak across time and space as well as audience levels is reinforced by puns and intertextual references, which one would expect to create distance, but which can also serve to enhance immediacy. Most strikingly of all, when Priam is described as a headless body on the shore, the implied author intrudes with a reference to contemporary Rome and Pompey's death in the civil wars. This, too, claims the universality and contemporary relevance of mythic storytelling and seems likely to intensify engagement. Finally, I look briefly at Genette's phrase 'Virgil "has Dido die"' and how the death of Dido fits into these ideas about grief and narrative.

Narrators in *Aeneid* 2: Aeneas and Sinon

Aeneid book 2 sets a story within a story within a story: the primary narrator, telling posterity about the adventures of Aeneas, gives way to the first-person narrative of the hero himself, to Dido at a Carthaginian banquet, which contains the story of Sinon, set up to deceive the Trojans into bringing in the Trojan horse. It is a book that is fundamentally concerned with the breaking of boundaries: spear violating horse, horse violating city, Greeks penetrating ever further into the innermost heart of Trojan power. It is also a book of deep and powerful emotional engagement, grief, and trauma. When Aeneas agrees reluctantly to tell the story, he figures the process as an act of reliving and recreating his own pain:

> *conticuere omnes intentique ora tenebant.*
> *inde toro pater Aeneas sic orsus ab alto:*

---

[8] Bowie (2008: 48) feels that 'we should not simply take Aeneas' narration as a long story within a story, as a "realist" text, but as something more complex into which the narrator's voice intrudes, in a manner very reminiscent of Ovid.'

'*infandum, regina, iubes renouare dolorem,*
Troianas ut opes et lamentabile regnum
eruerint Danai, quaeque ipse miserrima uidi
et quorum pars magna fui. quis talia fando
Myrmidonum Dolopumue aut duri miles Vlixi
temperet a lacrimis? et iam nox umida caelo
praecipitat suadentque cadentia sidera somnos.
sed si tantus amor casus cognoscere nostros
et breuiter Troiae supremum audire laborem,
quamquam animus meminisse horret luctuque refugit,
incipiam.'

(**Aen. 2.1–13**)

All grew silent and held their faces intently,
and from there on his high couch, father Aeneas
     began thus:
'Unspeakable is the sorrow, O queen, you order me
     to recreate,
how the Danaans overturned Trojan wealth and the
     kingdom
deserving lament, those most wretched events
     which I myself saw
and of which I was a great part. Which one, in
     speaking such things,
of the Myrmidons or the Dolopes or even which
     soldier of hard Ulysses,
could refrain from tears? And now the damp night
     falls headlong
in the sky and the falling stars encourage sleep.
But if you have so great a love to recognize our
     downfall
and to hear in a short time the final labour of Troy,
although my mind shudders to remember and flees
     back from grief,
I will begin.'[9]

The inclusion of lines 1–2 reminds the reader that this is a first-person narrative within a third-person narrative poem, emphasizing the circumstances

---

[9] The text of the *Aeneid* is that of Conte (2009); translations are my own, with no pretensions to elegance, but an attempt to show how I read the Latin.

of telling and dramatizing the high expectations of the internal audience. Lines 3–13 in contrast have many features of the proem of an epyllion: a dedication to the speaker's sponsoring audience, a statement of the subject matter, a claim of the speaker's own authority as narrator.[10] Discussion of metalepsis, as Matzner argues,[11] requires a sense of the frames which are set up to be broken. These lines establish the narrating context of *Aeneid* 2, and have a particular focus on grief. Line 3 defines the story of book 2 as an *infandum...dolorem* ('unspeakable grief'). The two words bracket the line, taking the key positions in it, and defining the act of narrative as essentially paradoxical: the act of storytelling recreates a situation so horrifically painful that it should not be spoken.[12] Aeneas is a reluctant narrator, acting on the orders of Dido (*iubes*). Most importantly, he presents himself as not just telling, but reliving the experience in the verb *renouare* ('renew'). The whole Trojan story has now become a cause of lament (*lamentabile*, 4), even if the various audiences can position themselves temporally before the downfall. Throughout this first-person narrative Aeneas will play with the double temporal perspective created by his position as both character and narrator, in a way that seems metaleptic to me. This is reinforced by generic expectations, in which epic is characterized as a third-person, omniscient genre, in which the gods participate as characters. The tensions between Aeneas' role as epic narrator and his limited perspective as a mortal frequently surface in book 2, continually putting the seams of epic on display. This too is anticipated in the proem, which does not invoke the gods, but instead presents Dido as inspiration and audience, driven by desire for knowledge. Instead, Aeneas emphasizes his own authority as both witness and participant: *quaeque ipse miserrima uidi | et quorum pars magna fui* ('those most wretched events which I myself saw | and of which I was a great part', 5–6). Similarly, tensions between acting and viewing will surface, which might potentially lay the narrator open to criticism, and invite the narratees, both internal and external, to exercise the evaluative function which is often an aspect of the narrator's intrusion into the narrative, by evaluating the narrator himself.[13] If he is watching, why was he not acting? If he was acting, why was he acting in that way?[14] Aeneas' narrative

---

[10] On Aeneas' proem, see Gasti (2006). Powell (2011: 195) shows that this beginning functions as an *exordium* to a persuasive speech.

[11] Matzner in this volume, pp. 19–23.

[12] See Thorne (2016) on trauma and unspeakable narration.

[13] On the evaluative function of the narrator see Culler (1981: 185); Labov (1972: 366–75).

[14] Powell (2011) brilliantly outlines the apologetic functions of books 2 and 3 of the *Aeneid* and their workings as a speech of self-justification.

continually questions his own reliability as narrator in a way that reminds us of its status as rhetoric. This is already implicitly happening in the proem: *quis talia fando | Myrmidonum Dolopumue aut duri miles Vlixi | temperet a lacrimis?* ('Which one, in speaking such things, | of the Myrmidons or the Dolopes or even which soldier of hard Ulysses, | could refrain from tears?', 6–8). On the surface, this is a claim that even the direst enemies of Aeneas would be moved by the story, a claim for universal emotional impact, emotional authenticity so overwhelming that it transcends even the bitterest enmity. But it also implicitly emphasizes the bipartisan nature of the conflict, that there might be a very different story if told by a Greek. In particular, this sentence evokes the most obvious previous model for Aeneas, the *apologia* of Odysseus in *Odyssey* 9–12.[15] Odysseus' story, too, is told in the context of his grief, as he reacts to Demodocus' song of the Trojan horse like a woman lamenting her dead husband and captured city (*Od.* 8.523–30), and Alkinoos asks him to explain himself. This is his opportunity to persuade the Phaeacians to help him, even at the risk of divine punishment themselves. As he starts his story, he is described as πολύμητις ('wily', *Od.* 9.1), and he begins by focusing on his desire to return to Ithaca (9.21–36). For Odysseus the act of listening is traumatic, while the act of telling is therapeutic.[16] Aeneas represents the act of telling itself as traumatic. This perhaps serves to underline his difference from Odysseus, his trustworthiness in comparison to Odysseus' clever manipulations of his audience. But the comparison always threatens to collapse into similarity rather than difference. If the epic audience should expect a slippery and complex narrative, is Aeneas' sincerity jarring? His final prefatory gesture is towards the incommensurability of narrative and reality: what he tells now in the space of a night will only be a brief (*breuiter*) retelling in comparison to the enormity of the grief and destruction, both final and climactic (*supremum*) toil/achievement (*laborem*).[17] The work of telling the story cannot match the sublimity of living through the events. Aeneas' mind flees again (*refugit*) just as his body actually did, horrified by the memory and the prospect of remembering. All of this functions as a teaser for the audience, a trailer, a claim of the importance and drama of the story to come. The proem sets up the frame of Aeneas' narrative, but also begins the play on first and third person, speaking of the unspeakable, Aeneas as poet versus Aeneas as participant, and the temporal dislocations

---

[15] On reading Odysseus as liar, see Parry (1994).
[16] On therapy in Phaeacia, see Race (2014).
[17] Powell (2011: 195) marks this as a rhetorical trope.

of multiple narratees which characterize the narrative as a whole. Although it can be read on the surface as perfectly naturalistic and appropriate for its context, the proem invites readers to see metaleptic moves that highlight the artificiality of the narrative and are calculated precisely to increase the emotional impact of the narrative on the various levels of narratees, from Dido to Augustus to posterity.[18]

Aeneas is a subjective narrator who frequently reminds us of his presence in the text.[19] Although he is not omniscient, he does have the benefit of hindsight, and takes on the role of epic narrator in his style and attitude. Aeneas' narrative interjections often work on more than one level: so at 54–6, he reflects that Laocoon's spear throw could have and should have revealed the truth about the Trojan horse.

> *et, si fata deum, si mens non laeua fuisset,*
> *impulerat ferro Argolicas foedare latebras,*
> *Troiaque nunc staret, Priamique arx alta maneres.*
>
> (*Aen.* 2.54–6)
>
> And if the fates of the gods, if the controlling mind
>   had not been unfavourable,
> he would have compelled us to violate the Greek
>   concealment with iron,
> and Troy would now stand, and you, citadel of
>   Priam on high, would now remain.

On the surface this passage represents the natural denial of the bereaved narrator. He desperately longs to tell a story with a different outcome. On another level, however, the equivalence between *fata* and *mens* in this passage could be taken to imply that the embedded narrator here is complaining about the choices of the poet. *Mens* is generally taken to refer to the attitude of the Trojan people who did not believe Laocoon, but it could also suggest a controlling providence, perhaps the mind of Jupiter.[20]

---

[18] A metapoetic reading is possible without creating metaleptic effects, and not every reader need take the metapoetic path. However, the close association between Aeneas as narrator and Virgil as poet does create some moments in the narrative that are more obviously metaleptic in their effects.

[19] Virgil as subjective narrator: Heinze (1993); on Virgil's polycentric narrative: Conte (2007).

[20] See Powell (2011: 197), Horsfall (2008: 91–2) for a summary of this debate.

Ultimately, neither Virgil nor Aeneas can change myth enough to prevent the fall of Troy. Aeneas as narrator can only remind his audiences that everything could have been different, bringing out the tragic irony of the Trojans' lack of knowledge and understanding, the tiny changes of causation which lead to massive outcomes, but the ultimate inevitability of myth and history.[21] This counterfactual certainly heightens emotional engagement and evokes lament: it also reminds us that this is a story being told by a character who was actually there, but now can no longer intervene.[22] Counterfactuals bring out the inner workings of myth as narrative.[23]

Aeneid 2 plays around even further with the mechanics of narration, going beyond the *Odyssey*, since Aeneas' narrative contains an inset narrative from a deliberately deceptive narrator, the Greek Sinon, who persuades the Trojans to bring the horse into Troy. The introduction of a false narrator inevitably reflects on the primary internal narrator and on narrative as an act of persuasion. The existence of Sinon to take on the role of 'lying Odysseus' could protect Aeneas by contrast from the accusation of inhabiting that role, or it could contaminate both the external and internal narrators with its problematization of narrative. Either way, narratees both internal and external must become more aware of the close connection between narrative and persuasion. Sinon also serves as object of blame, a way of grounding the inevitable anger of grief. When Aeneas introduces Sinon, he does so in didactic and evaluative mode, as an *exemplum* of Greek perjury:

> *accipe nunc Danaum insidias et crimine ab uno*
> *disce omnis.*
> *namque ut conspectu in medio turbatus, inermis,*
> *constitit atque oculis Phrygia agmina circumspexit,*
> *'heu! quae nunc tellus,' inquit, 'quae me aequora possunt*
> *accipere?'*
>
> **(*Aen.* 2.65–70)**

---

[21] Horsfall (2008: 198) shows how Aeneas creates degrees of identification and detachment from the Trojan perspective through his use of first-person and third-person plural verbs.

[22] Aeneas has a slightly Lucanian narrative voice, which is fundamentally a grieving voice, in that he desires to undo the story he is telling. He does not go as far as Lucan in viewing himself as actually recreating the events that he loathes, as in the *poeta creator* motif, explored by Lieberg (1982), but he does show some elements of the 'split voice', as discussed in Masters (1993). Narratives of grief, then, tend towards metalepsis.

[23] On counterfactuals see Cowan (2010).

> Hear now the treacheries of the Danaans and from
>   one crime learn all.
> For as he stood in the sight of all, disturbed,
>   unarmed,
> and looked around with his eyes at the Phrygian
>   columns,
> 'Alas! What land now,' he said, 'what sea can receive
>   me now?'

Aeneas as narrator makes his hindsight clear, along with his judgement and evaluation. Telling the story is equated to teaching, listening to learning. The very explicit narratorial push jars and invites resistance. But what do we learn? That vulnerability can be a position of strength, and suffering can be used to validate and persuade. Sinon's visibility should make him powerless, but he takes control of the gaze by assessing his audience (*circumspexit*, 'he looked around', 68). He begins by performing lament. More specifically, he uses his grief for Palamedes, and Palamedes' epic fame, to authenticate his own fictions:

> *'cuncta equidem tibi, rex, fuerit quodcumque, fatebor*
> *uera,' inquit; 'neque me Argolica de gente negabo.*
> *hoc primum; nec, si miserum Fortuna Sinonem*
> *finxit, uanum etiam mendacemque improba finget.*
> *fando aliquod si forte tuas peruenit ad auris*
> *Belidae nomen Palamedis et incluta fama*
> *gloria, quem falsa sub proditione Pelasgi*
> *insontem infando indicio, quia bella uetabat,*
> *demisere neci, nunc cassum lumine lugent'*
> (***Aen.*** **2.77–85**)

> 'I will confess all the things indeed to you, O king,
>   whatever will have happened,
> truthfully,' he said; 'nor will I deny that I am from the
>   Argive race.
> This first: if Fortune has modelled Sinon as wretched,
> she will not also model him wickedly as empty
>   and lying.
> If something by chance has reached your ears
>   from speech,

the name of Palamedes son of Belus and the fame
   of his renowned
glory, whom through deceitful betrayal the Pelasgians
sent down to death, innocent, in an unspeakable
   indictment, because
he forbade the war, now they grieve for the light
   in vain'

The densely packed words of speaking, confession, and fiction (*fatebor*, *negabo, finxit, finget, fando, fama, infando*) insist that the narratees be on the lookout for wordplay. Everything in this speech demands to be read on (at least) two levels, reminding us throughout that the speech is created by Sinon, Aeneas, and Virgil. First Sinon claims he will confess the truth, but the next clause underpins this claim with the sophistic argument that if Sinon is wretched he cannot also be a liar. The secondary internal (Carthaginian) and external audiences in fact know that Sinon is not wretched, but is a liar, while the immediate Trojan audience can take the statement at face value. Sinon uses his performance of grief to authenticate what he says and persuade the Trojans, but Aeneas uses his wordplay on the next level up of the narrative to play a trick for the audience to see through. Secondary narratees must read this speech differently from primary narratees. This interplay of different audience levels is created by Aeneas' hindsight and is almost certainly metaleptic for external narratees.

Later Sinon breaks off his speech to make sure that his audience are irrevocably hooked:

'*sed quid ego haec autem nequiquam ingrata reuoluo,*
quidue moror? si omnis uno ordine habetis Achiuos,
idque audire sat est, iamdudum sumite poenas:
hoc Ithacus uelit et magno mercentur Atridae.'
Tum uero ardemus scitari et quaerere causas,
ignari scelerum tantorum artisque Pelasgae.
prosequitur pauitans et ficto pectore fatur
                                                (*Aen.* 2.101–7)

'But why do I unroll this unwelcome tale in vain,
why do I delay? If you hold all Achaeans in one rank,

it is enough to hear that, take your punishment now:
the Ithacan wants this and the sons of Atreus are
   greatly rewarded.'
Then indeed we burn to know more and seek
   the causes,
unaware of such great crimes and Pelasgian skill.
He pursues panicking and speaks with deceitful heart

The act of breaking off the story symbolizes the breaking of its frame,[24] and the self-consciousness of Sinon's narrating tends towards narratorial metalepsis, bringing out the guiding presence of both Aeneas and Virgil. First he represents himself as a Roman reader winding back the roll (*reuoluo*).[25] Then *si omnis uno ordine habetis Achiuos* ('if you hold *all* Achaeans *in one rank*', 102) clearly echoes Aeneas' introduction *accipe nunc Danaum insidias et crimine ab uno | disce omnis* ('Hear now the treacheries of the Danaans and from *one crime* | learn *all*', 65–6), as *ficto pectore* from the internal narrator evokes the key repetition of *finxit…finget* (80) at the beginning of Sinon's speech.[26] Sinon thus slips into the role of self-conscious reader of the poem, while Aeneas uses Sinon's speech to reinforce his narrative evaluations for the reader.[27] There could also be a double meaning in his phrase *sumite poenas* ('take punishment', 103), which on the surface encourages the Trojans to extract punishment from Sinon, but might also imply procuring their own punishment by believing him.[28] Similarly, what Odysseus, Agamemnon, and Menelaus want is precisely that the Trojans should believe him, not that they should punish

---

[24] A similar break characterizes the transition from ekphrasis back into narrative at the end of the description of the gates at Cumae (6.30–9). Daedalus' depiction broke off with his inability to recreate the death of his own son; at the same moment of intensity, Aeneas' viewing is broken off by the Sibyl's intervention. Here too the movement between inset ekphrasis and framing narrative functions to draw back from and intensify emotional engagement. See Fitzgerald (1984).

[25] Horsfall (2008: 124) notes this metaphor.

[26] Possibly *ficto pectore* might reverse Aeneas' own ability to suppress emotions and fake for the sake of persuasion: *spem uultu simulat, premit altum corde dolorem* ('he pretends hope on his face, and presses grief deep in his heart', 1.209). While Sinon pretends to be in a state of grief but is actually hopeful, Aeneas pretends to be hopeful when he is actually grieving.

[27] Or, as Horsfall (2008: 128) following Servius puts it, 'V[irgil] is careful to remind his readers that they are still in the middle of a tissue of lies.'

[28] *OLD* 6a 'to take money, resources etc from a source, get, procure' is juxtaposed with 6b 'to exact (punishment or retribution)'.

him. The heavy irony and wordplay throughout Sinon's speech continually blurs the boundary between levels of narrative. A further level of irony exists for the external narratee, who can also see parallels between Aeneas and Sinon, Dido and the Trojans. As the Trojans react with desire to know (*ardemus*, 'we burn'), both levels of irony are activated: the city of Troy will burn, as will Dido (both emotionally and literally). The pleasure and horror of Aeneas' narrative lies precisely in the way his knowledge as narrator is overlaid on his experience as character. The *ars* of this speech is not just that of Sinon's Greek cunning, but also Aeneas as narrator and Virgil as poet, further brought out by the imitation of Sinon's stammering in *prosequitur pauitans*. The extreme artifice of the storyteller has as powerful an effect on the internal and external narratees as Sinon had on the Trojans. When Sinon literally breaks off his story he also breaks the frame of his story, and every word that he says keeps on breaking it. This irony is more characteristic of tragedy than epic, but cannot really be said to jar against the expectations of the external audience, given the story and the narrator.[29] Movement between narrative levels, rhetorical and ironic, here at least, is clearly an intensifier: in Carthage, Dido identifies intensely with Aeneas (but is this true of the other Carthaginians?); Roman readers and readers down the ages identify in a different way with Aeneas by doing the intellectual work to appreciate his double perspective. Heavy irony complicates and creates paradoxes, makes us desire more, just as the Trojans do. I'm a little in love with Aeneas myself at the moment. And Virgil.

Scene Changes and Metaleptic Moments

Metalepsis often occurs at the beginnings and ends of scenes or narrative units. As the story moves from one setting and group of characters to another, it is particularly noticeable that the narrative does not straightforwardly replicate reality. The choices of the narrator are particularly apparent. Fludernik discusses scene changes in novels, and the category of 'discourse metalepsis' or the deliberate filling of narrative time with narrator

[29] Mythical material encourages self-conscious reading, because readers always know in advance what the outcome is supposed to be and are always aware of different possible levels of reading it. The rhetorical education of ancient readers would also lend itself towards a heightened sensitivity to narrating situations. If the dominance of the realist novel as a narrative form creates the category of metalepsis, metalepsis must function differently in the rhetorical, mythical ancient world.

intervention that is particularly associated with temporal disjunctions or simultaneity: 'dear reader, while the characters walk, let us view the new setting'.[30] For me, this metaleptic move in realist fiction bears a close family resemblance to the use of ekphrasis at moments of narrative transition in ancient epic, particularly prevalent in Ovid's *Metamorphoses*.[31] But how metaleptic are these moments? Do we in fact expect a certain narrative tremor, as it were, at the edges of a narrative unit? *Aeneid* 2 has some striking scene changes and the book's most metaleptic moments come at the end of sequences. The counterfactual narrative interjection we have just examined comes at the end of the first Laocoon scene just before the arrival of Sinon is heralded with an *ecce* ('Behold!').[32] At 429–37, Aeneas and the scene move from a generalized battle in the streets of Troy to the sequence of events at Priam's palace:

> *nec te tua plurima, Panthu,*
> *labentem pietas nec Apollinis infula texit.*
> *Iliaci cineres et flamma extrema meorum,*
> *testor, in occasu uestro nec tela nec ullas*
> *uitauisse uices, Danaum et, si fata fuissent*
> *ut caderem, meruisse, manu. diuellimur inde,*
> *Iphitus et Pelias mecum (quorum Iphitus aeuo*
> *iam grauior, Pelias et uulnere tardus Vlixi),*
> *protinus ad sedes Priami clamore uocati.*
>
> (Aen. 2.429–37)

> Nor did your many kindnesses, Panthus,
> protect you as you slipped away nor the fillet
>   of Apollo.
> Ashes of Ilium and final flames of my own city,
> I call you to witness, that in your fall I did not avoid
>   any weapons
> or any dangers, and if the fates had been that I should
> fall by the hand of the Greeks, I deserved it. We are
>   torn away from there,

---

[30] Fludernik (2003b).

[31] On Ovid, transition, and ekphrasis see Lovatt (2013: 177–80). On duality of irony and empathy in the ekphrasis of Juno's temple, see Amir (2009).

[32] On scene changes in Virgil and Statius, see Lovatt (2019). This is a moderate scene change, part of the longer Trojan horse sequence, in the same location, but a significant change of direction with the entrance of Sinon. The word *ecce* signifies a sudden or 'quick cut' scene change. On the 'quick cut' in Tacitus see Waddell (2013).

> Iphitus and Pelias along with me (of whom Iphitus
> was now
> heavier through age, and Pelias slow through a
> wound from Ulysses),
> immediately we were called by the shouting to the
> palace of Priam.

This passage has several metaleptic features: the apostrophe of Panthus as he dies is a fairly standard epic feature, which the epic narrator uses to heighten the emotional connection with minor characters.[33] But this apostrophe is also in the voice of Aeneas, who can literally call on a friend from his past.[34] Further, it develops into a much more unusual address to the events themselves to prove the truth of Aeneas' narrative, which I think must have been jarring even in the context of ancient epic poetry in which apostrophe was much more common than in modern literature.[35] The apostrophes also mark an attempt by Aeneas the narrator to connect with the actions of his past self, at the same time that he justifies himself to his audience, displaying the guilt of the bereaved.[36] The change from the past tense of Panthus' death and the perfect infinitives of Aeneas' reflections on his past actions into the present passive of *diuellimur* suggests a resubmersion of Aeneas the narrator as character in the narrative, brought back to normal in the past tense of *uocati*, while the sense of *diuellimur* ('we are torn away') carries the opposite implication, creating a further paradox of immersion and alienation.[37] Emotion seems to intensify at the moment of rupture: perhaps emotion causes the narrator to break the narrative illusion in order to engage with his own guilt.

After the physical movement from one place to another, the huge battle at Priam's palace is described, including an anachronistic *testudine* ('tortoise

---

[33] Cf. Budelmann, De Jong, and Trimble in this volume on apostrophe, as well as Matzner in this volume on cultural-historically specific frameworks for any assessment of the impact of metalepses.

[34] Thanks to Gail Trimble for this point, and a possible connection with the shared lamentation at *Aen.* 1.217–22 where Aeneas and his men call on their lost comrades. Virgil's language suggests speaking to and calling on the dead: *amissos longo socios sermone requirunt* ('They search for their lost allies with long speech', 1.217); *nec iam exaudire uocatos* ('no longer hear when they are called', 1.219). Aeneas is presented here as using typically epic epithets to address the dead: along with *pius Aeneas* ('dutiful Aeneas') we have *acris Oronti* ('fierce Orontes', 1.220) and *fortem Gyan* ('strong Gyas', 1.222).

[35] On apostrophe in the *Aeneid*: D'Alessandro Behr (2005); on apostrophe as a trope of Roman epic: Georgacopoulou (2005), D'Alessandro Behr (2007).

[36] On typical stages and emotions of bereavement, see Parkes (1986).

[37] Thanks to Gail Trimble for this point.

formation', 441). Is this anachronism designed to create 'immediacy', as Horsfall suggests?[38] If this detail makes the fall of the city feel more familiar to a Roman audience, can it be felt to be metaleptic?[39] But the explicit involvement of the narrator's emotions is also a realistic representation of what it is like to hear someone telling a story. It is not at all clear that making the seams of storytelling visible distances rather than involves readers.

The transition to the next sequence, the climactic deaths of Polites and Priam, is completed at 453–9, with a brief ekphrasis and a change of perspective:

> *limen erat caecaeque fores et peruius usus*
> *tectorum inter se Priami postesque relicti*
> *a tergo, infelix qua se, dum regna manebant,*
> *saepius Andromache ferre incomitata solebat*
> *ad soceros et auo puerum Astyanacta trahebat.*
> *euado ad summi fastigia culminis, unde*
> *tela manu miseri iactabant inrita Teucri.*
>
> *(Aen.* **2.453–9)**

There was a threshold and dark doors and a way
    through
between the halls of Priam, an entrance abandoned
at the back, through which unfortunate
    Andromache, while
the kingdom was still standing, often took herself
    unaccompanied
to her parents-in-law and dragged the boy Astyanax
    to his grandfather.
I escape to the gables of the high roof, from where
wretched Trojans were throwing weapons from
    their hands in vain.

---

[38] Horsfall (2008: 342). Cf. Bing in this volume on anachronism.

[39] This example emphasizes the way that metalepsis is a matter of interpretation: if a reader stopped to think about whether or not tortoise formations were an appropriate thing to find in a narrative of the fall of Troy, that would inevitably break the frame of Aeneas' narrative and remind the external reader that this is in fact a fiction created by a Roman. But if they did not notice this as an anachronism, it would have the opposite effect by making them feel that ancient Trojans were more like them.

Here Aeneas takes the bird's-eye view of the omniscient epic narrator, but then literalizes that vertical perspective by claiming that he can see these events unfold from the roof of the palace. The shift to the roof is unexplained, and arguably jarring: Austin comments (*ad loc.*), 'Indeed one of the very few things in this Book that can be criticized is the amount of time spent by Aeneas on roofs.' Aeneas is claiming the ability to see into previously unseen spaces (hence *caecae*, 'blind', used for 'secret') and rationalizing the poet's decision to allow the narrator to see a number of key events which he probably would not have seen. This authorial metalepsis is muddied by Aeneas' explicit focalization through his narrating self, in which he connects the location with Andromache, soon to be widowed, and Astyanax, soon to be murdered, bringing out the dramatic irony of his position as both character and narrator, emphasized further by calling the Trojans *miseri* ('wretched') and their weapons *inrita* ('in vain'). The tensions between the traditional third-person narrative of epic and the first-person narrative of Aeneas are particularly evident in this passage.

There follows a description of Pyrrhus breaking into the palace, coming to a climax with Aeneas' listing of the famous moments of destruction that follow:

> *uidi ipse furentem*
> *caede Neoptolemum geminosque in limine Atridas,*
> *uidi Hecubam centumque nurus Priamumque per aras*
> *sanguine foedantem quos ipse sacrauerat ignis.*
> *quinquaginta illi thalami, spes tanta nepotum,*
> *barbarico postes auro spoliisque superbi*
> *procubuere; tenent Danai, qua deficit ignis.*
> *forsitan et, Priami fuerint quae fata, requiras.*
> (*Aen.* 2.499–506)

> I myself saw Neoptolemus
> raging in the slaughter and the twin sons of Atreus
>   on the threshold,
> I saw Hecuba and her hundred daughters-in-law
>   and Priam befouling
> the altars with blood, the altars which he himself
>   consecrated with fire.
> Those fifty bedchambers, such great hope of
>   descendants,

> the doorposts proud with barbarian gold and spoils,
> all fell; the Danaans hold them, where the fire fails.
> Perhaps also you might ask what was the fate
> of Priam.

Here the scene of general destruction in the palace of Priam moves into specific focus on Priam's death. Aeneas (and Virgil) bring this overview to a climax with the repetition of Aeneas' emphatic witnessing: *uidi ipse…uidi* ('I myself saw…I saw', 499, 501) and a roll call of the famous events in a nutshell: the key Greek aggressors, Neoptolemus, son of Achilles, Agamemnon, and Menelaus; Hecuba and Priam with their wealth and prolific family, all about to be wiped out. Priam's death is anticipated, out of narrative sequence, along with the ritual pollution and sacrilege of his death on the altars. The passage finishes with a change to the present tense, as if describing an image rather than narrating a sequence of events. The next scene is initiated with a move back to the perspective and experience of the internal narrator and audience, Aeneas anticipating questions from Dido, which can also, of course, function as a standard rhetorical question from author to reader, and is designed to move from summary and overview to the specific scene of Priam's death. It does break the rhythm of the preceding passage, but I am not sure whether that variation has a metaleptic effect.

We have certainly seen that the narrator comes to the surface at moments of transition, and that the ends of scenes are associated with high emotional intensity, although it is difficult to assess whether such climactic passages are distancing or suturing. It is possible that emotional intensity and immediacy allow the narrator (and author) to take greater liberties with narratee and audience expectations. In the heat of battle, as it were, the odd tortoise escapes notice.

Death and Epic: Polites and Priam

Scenes in epic often end with a simile. Similes are a key feature of epic style, and Aeneas uses them frequently, in a way that brings out the similarity of his first-person narrative to the main epic narrative.[40] I would argue that similes have a weak metaleptic effect, by evoking worlds and

---

[40] Horsfall (2008: xvii) argues that the total of nine (or ten) similes in the section 223–631 is significant, although books 9, 10, and 12 have higher total numbers. Book 2, of course, is a book of battle narrative.

ideas outside the narrative time and space. An extreme example of this is Valerius Flaccus' comparison of the battle with Cyzicus to the eruption of Vesuvius (3.208–11). Further, similes cause a pause in narrative progression, and put thematic and symbolic dimensions of interpretation at the forefront. Quite often, Aeneas' similes have additional twists of self-consciousness that increase this effect: at 304–8 the Greek overthrow of Troy, watched by Aeneas from his father's roof, is compared to both a forest fire and a river in flood (as if incorporating a battle of the elements), with the additional touch of an internal spectator: *stupet inscius alto | accipiens sonitum saxi de uertice pastor* ('shocked and unaware a shepherd hears the sound from the high peak of a rock', 307–8). The comparison at 355–60 of the band of young Trojans, resisting, to a pack of wolves defending their cubs, reverses normal expectations of wolf similes, where a pack of wolves is normally predatory, not defensive. Further, Aeneas follows this simile with the typical epic topos of narratorial inadequacy in the face of his material: *quis cladem illius noctis, quis funera fando | explicet aut possit lacrimis aequare labores?* ('Who might untangle the disaster of that night and the deaths by speaking, or who could equal the labours with his tears?', 361–2). Grief and confusion go hand in hand in this narratorial intervention, which both establishes Aeneas' authority as epic narrator, claims the sublimity of his subject matter, and emphasizes the overwhelming panic and grief which make any narrative ultimately an artificial reconstruction. At 376–83 a double reversal compares the Greek Androgeos realizing that he has been attacked by disguised Trojans to a man who steps on a snake without knowing it. The Trojans are assimilated to snakes, and the internal observer represents the Greek character: yet both snake and man are in danger of being destroyed. Similes do not create simple emotional identification: like anachronism they are seen as aiding immediacy, yet they require a step away from the narrative context and an act of (complex) interpretation. Further, at 416–19, the Trojans are caught up in attacks from all sides, which are compared to multiple storm winds creating a cosmic disturbance. This simile too goes beyond the normal equation of battle with storm, and evokes the magnitude and turbulence of the storm in *Aeneid* 1 (1.84–6 also mentions *Eurusque Notusque... Africus*; here we have *Zephyrusque Notusque et... Eurus*, 417–18). This arguably offers the opportunity to read a weak authorial metalepsis, since Aeneas cannot have known of the description of the storm in which he himself was almost killed, but it is not a jarring connection that demands reader attention. The most important simile in book 2 is probably 624–31 when Venus has given Aeneas temporary access to the divine gaze, allowing him to see the divine action missing from his first-person narrative. The gods, however, only appear in Venus' speech and through the simile which Aeneas uses to attempt to convey his sublime vision: the city literally subsiding, like a tree cut down by multiple axemen. The additional frisson of first-person narrative adds slightly more metaleptic force to epic similes, which both generate emotional power and create distance, play, and complexity. Aeneas' simile of the gods as axemen brings to a climax his narrative of the city's initial destruction, his resistance and witnessing, before the next sequence in which he persuades Anchises to escape from the city.

An even more metaleptic moment brings to an end the section describing the death of Priam. Priam's death is initiated by that of Polites, which also has metaleptic features:

> *ecce autem elapsus Pyrrhi de caede Polites,*
> *unus natorum Priami, per tela, per hostis,*
> **porticibus longis fugit et uacua atria** *lustrat*
> *saucius. illum ardens infesto uulnere Pyrrhus*
> *insequitur, iam iamque manu tenet et premit*
> *hasta. ut tandem* **ante oculos** *euasit et* **ora**
> > **parentum,**
> *concidit ac multo uitam cum sanguine* **fudit.**
> > (*Aen.* **2.526–32**)

> But look! Slipped away from the slaughter of
> > Pyrrhus, Polites,
> one of the sons of Priam, through the weapons,
> > through the enemies,
> *he flees through the long porticoes and* looks around
> > *the empty atria*
> wounded. Him, burning, hostile because of the
> > wound, Pyrrhus
> pursues, and now, now he has him by the hand and
> > presses
> with the spear. When at last he came out *before the*
> > *eyes and faces of his parents,*
> he fell and *poured out* his life with much blood.

Polites' sudden appearance creates a quick cut and models Aeneas' visual experience as witness. Nearly every word of this passage creates immediacy: the repetition of *per* shows him passing through one obstacle after another;

the verbs in the present tense (*fugit, lustrat*) display his panic as he searches for some sort of escape; the enjambment of *insequitur* mimics the pursuit of Pyrrhus, and *iam iamque* winds up the intensity still further. *Tenet* and *premit* give quick short movements, and the spear itself penetrates the next line. The moment of death is marked by a change back into the past tense. Yet even in this frenzy of action there is alienation and distancing. Pyrrhus is *ardens*, not just because he is very enthusiastic about killing Polites, but also because it is a pun on his name (Greek for fiery), which I would count as a weak authorial metalepsis.[41] The focalization moves from Aeneas to Polites (looking around) to Pyrrhus (desiring to kill) and finally back out to the whole scenario, with the epic audience watching the parents viewing as their son dies. The phrase *ante ora parentum* is loaded with gnomic and tragic significance: children should not die before their parents, in time and especially not in space.[42] Horsfall points out a number of occurrences of the phrase, and similar phrases, but not the connection that sprang first to my mind.[43] Aeneas himself at 1.95 wishes, in his first appearance during the storm, that he had died *ante ora patrum Troiae sub moenibus altis* ('before the faces of the fathers under the high walls of Troy', *Aen.* 1.95), and that he had 'poured out his life' (*animam effundere*, 98) at the right hand of Diomedes. While the death of Polites is unnatural, even criminal, because it takes place at the heart of his house and literally before the eyes of his parents, Aeneas longs for an appropriate epic death in battle, at home, protecting his father and his ancestral city. The long view of epic poetry requires that both ancestors and descendants are always watching, and this awareness of nested spectators never quite allows complete immersion in the moment.[44] The more intense the emotional impact, the higher the awareness that all those down the ages have been and will be watching.

---

[41] O'Hara (1996: 133). The self-consciousness of the pun is in contrast to the pace and immediacy of the surrounding narrative, and this contrast can work to remind us of the layers of narrating in operation here. Although Aeneas *could* make a pun on Pyrrhus' name, since he knows all the information required to do so (unless he is speaking Trojan, of course), the pun does seem much more in keeping with the narrative mode of the primary narrator, who is not reliving his own past trauma, but presenting a work of art.

[42] O'Sullivan (2009) explores the possible metapoetic resonances of the phrase.

[43] Horsfall (2008: 406) on this phrase plus *ante ora patris* and *ora parentum*: *Georg.* 4.477; *Aen.* 2.263; 2.681; 5.553; 5.576; 6.308; 11.887. The idea is found in Greek epigram and Greek literature about Roman civil war (Plu. *Sull.* 31; Cassius Dio 51.2.6).

[44] A macabre twist on the expansive epic audience are the ghosts of Amycus' victims watching his defeat at Valerius Flaccus 4.258–60, recapitulated with a ghostly audience for the duel of Polynices and Eteocles at Statius, *Thebaid* 11.420–3.

With the death of Priam himself this metaleptic effect goes a stage further. The final lines of the section sum up the horror of Priam's death, but end with a jarring reference to the world outside the text:

> *haec finis Priami fatorum; hic exitus illum*
> *sorte tulit, Troiam incensam et prolapsa uidentem*
> *Pergama, tot quondam populis terrisque superbum*
> *regnatorem Asiae. iacet ingens litore truncus,*
> *auulsumque umeris caput et sine nomine corpus.*
> *at me tum primum saeuus circumstetit horror.*
> *obstipui; subiit cari genitoris imago,*
> *ut regem aequaevum crudeli uulnere uidi*
> *uitam exhalantem;*
>
> (*Aen.* 2.554–62)

> This was the end of the fate of Priam; this death brought
> to him by lot, as he sees Troy burnt and Pergamum
> collapsed, once proud ruler of so many peoples
> and lands in Asia. He lies a huge trunk on the shore
> head torn from his shoulders and a body without
> a name.
> But savage horror then for the first time surrounded
> me.
> I was stupefied: the image of my dear father came
> to me,
> as I saw the equal-aged king with his cruel wound
> breathing out his life.

Priam has just been killed on the altar; why is he now suddenly a headless body? He was in the middle of his palace in Troy.[45] Why is he now suddenly lying on the shore? Servius gives an ancient (though still several centuries later) explanation of the lines: *Pompei tangit historiam, cum 'ingens' dicit non 'magnus'* ('This touches on the story of Pompey, since he says "huge" instead of "great"').[46] This pun on Pompey's epithet *Magnus* is metaleptic: there is no reason to think that Priam, an old man, was physically huge, although the significance of his death clearly was. Bowie

---

[45] Bowie (1990).
[46] Servius' interpretation evokes the rhetorical sense of metalepsis as a reference through the transferred meaning of words. See Matzner in this volume.

calls this 'a remarkable example of narrative dislocation'.[47] Servius also found the need to explain *litus*, not very convincingly, as a way of saying 'ground'.[48] Further arguments, following Bowie, for understanding this climactic description as a reference to the death of Pompey include the fact that Pompey and Priam are paired as examples of the fall of great men elsewhere in Roman discourse;[49] Priam is called *regnatorem Asiae* ('ruler of Asia'), where Pompey had his most significant victories; Pompey was renowned for his pride, brought out by the word *superbum*; Lucan seems to have made this connection in his description of the death of Pompey at *B.C.* 8.698–710. If we accept that these otherwise confusing lines are a reference to the death of Pompey, and current orthodoxy in the form of the most recent commentary by Horsfall does so, if rather grudgingly, then this is a convincing authorial metalepsis. The author breaks into Aeneas' narrative to sum up the moral lesson of the fall of Troy, and draw the attention of his Roman readers to recent parallels in their own history, which emphasize the contingency of history. At the emotional climax of Aeneas' story, the end of the sequence and the moment of his greatest pain so far, the narrative draws back from the immediate context to survey the wider implications of the fall of empires, and its relevance for contemporary Roman history. This metalepsis increases the sense of significance and universality for the narrative, as well as drawing on the emotional engagement of the Roman audience with their own recent involvement in civil war, violence in the city, and the death of a much-loved and admired historical figure. Grief tends to figure the personal as universal, and to create stronger empathy with similar situations: this drawing together of the tragedy of Troy with the tragedy of the Roman civil war surely increases the emotional power of Virgil's poetry.

---

[47] Bowie (1990: 473).

[48] There was a tradition, according to Servius, from Pacuvius, in which Priam was killed by Pyrrhus at the tomb of Achilles by the shore. But the narrative of *Aeneid* 2 focuses on the alternative tradition in which he dies at the altars in the palace in the middle of Troy. There are no hints to the alternative tradition to signpost a change to it: and even if this is the explanation for the confusing location of Priam's death, this too would be metaleptic since it would require readers to remember that there are multiple mythic traditions of the same event, and Aeneas as internal narrator does not and cannot know these traditions, so it would again make the primary narrator break into the secondary narrative. On Pacuvius in this episode see Horsfall (2010).

[49] Cic. *Tusc.* 1.85–6; *Div.* 2.22; Manilius 4.50–65; Juvenal 10.258–72, 283–6.

The Death of Dido

Genette uses the death of Dido as a key example of metalepsis.[50] He cites Fontanier's commentary on Dumarsais' *Tropes* for the idea that the poet 'himself brings about the effects he celebrates', as for instance 'when we say Virgil "has Dido die" in book IV of the *Aeneid*'.[51] If we look at the description of Dido's death, it is not clear in what sense 'Virgil has Dido die'. Dido is on the point of death, in Anna's arms at 690–2, when the perspective shifts to that of Juno:

> *tum Iuno omnipotens, longum miserata dolorem*
> *difficilisque obitus, Irim demisit Olympo,*
> *quae luctantem animam nexosque resolueret artus.*
> *nam quia nec fato, merita nec morte peribat,*
> *sed misera ante diem subitoque accensa furore,*
> *nondum illi flauum Proserpina uertice crinem*
> *abstulerat Stygioque caput damnauerat Orco.*
> *ergo Iris croceis per caelum roscida pinnis,*
> *mille trahens uarios aduerso sole colores,*
> *deuolat et supra caput adstitit. 'hunc ego Diti*
> *sacrum iussa fero teque isto corpore soluo':*
> *sic ait et dextra crinem secat; omnis et una*
> *dilapsus calor atque in uentos uita recessit.*
>
> (*Aen.* 4.693–705)

Then almighty Juno, pitying her long agony and painful dying, sent Iris down from heaven to release her struggling soul from the prison of her flesh. For since she perished neither in the course of fate nor by a death she had earned, but wretchedly before her day, in the heat of sudden frenzy, not yet had Proserpine taken from her head the golden lock and

---

[50] See Kearey in this volume in some detail on this as an example of 'secondary metalepsis', when a critic breaks through the frame between criticism and text.

[51] Fludernik (2003b: 396 n. 2); Genette (1972 = 1980: 234 n. 49). Genette's phrase is taken as referring to authors actually killing off their characters: see, for instance, on David Lodge, Morace (1989: 184). The section cited in Fontanier/Dumarsais does not mention Virgil or Dido, although there is an interesting discussion of Dido's death in the section on 'hypallage', about whether Virgil removes her soul from her body, or her body from her soul: Fontanier (1818: 233–6). On the ambivalence of the expression in the French original, see Matzner in this volume, p. 3 n. 6; for further discussion of its complexities of Genette's phrase, see Kearey, Matzner, and Trimble in this volume.

consigned her to the Stygian underworld. So Iris on dewy saffron wings flits down through the sky, trailing athwart the sun a thousand shifting tints, and halted above her head. 'This offering, sacred to Dis, I take as bidden, and from your body set you free': so she speaks and with her hand severs the lock; and therewith all the warmth passed away, and the life vanished into the winds. (Trans. Fairclough)

We would not perhaps expect an explicit reference to Virgil as poet deciding that Dido should die. The idea that 'Virgil has Dido die' comes rather from the tradition, possibly the oral tradition, of reading Virgil. In fact, it is Juno who makes that decision, so one would need to make an assumption that Juno is a figure for the poet here to read an authorial metalepsis. Iris has been ordered, against fate, and before the day when Dido should have died, to release her from her suffering: but she has been ordered by Juno. There is certainly imagery of rupture here, of going beyond what is expected, but we know too little about earlier versions of the Dido myth (say that of Naevius) to be sure that her death was in fact unexpected, even if it was not elsewhere caused by Aeneas.[52]

Was this passage felt to be jarring by readers of Virgil? How does the potentially metaleptic effect of Dido's death relate to the potential emotional effects? We can begin by noting that this is a key transitional moment in the text: the end of the first tetrad, corresponding to the triumph of Augustus in the shield at the end of book 8, and the death of Turnus at the end of book 12.[53] Aeneas finally finishes his wanderings and arrives in Italy. Dido's death is described in this way: *nam quia nec fato, merita nec morte peribat, sed misera ante diem* ('for since she perished neither by fate nor by a deserved death, but wretched before her day'). Commentators have written at length on these lines: already Servius found the contradiction between this line and *Aen.* 10.467 troubling. In that line Jupiter tells Hercules that his protégé Pallas is fated to die (*stat sua cuique dies*, 'his own day stands for each man'), using the example of the death of Sarpedon in the *Iliad* to affirm the inevitability of fate. Servius (*ad loc.*) explains away the contradiction by suggesting that there are two types of fate, decreed

---

[52] On other versions of the Dido myth see Davidson (1998).

[53] We could argue, as suggested by one of the anonymous readers of this piece, that both these climactic moments are also jarring and metaleptic. The abruptness of the ending of the poem clearly makes it jarring, and a number of markers emphasize textuality, such as the repetition of the line describing the death of Camilla (*Aen.* 12.952 = 11.831). This line emphasizes the transitional nature of death, as the soul moves from one realm to another. In book 8, ekphrasis and temporal play, especially with Aeneas' failure to understand the images, create a powerful effect of simultaneous distancing and familiarizing.

and conditional. The death of Dido apparently fits into the latter category, and it is possible to die in contradiction of a conditional fate. Virgil gives no sense, though, that this is a conditional fate, as for instance Homer does with the choice of Achilles at *Iliad* 9.410–16. Later commentators shy away from the contradiction. Henry (*ad loc.*) is keen to avoid any implication that Virgil arranges Dido's death against the decrees of fate, instead interpreting the phrase *nec fato* to mean 'Neither by a natural death', which he justifies by comparison to various Roman prose writers.[54] Conington (*ad loc.*) follows Henry's distinction between natural and violent death: 'her death was not predestined but sudden', but his caveat 'The distinction which Virgil suggests is practical rather than philosophical, and the words employed must not be weighed too nicely' suggests a certain unease.[55] Austin (*ad loc.*) interprets *fato* as 'equivalent to the fulfilment of time', avoiding the question of what Virgil meant without addressing the troubling aspects. Tellingly, Austin finds Dido's death tranquil ('the book ends in tranquillity like a Greek tragedy'), which may say something about the distancing effect of involving Juno and Iris and going from the hissing wound to the relatively tame act of cutting off a lock of hair. Juno's rather distant pity replaces the anguish of Anna. However, Austin also implies, by quoting Henry, that he finds the passage an example of 'ennobling, exalting, purifying contemplation of the grand, the beautiful and the pathetic'. For these four readers of Virgil, the final moments of *Aeneid* 4 are both difficult and sublime. There is, then, good evidence that this passage has been found jarring, and the efforts to explain away the narratorial comments *nec fato* and *ante diem* suggest that there is a sense in which the tradition of reading the *Aeneid* feels that Virgil 'has Dido die' here. It is not just the phrase *nec fato* but also the whole scene around it: the image of Iris physically breaking the link between body and soul, rupturing both the plans of fate and the life of Dido.

Epic characters do not normally die against the dictates of fate. There are instead many examples of epic characters who must die to keep the narrative on its fated course: this is a staple of the counterfactual in Homeric epic.[56] At *Odyssey* 1.34 Zeus refers to Aegisthus killing

[54] Henry (1878). Pliny, *Ep.* 1.12 talks of the death of Cornelius Rufus by his own hand as a particularly bitter loss because 'it seems neither from nature nor fated' (*quae non ex natura nec fatalis videtur*). The particular problem, then, with Dido's death, is the choice she made to kill herself.

[55] Conington and Nettleship (1884/1963/2007).

[56] See Louden (1993). Henry (1878: 324) suggests that Virgil's *nec fato* might correspond to the Homeric ὑπὲρ μοῖραν. At *Iliad* 20.366 Poseidon warns Aeneas to stop fighting Achilles in case he dies against fate; see also 2.155 (narrator: Argives would have accomplished their

Agamemnon ὑπὲρ μόρον ('against fate'), as an example of what happens if men ignore divine instructions; Aegisthus himself has been killed in return.[57] This story is, of course, famous for its tragic instantiations, while Odysseus survives in accordance with fate. Dido's death, then, is a moment of authorial transgression of the normal rules of epic narrative. The intervention of Iris (and Juno) can equate to the typical tragic ending of the *deus ex machina*, but in the Homeric counterfactuals gods intervene to set fate back on its course; here they intervene to change fate so that it falls in line with the narrative.[58] In epic, gods and author have a close kinship of perspective and power, and we can make a case that here the gods intervene as avatars of author and audience, moved by the character's suffering. Juno's involvement emphasizes the heroic stature of Dido and the disturbing emotional power of her death.

The death of Dido forms the emotional climax of the first third of the *Aeneid*. It has struck readers throughout the centuries as contradictory and confusing, indeed jarring, and it calls into question the relationship between poet, genre, gods, and fate. While Genette does not make an explicit claim for this passage, rather than the discourse about it, as metaleptic, the identification of metalepsis here makes sense: the removal from the intimacy of death and suffering to the grandeur of gods and fate and the sublimity of the many colours of the rainbow, as in the other examples we have looked at in *Aeneid* 2, both intensifies engagement and alienates readers. This is the fundamental emotional paradox of metalepsis in the *Aeneid*.

This chapter has shown the emotional complexity of metalepsis in the *Aeneid*, looking at two of the most powerful books of a central work in the Western canon, to offer a model for reading emotional intensity in terms of immersion and alienation. By performing the first analysis of multiple

return beyond fate if Hera and Athena had not intervened); 6.487 (Hector tells Andromache that no one can kill him unless it is his fate, and no one can avoid their fate); 17.321 (narrator warns that Trojans would have lost too soon to the Achaeans if Apollo had not encouraged Aeneas); 20.30 (Zeus worries that Achilles will take Troy too soon).

[57] While ὑπὲρ μόρον or ὑπὲρ μοῖραν are both used in counterfactuals to mean 'against fate' (*Od.* 2.155, 20.30, 20.336, 21.517), West (1998) *ad loc.* argues that 'what is contrary to fate simply cannot happen', and that fate is used here in the sense of 'what is fitting, right or reasonably to be expected', and that the uses at *Od.* 1.34 and 35 contain the idea of 'going beyond the normal limit'. On the difficulties of the term 'fate' in Homer, see Sarischoulis (2008); for an illuminating discussion of Zeus, fate, and narrative in the *Iliad*, see Myers (2019).

[58] The relationship between fate and narrative in the *Aeneid* is complex and paradoxical, as Armstrong (2002: 327) demonstrates; for fate as the immutable destiny of the winning side, see for instance Quint (1993: 92–5).

metaleptic features in *Aeneid* 2, the chapter has explored the complexity of layered first-person narratives in a culture of rhetoric, the connection between metalepsis and narrative transition, and the metaleptic effects of similes, as well as touching on apostrophe and anachronism. It also reinforces the importance of narrating trauma, death, and grief in Latin epic, and the need for a narratological commentary on the *Aeneid*, as well as a reassessment of emotional engagement in Latin epic. Finally, the chapter has investigated in what sense one can really say that Virgil 'has Dido die' and has shown the importance of grounding analysis of emotional reactions to ancient poetry in traditions of reading.

9

Secondary Metalepsis?

Talking to Virgil in Fulgentius' *Expositio Virgilianae Continentiae*

Talitha Kearey

Literature and literary criticism depend on one another. They blur at the edges, interact, and change themselves and each other through their interactions. While literature frequently functions self-reflexively to interrogate the category of literature, criticism, in turn, often displays an irresistible drive towards literariness as it deconstructs and reconstructs the inner workings of literary texts and, in so doing, refashions and rewrites them.

This chapter sets out, not to reinvent the metacritical wheel, but to fit it to the axle of narratology and take it for a spin. My interest here is in the particular fictions generated by the act of commenting on another author and in how these are variously sustained, destabilized, and manipulated by the critic who creates them. I argue that the concept of metalepsis, understood broadly as a transgression of distinct narrative levels, is a productive model with which to analyse these fictional turns. At the same time, I hope to show that considering the metaleptic dynamics of criticism—both ancient and modern, both 'nonfictional' and embedded within unequivocally fictional frames—can help refine our understanding of metalepsis more generally.[1]

* Many thanks to Sebastian Matzner and Gail Trimble, editors extraordinaires, for inviting me to contribute to this volume. I am grateful, too, to Emily Gowers, who generously read this chapter in draft and gave invaluable advice; to Shadi Bartsch, Siegmar Döpp, and Elena Giusti, who kindly shared their own research with me; and to the speakers and attendees at the Oxford conference in 2015. This work was supported by the Arts and Humanities Research Council [grant number AH/L503897/1].

[1] This definition of metalepsis is not one that ancient critics would have formulated in these terms: see Matzner in this volume.

Talitha Kearey, *Secondary Metalepsis? Talking to Virgil in Fulgentius'* Expositio Virgilianae Continentiae In: *Metalepsis: Ancient Texts, New Perspectives*. Edited by: Sebastian Matzner and Gail Trimble, Oxford University Press (2020). © The editors and Oxford University Press.
DOI: 10.1093/oso/9780198846987.003.0009

In a volume devoted to reconsidering the significance of metalepsis for classical literature, and vice versa, Genette's use of a Virgiliocentric example in his foundational definition of metalepsis makes for a good starting point.[2] In the first half of this chapter, I consider the implications of this example, arguing that it is better understood as an instance of 'secondary metalepsis' than within Genette's category of 'authorial metalepsis': the diegetic levels of author, narrator, and narrative are blurred not by that same author but by another, who employs the figure of the first author and their work within their own, secondary text. I then turn to Fulgentius' *Expositio Virgilianae Continentiae*, a sixth-century allegorical exegesis of the *Aeneid*. 'Secondary metalepsis', I argue, emerges as the driving motor of this bizarre text, underpinning its many hermeneutic flamboyancies: necromantic literary criticism, creative supplementation and impersonation, and the strange loop of narrativized metaphor and metaphorical narrative in which its reading of the *Aeneid* is entangled.

'Author's Metalepsis' Revisited

One of the examples Genette uses to illustrate his original formulation of the concept of metalepsis takes the form of an utterance of an imagined speaker: 'as when one says that Virgil "has Dido die" in the Fourth Book of the *Aeneid*.'[3] This example represents a category of metaleptic effects that Genette terms 'author's metalepsis'. This is familiar to classicists as the *poeta creator* motif (or something very close to it):[4] the common metafictional conceit whereby the author is represented as taking an active hand in the events of the plot, rather than merely narrating them. As a 'narrative figure',[5] 'author's metalepsis' remains in the realm of discourse rather than affecting the events narrated; by foregrounding the narrator's voice it highlights the fictive, non-mimetic nature of the narration and, says Genette, 'produces an effect of strangeness that is either comical...or fantastic'.[6] In this narrative

---

[2] On 'Virgil has Dido die' cf. Lovatt, Matzner, and Trimble in this volume.
[3] Genette (1972: 244): 'comme lorsqu'on dit que Virgile "fait mourir" Didon au chant IV de l'*Énéide*'. On the ambivalence of the expression in the French original, see Matzner in this volume, p. 3 n. 6. All translations in this chapter are my own, unless otherwise indicated.
[4] The term is from Lieberg (1982); formally the two concepts are similar, though Lieberg invests the *poeta creator* with religious significance that is not wholly convincing. Genette's term 'author's metalepsis' is derived from the French grammarian tradition ('les classiques', 1972: 244): here, Fontanier on Dumarsais (1818: 116). Cf. Nauta (2013a) and Matzner in this volume.
[5] Genette (1972: 244): 'la figure narrative...qui consiste à feindre que le poète "opère lui-même les effets qu'il chante"' (quoting Fontanier 1818: 116).
[6] Genette (1972: 244): 'produit un effet de bizarrerie soit bouffonne...soit fantastique'.

trick he sees something akin to the actual transgression of diegetic levels within a narration, and classes both under the umbrella heading 'narrative metalepsis'. His example of the latter is Cortázar's 'Continuidad de los parques', a short story in which the unnamed protagonist is encountered (and perhaps even assassinated) by a character from a novel he is reading.

Genette's brief paragraph has since come under scholarly fire from all directions. Is metalepsis a figure, a fiction, a trope, or something else entirely?[7] Does it enhance or disrupt the illusion of fictional narrative? How valid is his assertion that discursive metalepsis is related to its narrative cousin?[8] What kinds of metalepsis can we discern, and in what typological systems can we productively arrange and analyse them?[9] Throughout all this, Genette's test cases have remained central touchstones for discussions of metalepsis, as critics reuse them in their own formulations of the phenomenon and reassess their precise workings both in Genette's *Figures III* and in newer contexts. Thirty years after his first description of metalepsis, Genette was able to characterize the phrase 'Virgil has Dido die', not incorrectly, as the 'canonical example' of author's metalepsis.[10] This claim conceals his own role in elevating it to that status, just as his use of it in the first place helps to cloak his appropriation of the term 'metalepsis' from ancient rhetoric to twentieth-century narratology in a suitably classical reference.[11]

Despite such close attention, however, one aspect of Genette's citation of the phrase has largely escaped notice. Consider Genette's four examples of 'author's metalepsis' in his opening paragraph:

> . . . the narrative figure the classics call 'author's metalepsis', which consists of pretending that the poet 'himself brings about the effects he narrates', [i] as when one says that Virgil 'has Dido die' in the Fourth

---

[7] Cf. Matzner in this volume.

[8] Cf. e.g. Nauta (2013a: 477): 'the attempt to assign the figure [i.e. the *poeta creator* motif] to metonymy, or to metalepsis as a special kind of metonymy, has not proved successful'; Klimek (2010: 34–7).

[9] A good round-up can be found in Pier (2016), including typologies that roughly preserve Genette's bipartite distinction (e.g. Ryan 2004 'rhetorical/ontological', Whitmarsh 2013b 'weak/strong', Fludernik 2003b, Nelles 1997 'unmarked/distinctly marked', Pier 2005 'minimal/ascending or descending'), those concerned with direction of boundary-transgression (Wagner 2002, Meyer-Minnemann 2005, Schlickers 2005), and those concerned with metalepsis-adjacent phenomena (e.g. transfictionality, intertextuality, quotation: Lavocat 2016: 473–520). I favour Ryan (2004) as a basic working approach and critical shorthand, but appreciate Matzner's reassessment (in this volume) of the rhetorical grounding of narratological metalepsis (sc. 'figure' vs. 'trope'). Cf. also the typology of metalepsis suggested by Grethlein in this volume, p. 29.

[10] Genette (2004: 12): 'l'exemple canonique'.

[11] On this appropriation cf. Matzner in this volume.

Book of the *Aeneid*, **[ii]** or when Diderot, more ambiguously, writes in *Jacques le fataliste*: "What would prevent me from *marrying off* the Maître and *making* a cuckold out of him?", **[iii]** or even, speaking to the reader, "If it pleases you, *let us put* the peasant girl back in the saddle behind her companion, *let us let* them go, and *let us return* to our two travellers". **[iv]** Sterne went as far as to call for the reader's intervention, who he asked to close the door or help Mr Shandy get back into bed, but the principle is the same…[12]

Who exactly is it who 'pretend[s] that the poet brings about the effects he narrates'? In the second, third, and fourth examples, the metaleptic effect is controlled by the author, by Diderot or Sterne. It is the narrator, closely identified in each case with the author, who proposes that extradiegetic entities such as the author-narrator or the reader are capable of controlling, interfering in, or resisting the opportunity to meddle with diegetic events; Diderot, for example, threatening to 'marry off the Maître'. The metalepsis, if carried out—and note that all three examples remain potential, phrased as deliberative questions, hortative suggestions, and requests—would take place within a single text, under the ultimate control of the extradiegetic author. The central conceit is that each text is both written and narrated by the one who not only allows metaleptic boundary transgression but who will also, presumably, narrate it as it happens. Diderot steps into the position of *poeta creator*; Sterne, like Cortázar earlier, creates a fictional world within which the transgression of diegetic and extradiegetic narrative levels might be possible.[13]

---

[12] Genette (1972: 244) (emphasis original, numeration mine): '…la figure narrative que les classiques appelaient la *métalepse de l'auteur*, et qui consiste à feindre que le poète "opère lui-même les effets qu'il chante", [i] comme lorsqu'on dit que Virgile "fait mourir" Didon au chant IV de l'*Énéide*, [ii] ou lorsque Diderot, d'une manière plus équivoque, écrit dans *Jacques le fataliste*: "Qu'est-ce qui m'empêcherait de *marier* le Maître et de le *faire cocu?*", [iii] ou bien, d'adressant au lecteur, "Si cela vous fait plaisir, *remettons* la paysanne en croupe derrière son conducteur, *laissons*-les aller et *revenons* à nos deux voyageurs". [iv] Sterne poussait la chose jusqu'à solliciter l'intervention du lecteur, prié de fermer la porte ou d'aider Mr Shandy à regagner son lit, mais le principe est le même…'.

[13] Genette (1972: 244–5). It is interesting that both the third and fourth examples enlist the reader as accomplice in the author-narrator's metaleptic activity. Diderot's reader may be merely a passive extension of his narrator's exuberant first-person plural, but Sterne complicates matters throughout *Tristram Shandy* by requesting his reader to collaborate with him—notoriously, in some cases, by doing things they can actually do in the non-fictional world: taking a seat on a stack of the volumes of the novel already in print, or painting their own picture of a character onto a page left blank (Sterne 1769: 1, 146–7; my thanks to Gail Trimble for drawing my attention to this point). Genette here sidesteps the complexity of Sterne's narrative and material text, choosing a single example that retains authorial control of the

Something different, however, is going on in the first example: 'Virgil has Dido die'. To be sure, it is possible to analyse this example in the same way that I treated Genette's citation of Sterne: the speaker of the phrase momentarily creates a fictional world in which the character of 'Virgil', an author by trade, interacts metaleptically with the plot of the book he writes. Not just 'Virgil writes a plot in which Dido dies', but that he causes her death by some more tangible method, as if the two entities occupied the same plane of existence to enable such an interaction. On a formal level, such an analysis is entirely appropriate; indeed, it positions 'Virgil has Dido die' as the exact inverse of Cortázar's metalepsis.[14] But there are fundamental differences between the two examples. The phrase 'Virgil has Dido die' is not part of a narrative work, but instead purports to be a critic's comment on the *Aeneid* ('as when one says', 'comme lorsqu'on dit'). The speaker of the phrase is not exactly parallel to Diderot or Sterne: where the latter two paint themselves as capable of metaleptic leaps into their narrative, the speaker of 'Virgil has Dido die' attributes such capabilities to a secondary author, Virgil. It is not 'author's metalepsis' in the same way as the other examples are, but what we might call, provisionally, 'critic's metalepsis' or 'metalepsis of critical discourse'.[15]

As such, it has a different relationship with reality. Virgil exists outside the text of this sentence in a way that Genette's other metaleptic entities do not. Treacherous waters to navigate, here; the question of who or what 'exists' is a tortuous one in theories of fictionality, and the separation of fictional and factual discourse is by no means simple.[16] The distinction I am drawing here is not one that carries much weight in the realm of purely structuralist narratology, which remains largely uninterested in the

---

metaleptic effect: the reader knows that if anyone is going to be closing the door and putting Mr Shandy to bed, it will ultimately be the author.

[14] 'Virgil has Dido die': the extradiegetic speaker narrates how Virgil, a diegetic character, engages with his metadiegetic narration. Cortázar: a character from the metadiegetic narrative (the 'book within a book') engages with one from the diegetic level, as narrated by the extradiegetic speaker.

[15] On the fictionality of critical discourse: Pelletier (2003: 201–2) on 'Virgil has Dido die'; Fludernik (2003b) (393–4) (briefly 'extend[ing] the metaphorics of metalepsis to cover a critical use of metalepsis'); Matzner (2016a: 184) (on the 'postmodern... novelistic reification of the notoriously unstable text' troped in critical metalepsis). I will come back to this question of terminology (pp. 203–5 below).

[16] See, e.g., Pelletier (2003: 197–201), Cullhed (2015: 6–20). Questions of reality in metalepsis: Whitmarsh (2013b); Budelmann, Kennedy, and Trimble in this volume. Nauta takes an extreme approach: 'metalepsis is not defined from the contents of the story, but from the relationship between narrative levels' (2013a: 479–80).

truth-values of the narratives it describes.[17] Suffice it to say, for now, that the phrase 'Virgil has Dido die', as a fragment of critical discourse, rests on the assumption that 'Virgil' exists on the same level of reality *as the critic who speaks the phrase.*

Crucially, moreover, we are able to read the *Aeneid* without the (critic-) speaker's mediation, unlike, for example, the book read by Cortázar's protagonist, which is only available to us within Cortázar's narrative—and only partially, at that. The speaker of 'Virgil has Dido die' undoubtedly 'invents' both Virgil and the *Aeneid*, in so far as they are transformed into textual objects within a new literary setting, and thus controls the depiction of the authorial or narratorial relationship between the two. Nonetheless, we retain the ability to determine the extent to which this is a reasonable depiction by referring to the *Aeneid* itself, in its incarnation outside the phrase 'Virgil has Dido die'.[18]

The way that this example of 'author's metalepsis' is embedded within the secondary narrative of critical discourse, therefore, radically expands the range of interpretative possibilities available to us. Virgil inhabits the same level of reality as the scholar who writes these words, and his *Aeneid* is available on the same bookshelves as the commentary or monograph in which the words 'Virgil has Dido die' are to be found. Our access to the text of *Aeneid* 4, unmediated by either Genette or his imaginary scholar who utters the phrase, makes a concrete difference to the interpretative potential of this type of metalepsis and the ways in which it invites its reader to approach it. In particular, it prompts us to compare this assessment with our own perception of Virgil's narration. Should we understand 'Virgil has Dido die' as 'Virgil recounts that Dido dies'—the metonymic substitution suggested by Genette[19]—or as 'Virgil recounts that he has Dido die?' That is, does the speaker of the phrase invent a metaleptic relationship between Virgil and his text, or is it a valid third-person report of a metaleptic element that is *already* part of Virgil's authorial self-fashioning? If the former, are there any other ways in which this metaleptic invention still expresses something the critic perceives in Virgil's narration of the *Aeneid*? And whether or not it is somehow present in the *Aeneid*, what concepts of authorship, narration, fictionality, and literary interpretation does this critic's comment presume or demand?

---

[17] Cf., though, Matzner's discussion in this volume (following Fludernik 2003b: 384) of how Genette's 'author's metalepsis' supports or undermines expectations of truth-telling in narrative fiction.

[18] As is done by Lovatt in this volume.

[19] 2004: 12 (cf. n. 10): the phrase stands 'pour "raconte que Didon meurt"'.

The reader of *Aeneid* 4 knows that on the level of plot, at least, Virgil cannot be said to 'have Dido die'. Though blame for Dido's suicide proliferates wildly through Book 4—attaching itself to Dido herself,[20] Aeneas, Juno and Iris, Jupiter, the Fates, Iarbas, Mercury, Venus, monstrous *Fama* ('Rumour'), or wicked *Amor* ('Love')—an authorial or narratorial Virgil is not among the cast of scapegoats. The metalepsis of 'Virgil has Dido die' does not reflect a metaleptic authorial move in the *Aeneid* itself. But the critic who writes 'Virgil has Dido die' does perhaps pick up on something peculiar about the relationship between the narrator of Book 4 and the character Dido.

The narrator of the *Aeneid* is most tangibly a character when dealing with Dido.[21] He describes her like a personal favourite, and commiserates with her fate (*optima, pulchra, pulcherrima Dido*, or *infelix, miserrima*; 'best', 'beautiful', 'most beautiful', or 'unfortunate', 'most pitiable');[22] he apostrophizes her;[23] and, for the first time in the epic, he moves away from Aeneas' or the gods' point of view, and instead follows Dido around the palace and Carthaginian countryside. In fact, and rather disingenuously, the narrator seems particularly eager to let us know that he has no hand in causing Dido's death. He abandons the usual omniscience of an epic narrator for a more limited perspective: his apostrophe to Dido at 4.408–11 puts him at least momentarily in the same position as poor bewildered Anna, unable to comprehend her sister's emotions as Book 4 races to its tragic conclusion: *quis tibi tum, Dido, cernenti talia sensus,* | *quosue dabas gemitus…?* ('what was your state of mind then, Dido, when you saw these things? What sighs did you utter?').[24] When he cries *heu uatum ignarae mentes*, grieving Dido's (or her priests') fatal tunnel vision,[25] there is a

---

[20] The epic goes to extraordinary lengths to undermine Dido's control and agency; despite her suicide being pursued with increasing resolve, carefully plotted, elaborately staged, and doubly determined by both sword and fire, it is ultimately 'described by Vergil as in a sense not even *Dido's* act' (Hill 2004: 120). Besides the proliferation of causes (above), Dido even fails to finish the process of killing herself single-handedly: her death requires the intervention of Juno and Iris for its completion (4.693–705).

[21] Ancient critics, too, remarked upon Virgil's particular closeness with his character Dido. Servius, for examples, records that Virgil read Book 4 to Augustus, ventriloquizing one of Dido's speeches 'with immense passion' (*dicitur autem ingenti adfectu hos uersus pronuntiasse, cum…recitaret Augusto*, Serv. *ad Aen.* 4.323)—a story which seems to dramatize the literary character of the *Aeneid's* narration as a historical event.

[22] Aeneas' epithets lack this subjectivity: *pius, pater, Troius* ('dutiful', 'father', 'Trojan').

[23] On apostrophe and metalepsis, cf. Klooster (2013), Budelmann and De Jong in this volume.

[24] Cf. Anna's reactions at 4.500–2, 675.

[25] 4.65. The line is a crux interpretum: cf. Gildenhard's excellent discussion (2012 s.v.). Is *uatum* an objective genitive ('alas! minds ignorant of prophets') or possessive genitive ('alas! the unknowing minds of prophets')—or, in fact, deliberately ambiguous (O'Hara 1993)?

sense too of self-apostrophe, the *uates* castigating himself for his unexpected lack of foreknowledge.[26]

This narratorial closeness seems to come down to Dido's status as one of the epic's most overt and elaborate inventions.[27] Throughout the *Aeneid*, Virgil's newly created characters—or those newly given prominence, or drastically refashioned—receive narratorial attention of peculiar intensity and tenderness.[28] Where the author's hand is most visible in the *Aeneid*, the narrator's voice follows. It is this overlap of authorial and narratorial function, I think, that prompts the momentary metalepsis of the phrase 'Virgil has Dido die': the closeness of the narratorial voice to Dido is perceived as *authorial* closeness, and the author's direction of the plot is reframed as an interaction directly with the character.

Genette's quotation is brief and lacks context.[29] I hesitate to assert that the critic who writes 'Virgil has Dido die' would necessarily accept my characterization of its implications; after all, the use in literary criticism of verbs such as 'to have' or 'to make' (*faire, facere*, etc.) to denote an author's direction of the plot is idiomatic and generally unmarked.[30] Not every use of the formula 'X author has Y character do Z' corresponds to a specific narratorial feature in the text under discussion. But critics *can* choose to exploit its metaleptic potential to concrete ends. In his famous article 'The Two Voices of Virgil's *Aeneid*', for example, Parry offers one explanation for the narrator's troubling sympathy for Dido: 'another theory is that Virgil somehow fell in love with, and was carried away by, his own heroine'.[31] Parry's comment is clearly facetious: he displaces it onto other unnamed critics (as Genette does) and leaves its mechanisms unexplained ('somehow'). The metalepsis comes down to a pun: Virgil 'gets carried away' in his imaginative excesses, which Parry literalizes as his own character sweeping him off his feet, the intrepid bride carrying her groom over

---

[26] The narrator proclaims himself *uates* at 7.41. Note that in the *Aeneid* the exclamation *heu* is almost always found in character-speech: twenty-nine of thirty-three occurrences are in direct speech, two more focalized as Aeneas' turbulent indecision (*heu, quid agat?*, 'alas! what should he do?': 4.283, 12.486), and another seems focalized through the unfortunate *agricolae* in a pastoral simile (12.452). *heu* at 4.65 is, uniquely, in the narrator's own voice.

[27] On Virgil's 'invention' of Dido, cf. Wigodsky (1972: 29–34), Horsfall (1973: 8–12), Hexter (1992: 338–9), and Giusti (2018). Cf. Macrobius 5.17.5–6, especially *fabula lasciuientis Didonis, quam falsam nouit uniuersitas* (5.17.5, 'the story of lustful Dido, which [or "whom"?] everyone knows to be a fabrication').

[28] The list of major characters who receive narratorial apostrophes is almost identical to that of Virgil's invented or significantly elaborated characters: Dido, Palinurus, Nisus and Euryalus, Pallas, Turnus, Lausus, and Camilla.

[29] Cf. Lovatt in this volume on its relationship to the actual text of Fontanier/Dumarsais.

[30] Cf. Nünlist (2009: 26–7, 133); Nauta (2013a: 478 and n. 40).

[31] Parry (1963: 77).

the threshold.[32] But it is notable that this fanciful metalepsis occurs in the context of his proposition of a 'second voice' in the *Aeneid*, a 'private' undercurrent of anti-epic regret and ambivalence that he attributes not to the narrator alone but to Virgil himself, and which he locates at moments of marked authorial invention and narratorial involvement. Indeed, his broader argument turns on his discussion of *Aeneid* 7.750–60, where Virgil invents the priest Umbro only to grieve his imminent death in a narratorial apostrophe (759–60).[33] For Parry, the narrator's inclinations are aligned with the author's; his metaleptic characterization of Virgil's authorship, however sarcastically or warily expressed, brings the two even closer together.[34]

The Case for 'Secondary Metalepsis'

At this point I would like to propose a new paradigm within which to understand constructions like the unnamed critic's 'Virgil has Dido die' or Parry's 'Virgil somehow fell in love with, and was carried away by, his own heroine'. The feature that distinguishes these phrases from Genette's other examples of 'author's metalepsis' is that the diegetic levels of author, narrator, and narrative are blurred or transgressed not by a single author, within a single work, but by a secondary one, who employs the character and literary output of the source author within a new work on a (now) shared narrative plane. For phrases like this—fragments of literary criticism which fleetingly construct a metaleptic relationship between the author under discussion and their text, whether that author employs that motif in their own work or not—the term 'critic's metalepsis' is of course a good one. The echo of Genette's term 'author's metalepsis' is fitting: the figure is common enough in literary criticism as to be something of a cliché, and is unmarked or insignificant in most instances.[35] But I would argue that the

---

[32] Virgil momentarily takes the place of his own hero Aeneas. Note that the phrase 'Virgil has Dido die' also puts Virgil in one of the roles filled by Aeneas in the plot of the *Aeneid*. Is Virgil the true protagonist of his own epic? Ancient biographers were certainly keen to parallel the two: cf. Ziogas (2017) on Virgil's recitation to Octavia as a double for Aeneas' speeches to Dido.

[33] Parry (1963: 66–9).

[34] Parry's phrasing recalls the Pygmalion myth, itself intensely metaleptic: *operisque sui concepit amorem* ('[Pygmalion] conceived a love of his own creation', Ov. *Met.* 10.249; cf., brilliantly, Sharrock 1991). Erotic encounters between creating artist and created beloved are of course a staple of Latin elegy (cf. Wyke 1987 on Propertius' *scripta puella,* and see already Homer in love with Penelope at Leontion fr. 3.27–34); small wonder, then, that Parry's metaleptic turn expresses his theory of a grieving Virgilian narrator, who emerges at particularly elegiac moments in the *Aeneid*.

[35] Cf. Matzner's suggestion (in this volume) of 'dead' metalepses.

category of secondary metalepsis—metalepsis at one authorial remove, as it were—is broader than this alone. It extends to include not only the discursive or rhetorical 'critic's metalepsis' seen in 'Virgil has Dido die', but its narrativized (or 'strong', or 'ontological') equivalent. Just as Genette sees in 'author's metalepsis' the seeds of fully fledged metaleptic narratives such as that of Cortázar's 'Continuidad de los parques', so too, I posit, 'critic's metalepsis' contains within it the potential for development into more elaborate and explicit forms of secondary metalepsis, in which the relationship between authors and their texts becomes the subject of a new fiction recounted by another author.

This is a different phenomenon from those accommodated by most other theorizations and typologies of metalepsis. It has something in common with the category termed 'horizontal metalepsis' by some theorists: the transgression of boundaries not between different narrative levels (conceptualized as vertical layers) but between wholly different fictional 'worlds' of the same narrative level.[36] One famous example of this in ancient literature might be Ovid's Ariadne, who seems in *Fasti* 3.469–75 to recall her previous, Catullan incarnation.[37] What I propose to call 'secondary metalepsis', however, is more diagonal than purely horizontal, following this spatial model: the portrayal of the first *author* within the second's text transgresses boundaries both horizontal and vertical, whereas Ariadne remains at the same narrative level in whichever text she is found.

I am particularly interested in a certain degree of continuity between 'discursive' and 'ontological' types of secondary metalepsis, something not well supported or emphasized by the spatial model.[38] Genette's original insight lay in uniting the two types, although he glossed over the precise relationship between them by presenting 'ontological' metalepsis (as, for example, in Cortázar) as an 'extreme' version smoothly derived from 'discursive'

---

[36] Cf. Meyer-Minnemann (2005: 140), Saint-Gelais (2011: 11) (and cf. 'heterometalepsis', Rabau 2005; 'intertextual metalepsis', Wagner 2002: 247). In theory this can apply to works by the same or by different authors. It is perhaps most commonly seen in contemporary fan fiction, especially in 'crossover' works which blend elements of two or more different sources (especially their characters and settings) in a new text. When this model is applied to narratives within the *same* text (e.g. two stories told by a character within a novel), it is not strictly metalepsis: cf. Klimek (2011: 25–6), Lavocat (2016: 498–9). On the suitability or otherwise of the term 'fan fiction' to ancient literature, cf. Peirano (2012: 10–13) and the papers in Willis 2016.

[37] On metaleptic Ariadne, cf. Conte (1986: 60–3), Nauta (2013b: 223–5), and Trimble in this volume.

[38] In this model the two would be called 'diagonal metalepsis of enunciation' and 'diagonal metalepsis of the enunciate' or 'diagonal metalepsis *in uerbis*' and '*in corpore*' (Meyer-Minnemann 2005), cumbersome terms which serve to separate rather than unite the two categories.

metalepsis (as in 'Virgil has Dido die').[39] Subsequent narratological analysis, with its typologizing tendencies, has generally worked to separate the two rather than unite them. Where secondary metalepsis is particularly pronounced, however, I would argue that slippage between 'discursive' and 'ontological' modes is a central feature of the phenomenon.

A hypothesis naturally demands a case study. The remainder of this chapter steps back in time from twentieth-century discussions of Virgil to those of the sixth century, taking as its focus Fulgentius' *Expositio Virgilianae Continentiae secundum philosophos moralis* ('Exposition of the Contents of Virgil according to moral philosophy').[40] This extraordinary piece of late antique Latin scholarship, I argue, exemplifies the overlap between literary criticism and outright fiction—and the slippage between 'discursive' and 'ontological' metalepsis—that, I believe, particularly characterizes secondary metalepsis.

Fulgentius' *Expositio Virgilianae Continentiae*

Very little can be said of Fulgentius by way of authorial biography, other than that he was probably a sixth-century Christian from North Africa.[41] As well as the *Expositio Virgilianae Continentiae* (henceforth '*Expositio*'), he wrote a three-book allegorical interpretation of classical myth (*Mitologiae*), a lipogrammatic history of the world (*De aetatibus mundi et hominis*), and an antiquarian treatise on archaic words (*Expositio sermonum antiquorum*). The *Expositio* is an allegorical reading of the *Aeneid*, subordinating the whole poem to a Christianizing schematics of man's life and moral development: the *Aeneid* is taken as an allegory for Everyman's journey through life.[42]

---

[39] 1972: 244: 'c'est là une forme inverse (et extrême) de la figure narrative que les classiques appelaient la *métalepse de l'auteur*' ('this is an inverse (and extreme) form of the narrative figure the classics call "author's metalepsis"'). Note that even the sceptical Nauta finds this original move persuasive (2013a: 478: 'crucially, he then realized…'), though he goes on to criticize Genette's attempts to explain as obfuscations (479: 'uncharacteristic lack of precision').

[40] I quote Fulgentius in Latin from Helm's 1898 Teubner by page and line number throughout; translations are my own. Hays's edition and translation of Fulgentius is eagerly anticipated; in the meantime, he provides an abridged text and translation in Ziolkowski and Putnam (2008: 660–72).

[41] On Fulgentius' dates, geographical provenance, and identity, cf. (persuasively) Hays (2003). I do not believe this Fulgentius to be the homonymous Bishop of Ruspe (cf. Hays 2003); I also exclude the pseudo-Fulgentian *Super Thebaiden*. Lengthier bibliographies: Wolff (2009) and Hays (2013).

[42] The unfinished *De aetatibus* similarly attempts to align the ages of the world with the ages of man. The preeminent work of allegorical interpretation of the *Aeneid*, (pseudo-)

Fulgentius' *Expositio* is remarkable for several reasons. It is the first explicitly Christian scholarly work on the *Aeneid*, and the first to apply a comprehensive process of *allegoresis* to the whole poem.[43] Most striking, however, is its central necromantic conceit: after a brief epistolary opening addressing the tract to an unnamed deacon (*Leuitarum sanctissime*, 83.1), the exegesis takes the form of a dialogue in which the majority of the explanation is not Fulgentius' but is instead delivered by the shade of Virgil himself, summoned from the dead by Fulgentius' invocation to the Muses near the opening of the tract (85.2–17):[44]

ego uero . . . Musis aliquid blandius fabulabor:
> *uos, Eliconiades, neque enim mihi sola uocanda est*
> *Calliope,[45] conferte gradum, date praemia menti.*
> *maius opus moueo; nec enim mihi sufficit una.*
> *currite, Pierides, uos enim mea <maxima cura,>*
> *Parrasias niueo conpellite pectine cordas.*

haec tam parua precatio credo quod Virgilianis satisfecerit Musis. cede mihi nunc personam Mantuani uatis, quo fugitiuos eius in lucem deducamus amfractus. nam ecce ad me etiam ipse Ascrei fontis bractamento saturior aduenit, quales uatum imagines esse solent, dum adsumptis ad opus conficiendum tabulis stupida fronte arcanum quiddam latranti intrinsecus tractatu submurmurant. cui ego . . .

Bernard Silvestris' twelfth-century *Commentum super sex libros Eneidos Virgilii*, takes the same topic as its key.

[43] On Fulgentius' *allegoresis*: Edwards (1976), Bartsch (2018).

[44] Cf. Laird (2001: 60–7) and (2009: 3–4).

[45] A reference to his earlier encounter with Calliope and the Muses, similarly summoned up by poetic invocation, in the prologue to *Mit.* 1 (8.10); cf. Döpp (2013: 453–5), Cullhed (2015: 414–32). Fulgentius is there similarly self-conscious as a narrated character (note *index te libelli fefellit*, 'the title of this book deceived you', 10.19). Calliope, too, is an unsettlingly metaleptic apparition in the narrative (cf. Fulkerson in this volume on divine apparitions)—but there is no suggestion that she belongs to the same narrative level as Fulgentius (unlike Virgil in the *Expositio*). She is easily reduced to allegory (cf. Philosofia, Satyra: 12.10–13) as a personification of pagan literature; the attractive seductions offered by her and her companions (cf. *lasciviens amica*, 12.11, and her appearance in Fulgentius' bedroom, 13.19) are contrasted with Fulgentius' jealous wife (*liuens zelo . . . coniugium*, 12.16), an allegory for Fulgentius' Christian faith (cf. Relihan 1993: 158, Hays 2003: 212 n. 140). Fulgentius systematically uses female familial relations to allegorize one's affinity to abstract concepts: cf. *felicitatis . . . nouerca fortuna*, 4.18; *libido . . . honestatis nouerca*, 54.4; *curiositatem . . . salutis nouercam*, 68.4. Jerome, more sinisterly, quotes Deuteronomy 21:10–13 to characterize Christian reuse of classical text as a rape, 'taming' a foreign captive into a wife: *deponet uestem . . . et postea intrabis ad eam, dormiesque cum illa, et erit uxor tua* ('strip off her clothes . . . and afterwards you should go in to her, and sleep with her, and she will be your wife', *Ep.* 70.2). On the text as woman in ancient and medieval hermeneutics, cf. Dinshaw 1989: 18–25.

But now I will make up something more pleasing to the Muses:
> 'O Muses of Helicon—and I do not call only on
>   Calliope—
> Draw near, and grant your favour to my mind.
> I undertake a greater task; a single Muse is not
>   enough for me.
> Run, Pierian Maidens, you are my greatest care.
> Strike the Arcadian strings with an ivory plectrum.'

I think this little prayer will satisfy the Virgilian Muses. Grant me now the Mantuan bard in person [or: 'the *persona* of the Mantuan bard'],[46] so that I may lead his elusive circumlocutions out into the light. And behold: he comes toward me, all drenched with a draught of the spring of Mount Helicon. He looks just as the pictures of bards do, with their tablets raised in order to compose their work, wearing a dazed expression, while they murmur something mysterious, dragged out from within them and resounding like a dog's bark. I said to him . . .

The two speakers, Virgil and Fulgentius, assume the roles of schoolmaster and student and proceed to make their way through the twelve books of the *Aeneid*.[47] Virgil explains how each represents a distinct stage in the growth and moral development of a generic Everyman, drawing on symbolism, parallels with other texts, and (especially) etymologies to explain his allegories.[48] To Virgil's generalizing readings, Fulgentius replies with a parallel, an explanation, or a comment drawn from Christian scripture or teachings.[49] The dialogue ends abruptly: 'The End', *finit* (107.4), and a final note to the recipient of the letter advising caution in reading it.

The dialogue structure clarifies and enacts Fulgentius' aims in the *Expositio*: to simultaneously demolish the pagan significance of pre- and non-Christian classical antiquity and preserve its importance, refitted for Christian

---

[46] Discussed below at pp. 216–19.

[47] Cf. Jones (1964); Cullhed (2015: 404–6, 411); Bartsch (2018). Fulgentius asks Virgil for 'only those trifling things that—for a monthly fee—grammarians dissect for their audience of little boys' (*tantum illa . . . leuia, quae mensualibus stipendiis grammatici distrahunt puerilibus auscultatibus*, 86.4–6), though in the end he gets significantly more than this. Virgil's attitude is parodically schoolmasterly: he chastises and insults Fulgentius (86.7–10, 102.19–20), tests Fulgentius on his catechism (the synopsis of *Aeneid* 1, 90.20), and puts forward the acquisition of knowledge as the topic of the allegory of Book 6 (95–103).

[48] On the tangled relationship between allegory and etymology, see Del Bello (2007), Most (2016).

[49] Christian scripture cited at 87.7–10 (1 Corinthians 23–4), 89.4–10 (Psalms 1:1), 96.14–18 (Psalms 50:19), 97.18–22 (Joshua 7:21).

consumption.[50] Central to Fulgentius' tactics is the conceit that he is not imposing new meaning on the text, nor integrating it unchanged into Christian culture, but rather uncovering and extending meanings already present in the text, authorized by Virgil himself. He enables this by employing two distinct discursive stages in his process of allegorical interpretation. First, Virgil—resolutely pre-Christian[51]—reveals the generalized truths about human nature, the 'real' contents of the *Aeneid*, which he hid behind the poetic apparatus. At that point, the soberly Christian Fulgentius can complete the process by interpreting this 'real' meaning in the light of Christianity.[52] This allows Fulgentius to distance himself not only from the original text of the *Aeneid*, itself still a slightly suspect choice of source from which to derive moral Christian truths, but also from the act of interpreting it.[53] By the time the character 'Fulgentius' reaches the point of applying critical thought to the text, it has been defanged and neutralized. Virgil transforms it into a generic set of truths, though still unaware of their ultimate significance,[54] and Fulgentius need only align these predigested interpretations with Christian thought to redeem the *Aeneid* in its entirety.[55]

Metaleptic Fulgentius

Fulgentius' dramatic scenario is shot through with metalepses. Döpp has explored the ways in which Fulgentius blurs the lines between his various first-person authorial and narratorial roles: he slips between his incarnations

---

[50] Bartsch (2018) explores the *Expositio*'s theological elements.

[51] Cf. 89.10–13, 103.7–10.

[52] Compare the presentation of Virgil as raving bard or severe *magister* with Fulgentius' scholarly and pious self-presentation throughout the *Expositio*. The Fulgentius of the *Mitologiae* caricatures (pagan) vatic wildness: 3.19–20, 8.11, 13.18–19 (cf. Cullhed 2015: 415).

[53] Cf. e.g. MacCormack (1998: 21–44). Fulgentius distances himself from impropriety: *uae inquam nobis, aput quos et nosse aliquid periculum est et habere* ('woe, I say, to me, if there is among these subjects anything dangerous to know and believe', 83.7–9).

[54] Fulgentius neatly avoids the problem of attributing Christian sentiment to the pre-Christian Virgil, even as a quasi-unconscious allegory; cf. Cullhed (2015: 407).

[55] Only one disagreement: Fulgentius deplores Virgilian metempsychosis in *Aen.* 6. He accuses Virgil of uncharacteristic stupidity (102.18–20), citing *Eclogue* 4 as proof of Virgil's usual quasi-Christian insight; Virgil cheerfully accepts the charge, blaming his pagan incomprehension (103.7–13). Bartsch (2018) suggests that Virgil's very presence in Fulgentius' dialogue negates the theory of metempsychosis: Virgil would have become someone else by the time of Fulgentius, rather than a lingering ghost. (*Contra*: Anchises specifies a Platonic thousand years between reincarnations: *mille…annos, Aen.* 6.748. But would Fulgentius care about this philosophical nicety?)

as extratextual author of the *Expositio*, as letter writer, and as the character within the fiction of the dialogue who summons Virgil from the dead and speaks with him.[56] This close overlap between author and narrator is not particularly remarkable in itself.[57] More interesting is Fulgentius' willingness to break the illusion of his fiction of necromantic dialogue by drawing attention to its fictitious nature—the 'suspension of the suspension of disbelief' so characteristic of metalepsis. When Virgil offers to explain the numerological significance of the number seven, in allegorizing the seven Trojan ships that survive the storm of *Aeneid* 1, Fulgentius turns him down (91.20–92.6):

'*...cuius formulam, si uidetur, breuiter explanabo.*' *cui ego: saturanter haec in libro fisiologo quem nuper edidimus de medicinalibus causis et de septenario et de nouenario numero omnem arithmeticae artis digessimus rationem, eritque perissologiae nota si, quae in uno libro descripsimus, etiam aliis inseramus. ergo qui ista discere cupit, nostrum fisiologicum perlegat librum. nunc uero a te quae restant expeto.*

'...I will briefly explain this principle to you, if you would like.' I replied, 'I have already discussed to exhaustion the whole art of arithmetic concerning the numbers seven and nine, in the book on physiology dealing with medical matters which I have recently published. It will be a mark of otiose verbiage if I put in one book topics I've already outlined in another. And so anyone who wants to learn about those matters can read my physiological book. But now I want to get the rest of it from you.'

Fulgentius' citation of his own back issues (*in libro fisiologo*) shores up the autobiographical fiction of the *Expositio*, that Fulgentius actually met the ghost of Virgil and spoke with him. The *ego* of the dialogue claims the same identity as the Fulgentius who writes the *Expositio*, as well as his other books.[58] But the next sentence shatters the fiction: this *ego* is paradoxically aware that he is a fictional construct existing within the pages of a book (*in uno libro*), even as he speaks. The ground shifts from under our own feet,

---

[56] Döpp (2013: 455–8); cf. already Edwards (1976) and Lerer (1985: 62–3).
[57] Cf. Whitmarsh (2013a: 235–8).
[58] I presume it is a quirk of textual transmission that this *fisiologicum librum* of Fulgentius' is no longer extant—but we twenty-first-century readers cannot help but notice that it is, for us, as fictional as the shade of Virgil himself.

too: we may have fancied ourselves invisible eavesdroppers on Fulgentius' and Virgil's *tum ille/cui ego* back-and-forth banter, but now Fulgentius meets our eyes over Virgil's shoulder and drops us a wink, before turning back and pretending he has not seen us (note the overtly innocuous third-person *qui ista discere cupit*, 'anyone who wants to learn about those matters'). Döpp sees in Fulgentius' self-consciously metaleptic narration a 'downright mischievous game with the entities of author and narrator', typical of late antique Latin writing and especially characteristic of a certain *spoudogeloion* tone.[59] Fulgentius' playful approach allows him to stop short of wholeheartedly committing to the fiction he uses to convey his reading of the *Aeneid*, instead holding it comfortably at arm's length.

Metaleptic Virgil

So far, so metaleptic. But it seems to me that for a fuller account of metalepsis in the *Expositio* we must turn not only to Fulgentius but to Virgil too, rather unexpectedly summoned up from the dead by Fulgentius at the beginning of the tract. The appearance and speech of a historical figure in a 'fictional' work is not, of course, automatically metaleptic. There is no reason to see Lucan's Pompey, a priori, as a metaleptic entity, nor Ovid's Numa;[60] neither is represented as transgressing the boundaries between reality and fiction, or between different narrative levels.[61] But something else happens when *authors* are depicted within another's fiction.[62] Critical discourse is always potentially metaleptic, reshaping as it does the relationship between author and text to produce a new model (or fiction) of authorship. The actual appearance of the author within the critical text goes one step further, fully realizing the metaleptic potential of critical discourse. What we have here, I argue, is a case of 'ontological' secondary

---

[59] Döpp (2013): 'ein geradezu mutwilliges Spiel mit den Instanzen von Autor und Erzähler' (458); 'die Interpretation Vergils…ihren besonderen Reiz aus metaleptischen Akten gewinnt' (455–6) ('the interpretation of Virgil…takes its particular charm from metaleptic events'). On Fulgentian *spoudogeloion*, cf. Venuti (2015) (*Mitologiae*), Wolff (2003: 439–40) (*Expositio*).

[60] Pompey: Lucan, *Bellum Ciuile*. Numa: Ovid, *Fast.* 3.259–398, 4.629–76, *Met.* 15.1–487.

[61] By contrast, Nisard's comment on Lucan's Pompey—that the character is ridiculous, but the poet has not noticed this and has therefore been fooled by his own creation ('il est ridicule, et personne autour de lui ne trouve ridicule; ce qui prouve que le poëte ne s'en est pas aperçu, et qu'il est dupe de son héros', 1867: 156)—is an excellent example of secondary metalepsis: Nisard fashions a relationship not between character and narrator, but between character and *author*. Compare Parry (1963: 77), discussed above (pp. 202–3).

[62] Cf. Trimble in this volume, pp. 144–5, on Catullus' appearances in the works of others.

metalepsis: Fulgentius' conceit is that the author Virgil, who exists (or existed) on the same plane of reality as Fulgentius himself, finds himself within the fiction of Fulgentius' narrative. At the same time, the reverse is true: there is a sense that Fulgentius has slipped into a world of Virgil's own making, in which ghosts appear to expound secret mysteries, Virgil resumes his narration of the *Aeneid*, and even Fulgentius begins to speak in sonorous Virgilian cadences.

I suggested above that this 'ontological' form of secondary metalepsis should be viewed within the same category as milder 'rhetorical' forms, such as 'Virgil has Dido die'. In a sense, then, the apparition of Virgil in the *Expositio* is merely a hyper-logical extension of the common scholarly habit—as pervasive now as in antiquity—of ventriloquizing the author to express the interpretation of the text.[63] When Servius introduces a gloss, paraphrase, or exegetical remark with *Vergilius dicit* ('Virgil says') or *hic poeta loquitur* ('the poet says here'),[64] for example, the underlying conceit is that Servius' interpretation is not only Virgil's own sentiment expressed more clearly, or 'translated' into a mode Servius' audience will understand more naturally, but in some way even identical to the text under consideration. The commentator purports to have no active role in the elucidation of the text, but rather to serve merely as a conduit for the author's own sentiment, in the author's own words. In its metonymy of 'author' for 'work' and 'saying' for 'meaning', too, this discursive mannerism shares some conceptual space with the critical maxim Ὅμηρον ἐξ Ὁμήρου σαφηνίζειν ('explaining Homer from Homer' or 'Homer must be his own interpreter')—that is, the principle that criticism of a text should rely on what is known of the author's literary habits and biography.[65] Fulgentius literalizes the metonymic shorthand, bringing the dry idiom to life: Virgil himself acts as his own interpreter (*narrator*, 103.11). His speech in the *Expositio* is hinted to be both an exegesis of the *Aeneid* and, at the same time, a replay of the *Aeneid* itself, the epic retold by the same author. Virgil appears already singing

---

[63] Matzner (2016a) explores the ways in which literary-critical writing is (and figures itself as) a form of ventriloquism, and discusses postmodern fictional representations of this relationship with antiquity: passim but esp. 186, 189–90, 196 n. 30, 201 n. 65.

[64] E.g. Servius *ad Aen.* 1.20: TYRIAS ARCES *Carthaginem dicit, quam Tyrii condiderunt* ('TYRIAN CITADELS: he says [i.e. 'means'] "Carthage", which the Tyrians founded'). *dicere* and *loqui* are also used to introduce direct quotations from the text: e.g. *ad Aen.* 1.32: ACTI FATIS *si odio Iunonis fatigabantur, quo modo dicit 'acti fatis'?* ('DRIVEN BY THE FATES: if they were tormented by Juno's hatred, why then does he say "driven by the fates"?')

[65] The aphorism is found in Porphyry (*Quaest. Hom. Il.* 297) but associated with Aristarchus. The second translation given above is Pfeiffer's (1968: 3). Cf. Pfeiffer (1968: 225–7), Porter (1992), and Struck (2004: 21–3).

(*submurmura[n]t*, 85.16) and grasping his writing tablets (*adsumptis ad opus conficiendum tabulis*, 85.14–15), ready to finish the poem he left abandoned at his premature death.[66]

Fulgentius' innovation lies in taking this scholarly idiom writ large, shaping it as a sustained *nekyia* or *katabasis*, and blending it with the long-established form of scholarly dialogue seen in, say, Plato, Cicero, or Macrobius.[67] The motif of a particularly significant shade employed to expound secret mysteries allows fictional fulfilment of the perhaps universal desire, impossible in reality, to converse with and obtain answers from the dead. To actually stage a scholarly exegesis within a *nekyia*, as Fulgentius does, is a critic's dream: to be able to demand that the author himself decipher and explain the deep meanings hidden beneath his poetry's outward form is the ultimate form of recourse to the author's intentions.

Fulgentius builds here on a long tradition of necromantic literary criticism, improbable as that subgenre may sound.[68] In Plato's *Theaetetus*, Socrates confronts the problem of interpreting a text in the absence of its author; having reached an impasse over the meaning of a Protagorean maxim, he imagines the head of the long-dead Protagoras emerging from the ground before him and his interlocutor (171c–d).[69] The prospect of such recourse to the author's intentions is, however, phrased as purely hypothetical, and Socrates immediately dismisses it as impossible: ἀλλ' ἡμῖν ἀνάγκη, οἶμαι, χρῆσθαι ἡμῖν αὐτοῖς, ὁποῖοί τινές ἐσμεν ('but we, I think, must depend on ourselves, such as we are', 171d). Plato's summoning of the dead Protagoras is a fleeting contrafactual, an impossibility

---

[66] The simultaneous focus on orality and textuality here perhaps reflects both Virgil's extratextual authorial role and his narratorial illusion of performance (*cano*, 'I sing', *Aen.* 1.1).

[67] Boethius' allegorical dialogue, the *Consolatio Philosophiae*, makes a fascinating parallel to Fulgentius' *Mitologiae* and *Expositio* (cf. Lerer 1985), though priority is not clear (cf. Hays 2003: 169–73).

[68] I do not mention here Aristophanes' katabatic literary criticism (*Frogs*, *Thesmophoriazusae*). A discussion of the trope's use by modern classical scholars would be a whole other chapter: cf. e.g. Page's interrogation of Aeschylus (Denniston 1957: xxvi–xxviii), Goold's of Servius (1970: 135–6, densely contrafactual), or Anne Carson's of Mimnermus and Stesichorus (1995: 18–26; 1999: 18–20). Jackson Knight's spiritualist communications with Virgil are notorious (cf. Wiseman 1992: 171–209, Richardson 2016), and Horsfall's commentary on Virgil's *katabasis* is in on the game too (2013: 639: 'if the shades of Oliver Lyne and Don Fowler were to drink blood at the trench and ask me...'). Cf. Matzner 2016a on postmodern novelistic treatments of this scholarly turn; Richardson 2016 on the nineteenth- and twentieth-century spiritualist turn towards 'ghostwritten classics'. My thanks to the audience at the original conference (Oxford, 2015) and to Bram van der Velden for pointing me to some of these works.

[69] καὶ εἰ αὐτίκα ἐντεῦθεν ἀνακύψειε μέχρι τοῦ αὐχένος... ('and if he were to emerge from the ground right here, as far as his neck...'). Cf. Ford (1994) on this image's role in Plato's discussion of problems of authorial intention and fragmented texts. Augustine likewise imagines consulting Moses at *Conf.* 11.3.5.

against which more practical methods of philosophy and interpretation can be measured.[70] Centuries later, Lucian develops the same topos into a pointed parody of clichéd modes of critical discourse. The narrator of the *Verae Historiae* ('Lucian') travels to the Isles of the Blessed, finding them crammed to bursting with the glorious dead—among them not only the luminaries of Greek intellectual history but characters familiar from Greek literature too.[71] 'Lucian' meets Homer and quizzes the long-dead bard about stale topics of scholarly contention: his birthplace, suspected interpolations in his text,[72] his choice to begin with the wrath of Achilles, the order of composition of the *Iliad* and *Odyssey* (*VH* 2.20). Homer obliges, and 'Lucian' gleefully contrasts this sciomantic shortcut to knowledge verified by the author himself with the futile efforts of scholiasts and grammarians, who can but grope at straws with no hope of a definitive answer: κατεγίνωσκον οὖν τῶν ἀμφὶ τὸν Ζηνόδοτον καὶ Ἀρίσταρχον γραμματικῶν πολλὴν τὴν ψυχρολογίαν ('consequently I condemned the grammarians Zenodotus and Aristarchus for the highest degree of nonsense'). This is a prime example of secondary metalepsis.[73] Indeed, the *Verae Historiae* stages encounters not just between 'Lucian' and Homer, but between the long-dead bard and his own Iliadic and Odyssean characters too: Thersites arraigns his creator on the charge of libel (ὕβρεως... ἐφ' οἷς αὐτὸν ἐν τῇ ποιήσει

---

[70] Pliny is similarly scathing about the prospect of literary necromancy in his attack on magic in *Nat.* 30. He reports that Apion once told him that he had summoned the ghost of Homer and quizzed him about his origins—but the story closes bathetically with the renowned scholar ultimately refusing to reveal the answers he received (*non tamen ausus profiteri quid sibi respondisse diceret*, 30.18.8): Apion's silence betrays the fraudulence of his claims. It is interesting, however, that Pliny's encounter with Apion is itself described a little like a necrological apparition: Apion 'appeared' to Pliny (*adulescentibus nobis uisus Apion*, 30.18.2; cf. Dillery 2003: 386), and Pliny admits that magic—in all its falsity—still has something of a 'shadow' (or 'ghost') of the truth about it (*intestabilem, inritam, inanem esse, habentem tamen quasdam ueritatis umbras*, 30.17.6).

[71] *VH* 2.4–29. Lucian follows Socrates in peopling the underworld with both fictional and historical personages: cf. Pl. *Ap.* 40e–41c, ἅπαντες οἱ τεθνεῶτες... Ὀρφεῖ... καὶ Μουσαίῳ καὶ Ἡσιόδῳ καὶ Ὁμήρῳ... Παλαμήδει καὶ Αἴαντι ('all the dead...Orpheus and Musaeus and Hesiod and Homer...Palamedes and Ajax'). Contrast the notable absence of 'real' poets and authors from Virgil's underworld: Orpheus and Musaeus (*Aen.* 6.45–78), but not Homer or Hesiod. (At the dramatic date of the *Aeneid*, are these last two perhaps still alive, or not yet born?)

[72] Lucian himself enacts even greater interpolations into the Homeric canon: an epigram (2.28), an Odyssean narrative in miniature (2.35), and even an entire military epic subsequently misplaced by 'Lucian', with the exception of its opening line (2.24). Cf. Ní Mheallaigh (2009: 20–8) on Lucian's authorial games (a 'self-ironising critical loop', 26) in *VH* 2; Kim (2010: 140–74) explores Lucian's self-conscious fictionality.

[73] On metaleptic Lucian, cf. Whitmarsh (2009, 2013a: 242–4).

ἔσκωψεν, 2.20), which he escapes with the help of his honey-tongued lawyer, Odysseus.[74]

Lucian situates his encounter with Homer in the radically destabilized fiction of the *Verae Historiae*, a carnivalesque piece best viewed as a riot of 'metaleptic anarchy'.[75] He lays out his mendacity with disarming honesty in the prologue (1.1–4), warning us at the outset not to believe a single word he tells us.[76] It is certainly difficult to take Lucian's Homer—flippant, unthinking, scarcely recognizable as the revered bard—at all seriously, despite the narrator's constant assurances of autopsy and true experience.[77] Fulgentius' narration, too, plays with belief and disbelief, authority and subversion, reality and invention; even more than Lucian's, it resists resolution one way or the other. The metaleptic apparition of the ghostly Virgil comes to function as a focal point for this complex ambiguity: it simultaneously demands to be taken seriously as a representation of the actual historical Virgil and systematically undermines any possibility of being taken as such.

For one thing, Virgil—like Fulgentius himself—is unnervingly aware of his own status as a character sprung from someone else's imagination (103.11–13):

neque enim hoc pacto in tuis libris conductus narrator accessi, ut id quod sentire me oportuerat, disputarem et non ea potius quae senseram lucidarem. audi ergo quae restant.

For I did not take on the job of appearing as a speaker[78] in your books on these terms—to argue about what I should have known, rather than to shed light on what I did know. Listen, then, to the rest of it.

---

[74] Compare the anonymous epigram in Dido's voice, similarly accusing Virgil of libel: Πιερίδες, τί μοι ἁγνὸν ἐφωπλίσσασθε Μάρωνα | οἷα καθ' ἡμετέρης ψεύσατο σωφροσύνης? ('Muses, why did you arm virginal Maro against me to slander my chastity like this?', *AP* 16.151). The trope reappears in modern metaleptic fiction: Flann O'Brien's *At Swim-Two-Birds* revolves around fictional characters subjecting their creator to trial (cf. Malina 2002: 11–14).

[75] Ní Mheallaigh (2009: 27).

[76] κἂν ἓν γὰρ δὴ τοῦτο ἀληθεύσω λέγων ὅτι ψεύδομαι ('I shall at least be truthful in admitting that I lie', 1.4). Lucian cites 'Homer's Odysseus' (ὁ τοῦ Ὁμήρου Ὀδυσσεύς, 1.3) as an illustrious predecessor in this practice of lying; cf. Kim (2010: 151–5).

[77] He reveals himself to be Tigranes the Babylonian, fully sighted, and prone to impulsive poetic decisions: he began the *Iliad* with μῆνιν ('wrath') simply because it came to him on a whim (οὕτως ἐπελθεῖν αὐτῷ μηδὲν ἐπιτηδεύσαντι, 2.20).

[78] *narrator* (one who narrates; a speaker) is unexpectedly rare in Latin: Cicero speaks of *narratores* in terms of the crafted nature of their speech (plain-speaking in contrast with fanciful *exornatores*, 'embellishers', at *De Or.* 2.54.3; 'skilled', *facetus*, and paralleled with 'mimics', *imitatores*, at 2.219.5); Quintilian and Silius Italicus associate *narratores* with specifically

Invented interlocutors are nothing new in ancient dialogues, of course: think of Persius' open admission of fabrication in his first *Satire*, when he addresses 'you, whoever you are, whom I've conjured up to put the opposite case' (*quisquis es, o modo quem ex aduerso dicere feci*, 1.44).[79] But Fulgentius' Virgil occupies a curious position, self-aware as a narrative fiction yet also determined to retain autonomy as a peculiarly authorial figure (*narrator*). There is a strange combination in this passage of surrendered agency and tacitly reasserted authority. Like Lucian's Thersites (*VH* 2.20), Fulgentius' Virgil knows that he is somebody else's fiction: he appears *in tuis libris*, 'in your books'. Yet by framing this as an agreement or concession that he has made prior to the narration of the *Expositio* (*neque... hoc pacto*, 'not... on these terms'), he asserts his external existence.[80] Note, too, that his statement of metaleptic self-awareness here mirrors Fulgentius' earlier version (92.3–4): both pause to define more precisely their exegetical role, stating exactly what they will and will not do, and prompt the resumption of the dialogue by referring to *quae restant* ('the rest of it', 92.6, 103.13). By the very structure of his speech, Virgil lays claim to the same degree of reality as that possessed by Fulgentius.

A closer look at the moment of Virgil's sudden intrusion into the world of the *Expositio* reveals a similar oscillation between assurances of realism and self-conscious fictionality. Here is the passage again (85.2–17):

ego uero... Musis aliquid blandius fabulabor:
>*uos, Eliconiades, neque enim mihi sola uocanda est*
>*Calliope, conferte gradum, date praemia menti.*
>*maius opus moueo; nec enim mihi sufficit una.*
>*currite, Pierides, uos enim mea <maxima cura,>*
>*Parrasias niueo conpellite pectine cordas.*

autobiographical narration (*Inst.* 11.1.36, *Pun.* 6.529–30). I wonder if Fulgentius' *narrator* carries the sense of *enarrator* ('interpreter' or 'expositor'), a more common term in scholarly works (cf. Gellius, *Noctes Atticae* 13.31.1, 18.4.2, 18.6.8; Porphyrio *ad Epist.* 2.1.230): Fulgentius' Virgil rivals Fulgentius himself in taking on the role of (self-)critic.

[79] Persius' *Satires* are particularly multivocalic, full of interrupting interlocutors, split personalities, and self-interrogation: cf. Gowers (1994), Hooley (1997: 67–80).

[80] I am reminded here of Roderick Townley's *The Great Good Thing* (2001), in which the characters of a book within the novel know themselves to be characters, bound by the rules of the book's genre and plot. When the book is destroyed, they escape into their reader's imagination. Compare the characters in Cornelia Funke's *Inkheart* (2003): while they are drawn out of a book into the diegetic narrative, prior to that metaleptic leap they remain unconscious of their fictional nature. Fulgentius' Virgil speaks of *tui libri*, 'your books'; does this imply that he too might escape into someone else's books, or his own, or his readers' minds?

haec tam parua precatio credo quod Virgilianis satisfecerit Musis. cede mihi nunc personam Mantuani uatis, quo fugitiuos eius in lucem deducamus amfractus. nam ecce ad me etiam ipse Ascrei fontis bractamento saturior aduenit, quales uatum imagines esse solent, dum adsumptis ad opus conficiendum tabulis stupida fronte arcanum quiddam latranti intrinsecus tractatu submurmurant. cui ego...

But now I will make up something more pleasing to the Muses:
    'O Muses of Helicon—and I do not call only on
      Calliope—
    Draw near, and grant your favour to my mind.
    I undertake a greater task; a single Muse is not
      enough for me.
    Run, Pierian Maidens, you are my <greatest care.>
    Strike the Arcadian strings with an ivory plectrum.'

I think this little prayer will satisfy the Virgilian Muses. Grant me now the *personam Mantuani uatis*, so that I may lead his elusive circumlocutions out into the light. And behold: he comes toward me, all drenched with a draught of the spring of Mount Helicon. He looks just as the pictures of bards do, with their tablets raised in order to compose their work, wearing a dazed expression, while they murmur something mysterious, dragged out from within them and resounding like a dog's bark. I said to him...

Fulgentius' Virgilian pastiche of an invocation seems to please the 'Virgilian Muses'; they send him the *persona Mantuani uatis*. But the precise nature of this *persona* is not immediately clear.[81] Does it denote 'Virgil in person', that is, a thoroughly metaleptic appearance of Virgil in Fulgentius' narrative? Or does Fulgentius instead ask for the Virgilian *persona* or 'mask' of authorship, an imitation of Virgil's style, authority, and understanding that is necessarily transferable and impermanent? That is, is this truly the ghost of Virgil, or merely an exercise in prosopopoeia?[82]

---

[81] Ancient critics were acutely conscious of the distinction between *persona* and external authorial reality (*poeta*). Servius, for example, devotes an extensive note to the problem (*ad Ecl.* 3.1), contrasting poetry in which the poet speaks directly (*Ecl.* 4 and 10) and that in which he uses characters (*personae*). The Virgilian narrator is conceived of as another 'character' whose action is limited to the business of narrating.

[82] On prosopopoeia, cf. Peirano (2012: 26–8), Whitmarsh (2013a: 241). Cic. *Amic.* 3–4 is instructive; cf. Stroup (2013: 143–50).

To a certain degree, this passage sustains the fiction of Virgil's presence. The ghost sounds like Virgil: his speech occasionally veers into quotation from his own works, as if to validate that this is the very Virgil who wrote them.[83] The rest of the dialogue remains attentive to Virgil's characterization: his philosophical preoccupations and his interest in etymological wordplay and multivalent systems of symbolism are as recognizably Virgilian to a modern audience as to Fulgentius'. The ghost looks like Virgil, too, in his appearance as a pagan *uates* in the grip of divine inspiration (85.14–16). He is described in straightforward visual terms, as if the tangible solidity of his materialization could in no way be called in question—this is no *umbra tenuis* ('insubstantial shadow', *Georg.* 4.472, *Aen.* 10.636), no *uanum* or *falsum insomnium* ('empty' or 'false dream', *Aen.* 6.283–4, 896). Fulgentius' account of Virgil's apparition is a marvel of no-nonsense narration: *ecce ad me etiam ipse… aduenit*, he says, 'behold: he himself comes towards me' (85.13–14); no hand-wringing here over the ontological status of the apparition.[84]

But other elements of this passage arouse rather more unease about the stability of the *persona Mantuani uatis*. Virgil's apparition in this passage follows the contours of certain different types of encounters: dreams, ghostly visions, *katabaseis* and *nekyiai*, divine epiphanies. All of these purport to be mechanisms of authority, allowing the communication of privileged information—but in ancient literature and culture, and perhaps especially in Virgil, they frequently turn out to signal narrative instability, dubious authenticity, or even outright fictitiousness.[85] And Fulgentius in fact sets this exact ambiguity in motion in the opening line of the passage. He marks the transition between his opening discussion of Virgil's work (83.1–85.2) and the dialogue that makes up the bulk of the *Expositio* with the declaration *ego uero…Musis aliquid blandius fabulabor* ('but now I will make up something more pleasing to the Muses', 85.2–4).[86] Within

---

[83] Direct quotations: *Aen.* 6.552–4 (100.1–3); *Aen.* 6.724–5 (102.14–15); lemmata passim (incl. *Aen.* 1.1, at 87.4). Virgil's paraphrases of the *Aeneid* sometimes drift into quotation: e.g. *animum pictura inani quod pascit* ('the fact that [Aeneas] feasts his soul on the picture in vain', 93.6) from *animum pictura pascit inani* ('[Aeneas] feasts his soul on the picture in vain', *Aen.* 1.464).

[84] Fulgentius is resolutely uninterested in any metaphysical discussions that might explain Virgil's appearance to him: *quaerimus…nec illa quae…aut Battiades in paredris aut Campester in catabolicis infernalibusque cecinerunt* ('nor do I seek [to learn about] what Battiades sang about familiars [or "daemons", or "spirits"?], or Campester about ghosts or underworld spirits', 85.20–86.4).

[85] Cf. e.g. O'Hara (1990), Harris (2003), Gowers (2005), Casali (2010), Kearey (2018), and Fulkerson in this volume.

[86] *fabula* is reserved in the *Expositio* specifically for *invented* narrative: the plot of the *Aeneid* (90.19), stories told to children (93.20), the myth of Tricerberus (98.24).

the fiction of Virgil's apparition to Fulgentius, this *aliquid blandius* refers to the invocation that follows. But there is an unavoidable sense too in which it applies to *all* that follows, as an admission that the entire encounter is a self-conscious fabrication.

In this context, taking the phrase *persona Mantuani uatis* as an admission of fabrication or impersonation can help explain some curiosities of the *Expositio*. In particular, it helps us reckon with the fact that, although Fulgentius relies upon his dialogue structure and its concomitant separation of the two characters' voices, the two are uncomfortably prone to blurring. Indeed, in the passage quoted above, Fulgentius sounds more like Virgil than Virgil does. It is Fulgentius, now, who declares *maius opus moueo* (85.7 = *Aen.* 7.45). Laird notes that the exclamation *ecce* 'heralds the appearance of Palinurus [and] introduces the apparition of the dead Hector in Aeneas' own narrative of his dream' (*Aen.* 6.337, 2.270): Fulgentius takes on the voice of the protagonist of the *Aeneid*, as well as its narrator.[87]

More troublingly, Fulgentius' voice sometimes seems to issue forth from Virgil's own mouth. We must note that Virgil has remained pagan, but is aware of Christianity; like Anchises, who perceives time passing even while confined to the underworld,[88] Virgil too seems to have kept up with the literary scene after his death and therefore cites post-Virgilian authors (Tiberianus 97.9, Petronius 99.1–2, Porfirius 100.19–101.4). While somewhat jarring in effect, these remarks do not entirely ruin the illusion of Virgil's presence. But something goes more seriously awry when Virgil discusses the story of three-headed Cerberus (98.23–99.2):

> *Tricerberi enim fabulam iam superius exposuimus in modum iurgii forensisque litigii positam; unde et Petronius in Euscion ait: 'Cerberus forensis erat causidicus'.*

> I have already explained in my previous book that the story of Tricerberus works as an allegory for quarrelling and courtroom litigation. Because of this, Petronius writes of Euscios, 'Cerberus was a trial lawyer'.

---

[87] Laird (2001: 66).

[88] Anchises' first words in Book 6 are *uenisti **tandem*** ('you have come *at last*', *Aen.* 6.687), and he continues to refer to the length of time since he has seen his son Aeneas: 'counting out the hours' (*tempora dinumerans*, 6.691), 'for a long time I have wanted to tell you' (*memorare tibi . . . iampridem . . . cupio*, 6.716–17). Fulgentius emphasizes his own temporal distance from Virgil—contra Greene (1982: 17), who declares, 'no one before Dante could have described Virgil as hoarse from long silence because no one was capable of measuring his own anachronistic distance from Virgil.'

The voice of Virgil momentarily claims authorship of *Fulgentius'* works. The mask slips; we see that behind it has been Fulgentius all along. The reader is jolted out of comfortable suspension of disbelief into renewed awareness that 'Virgil' is merely a narrative device and the mouthpiece for Fulgentius.[89]

I would argue that this wavering between semi-serious realism and self-conscious, self-deflating fictionality is key to Fulgentius' deployment of secondary metalepsis. As with 'Virgil has Dido die', or Parry's more elaborate but more cautious formulation, the illusion is not to be entertained for too long. Fulgentius' readers must stay aware that this is a work of literary criticism, and even if the *jeu d'esprit* supports, or derives from, or adds to the more po-faced interpretative work, it should not overpower it. In a way, too, this reduction to prosopopoeia allows the author Fulgentius to reassert control, proving himself ultimately responsible for the readings presented in the *Expositio*. After all, as far as Fulgentius is concerned, the death of the author does not remove him from critical consideration; instead it allows him even more interpretative control, if allowed to slip metaleptically into Fulgentius' work.

A Light in the Darkness

I end with a postscript on one further facet of Fulgentius' necromantic hermeneutics.[90] Let us turn once more to Virgil's entrance into the *Expositio*, where Fulgentius pauses to state his purpose in all of this (85.11–12):

(1)   *cede mihi nunc personam Mantuani uatis, quo fugitiuos eius in lucem deducamus amfractus.* ('Grant me now the *persona* of the Mantuan bard, so that I may lead his elusive circumlocutions out into the light.')

Here Fulgentius defines his own interpretative process: *allegoresis* consists of drawing deeper meanings out of the murkiness of their original phrasing and context into the light of purer knowledge and truth. Looking

---

[89] That is, Virgil is simply a 'mask' (*persona*) through which Fulgentius can speak (*per-sonare*). The etymology is probably spurious (note the vowel difference: *persōna*, but *personāre*), but was popular in antiquity. Gellius proclaims the derivation 'damned elegant and witty' (*lepide, mi Hercules, et scite*, 5.7.1), but dodges the problem of vowel length ('*o*' *littera propter uocabuli formam productiore*, 'the letter "o" is lengthened because of the formation of the word', 5.7.2). Cf. Ahl (1985: 54–7) on Latin puns which ignore vowel length; e.g. Plaut. *Am.* 723, *et malum et mālum dari* ('to be given a beating and an apple').

[90] I owe the sparks of the ideas in this section to Laird's article (2009).

further into the *Expositio* we find that the same metaphor recurs over and over again, mostly now in Virgil's voice:[91]

(2)   Virgil accuses Fulgentius of stupidity, calling him *creperum* (lit. 'dark', 86.7); cf. *claritatem facundiae* ('the brightness of eloquence', 97.6)

(3)   *ueritas…tamen ceca quadam felicitate etiam stultis mentibus suas scintillas sparsit* ('nonetheless, [Christian] truth still sprinkled its sparks in my uncomprehending mind with a sort of blind happiness', 89.12–13)

(4)   On the blinding of the Cyclops: *id est: igne ingenii uana gloria cecatur* ('that is: vainglory is blinded by the flame of understanding', 94.7–8)

(5)   On the burning of the ships in *Aeneid* 5: *igne ingenii superexcellente haec omnia consumuntur* ('they are all destroyed by the marvellous flame of understanding', 95.11–12)

(6)   Fulgentius: *itane tuum clarissimum ingenium tam stultae defensionis fuscare debuisti caligine?…* Virgil: *nullo enim omnia uera nosse contingit nisi uobis, quibus sol ueritatis inluxit* ('Fulgentius: "why did you obscure the brightness of your intelligence in the gloom of such an idiotic line of defence?"…Virgil: "for the whole truth can only be known to those of you on whom the sun of truth has shone"', 102.19–103.10)

(7)   *ut id quod sentire me oportuerat, disputarem et non ea potius quae senseram lucidarem* ('to argue about what I should have known, rather than to shed light on what I did know', 103.12–13)

I do not think this is a dead metaphor (to use an uncannily appropriate metaphor in itself). Throughout the *Expositio* Fulgentius expands its meaning: sometimes it describes the process of allegory (passages 1, 3, 7), sometimes the capacity to *perceive* allegory (2), sometimes the *lux ueritatis*, the specifically Christian light of truth (3, 6, 7), and sometimes the allegorical meaning of a passage of the *Aeneid* (4, 5). This is Fulgentius up to his old tricks again: this multivalent use of light and shadow literalizes a technical term of literary criticism, since in late antiquity *umbra* ('shadow') was jargon for 'allegory' and 'impersonation'.[92]

---

[91]   The tone is set before Virgil's appearance by Fulgentius' first quotation, a passage from the *Eclogues* describing the omen of a sudden blaze of fire (*Ecl.* 8.105–8, cited by Fulgentius at 84.4–6). I do not think it is coincidence that both Virgil's bough (96.22–98.3) and Hercules' Hesperidean apples (84.19–22) are golden.

[92]   Laird (2009: 4); cf. *OLD* s.v. 10. Auerbach (1984: 44) notes that *imago* also denoted 'allegory'; cf. *imagines*, 85.14. Augustine speaks of *adumbrata persona* ('assumed characters') for both prosopopoeia (*Conf.* 1.17.27) and allegory (*C.D.* 10.27); cf. *OLD* s.v. *adumbro* 3–4 ('counterfeit', 'imitate'). Cf. Cullhed (2015: 16).

But there may be further significance in this metaphor. *umbra* is also the standard term for a ghost. What's more, it is a particularly Virgilian term, not only for ghosts but for Virgil and his authorial self-fashioning as well. His use of *umbra* famously circumscribes his poetic career. Shadows open his first poem (*Ecl.* 1.1, *sub tegmine fagi*), and at the end of each work— including the one that supposedly coincides with the end of his own life, in the traditional equation of his literary and literal *corpus*—we encounter yet more shadows (*Ecl.* 1.83, 10.76; *Georg.* 4.566 = *Ecl.* 1.1; *Aen.* 12.952).[93]

Virgil is a shadow; his death cast shadows over both him and his works. Fulgentius, by contrast, gleams. His name derives from *fulgens* ('shining'), something this most etymologically minded of mythographers would never let pass without emphasis: the first occurrence of his name in the *Mitologiae* (*Fulgenti*, 12.24) comes soon after a reference to 'the fire of the sun's *radiance*', *sol*[*is*] *fulgoris igne* (11.14).[94] Like Dante, who transforms Virgilian *umbrae* into stars (*stelle*) in the final word of each cantica of the *Divina Commedia*,[95] Fulgentius burns with the flame of Christian truth, and throws light on the most shadowy of pagan poets. Indeed, the way this metaphor resonates with Virgil's writings ultimately produces something of an aetiology or rationale for his presence in the *Expositio*. Consider Virgil's gnomic comment at *Ecl.* 10.75: *solet esse grauis cantantibus umbra* ('the shade is dangerous to singers'). Does Virgil's line find fulfilment and reversal in Fulgentius, where it is first his 'elusive circumlocutions' (*fugitiuos...amfractus*) and then, ineluctably, the singer himself (*persona Mantuani uatis*) which are drawn into the light?[96]

It is difficult to walk a linear path through these interweaving semantic and thematic associations. None are fully complete: is it possible to draw the poet into the light when the poet himself is an *umbra*? Is the *umbra* Virgil, or allegory, or the underworld, or hopeless obscurity? Is Fulgentius 'knowledge' itself, or is Virgil?[97] Nonetheless, the repetitive imagery,

---

[93] Theodorakolopoulos (1997: 162–4).

[94] This phrase too occurs in the context of Fulgentius' allegorical hermeneutics: *mutatas itaque uanitates manifestare cupimus, non manifesta mutando fuscamus* ('I wish to bring the falsehoods altered [away from the truth] into the open; I do not obscure what is already clear by altering it', 11.12–13).

[95] *Inf.* 34.139, *Purg.* 33.145, *Par.* 33.145. Compare the shadowy woods at the opening of the work: *una selua oscura* (*Inf.* 1.2).

[96] Fulgentius' term is *deducamus* (85.12); compare Virgil's *deductum carmen* (*Ecl.* 6.5).

[97] Fulgentius' Virgil says he used the Golden Bough to allegorize 'knowledge' because he knew his mother dreamt she gave birth to a branch (97.1–3). The detail is from Virgilian biography: cf. *Vita Suetonii-Donati* 3 (Putnam and Ziolkowski 2008: 182, 190), relying on the etymological links *Maro ~ ramus* ('bough') and *Virgilius ~ virga* ('stick', 'wand'). Fulgentius' triangulation of these elements—Virgil, branch, knowledge—closes the loop to imply that Virgil himself is, in some sense, knowledge itself.

allusions to Virgil's works, and his metapoetic self-identifications all work cumulatively, building up a sense of complex symbolic or mystical connection without ever quite pinning it down with precision. In this sense, the metaleptic conceit of the ghostly Virgil can be seen as far more than a humorous framing device alone; it is instead a figure integral to and inevitable from the allegorical mode of interpretation itself.

10
Metalepsis and Metaphysics

Duncan Kennedy

Dreaming, with Christopher Nolan and Descartes

> Dreaming, seemingly so inconsequential, has the curious attri-
> bute of leading us on into deeper and deeper philosophical
> topics.
>
> **Hacking (2002: 233)**

Metalepsis as a narratological term was first proposed by Genette, and
defined by him as 'any intrusion by the extradiegetic narrator or narratee
into the diegetic universe (or by diegetic characters into a metadiegetic
universe) or the inverse.'[1] Perhaps the most interesting recent venture to
exploit the narratological model of metalepsis is Christopher Nolan's 2010
movie, *Inception*. Three distinct narrative levels 'down' (the van chase; the
tilting hotel; the fortress hospital) are troped as dreams and dreams within
dreams, with a fourth, limbo or unconstructed dream space below that.
Metalepsis thus becomes a 'diegetic concept'[2] within the movie, and is
visualized as a cartoonish machine that, complete with large button, enables
the metaleptic jump down between dream levels. The orchestrator of these
embedded narratives is Cobb, together with the team he has assembled,
and the plan is, at the instigation of a Mr Saito, to insert an idea (breaking
up his father's business empire after his death) into the mind of Robert
Fischer, Saito's business rival, in such a way that it will seem to have

* I am very grateful to the editors of this volume for their meticulous and astute com-
ments on an earlier draft of this chapter. In the process of its coming into being, many others
have helped with their comments, including Benjamin Folit-Weinberg, Genevieve Liveley,
Charles Martindale, Pantelis Michelakis, and Ellen O'Gorman.

[1] Genette (1972 = 1980: 234–5).   [2] This term is taken from Kiss (2012).

Duncan Kennedy, *Metalepsis and Metaphysics* In: *Metalepsis: Ancient Texts, New Perspectives.* Edited by:
Sebastian Matzner and Gail Trimble, Oxford University Press (2020). © The editors and Oxford University Press.
DOI: 10.1093/oso/9780198846987.003.0010

occurred spontaneously to him as the right thing to do ('inception' in the movie's terminology); the lower the dream level at which the idea is inserted, in the movie's premise, the more likely it is to take hold. Explaining the potential effects of inception, Cobb says: 'The seed of the idea we plant will grow in this man's mind. It'll change him. It might even come to define him.'[3] The team carry out this plot in the course of a flight from Sydney to Los Angeles long enough that they can use the machine to put Fischer and themselves into a drug-induced sleep and enter a shared dream space with the levels they have designed. Only one person is dreaming at each level; the others are within that dreamer's dream.[4] The characters go back up through the dream levels either by means of a 'kick', a physical jolt of some kind, or by dying within a dream.

Cobb believes inception to be possible because, he reveals to his protégée dream architect Ariadne,[5] he has done it before: trapped in limbo after going down through dream levels with his wife, Mal, he inserted the idea that 'our world was not real'. This has catastrophic consequences for Mal (and Cobb), for she tries to persuade him on their wedding anniversary to join her in (yet another) suicide pact that will project them up to what she believes will be reality (they have killed themselves at least once before to rise up through the dream levels). When she fails to persuade him, she throws herself from the hotel window ledge in what she herself describes, echoing Cobb's own words in a previous suicide pact revealed in flashback, as a 'leap of faith'. Cobb tells Ariadne that the authorities believe he has murdered Mal, and he has had to flee the United States, leaving behind their children; Saito induces Cobb to accept the job by promising him that if inception works with Fischer, he has the influence to get Cobb safely back home. The movie ends with the apparent success of Cobb's plan: the plane lands and he is readmitted to the US. But at the point Cobb is about to be reunited with his children, Nolan introduces a metaphysical conundrum characteristic of his plots. As Cobb goes out into the garden to see his children, the camera focuses in on the spinning top which he has repeatedly resorted to as what he calls a 'totem' to reassure himself, when it

---

[3] Nolan (2010: 84–5).

[4] In the scenario of *Inception*, one of Cobb's team is the designated dreamer of each level (the chemist Yusuf of the van chase; the point man Arthur of the tilting hotel; the forger Eames of the fortress hospital), and does not descend to a lower dream level.

[5] The name will be rich in resonances for readers of Latin literature. For Catullus' Ariadne as a metaleptically self-conscious figure cf. Trimble in this volume. Nolan's Ariadne becomes metaleptically self-conscious in the course of *Inception*, but is also a creator figure who designs dream worlds and fills them with, as Cobb puts it, 'things that have never existed, things that *couldn't* exist in the real world': Nolan (2010: 60–1).

topples, that he is not 'within' a dream—his own or someone else's. But before we know whether the top will fall *this* time, Nolan cuts to black, generating a trope for the moment metalepsis gives way to metaphysics. Is this level Cobb's 'reality', or is he still within a dream?

According to Genette, 'The most troubling thing about metalepsis indeed lies in this *unacceptable* and *insistent* hypothesis that the extradiegetic is perhaps always diegetic, and that the narrator and his narratees—you and I—perhaps belong to some narrative.'[6] Narratology can be averse to probing its metaphysical assumptions, and Genette's reluctance to do so is palpable here. Perhaps with a little help from *Inception*, we can administer the necessary 'kick' to awaken us to them. Genette associates this kind of metalepsis with the literary 'fictions' of writers such as Sterne or John Fowles. But things like this never happen 'in real life', do they? Hence 'unacceptable'. And if metalepsis doesn't exist 'in reality', hence the need for a fantastic metalepsis machine in *Inception*—a 'plot device' if ever there was one![7] But if 'unacceptable', why is it 'insistent'? What Genette resists is the notion that for many who inhabit the world of empirical experience (though the crucial theoretical question is: for most, or even for all—including 'you and I'?), their world is *not* 'reality' or 'ultimate reality', which lies at one level removed. We shall return to this (section 'Metalepsis and Classical Metaphysics' below).

Nolan's choice of the trope of dreaming evokes a famous debate in the metaphysical tradition. For Descartes, the very distinction between dreaming and waking was crucial to the sceptical enquiry into the evidence of the senses and the beliefs that are based on it: how do you know that what you are experiencing is not a dream? In the first of his *Meditations on First Philosophy* (1641) he presented himself sitting in front of his fire, wearing his dressing gown, holding a piece of paper in his hands, and pondering that very question: are the objects in front of him real? Of course they are . . . and yet:

> How often, asleep at night, am I convinced of just such familiar events— that I am *here* in my dressing gown, sitting by the fire—when in fact I am lying undressed in bed! Yet *at the moment* my eyes are certainly wide awake when I look at *this* piece of paper; I shake *this* head of mine and it

---

[6] Genette (1972 = 1980: 236); my emphases. Cf. on this idea Trimble in this volume, p. 144.

[7] Strictly speaking it is a 'Portable Automated Somnacin IntraVenous (PASIV) Device', MV-235A. Nolan (2010: 220–7) contains badly aligned and grainy 'photocopies' of its instruction manual.

is not asleep; as I stretch out and feel *this* hand here I do so deliberately, and I know what I am doing. All this would not happen with such distinctness to someone asleep. Indeed! As if I did not remember other occasions when I have been tricked by exactly similar thoughts when asleep! As I think about this more carefully, I see plainly that there are never any sure signs by means of which being awake can be distinguished from being asleep. The result is that I begin to feel dazed, and *this* very feeling only reinforces the notion that I may be asleep.[8]

What seems so vivid and immediate—*this* piece of paper, *here, at the moment; this very feeling*—could, he thinks, be as much a feature of dreaming as of waking experience in such a way as to make it impossible to distinguish between the two. By the end of his sixth and final *Meditation*, Descartes believes he has found a solution:

The exaggerated doubts of the last few days should be dismissed as laughable. This applies especially to the principal reason for doubt, namely my inability to distinguish between being asleep and being awake. For I now notice that there is a vast difference between the two, in that dreams are never linked by memory with all the other actions of life as waking experiences are. If, while I am awake, anyone were suddenly to appear to me and then disappear immediately, as happens in sleep, so that I could not see where he had come from or where he had gone to, it would not be unreasonable for me to judge that he was a ghost, or a vision created in my brain, rather than a real man. But when I distinctly see where things come from and where and when they come to me, and when I can connect my perceptions of them with the whole of the rest of my life without a break, then I am quite certain that when I encounter these things I am not asleep but awake.[9]

---

[8] Descartes (2013: 24–5): *Quam frequenter vero usitata ista, me **hic** esse, toga vestiri, foco assidere, quies nocturna persuadet, cum tamen positis vestibus jaceo inter strata! Atqui **nunc** certe vigilantibus oculis intueor **hanc** chartam, non sopitum est **hoc** caput quod commoveo, manum **istam** prudens et sciens extendo et sentio; non tam distincta contingerent dormienti. Quasi scilicet non recorder a similibus etiam cogitationibus me alias in somnis esse delusum; quae dum cogito attentius, tam plane video nunquam certis indiciis vigiliam a somno posse distingui, ut obstupescam, et fere **hic** ipse stupor mihi opinionem somni confirmet.* I have slightly adapted Cottingham's translation to bring out Descartes' use of deictic words, an aspect of metaphysical language that will be important in what follows. For the importance of the physical gesture of pointing and the associated deictic dimension of language in metaphysical thinking, cf. Tallis (2010) and Kennedy (2013a: 11–19). Unless otherwise indicated, all translations are my own.

[9] Descartes (2013: 124–5).

Descartes sounds very confident here, but has not said the last word, as we shall see. Dreams remain an important way of critiquing metaphysical assumptions.

Hacking has asked us to reflect upon the culturally specific way 'my culture' (by which he means 'relatively high European literate culture, as traditionally conceived, with Greek and Judaic origins') has come to think about dreaming: 'One important difference between my culture and what appears to be the case in many others is that there is a definitive break between waking and dreaming life. When someone's dreams and waking life flow into each other, the person is considered mad'[10]—as Descartes himself anxiously observes at the beginning of his first *Meditation*. By way of contrast, Hacking adduces the work of the Brazilian ethnographer Viveiros de Castro on Amazonian peoples: 'In the Amazonian group dreams are integral to the whole of life. Our sharp distinction of waking/dreaming does not make much sense to them.'[11] Hacking here gestures towards a current argument that treats metaphysics, against the universalizing pretensions so often attributed to it, as having specific historical and local manifestations.[12]

Put crudely, what 'our culture' calls 'metaphysics' has seen its task as exploring the distinction between being and seeming, between reality and appearance, and between what we can sense and what lies beyond our senses. The term itself is quite late in appearing, and although one of Aristotle's treatises has the title *Metaphysics*, he himself doesn't use the word. The story goes that when his various treatises were classified in the library of Alexandria by Andronicus of Rhodes in the first century BC, there were the political texts, the moral texts, the rhetorical texts, and so on. Then there were a number of texts on physics, after which came a number of books which didn't fall into any of the previous categories and were lumped together as τὰ μετὰ τὰ φυσικά, the things that come after physics (τὰ φυσικά). Aristotle himself talks of θεολογική and φιλοσοφία πρωτή, 'first philosophy', when he wants to refer to that realm of knowledge (ἐπιστήμη) that deals not with the being of specific things, such as living things (biology) or human societies (politics), but with being as such in its universality or generality. Descartes adopted this terminology

---

[10] Hacking (2002: 228).   [11] Hacking (2002: 233).
[12] See now Viveiros de Castro (2014), provocatively entitled *Cannibal Metaphysics*. He challenges occidental metaphysics through a methodology called 'symmetrical anthropology' in which the ways anthropologists and their subjects make sense of each other are placed on an equal footing; see especially Latour (2010) and (2013), Descola (2013), Maniglier (2014), and Lloyd (2015).

and some of the characteristic questions of metaphysics in the title he gave to his *Meditationes de prima philosophia*, with its subtitle *in quibus Dei existentia et animae humanae a corpore distinctio demonstrantur* ('in which are demonstrated the existence of God and the distinction between the human soul and the body').[13]

In ordering Aristotle's works as he did, Andronicus was not simply looking for spare shelf space.[14] Metaphysics involves thinking about 'first philosophy', the 'principles' back beyond which it is impossible to go (etymologically, *principle* comes from *primus* and *capio*, and suggests occupying first place), but for Andronicus it lies 'after' τὰ φυσικά, a cataloguing that reflects the way that what I shall call 'classical' metaphysics envisages a separation of realms of being that is often *hierarchical*, reflected in a distinction between the natural and the *super*natural, what is part of human experience and what lies *beyond* it. Metalepsis can provide a way of thinking about how this separation is effected, as we shall see in the cases of Plato (see next section) and other ancient writers (see section 'Metalepsis and Classical Metaphysics'). But this is not the only way of thinking metaphysically, as we shall explore when we encounter metaphysical approaches that resist assent to hierarchical levels of being—what I shall refer to as 'counter-classical metaphysics' (see section 'Metalepsis and Counter-Classical Metaphysics'). Metalepsis can be seen to be no less a feature of such world views, though it operates differently to different effect,[15] and arguably it assumes a much greater importance in fashioning our experience of 'reality' than the paradoxical device of literary fictions Genette makes it. That discussion will also help us to understand the tension Genette feels in his own use of the term.

Dreaming and Metalepsis in Plato

Consider Plato's Forms: how do we know them? *Do* we know them? Plato's works usually consist of reported dialogues embedded within a narrative

---

[13]   As this subtitle suggests, θεολογική is a crucial element of Western metaphysical thinking, in both what I shall shortly refer to below as its 'classical' and 'counter-classical' traditions.

[14]   Even if not true, the story is revealing. Lear (1988: 248 n. 63) remarks: 'I don't believe this story; or, at least, if a librarian did place the *Metaphysics* after the *Physics*, he did so because he was a very smart librarian and had a deep reason for doing so.'

[15]   Cf. Matzner in this volume on the relevance of specific frameworks for assessment of the effect of metalepsis.

frame, representing in 'dramatic' time, as it were, the attempts of Socrates and his interlocutors to argue through a particular issue. Characteristic of the Platonic dialogue is that the issue is clarified rather than concluded; the day ends, the interlocutors disperse, and the argument is put to one side for the moment. Not even Socrates himself claims knowledge of the Forms, which lie beyond immediate human experience, and are elusive. Thus, in *Cratylus* 439c, Socrates remarks to Cratylus: 'Consider the thing I often *dream* about, my worthy Cratylus: should we say, or shouldn't we, that there is a beautiful in itself or a good in itself, and in this manner each one of the things that are?'[16] It would be easy to take this reference to dreaming for granted and to overlook the heavy metaphysical lifting it is doing. Let us accept Hacking's invitation to think about how the meta-physical entailments associated with dreaming may be not simply cultur-ally but historically specific as well. Classical Greek had two words for dreaming, ὄναρ and the curious word ὕπαρ, and Plato repeatedly exploits his own distinction between the two. In an important article, Miller has observed that in Penelope's account of her dream of the eagle and the geese in *Odyssey* 19.547–50, a passage Plato alludes to in the *Republic*, she contrasts ὄναρ and ὕπαρ in such a way as to suggest that both occur in sleep, but whereas ὄναρ suggests a misleading dream, ὕπαρ denotes a reli-able one.[17] In *Republic* 476c Socrates gives a remarkable twist to this dis-tinction between ὄναρ and ὕπαρ to talk about the relationship of lived experience to the Forms in what Miller argues is 'a problematic and self-referential meditation on the simultaneous necessity and impossibility of distinguishing between being and seeming'.[18] Socrates says (in Miller's translation but with my emphases): 'The one who believes in beautiful things on the one hand, but who neither believes in beauty itself nor, should someone lead him to the knowledge of it would be able to follow, *does he seem to you to live a dream* [ὄναρ] *or be awake* [ὕπαρ]? Is dreaming not the following: whenever someone, *awake or asleep*, believes the like (ὅμοιον) is not the like (ὅμοιον) but the thing itself (αὐτό) to which it resembles (ἔοικεν)?'[19] Socrates suggests you can be 'dreaming' when you

[16] σκέψαι γάρ, ὦ θαυμάσιε Κρατύλε, ὃ ἔγωγε πολλάκις ὀνειρώττω. πότερον φῶμέν τι εἶναι αὐτὸ καλὸν καὶ ἀγαθὸν καὶ ἐν ἕκαστον τῶν ὄντων οὕτω, ἢ μή;
[17] Miller (2015: 43).   [18] Miller (2015: 37).
[19] ὁ οὖν καλὰ μὲν πράγματα νομίζων, αὐτὸ δὲ κάλλος μήτε νομίζων μήτε, ἄν τις ἡγῆται ἐπὶ τὴν γνῶσιν αὐτοῦ, δυνάμενος ἕπεσθαι, ὄναρ ἢ ὕπαρ δοκεῖ σοι ζῆν; σκόπει δέ. τὸ ὀνειρώττειν ἆρα οὐ τόδε ἐστίν, ἐάν τε ἐν ὕπνωι τις ἐάν τε ἐγρηγορὼς τὸ ὅμοιόν τωι μὴ ὅμοιον ἀλλ' αὐτὸ ἡγῆται εἶναι ὧι ἔοικεν; ὕπαρ is a peculiar word, an indeclinable noun, which is used quasi-adverbially here, and attracts ὄναρ (normally declinable) into a similar function. For ὄναρ and

are awake, when you mistake the resemblance (ὅμοιον) for the thing itself (αὐτό). In *Inception*, recall how Mal, when she tries to persuade Cobb he's dreaming, tells him that these are not their children (i.e. they are ὅμοια, resemblances she believes to be resemblances), whereas he firmly believes they are not resemblances but the real thing (αὐτό) with whom he is determined to be reunited.

Socrates uses the distinction in *Theaetetus* 158b to touch on the sceptical argument that Descartes was to develop and which provides the scenario for the closing scene in *Inception*: you may believe yourself to be awake, but how do you know you're not dreaming? Socrates asks what evidence you could put forward to settle the question for yourself: 'What proof you could give if someone should ask us now, at the present moment, whether we are sleeping and are dreaming all the things we are thinking of, or whether we are awake and talking with each other ὕπαρ.'[20] The operative contrast is not simply between sleeping and dreaming on the one hand and being awake on the other, but sleeping and dreaming, and knowing that the experience is a dream on the one hand, and on the other experiencing a context of such verisimilitude in all its detail that it convinces us of its reality—not a dream we know is a dream (ὄναρ) but a dream so vivid in its every particular that we don't know it's a dream (ὕπαρ). Theaetetus responds that he can't see what proof could be given. Any evidence to distinguish waking from dreaming would have to consist of something whose presence is held to characterize or guarantee our waking experience. And whatever is suggested, an object like the spinning top totem in *Inception* or a more general feature such as coherence, it is always an intelligible supposition that one might be *dreaming* that that object or feature is present.[21]

ὕπαρ contrasted in Plato, cf. *Phaedrus* 277d, *Republic* 520c, 533b–c, 574d (and cf. 576b), *Statesman* 277d, 278e.

[20] τί ἄν τις ἔχοι τεκμήριον ἀποδεῖξαι, εἴ τις ἔροιτο νῦν οὕτως ἐν τῶι παρόντι, πότερον καθεύδομεν καὶ πάντα ἃ διανοούμεθα ὀνειρώττομεν, ἢ ἐγρηγόραμέν τε καὶ **ὕπαρ** ἀλλήλοις διαλεγόμεθα.

[21] As we saw in the previous section, Descartes at the end of the final *Meditation* resorted to the coherence argument. Although Hacking believes that Descartes had genuinely experienced acute sceptical anxiety, he gives this short shrift: 'Coherence arguments like that are two a penny in the history of philosophy…At the end of the *Meditations* he recites the old stuff, the coherence argument, but only because *by then* he has convinced himself that he no longer experiences live skepticism' (2002: 241; my emphasis). Coherence arguments persist (notably in Malcolm 1959), but Hacking's point is that they are deployed by those who *have made up their minds* they know the difference between dreaming and being awake. Furthermore, as Reid (1992: 9) argues, perceptions of coherence—and, we may add, incoherence—depend on acts of framing (cf. Matzner in this volume, pp. 19–23). Distinctions between dreaming and being awake can provide just such acts of framing. More on the importance of framing in the final two sections of this chapter.

In developing the ὄναρ/ὕπαρ distinction as he does, Socrates is not trying to advance the radical scepticism that would so disconcert Descartes,[22] rather to stress the limits of our waking experience (which seems so substantial). To revert to the argument in *Republic* 476c, our waking experience reveals not the real thing (αὐτό), but likenesses (ὅμοια); if we recognize them *as* likenesses, likenesses of the real thing but significantly different from it, we gain a sense that appearance is not the same as reality, that seeming is distinct from being. In *Inception*, Cobb is (too?) ready to invest in present appearances, while Mal so believes in the metaphysical idea that 'this world is not real' that she (physically!) acts precipitately upon it in her 'leap of faith' from the window ledge. In the divergent conclusions they jump to, Cobb and Mal both ignore the distinction between appearance and reality which provides that very space of questioning, of irony, that Socrates is at such pains to develop.[23] Socrates might concede that in important respects 'our world is not real', but would argue that 'our' world is not one we can readily escape from; the world of the Forms is one he can, as we heard him say in *Cratylus* 439c, only 'dream of', not enter. Sedley remarks of this passage: 'This metaphor of dreaming does not imply, as it might in modern English, a wish or hope. Rather it is Plato's device for describing a *hypothetical* grasp of something—trading on the way that in dreams we treat things *as if* they were true or real, without knowing whether they actually are.'[24] In Plato's writings the distinction of ὄναρ and ὕπαρ thus sets in motion a complex interplay between waking and dreaming experience in such a way as to forge a distinction that is at once metaphysical and hierarchical between waking experience and the world of the Forms. Where Sedley speaks of the *metaphor* of dreaming, I think we could see Socrates' reference to dreaming rather, within the specific narrative framework of the *Cratylus*, as a fleeting *metaleptic* moment: through a single word, it serves to break the narrative frame of the immediate ongoing experience of its participants in order to appeal to or gesture towards, *though not enter*, the realm of the Forms. Socratic

---

[22] Cf. Burnyeat (1982).

[23] Cf. Miller (2015: 47) (original emphasis): 'The critical question is not, then, between appearance and reality, but between appearances that offer the promise of a certain self-transcendence, and therefore offer the possibility of self-criticism, and those that return always and only to the realm of the immediate. Thus the question is always *precisely* a question, an ironic moment in which a dream (ὄναρ) promises to be something more than just a dream (ὕπαρ), when appearance appears other than itself, but does not therefore reveal or produce a doctrine that introduces a set of transcendental guarantees allowing unimpeded access to "the way in which the thing that is is." '

[24] Sedley (2003: 165); original emphasis.

irony presents a philosophical *aporia* (etymologically 'the lack of a way through'), through which this metaleptic trope can at least point in the desired direction.

I have spoken of a metaleptic moment, a single word such as 'dreaming' that points to an alternate world that lies beyond or transcends immediate experience. This could be seen as the product of a narrative condensation that precipitates the metaphysical resonances that become associated with such terms. In adumbrating separate metaphysical 'realms', not only a realm of Forms but of an afterlife as well, to which we have no direct access, inset narratives have a crucial role to play, as the Myth of the Cave in *Republic* 7 (514a–517a) and the Myth of Er in *Republic* 10 (613e–621d) illustrate. As Nightingale has argued, the Myth of the Cave is structured in narrative terms on the Greek social institution of *theōria*, in which a representative of the city visits a Panhellenic festival, observes, and then reports back to the citizenry.[25] The Myth of the Cave, with its journey upwards to the light and its journey back to inform the prisoners below, thus precipitates a term, *theory*, that is freighted with the metaphysical baggage associated with Platonic thinking: the search for truth, and, in Plato, related to divine rather than human knowledge, as Socrates suggests in his commentary on the myth (517b): 'And if you connect the journey upwards and the sight of the things up there with the ascent of the mind into the intelligible region, you won't misunderstand my surmise, since that is what you are eager to hear; *but only god knows, perhaps, if this is the truth.*'[26]

The Myth of Er shares the narrative structure of a return journey. Socrates tells Glaucon how Er returned from the dead after twelve days, sent, Er says, as a messenger to recount to humankind what he had seen 'over there' (ἐκεῖ, 614d).[27] The function of the story, according to Socrates, is to induce *belief*. Unlike the other souls, Er was prevented from drinking of the waters of forgetfulness, 'and so, Glaucon, his tale was saved and did not perish, and it may save us, *if we believe it*' (621b–c).[28] In general terms we might call such narratives 'metaphysical journeys', to suggest a journey,

---

[25] Nightingale (2004).

[26] τὴν δὲ ἄνω ἀνάβασιν καὶ θέαν τῶν ἄνω τὴν εἰς τὸν νοητὸν τόπον τῆς ψυχῆς ἄνοδον τιθεὶς οὐχ ἁμαρτήσει τῆς γ'ἐμῆς ἐλπίδος, ἐπειδὴ ταύτης ἐπιθυμεῖς ἀκούειν· **θεὸς δέ που οἶδεν, εἰ ἀληθὴς οὖσα τυγχάνει.**

[27] The deictic ἐκεῖ is frequently used in the *Republic* to 'point' to other realms: in the Myth of Er cf. also 614b (in 619b, Er is described as 'the messenger from over there' [ἐκεῖθεν]); and of the afterlife elsewhere 330d, 365a, 498c. In 500d it refers to the world of the Forms, and in 516c and 520d to the world of the Cave.

[28] καὶ οὕτως, ὦ Γλαύκων, μῦθος ἐσώθη καὶ οὐκ ἀπώλετο, καὶ ἡμᾶς ἂν σώσειεν, ἂν πειθώμεθα αὐτῶι.

there and back, to another realm that we cannot take 'physically': we are the beneficiaries of a report from one who has been able to make that journey and return. To put this in narratological terms, a secondary diegetic sphere, Er's account of what happens to the soul after death, is embedded within a primary diegetic sphere, Socrates' discussions with his interlocutors in the *Republic*, the metaleptic link being Er's *theōria*, his report back to the living of what happened to him after his death. The embeddedness is in fact more multi-layered than this, since the dialogue of Socrates and his companions is itself presented as a report of their discussions inset into a narrative frame by Socrates himself ('I went down yesterday to the Piraeus with Glaucon, son of Ariston' [*R.* 327a]). For all that the discussions of Socrates and his companions seem vividly present to readers of the *Republic*, they are a report from a world that is *forever* temporally absent ('I went down *yesterday*'). This structures Socratic dialogues like the *Republic* as *theōria*. Let us explore this further, now also keeping in view the hitherto shadowy figure of Plato.

In the *Republic*, Socrates goes to considerable pains to portray the philosopher as a particular kind of artist, not one who 'imitates' particular objects that presently exist in the world, which is the realm of the senses, but one who, as Allen has put it, makes 'models that can be "used" by listeners and readers *to gain concepts* that help them toward cognitive access to what really is'.[29] Key examples of such models (παραδείγματα) are the 'myths' that punctuate Plato's dialogues, and that precipitate concepts such as *theory*. In *Republic* 2, the education of the young in the ideal city involves 'myths' that are openly acknowledged as ψεῦδος (377a), fictions that, taken as a whole, are 'a lie' but 'contain some truth'. Their function, for grown-ups as well as children, is not the *representation* of 'truth' or 'reality'. They are 'make-believe', but if they are effective they *make us believe*. Plato's dialogues themselves are large-scale examples of such παραδείγματα. They do, of course, deploy all sorts of things familiar from experience (e.g. Socrates, Glaucon, the port of Piraeus, the festival of Bendis at the beginning of the *Republic* [327a]), but such stories are not documentaries.[30]

---

[29] Allen (2010: 45) (my emphasis); she suggests that 'it is fair to say that [Plato] discovers the distinction between depicting a particular object and modelling a general idea, and therefore also the distinction between representation and visualization' (2010: 44). Cf. also Miller (2015: 47–9).

[30] Reference, in the sense of information about what Socrates was up to on a particular day, is not the primary motivation of such narrative details. Rather they provide an easily recognizable set of bearings that serve to orientate us on the 'journey' we are being asked to make in reading the *Republic*.

Collectively, they precipitate a concept, *dialectic*, which is Socrates' preferred 'method' of trying to help us, as Allen put it, 'toward cognitive access to what really is'. In the *Phaedrus* (276b–e), Socrates develops the image of discourse (*logos*) as a seed planted in the recipient's mind which can be tended so as to develop, bear fruit, and be disseminated (not so far, perhaps, from the eponymous theme of *Inception*); and the best discourse is, of course, the 'dialectical technique' (276e). The seeds so planted could be 'this world is (in important respects) not real' and 'there is a way to truth (the dialectical technique)'. 'Theoretical' knowledge that seeks to move beyond immediate human experience figuratively involves a journey. It can be no coincidence that the *Republic* begins with the narrative of a journey—but this is a journey that is transformed from a *hodos* to a *methodos* (the preferred 'path to follow' on a metaphysical journey) by the nesting of diegetic spheres linked by metaleptic chains.[31]

The Platonic 'method' was to grow into a branching problem the subsequent philosophical tradition saw its job as addressing: the issue of Being. Behind Plato in the fifth century BC lies Parmenides. His poem sets up a sharp distinction between the 'Way of Truth' and the 'Way of Opinion'. He too sets up his thinking with the report of a journey. In the prologue to the poem, a young initiate travels on a chariot from the world of daily life to the place where day meets night. There he is instructed by an unnamed goddess that thought must have something to think about: 'it must be the case that what can be talked about and thought about exists; for it is possible for that to exist, but it is not possible for nothing to' (B 6.1–2).[32] This assumption, taken to be fundamental, is expressed by the word ἔστι; on the other hand, 'you cannot say or think that it is not (οὐκ ἔστι, B 8.8–9)'.[33] On this basis she deduces that whatever can be talked about must be 'without birth or death, whole, the only one of its kind, motionless and complete, nor was it, nor will it be, since now it is, all together, one, continuous' (B 8.3–6).[34] That is to say, any talk of temporal change, of coming into being and passing away, of plurality, contrasts, and qualitative change, or of non-existence, violates this assumption. So, although Parmenides uses a

---

[31] διήγησις is etymologically associated with the verb ἡγέομαι, which encompasses acting as a guide to a route and believing.

[32] χρὴ τὸ λέγειν τε νοεῖν τ᾽ ἐὸν ἔμμεναι. ἔστι γὰρ εἶναι, | μηδὲν δ᾽ οὐκ ἔστιν.

[33] οὐ γὰρ φατὸν οὐδὲ νοητόν | ἔστιν ὅπως οὐκ ἔστι.

[34] ὡς ἀγένητον ἐὸν καὶ ἀνώλεθρόν ἐστιν,
οὖλον μουνογενές τε καὶ ἀτρεμὲς ἠδ᾽ ἀτέλεστον,
οὐδέ ποτ᾽ ἦν οὐδ᾽ ἔσται, ἐπεὶ νῦν ἐστιν ὁμοῦ πᾶν,
ἕν, ξυνεχές.

narrative to set up his argument, he asks you to accept that the things narrative articulates—time, change, and the means by which it does so, language—are illusory; to access truth, you must reject this world for another which is exceedingly strange, the world of ἔστι, absolutely static and without qualities.

Effectively, Parmenides reduces language to the single word ἔστι. Later generations still struggle to parse this: the third-person singular of the verb 'to be', grammatically a present indicative, but in effect a tenseless present, a linguistically minimalist expression (thrust into a syntactic and semantic isolation) that inaugurates a tradition of thinking that would come to be criticized in the twentieth century as the 'metaphysics of presence'. The contextualizing frame which has precipitated the term ἔστι is elided or rendered invisible, and narrativity in the realm of ἔστι is reduced towards zero. The legacy of Parmenides is to see being as existing outside of time and change, and this tradition has characteristically sought reality and truth, as Parmenides did, in the transcendence of language—and yet manipulates language and narrative to fashion this separate realm and to articulate our relationship to it, before dismissing them as illusory. Rather than the 'metaphysics of presence', we might speak of the 'metaleptics of presence', a phrase that points up a distinction between the world of experience articulated in narrative and a world of timeless, changeless Being. The distinction is hierarchical—*this* world is not real, *that* one is— and we gesture to it from this side through a series of deictic metaphors: of levels, lower and higher; of modes of access ('breaking and entering', if you will, though *theory*, thanks to Plato, is a term that allows us to feel a cut above your average burglar); dreams; prayers; leaps of faith; death.

Metalepsis and 'Classical' Metaphysics

For many who inhabit the world of empirical experience, *this* world is not 'reality' or 'ultimate reality', which rather lies *over there*, at one level removed, above, below, or beyond. *Pace* Genette, who deems it 'unacceptable', people have, in fact, readily seen themselves as characters 'within' some grander narrative that they have only fleeting intimations of. Think of Virgil's *Aeneid*, where (as in *Inception*) metalepsis is a diegetic concept. No machine here, however, rather the irruption of specific manifestations of narrative, such as oracles and dreams, that suggest, and seem to give glimpses of, a level of reality that exists beyond everyday experience, and endows it with meaning that is not immediately apparent. Thus the metaphysical journey of Aeneas to the underworld, in which he sees the souls of those who have died and of those yet to be born, is troped as a dream: at the end of the journey, we hear of the twin gates of sleep, the one of horn by which a ready exit is given to true shades; and the other of ivory, by which Aeneas and the sibyl leave, 'the Manes send false dreams to the world above' (6.893–8). Arguably the most important manifestation of metaleptic narrative in the *Aeneid* is what, from a human perspective, is called 'prophecy': the poem suggests that, beyond any account of history you or I or the Virgilian narrator could construct in our world, which would be imperfect (literally 'incomplete'), lies a master narrative, the definitive version that fully embraces not only the past but the future as well, in such a way as to make sense of events that may seem pointless—that seem, precisely, to lack coherence, when viewed within a narrower frame. In the *Aeneid*, that version is associated with Jupiter, the supernatural narrator of the story of Rome's 'empire without boundaries of time and space' (*imperium sine fine*) in 1.257–96.[35] This perfect version is a narrative framing of history without any of the limits we bump up against, notably ignorance of events that have not yet happened. It extends the frame of interpretation to include *everything*. Precipitated from this metalepsis is the idea of Fate or History—the grand 'plot' that (if we believe in it) transcends, and ultimately explains, our immediate historical experiences.

A realm that transcends the temporal situatedness of human narratives is a feature of many theological discourses. Augustine addressed some of the metaphysical challenges in his autobiographical *Confessions*.[36] When he turns from the books he has written on himself and on the subject of memory (1–10), he addresses God and says (11.1.1): 'Lord, eternity is yours, so you cannot be ignorant of what I tell you. Your vision of occurrences in time is not temporally conditioned. Why then do I set before you an ordered account of so many things (*cur ergo tibi tot rerum **narrationes** digero*)?'[37] Augustine's God isn't a reader and doesn't narrate—existing outside time, he doesn't need to; unlike human beings, who must narrate from a point in time, God knows the complete intentional and consequential significance of any event. The narration of the *Confessions* is not directed towards God, then, but towards his fellow human beings (cf. 2.3.5 *cui narro haec*? 'To whom do I tell these things? Not to you, my God. But before you I declare this to my race, to the human race'). But 11.1.1 instantiates the

---

[35] See further Kennedy (2013a: 43–83).
[36] What follows is discussed in greater detail in Kennedy (2013a: 2–42).
[37] Translations from Augustine are taken from Chadwick (1991).

master trope of the work, apostrophe ('Lord, eternity is yours'),[38] the second-person address of confession and prayer, broadcast to eternity from within the temporal situatedness and sequentiality of human existence. Apostrophe and confession run athwart and seek to break out of the narrative framing of memory, experience, and the stories we tell of ourselves. Breaking the frame, though not entering the realm of eternity: only his death will bring Augustine fully into the presence of God.

There is, of course, resistance to such appeals to a 'higher' reality, and in particular to the association of a realm of true knowledge with the divine or the supernatural, most notably in Lucretius' exposition of the philosophy of Epicurus. In the first of the great set pieces praising the achievement of Epicurus (*De rerum natura* 1.62–79), humankind is depicted grovelling on the ground oppressed by Religion (62–3), personified as a figure 'showing its head from the regions of the sky', and 'standing over' (*super... instans*) mortals (64–5). Epicurus is the first human being 'to raise mortal eyes against it and to stand up against it' (66–7). He goes on a journey 'beyond the flaming ramparts of the world' (73), and 'surveys the immeasurable universe in his mind and spirit' (*omne immensum peragrauit mente animoque*, 74). This superhuman journey across what for Epicureans was a universe infinite in space and time takes place not in body but in thought, and is, like the Myth of the Cave, structured in narrative terms as the journey there-and-back-again of *theōria*: Epicurus 'reports back to us' (*refert nobis*, 75) 'the explanation according to which* what can and cannot come into being, in short how each thing has its powers limited' (*quid possit oriri, | quid nequeat, finita potestas denique cuique | quanam sit ratione*, 75–7)—the theory of the atom. Crucially, Epicurus' metaphysical journey across an infinite universe eliminates time and space from explanation of natural phenomena and offers, precisely, universality: no matter where you look, no matter when you look, Epicurean *theory* offers a true explanation of what you see, the reality behind visual appearances.[39] As a result of Epicurean theory, Religion is trampled beneath our feet, and we are elevated to the place formerly associated with it, up there in the sky (78–9). Elsewhere, in rejecting that other realm associated with metaphysical thinking, the afterlife, Lucretius similarly appropriates the deictic and orientational terms that refer to it: 'nowhere appear the regions of Acheron, and the ground does not stand in the way of our seeing everything that goes on beneath our feet *below* throughout the void' (*sub pedibus*

---

[38] On metaleptic apostrophe cf. Budelmann, De Jong, and Trimble in this volume.
[39] Cf. Kennedy (2013b).

quaecumque **infra** *per inane geruntur*, 3.25–7). There is no such 'other realm', only the ceaseless movement of atoms within empty space. So is it the case that τὰ φυσικά triumph and τὰ μετὰ τὰ φυσικά, whether above, below, or after, are given the boot? Not so fast.

Epicurus' metaphysical journey returns with the theory of the atom that has two aspects: a *physical* entity that, we are told, was never created, will never be destroyed, and is eternal and unchanging; but also an *explanatory* entity that, in Lucretius' terminology, is the 'first beginning', *principium*, back to which, but never beyond which, any phenomenon is to be referred—the sort of ultimate explanation sought by what Aristotle called φιλοσοφία πρωτή. Is the journey needed? The answer seems to be yes. Wardy has said: 'From antiquity to the present day atomic theory has demanded that people confront a startling idea: that the world, on scales both very small and very large, is not *faithfully* represented by the experiences of human subjects... Theory reveals to *the mind's eye* a stark, pure vista of colorless, odorless, tasteless, soundless atoms traveling through the never-ending void. It opens a gap between basic *reality* and at least the most familiar or basic *appearances*, threatening to make strangers of us in our own world.'[40] Lehoux has analysed how Lucretius, paradoxically, uses the language of 'seeing' repeatedly in relation to what he emphasizes cannot be physically seen, atoms, and which lack the (so-called 'secondary') qualities apprehended by the human senses.[41] Recall Wardy's terms that I've emphasized: the well-worn cliché of 'the mind's eye'; 'the world...not faithfully represented by the experiences of human subjects'. Plato and Lucretius are in many ways poles apart philosophically, but in others they are not. Both regard the knowledge provided by human experience to be of itself inadequate and to require the supplement of *theory*; both make an appeal to a theoretical realm of stable truth beyond experience and ask us to make a leap of faith and invest our belief in that realm. Both are idealists, Plato of form, Lucretius of matter. Both are in the business of *make-believe*. The *evidence*, what (etymologically) we can see (*uidere*), provides a limited sort of knowledge; absolute knowledge beyond that involves putting one's trust that there *exists* some thing that guarantees a true explanation. Consider this too in relation to Virgil and Augustine. As with Lucretius, they too make appeal to an eternal unchanging order beyond that of human experience, but one whose effects we sense in our world—the *eureka* moment of discovery or revelation of what has been *there* all along had we

---

[40] Wardy (1988: 112); my emphases.   [41] Lehoux (2013).

only the wit to *recognize* it: I see this phenomenon (i.e. this appearance presented to my sensory experience) and can 'point' to, in the case of Lucretius, the activity of the atom; in Virgil's *Aeneid*, a particular event makes ultimate sense in the 'light' of the preordained pattern of History; for Augustine, the action of God's grace in the world becomes apparent as one opens the scriptures and sees oneself addressed in them, as if this were God's apostrophe to you from beyond.

But theorizing is something we do the whole time. How many of us have never uttered words along the lines of 'this is *really* all about such-and-such', appealing to some explanatory entity or order that lies behind initial appearances? Might we even associate such a hierarchy of levels with the principle of reason itself? The stories we narrate, whether the narrator is Parmenides, Plato, Lucretius, Virgil, Augustine, or ourselves, precipitate concepts in which we, to a greater or lesser extent, invest belief, and which we consider to *underlie* and explain the immediate evidence. Moreover, Hacking suggests that concepts create identities. He describes what he calls 'looping effects' in which people come to see themselves through the lens of a new concept and define themselves in its terms— more or less what Plato suggests in the *Phaedrus*, or what Cobb claims for inception.[42] In some cases, the concept purports to be eternal and overtly providential (Virgil's Fate, Augustine's God), to the extent of being personified; in some cases eternal but non-providential (Lucretius' atom). But the list can be extended: one might also see this in providential (personified) or quasi-providential (non-personified) modes of explanation (Augustine's *City of God*, Marxism, or Fukuyama's 'end of History'; or the 'Invisible Hand' of Adam Smith's *Wealth of Nations*, or Hegel's Reason)[43] that project some kind of transcendent entity that operates upon us in a way that cannot be reduced to human will or intention but that expresses itself in human action with effects that we (sometimes) think we can dimly 'discover'; the test is do we *believe* that that entity *really exists*? Lucretius represents Epicurus as rebelling against a religion that 'stands over' (*super...instans*, 1.65) humankind, and many would raise their eyes and stand up against equivalent modern 'superstitions' that similarly enjoin submission and obeisance—the Market of neo-liberal economics, perhaps, though examples of such fetishisms could readily be multiplied from across the ideological spectrum, not least at the moment in the oppressively dogmatic world views of religious or scientific fundamentalism.

---

[42] Hacking (1994).   [43] Cf. Kennedy (2013a: 98–9).

Such discourses continue to posit an 'other world' which harbours the truth beneath the veil of illusion, often accompanied by an alleged 'vision' of this salvific realm, whether it be a paradise peopled with various fantasies of fulfilment, or the 'singularity', that moment of rapture when human consciousness shall be gathered up and rendered immortal as bytes.[44] But there are more things in heaven and earth than are dreamt of in *this* tradition of metaphysics.

Metalepsis and 'Counter-Classical' Metaphysics

Standing up against such ideologies involves a mode of metaphysical thinking in which concepts are viewed not as eternal, nor providential, entities but, precisely, as provisional, human explanatory formations that are 'transcendental' only to the extent that they are the objects of temporary ontological and metaphysical investment. One can thus inhabit the Socratic space between appearance and reality so as to resist, rather than give in to, the temptation to believe. There are many examples of this approach one could adduce. For example, in the natural and social sciences what Daston calls 'applied metaphysics', the coming into being and passing away of objects of scientific study: dreams, atoms, culture, value, cytoplasmic particles, the self.[45] Similarly, in the philosophy of history, there is Koselleck's *Begriffsgeschichte*, 'conceptual history' that (as the book's blurb has it) 'focuses on the invention and development of the fundamental concepts underlying and informing a distinctively historical manner of being in the world'.[46] As we have seen, you can subject 'metaphysics' itself to this kind of analysis, as the product of a particular time and a particular place. If, however, such concepts are invested with a theoretical reality, they can be applied hypothetically across time, so as to view Parmenides and Plato as (if) metaphysicians—or, indeed, to treat the narratological use of metalepsis (originally formulated by Genette in 1972) as (if) operative in Plato or Virgil.

The prominence of such approaches in recent times owes much to the phenomenological tradition (the discourse [*logos*] that takes as its starting point the study of appearances [*phenomena*]), and in particular to

---

[44] Cf. Kurzweil (2006).

[45] Daston (2000). Hacking (2002: 1–26) offers a useful critical survey of the major figures he gathers in the field he calls 'historical ontology'. As he remarks (2002: 4–5), 'The comings, in comings into being, are historical.'

[46] Koselleck (2002).

Heidegger's critique of classical metaphysics in *Being and Time*, which seeks to explore 'the question of Being' within time rather than assume it exists outside time.[47] But once you admit time, you throw open the borders to all the things Parmenides sought to exclude. Instead of singularity (Being) you get plurality, swarms of beings, not of a single type but of many types and colours, all with their histories; you get languages, with their competing vocabularies and multiple narratives. This is a metaphysical turn, to be sure, not only a return to metaphysics, but a metaphysics whose perspective has been turned through 180 degrees—what I therefore call counter-classical metaphysics.[48] Rather than being 'epiphenomena', as classical metaphysics would have them, plurality, time, language, and narrative assume the place of principles (note the plural) in this counter-classical turn. Counter-classical metaphysics admits the existence of many, many things—but seeks to exclude one. As Gabriel has put it in *Why the World Does Not Exist*: 'In this book I will develop the outlines of a new philosophy, which follows from a simple, basic thought, namely the idea that the world does not exist.[49] As you will see, this does not mean that nothing exists at all. There are planets, my dreams, evolution, the toilet flush, hair loss, hopes, elementary particles, and even unicorns on the far side of the moon.'[50] Innumerable things exist: they come into being, and they can also pass away. The crucial question for a counter-classical metaphysics which explores being in time is not whether such entities exist per se, for, if we imagine them, they *do* exist *in some sense*, as unicorns on the far side of the moon exist as the objects of Gabriel's imagination or a metalepsis machine exists in *Inception*. Odysseus exists no less than Sebastian Matzner or metalepsis, though they do not exist in the same sense. As Latour suggests, their *modes* of existence, the ways in which their existence comes about and is (or is not) maintained, differ.[51]

---

[47] Heidegger (1962).

[48] In keeping with the emphasis of this chapter on the historicity of varieties of metaphysical thinking, one could point to ancient instances of a counter-classical mode: the *Metamorphoses* of Ovid spring to mind as (if) a particularly refined example, counter-Virgilian metaphysically, as in many detailed ways. However, as I argue in Kennedy (2020), a companion piece to this one that elaborates a number of the arguments here, the texts of Plato and Lucretius can be remarkably responsive to a phenomenologically inflected reading. My contrast of 'classical' and 'counter-classical metaphysics' is thus a convenient mnemonic for the purposes of the present argument; these are not a couple of definitive categories into one or other of which any text can be unreflectively put.

[49] Yes, he has been watching *Inception*: Gabriel (2015: 20, 42, and 187).

[50] Gabriel (2015: 1).

[51] Latour (2013) suggests fifteen such modes of existence (two that intersect we will focus on presently), but emphasizes that his work is part of an ongoing experiment in metaphysics and invites the suggestion of further ones. For a perceptive commentary see Maniglier (2014).

Maniglier has put it thus: '"To be" does not mean the same thing for a Higgs boson as it does for the Argentinian peso, but both equally *are*, and the task of the metaphysician is to exhibit that equality and that diversity.'[52] Crucially, nothing exists in isolation. For Gabriel, 'If we know something about an object, we know some of its properties. By virtue of these properties, the object stands out among other objects. The idea of existence comes from the Latin (with an ancient Greek pre-history). The word "existere" means "to originate," "to come forward." Translated literally, it means "to stand out," "to stick out," or "to step out." What exists sticks out; it sets itself apart from other objects by virtue of its properties.'[53] It is clear that a Higgs boson does not exist *in the same sense* as the Argentinian peso. The notion of framing is essential to this way of thinking, and Gabriel talks of 'fields of sense'. Thus a Higgs boson exists in the field of sense of particle physics (a very large field that includes the Large Hadron Collider, thousands of scientists with their recording devices and protocols of argumentation, funding bodies, and much more).[54] But particle physics is not the field of sense in which the Argentinian peso exists: 'Fields of sense are determined through the objects that appear in them.'[55] Fields of sense are unlimited in number; the worlds they constitute 'partly overlap, but are also partly independent of one another.'[56] Fields of sense are frames, and the size and extension of these frames can be extended. However, no one field of sense, no matter how developed or sophisticated, not science, nor religion, nor economics, can claim to be the arbiter of reality more generally. Here we can return to consider how to account, given the plurality of things that *do* exist in some sense, for the one thing that, according to Gabriel, does not exist. 'The world', in the sense of that which encompasses everything that could exist, cannot exist, for the number of things that could exist is limitless (like whole numbers, to which you can always add another one). Dream of it though one may, the God's-eye view of classical metaphysics, which can view everything that exists from the outside, does not make sense in the counter-classical perspective.

Importantly, there is no *given* hierarchy of fields of sense: one is not inherently more or less real than any other. Gabriel suggests that fields of sense can (be made to) overlap. Though they do not exist in the same sense, it is possible to put 'Odysseus', 'Sebastian Matzner', and 'metalepsis' meaningfully into the same field of sense, just as Plato puts Socrates,

---

[52] Maniglier (2014: 42).   [53] Gabriel (2015: 54–5).
[54] Cf. the actor–network theory developed by Latour, especially in Latour (2005).
[55] Gabriel (2015: 87).   [56] Gabriel (2015: 65).

Glaucon, the port of Piraeus and the festival of Bendis into the field of sense he lays out in the opening of the *Republic*. One of the 'modes of existence' Latour suggests is what he signals by his idiosyncratic typography, *[FIC]TION*.[57] The alteration fiction brings about, Latour says, is to 'multiply worlds'. It can 'multiply worlds'—create fresh fields of sense, if you will—through verbal means, but also through performative, plastic, pictorial, musical, or sonic means, fields differently configured in different genres. Another mode of existence is *[ORG]ANIZATION*, which can 'change the size or extension of frames'.[58] One result of the intersection of these two modes are the narratives (Latour himself tends to use the term 'scripts') we live by.

Latour's notion of 'scripts' finds a recent counterpart in theoretical studies of narrativity. Coming from the direction of discourse analysis and cognitive linguistics, Fludernik has developed an approach she calls 'natural narratology' that posits a fundamental connection (hence 'natural') between 'real-life' experience and the frames and concepts of storytelling.[59] Our emotional investment in and desire to understand, evaluate, and shape our experience generate the cognitive drive that *constitutes* narrativity, and thence the frames (what we refer to with terms such as 'genres' or 'plots') that have emerged and continue to emerge over time. To translate this back into Latour's terminology, *[FIC]TION* is a primary mode of human experience of the world. From this perspective, literary and artistic 'fictions' are a special subset of the fictions or 'scripts' we live by—which, as we have seen, are shot through with historically specific metaphysical assumptions about what it is to be a human being.

Narratives are thus not simply stories the masters of make-believe (poets, novelists, film-makers, and even philosophers and literary critics) tell. Rather, narratives are amongst the most important ways by which you and I seek to structure our ongoing experience and generate what we call (for the most part, unreflectively) 'reality'. Works of *[FIC]TION* are, Latour suggests, *anthropogenic*: we make them, of course, but crucially they *make* us what we *are*. So, let us consider how narratives make us what we are, and the role metalepsis plays in this counter-classical metaphysics. Once upon a time, Gail Trimble and Sebastian Matzner put their heads together and said, 'Let's have a conference on metalepsis.' When they did so, they split themselves into what I have elsewhere called their narrating selves

---

[57] Latour (2013: 233–57).   [58] Latour (2013: 381–411).
[59] Fludernik (1996). I am grateful to one of OUP's anonymous referees for drawing this to my attention.

and their narrated selves;[60] we relate to ourselves as if we were another person, existing in another field of sense. Their narrating selves construct a narrative that has its planned climax or *telos* on 3–5 September 2015, and they project their narrated selves as characters within that script, characters who transcend time in that, from the moment of conception, they can inhabit any and all of the events within that script that work towards that *telos*. Their narrating selves thus created a frame, which, like the dream-architect Ariadne in *Inception*, they proceeded to populate with beings of various sorts: not only their narrated selves but the speakers they would invite, the Ioannou Centre in Oxford as its setting, the funding they would apply for, data projectors, cups of coffee, and not least (the Hamlet of this particular script!) the idea of metalepsis as a focus for discussion.

They *created* a world, but how do they *make* it 'reality'? Once upon a time, my narrating self too had created a script, in the genre 'holiday plan', which was also to have its culmination in September 2015, a world richly populated with its own beings—my narrated self, a secluded cottage set in the landscape of Scotland, long walks, my cosy jacket, an open fire, glasses of single malt, and, for my companions, DI Rebus and Richard Hannay. I think, therefore I am—there, then! In my dreams…Here comes the kick, the metalepsis. Other scripts are constantly intruding to disrupt and disorganize the narratives we have framed for ourselves, for many versions of our narrated selves are circulating out there in other frames, and they are not set in train by our narrating selves alone. In issuing their invitation (a classic metalepsis machine, still in excellent working order), Gail and Sebastian were breaking and entering my frame, and when I accepted it, my frame disappeared. Instead, I came to inhabit the frame they had created, and, in submitting to the agenda of their script, I became subject to a kind of determination and necessity, as I subordinated myself to their narrative by fulfilling the role they had designated for me with all the dutifulness of an Aeneas: earnestly thinking about metalepsis, booking train tickets, packing my case, and duly rocking up to the Ioannou Centre on 3 September 2015. Other scripts, other worlds could have broken *their* frame and disorganized it, a speaker pulling out, the Chancellor of the Exchequer abolishing the AHRC, even to the extent of stripping that frame of everything that would give it, eventually (in the outcome), reality. But at the precise moments the refreshments are served, we meet and greet and give and listen to our papers, the script (perhaps with some rewrites

---

[60] Cf. Kennedy (2008); (2013a: 4–11).

along the way) has achieved its outcome and become invisible, having rendered us—and the idea and the texts we discuss—the beings we and they are now become. This is, of course, the usual way realism works: when we accept something as reality, the modes of representation (what Latour calls *[FIC]TION* or the fields of sense of which Gabriel speaks) become invisible. We are at any moment characters within many frames, our own and others', frames of memory and of imagination, which again and again impinge metaleptically on each other, 'small trips', as Gabriel puts it, 'through fields of sense which we take a hundred times a day'.[61] From a metaphysical perspective different from Genette's, metalepsis is so insistent a feature of the creation and production of what we experience as reality that we accept it largely without question. A small mercy, perhaps, since, as Latour has said, it is 'impossible for any human to unify in a coherent whole the role that the scripts have assigned him or her'.[62]

---

[61] Gabriel (2015: 95).   [62] Latour (2013: 393).

11

Epilogue

Metaleptically Ever After

Sebastian Matzner and Gail Trimble

[Metalepsis is] any intrusion by the extradiegetic narrator or narratee into the diegetic universe (or by diegetic characters into a metadiegetic universe, etc.) or the inverse … [T]he narrative figure the classics called author's metalepsis … consists of pretending that the poet …

Genette (1972 = 1980: 234–5)

… himself brings about the effects he celebrates …

cf. Fontanier (1818: 116), Dumarsais (1730)

… as when we say that Virgil 'has Dido die'

Genette (1972 = 1980: 234)

quis tibi tum, Dido, cernenti talia sensus,
quosue dabas gemitus, cum litora feruere late
prospiceres arce ex summa, totumque uideres
misceri ante oculos tantis clamoribus aequor!

What were your feelings then, Dido, as you looked on what was happening? What groans did you give, when you looked out from the height of your citadel to see the shores seething far and wide, and the whole sea in turmoil before your eyes with such overwhelming noise?

Virgil, *Aeneid* 4.408–11
[translation our own]

One of the more peculiar realizations in our work on this volume has been the discovery that thinking about metalepsis is laced with a thread of

Sebastian Matzner and Gail Trimble, *Epilogue: Metaleptically Ever After* In: *Metalepsis: Ancient Texts, New Perspectives*. Edited by: Sebastian Matzner and Gail Trimble, Oxford University Press (2020). © The editors and Oxford University Press.
DOI: 10.1093/oso/9780198846987.003.0011

Virgilian moments. In the twentieth century, Genette defined 'author's metalepsis' by means of a famous sentence in *Figures* III centring on 'Vergile fait mourir Didon' ('Virgil has Dido die'/'Virgil kills Dido')[1] which several contributors to this volume subject to critical re-examination. The Virgil/Dido example was Genette's addition to a suggestion that authors may 'themselves bring about the effects they celebrate' which he took from the neoclassical rhetorical treatises of eighteenth- and nineteenth-century France.[2] And in the rhetorical writings of late antiquity, grammarians and critics quote from Virgil's *Aeneid* and *Eclogues* to illustrate their foundational definition of metalepsis as the trope that allows a character to say 'gloomy' and mean 'deep', to say 'corn ears' and mean 'years'.[3]

Perhaps the fact that we were intrigued by this was the result of our own professional deformation. Then again, perhaps, we should not have been surprised at all. Down the centuries, readers and writers for whom Virgil is a (or *the*) canonical author have felt compelled to explore the level of control he has over his language, over his plots, and over one particular character in his epic poem—Dido, who seems to have been especially engaging not just to the protagonist of the *Aeneid* but even to its author, and, last but not least, to the readers themselves.

On the one hand, Dido is a character on the boundary between familiar, shared myth and innovative fiction: it seems that Virgil can 'kill' her because she is essentially his own contribution to the mythical story he is telling,[4] and that an author's metalepsis such as this one—if that is indeed what it is[5]—highlights the way in which the author controls the events of the fiction. Matters may not be so straightforward, we might think, in classical texts that feature characters positioned on different boundaries

---

[1] On the ambivalence of the original French expression, see Matzner in this volume, p. 3 n. 6.

[2] Genette's 'quotation' of Fontanier/Dumarsais is in fact a condensed paraphrase. The original reads: 'La métalepse fait bien plus encore que transformer les poètes en héros des faits qu'ils célèbrent; elle fait bien plus que les représenter comme opérant eux-mêmes les effets qu'ils peignent ou chantent', 'Metalepsis does much more than transform poets into the heroes of the deeds they celebrate; it does more than represent them as themselves bringing about the effects they paint or sing' (Fontanier 1818: 116. Unless otherwise indicated all translations are our own). For more on this passage of Fontanier/Dumarsais and its use by Genette, see in this volume Matzner (p. 6), Lovatt (pp. 189–90), and Kearey (pp. 196–203).

[3] Discussed by Matzner in this volume, p. 16 (the example here is from Charisius, *Inst. Gramm.* 273).

[4] Kearey in this volume, p. 202.

[5] Compare Kearey in this volume, pp. 196–203, with Lovatt in this volume, pp. 189–92.

between myth, fiction, and real life, such as divinities,[6] or the difficult-to-control *puellae* of those Roman poets who wrote about their 'own' experience of love.[7] The very nature of these entities, and the way they characteristically function in literary texts, would rather seem to demand that their agency is independent from (and indeed sometimes threatening or overpowering that of) the author and/or narrator.

On the other hand, however, Virgil's status as an author-narrator separate from and in control of his text can appear most in doubt precisely when he writes about Dido. His use of emotive, affectively engaged adjectives renders the relationship between author-narrator and character more intense and interwoven than their respective positions on different narrative planes might seem to permit.[8] The (semblance of) immediacy of contact generated by his apostrophe to her at *Aeneid* 4.408–11 (cited above, p. 247) can be taken as indicative of Dido's potential 'availability' for interaction with her author (and perhaps also with readers) across the ontological boundary between text and reality;[9] alternatively, it may reveal that Virgil is, at least for the moment, on the 'wrong' side of that ontological boundary, temporarily becoming a character in his own text.[10] The recurrent interest in apostrophe that runs through this volume (and through other work on ancient metalepsis) is not simply a result of the frequency of the phenomenon in classical literature.[11] Apostrophe highlights a (potential) moment of communication between two figures—usually author and character—who are or ought to be separated from each other by the boundary between narrative worlds. But the more 'ancient', the more 'classical' the apostrophic text becomes, the less significant is that separation in the eyes of readers who are separated from Virgil and Dido, Sappho and Aphrodite, Catullus and Lesbia by the now more significant boundary of hundreds or thousands of years. For modern readers, both ancient authors and ancient characters— fictional or not—are, in effect, inhabitants of another 'world', a world accessible to us only by means of classical texts and the whole subsequent

---

[6] See Budelmann, De Jong, Bing, Fulkerson, and Kennedy in this volume, and further discussion below, pp. 253–5.

[7] See Trimble and Fulkerson in this volume.

[8] Cf. Kearey in this volume, p. 201, arguing that '[t]he narrator of the *Aeneid* is most tangibly a character when dealing with Dido'.

[9] On the 'availability' of apostrophized characters, and on the author's interaction with them as providing a model for the reader's interaction, see Budelmann in this volume.

[10] Kearey in this volume, p. 201, compares his attitude at this moment to that of Dido's sister Anna.

[11] This pronounced interest is noted especially by Budelmann in this volume, p. 60, who also comments on the prominence of apostrophe in De Jong (2009) and Eisen and von Möllendorff (2013b).

disciplinary traditions of Classics and of literary criticism and theory. Studying instances of metalepsis in ancient literature may therefore prompt us to consider just what, if any, possibilities might exist for crossing the fundamental boundary that separates the ancient world from ours.

Setting out to reconsider metalepsis from a classical perspective is further complicated by the particularly wide disciplinary breadth of Classics, which at once renders any attempt at comprehensive treatment from this perspective virtually impossible. For the purposes of this book, however, no such comprehensiveness is necessary. The present volume's core aim is to explore how metalepsis can be understood when it is studied outside the typical context for its theorization, that is, (post-)modern novelistic prose and film. To achieve this, the volume effects a double displacement, not only of the usual time (from modern to ancient via everything in between), but also of the usual literary and artistic forms. While some contributors focus on ancient genres that are more straightforwardly narrative, notably epic (the 'novel' of antiquity, perhaps), several spread their attention more widely to take in less obviously narrative material, including the variously refracted or compromised narratives of large-scale lyric, elegiac, and bucolic poetry; the 'technical' prose of ancient philosophy and literary criticism; the sometimes fragmentary snapshots of the shortest lyric and/or personal poems; and, by way of adding a further, intermedial perspective, the complex case of 'narrative' in vase-painting. The case studies gathered here thus come from a deliberately wide range of Greek and Roman sources, but make no claim to comprehensive coverage of 'metalepsis in classical literature (and art)'. What the volume seeks to offer is nothing more and nothing less than what is promised in its subtitle: ancient texts, new perspectives. We hope, however, that further work on metalepsis in classical texts and culture is provoked by the absences that punctuate this volume and which include (in prose) historiography, oratory, and the ancient novel; (in verse) comedy, satire, and didactic poetry; as well as further non-literary manifestations of metalepsis in different media.

It follows from the exploratory nature of our project, to rethink metalepsis from a perspective—or better: a range of perspectives—steeped in classical literature, art, and thought, that it is neither possible nor indeed desirable to synthesize at this point the positions of the various chapters into a conclusive, homogeneous, monolithic notion of metalepsis in general and of metalepsis in ancient literature and art in particular. Nevertheless, we wish to take stock of the emerging common ground that can be established among the different contributions, and also to explore the differences and productive tensions that remain.

Across the various contributions that make up this volume, a set of recurring concerns emerges. Broadly speaking, these cluster around issues of historically contingent reception aesthetics; narrative and historical ontology; modes and modalities of affective engagement; and the idiosyncrasies of different performance situations, different media, and different genres. If one seeks a common denominator for such seemingly diverse concerns, then the strongest candidate is the consistent pull towards examining the frames and frameworks that variously emerge as the point of reference for the wide range of transgressions and slippages considered in this volume as instances of metalepsis. By studying different phenomena—from apostrophe and anachronism to poetic epiphanies and everyday metaphysics—and pondering whether and in what way they can be deemed to constitute cases of metalepsis, each contributor invariably confronts the question of just which frame(work) exactly is being transgressed, what boundaries exactly are crossed or become blurred in each respective case. For metalepsis to be perceived—whether strongly or weakly, whether by everyone or only by attentive connoisseurs—there always needs to be a norm, or set of norms, or habitual expectations that draw the dividing lines which metalepsis then recognizably overrides. Metalepsis, in other words, only becomes visible against, and gains its form and effect according to, the frames of reference which it takes the liberty of temporarily dislodging.[12]

This has two major consequences. On the one hand, what the case studies in this volume powerfully demonstrate is the high degree of specificity—and historical changeability—of the frames of reference that thereby come into view. Grethlein, for instance, shows how studying metalepsis in ancient vase-painting necessitates several adjustments and qualifications to our notions of the frames and framings at issue here. It emerges that a key differentiator between textual and visual metalepsis is the absence of a noticeable 'narrator' in visual art. This eliminates some forms of metalepsis. In visual art there can be no 'inward metalepsis' like apostrophe, since no narrator is palpably present who could turn to address a character across a divide of their own making: there is no one here who could ask 'What now, Dido?'—and some of the power of ekphrasis stems from the fact that it can supply in an artwork's textual representation precisely this function that cannot occur in a visual representation. This observation, in

[12] Cf. Matzner in this volume, pp. 19–23, in keeping with that argument, we continue to understand metalepsis as a phenomenon that is always specific and/or temporary in scope, rather than something all-pervasive in literature, in narrative, or even in certain texts.

turn, prompts a wider reconsideration: who or what constitutes the differ-
ent narrative levels that are traversed in metalepsis if we take narrators out
of the equation? Or if we take narrativity as a whole out of the equation?
Rather than orienting our analyses towards narrative agents—by asking:
'whose narrative is this (in)?', as most scholars, including in this volume,
do—Grethlein instead proposes to think of metalepsis as a traffic between
and across different levels or worlds of representation (what is represented,
the representation itself, the medium of representation, who perceives the
representation, etc.).[13] This move not only makes it possible to integrate
non-visual and non-narrative or less narrative works into the analysis; it
also makes clearer how pragmatic dimensions influence the frameworks
in which metalepsis operates. For vase-paintings, this includes the fact that
material parts of the object carrying the representation (handles, rims, etc.)
not only function as the representing medium but also inevitably feature
themselves in the pictured scene. This strong material presence of the
medium itself stands in marked difference from verbal artworks, on the
one hand, and from modern visual artworks, on the other. While the
results of the interaction of the medium (vessel) and representation on the
medium (vase-painting) may be at times strikingly metaleptic to modern
viewers, Grethlein questions whether this perception would have occurred
in antiquity, given that it is fully in keeping with conventions—and thus
expectations—for ancient vase-painting. What might seem metaleptic to
us may not have done so in antiquity. The difference in ancient and modern
expectations is accentuated further by the greater separation of most mod-
ern literature and art from daily life; removed from a 'Sitz im Leben' that
imbricates the work with one's ordinary reality, it is relegated instead to
the separate realm of the aesthetic. Modern expectations of aesthetic
autonomy thus consolidate and sharpen assumptions regarding the sep-
aration of distinct levels of representation (including between representa-
tion and referential reality) that foster the perceptibility of their
transgression in instances of metalepsis.

Slippages between representation and referential reality (and the ques-
tion of what counts as which) constitute a major area where working with
ancient material forces us to think differently. Vase-painting, with its
pragmatic embeddedness in sympotic settings and practices, is only one
of many ancient art forms which differ from much modern art in that

---

[13] Compare and contrast Becker (1995: 42–3, referred to by Trimble in this volume,
p. 122), on levels of representation in ekphrasis. Grethlein generally prefers the less hierarchical
concept of worlds.

they are simultaneously conveyors of a representation and part of that representation itself. For instance, Greek lyric—such as epinician poetry— and Athenian drama likewise operate in 'real-life' settings (especially at their original performance) where their material grounding in the given context enables them to be active in two dimensions at once: the here and now of their material, embodied presence and the then and there of their representation.[14] This duality affords them with moments of punctual convergence of these two dimensions. Thus, the (first) performance of a Pindaric ode may be accompanied by gestures that ground the words of the text (notably via demonstratives and underdetermined personal pronouns) in a particular contextual reality. This results in an osmotic relationship between representation (text) and reality (context) that changes or vanishes as the performance context changes or disappears into reading. The same is true for plays performed at the theatre in Athens where the visual backdrop of the city combined with a cast (and audience) of citizens allows for moments of metaleptic convergence between what is represented and the setting of the representation, which can add to a play's significance and appeal.

Questions regarding the boundaries of representation and reality also arise when divine and heroic personages make an appearance in ancient texts.[15] Their ontological status is complicated by the fact that they are also considered as inhabiting a plane of existence which is outside the text in which they appear as characters, yet at the same time constituted differently from ordinary referential reality. This means that here, too, we find a potential for metaleptic convergences between what is inside and outside the text, as deities and heroes can be thought of as existing in a permanent contemporaneity and even copresence with the texts in which they appear. In that case, any direct address to them has the potential to point in two directions at once: to the character in the text and to the entity outside the text. Alongside questions of the literary genealogy of lyric apostrophes in relation to hymnic forms, there is therefore, as it were, a structural potential for a metaleptic hymnic access to the divine when speaking about, and especially when speaking to, divine characters. For heroes, as De Jong shows,[16] there is moreover the particular conundrum of the 'gear changes' of their ontological status at different points in time,

---

[14] On such metaleptic moments in epinician poetry, see De Jong (2013) and in this volume; in Greek drama, see Whitmarsh (2013b).

[15] See Budelmann, De Jong, Bing, Trimble, and Fulkerson in this volume.

[16] See De Jong in this volume.

that is, on their trajectory from time- and space-bound mortal to godlike hero. This causes past, present, and future to become somewhat permeable in references to heroes, since each stage and status contains traces of the others, allowing for slippages between the boundaries of time and temporalities that otherwise separate the hero's different instantiations and narrativizations. When a narrator addresses a hero as if that hero was presently available, do they assume, by means of this presence and availability, the hero's status as already godlike, do they anticipate it, or do they seek to immerse the reader in a merger of worlds?

If heroes in works of literature can thus confuse frameworks of temporal and ontological orders, then gods here come into view as confusing frameworks of authorial authority. One often discussed version of metalepsis consists in a greater than usual presence of the author, who comes into view as lurking behind narrator and characters and can be seen as manipulating them and the narrative. In ancient literature, a further level opens: gods can come into view as lurking behind authors, manipulating the entire act (and fact) of narration itself. The relationship between poet and Muse is a case in point, raising the question: where exactly does the narrative come from? Fulkerson's chapter discusses the disruptive narrative potential caused by epiphanies, examined here as a metaleptic intrusion of a deity into an elegiac poem. As Fulkerson argues, prophetic epiphanies to characters remain within the storyworld, but scenes of poetic inspiration jump out of the narrative itself in the sense that they have real-world textual implications for what is told, why, and with what authority, in the first place. In elegy, where author and protagonist share a name, both scenarios tend to blend. One result of epiphanies is that they can remind readers of that conflation, a fundamental conceit at the very heart of the elegiac genre. As Fulkerson notes, 'this is how both narrative and literary depictions of divine epiphany tend to work; we are normally forgetful of authors' control over their material until they remind us by inserting an extradiegetic comment'.[17] Literary appearances of deities along such metaleptic lines show that the divine and human spheres may be distinct, but also mutually interpenetrating. They afford special status to the poet who is able to discern and engage with divine presences and actions in a way that nobody else can, while at the same time distancing the poet from any blame for the narrated events or their narration: they can tell the tale without bearing responsibility for it. Thus deities, not least vengeful ones,

---

[17]   See Fulkerson in this volume.

appear in ancient literature as the ultimate arbitrators of narrative content, form, and whether or not the act of narration takes place. Be it Ovid's forcible reorientation from epic to elegiac poetry at the hand of Amor in *Amores* 1.1; be it the divinely coerced 'new and revised version' of Helen's story in Stesichorus' *Palinode*, discussed by Bing;[18] be it the set-up of [Tib.] 3.4 where Apollo's appearance enables the wronged lover Lygdamus to vent his feelings, even though he himself could not possibly bring himself to say anything bad about his beloved—all of these cases (and many more) illustrate the power of deities to intervene and bend authors to their will. Such interventions are often dramatically represented in literary texts, but chronologically and ontologically positioned as 'real-world' occurrences prior to (and formative for) these texts.

Studying deities and heroes in classical literature through the prism of metalepsis thus shows us that not all literary characters are created equal and that narratological considerations must here make due allowance for differences between ancient and modern conceptual universes.

Yet we would be mistaken to think that we are on terra firma as long as we stick to human beings. The chapters by Kearey and Kennedy do what many of the most powerful metalepses do: they bring us ourselves into the picture, when we least expect it. Kearey's contribution does so through her notion of 'secondary metalepsis', that is, instances where 'the diegetic levels of author, narrator, and narrative are blurred not by that same author but by another, who employs the figure of the first author and their work within their own, secondary text'.[19] This may seem a quite distinctive and peculiar scenario, explored in fictional narratives such as the author's encounter and philological discussion with Homer in Lucian's *True Stories* or indeed Fulgentius' extended engagement with Virgil and his work in his *Expositio*, which forms the centre of Kearey's study. The core structure of this scenario, however, also fundamentally characterizes what Kearey calls the 'metaleptic dynamics of criticism—both ancient and modern, both "nonfictional" and embedded within unequivocally fictional frames'[20]— and this is where we, as critics, enter the picture. Do we, in our own scholarly practice, not also engage in manoeuvres and practices that, on reflection, are not altogether unlike those of Fulgentius in his tête-à-tête with Virgil? Turning her attention to the sentence 'Virgil has Dido die',

---

[18] Compare with this also De Jong's discussion of the recurrent use of metaleptic apostrophe to mark a poet's intervention in the wider literary tradition, as Pindar's address of a hero at moments where myths are 'corrected'; see p. 92.

[19] Kearey in this volume, p. 196.

[20] Kearey in this volume, p. 195.

Kearey points out—contra Lovatt—that this is not so much a case of 'authorial metalepsis' (in that it does not reflect an authorial move in the *Aeneid* itself) but rather a case of 'critic's metalepsis' or 'metalepsis of critical discourse'.[21] After all, she argues, 'the phrase "Virgil has Dido die", as a fragment of critical discourse, rests on the assumption that "Virgil" exists on the same level of reality *as the critic who speaks the phrase*'.[22] In a move akin to Genette's (in-)famous statement, that the whole of Homer's *Odyssey* could be seen—and analysed—as a large-scale amplification of the kernel sentence 'Ulysses comes home to Ithaca',[23] Kearey considers the metalepsis in the critic's utterance 'Virgil has Dido die' to be a kernel version of the whole extended narrative set-up of Fulgentius' *Expositio*, which also features a critic speaking (as a character), here in dialogue with Virgil, himself another author-turned-character. Musonius' discussion of—and with—Euripides as part of his *Ninth Discourse* on exile, as analysed by Budelmann, is another case in point, likewise illustrating in the narrativized form of a developed conceit the metaleptic dynamics of criticism. This means, however, that modern academic critical commentary, objective and external to its objects of study though it may seem, also comes into view as a genre that relies on metaleptically facilitated encounters of critics, authors, and characters on a newly shared plane, a meeting (and meeting space) that is likewise predicated on a certain dissolution of boundaries to enable this encounter. What distinguishes Fulgentius' Virgil criticism from ours is that his text works hard to 'lay bare the device',[24] to mark the crossings, gear changes, and slippages between different levels of representation that modern criticism tends to elide: he presents himself intrafictionally as (if) in an authentic dialogue with Virgil, but he also steps back and shatters that illusion in brief third-person comments that pertain to the reader (oblique apostrophes of extradiegetic narratees, as it were). The result is an 'oscillation between assurances of realism and self-conscious fictionality',[25] which hinges not least upon each agent's awareness of their own status (author as author, character as character) and renders visible their jostling to determine what kind of authority and power that gives whom over whom. Do modern scholars stand to learn something from the more upfront *mise en scène* of the encounter with authors, narrators, and literary characters we witness in the works of these ancient critics?

---

[21] Compare and contrast, however, Lovatt's productive pursuit of just such an authorial reading in this volume, pp. 189–92.

[22] Kearey in this volume, p. 200.   [23] See Genette (1972 = 1980: 30).

[24] Compare Matzner's differentiation between metalepsis as trope or as figure in this volume, pp. 10–22, esp. p. 21.

[25] Kearey in this volume, p. 215.

With Musonius, Fulgentius, and Kearey, we may begin to embrace sec-
ondary metalepsis as every critic's fate. With Kennedy, we are challenged
to think further still along such lines as he ponders the 'metalepses we live
by'—not just critics, but everyone. If this volume as a whole mobilizes
classical perspectives to reconsider metalepsis as a phenomenon hitherto
largely theorized on the basis of postmodern cultural products, then
Kennedy radicalizes that programme by turning the tables of the classical
and the postmodern: what can metalepsis mean under the conditions of
postmodernity, especially in the light of the anti-foundationalism that char-
acterizes post-structuralist thinking? Is there a lingering attachment to clas-
sical metaphysics operative in narratological theorizations of metalepsis
that, under closer scrutiny, jars with postmodern thinking at large? Kennedy
probes such metaphysical assumptions by examining metalepsis 'in real life'.
In order to make sense of our experience, even to have experiences that can
be grasped and processed as such, human beings rely on narrativization
and narrative frameworks. In Kennedy's words: 'perceptions of coherence—
and, we may add, incoherence—depend on acts of framing. Distinctions
between dreaming and being awake can provide just such acts of framing.'[26]
He goes on to argue that a hallmark of 'classical metaphysics', both ancient
and modern, is the gesture of pointing to an assumed 'alternate world that
lies beyond or transcends immediate experience'.[27] A broad range of higher-
level, that is, higher truth-level, worlds comes into view here: from Platonic
Forms, Virgil's divinely ordained destiny of Roman history, Augustine's
God, Hegel's Reason, Marx's materialist dialectic, Smith's 'invisible hand' of
the market—whatever the 'theory' in question, Kennedy invariably recog-
nizes the same metaleptic gesture, 'a phrase that points up a distinction
between the world of experience articulated in narrative and a world of
timeless, changeless Being'.[28] Crucially, however, it is not only the appeal to
such *grands récits* (or 'master-'/'meta-narratives') that sees us reaching met-
aleptically beyond the narrative world we inhabit; rather, for Kennedy,
'theorizing is something we do the whole time. How many of us have never
uttered words along the lines of "this is *really* all about such-and-such",
appealing to some explanatory entity or order that lies behind initial
appearances?'[29] Probing into the metaphysics of metalepsis—in a manner
more rigorously postmodern than most of its postmodern theorizing—
shows that any attempt to differentiate between narrative and ontological
metalepsis here at once collapses: we are always inside a storyworld and any

---

[26] Kennedy in this volume, 230 n. 21.   [27] Kennedy in this volume, p. 232.
[28] Kennedy in this volume, p. 235.   [29] Kennedy in this volume, p. 239.

appeal to anchor our experience to realities outside of it only brings us to yet another framing ('il n'y a pas de hors-cadre', 'there is no outside-frame', as it were). If we are serious about letting go of foundational assumptions and the universalized ultimate reference frames they provide, then we need to turn to 'metaphysical approaches that resist assent to hierarchical levels of being (what I shall refer to as "counter-classical metaphysics")'.[30] For Kennedy, this means acknowledging the dynamics in which our individual stories are shot through, disrupted, and reorganized by the inferences of the scripts of others, who become co-authors of how we narrativize our own lives. Metalepses we live by indeed.

The same question—what happens to boundary-crossing or boundary-collapsing metalepsis under the conditions of a marked absence of stable, ultimate boundaries?—recurs in different form in Trimble's close reading of Catullus' poetry. Not metaphysics without foundational assumptions, but literature without solid narrative frames here takes centre stage as Trimble ponders the possibilities for metalepsis in lyric—a famously self-conscious genre where narrative levels and agents are often either altogether absent or else only vaguely or unstably present. The metaleptically self-conscious figure of Ariadne acts a linchpin both for Kennedy (via the 'dream-architect' of that name in Christopher Nolan's film *Inception*) and for Trimble (via the heroine's depiction on the coverlet in Catullus' ekphrastic poem 64). Trimble traces how Ariadne—as a figure and a topic—crosses from one narrative level to another, and in the process threatens to derail the poem and its (framing) narrative. Observing a similar 'metaleptic movement' in the treatment and presence of Troy in poem 68, she asks whether such cross-traffic constitutes a particular, lyrical form of metalepsis, or whether such dynamics should be considered an inherent feature of how lyric qua lyric works, in its associative leaps and connections. In her analysis, it becomes 'possible to see the multiplicity and confusion of addressees and narrative levels in Catullus 68 as tending to create, overall, a single level, world, or poetic "moment" on or in which everything in the poem exists'.[31] The chronotope of lyric, at once unified and multiplicitous, given its shifting or indiscernible frame(s) of reference, poses unique challenges for the possibility of crossing or breaking the frame, making it a strong (genre-)specific test case for the general principles set out by Matzner in the opening chapter.[32] Yet, as Trimble shows, this does not mean that there would be no place for metalepsis in lyric. To the contrary,

---

[30] Kennedy in this volume, p. 228.   [31] Trimble in this volume, p. 135.
[32] See Matzner in this volume, pp. 19–23.

there is a particular power, and melancholy, to the moments of 'failed metalepsis' discernible in Catullus, where the poet's voice seeks to reach out across a divide but cannot seem to get through (to his dead brother in 68, to Ariadne in 64); just as it is the sustained tension between the immersion in and alienation from the mythical world of poem 64 which leaves it unclear how separate, accessible, or controllable this world is from the world of the reader.

In the light of the enormous plethora of different framings and frames of reference extrapolated across this volume, one broad consensus can be seen to emerge: that in order to talk about metalepsis in a meaningful way, we need to historicize, contextualize, and sometimes even individualize the wide array of frameworks at play in metaleptic constellations. Even though most chapters take at least their cue from metalepsis as conceptualized by Genette and later narratologists, many of them move away from or complicate classic structuralist perspectives. Structures—and their violation, elision, or rendering visible—must, it seems to us, be a feature of any discussion of metalepsis, since the core dynamics of metalepsis cannot be thought of (or experienced) without some kind of awareness of them. Yet the universalist, ahistorical orientation of structuralism proves time and again too blunt an instrument to grapple with the variables and variabilities involved in the study of metalepsis across time and in different genres and media. The rich array of different structures and frameworks that emerge as potentially significant here, along with their diverse conceptualizations and pragmatics, must inflect the theorization of an intrinsically structure- and framework-based phenomenon such as metalepsis. What follows from this critical insight is the fundamental recognition that metalepsis should be counted among those literary-critical terms which heuristically describe a transhistorically and transculturally recognizable literary phenomenon, but whose realization in concrete literary (and non-literary) instantiations shape-shifts in different periods, literatures, media, genres, and cultures. We can examine what metalepsis is, in general and in principle, but we may not be able to pinpoint the formal properties of any concrete phenomenon as constitutive of metalepsis per se, that is, of instances of metalepsis in any and every given literary and cultural context.

The second consequence that follows from the prominent place taken up across this volume by reflections on the framings and frameworks against which metalepsis occurs points to the particularities not of the classical material studied, but of the classicists studying it. If, as Matzner proposes, we understand metalepsis either as a narrative trope, namely where it comes into view as a recognizable deviation from ordinary narrative (that is, from what one might expect in standard narrative); or as a narrative figure, namely where it comes into view as a particularly marked and visible usage of established, standard means and features of narrative; then metalepsis hinges to a significant degree upon what we consider to be 'standard narrative' and 'standard narrative means'—considerations that fall squarely into the daily business of the literary critic. Observing the critics at work renders visible the central importance of our own critical assumptions for whether, how, and where we perceive metalepsis and how strong or weak we consider its effects to be. It also bespeaks the inevitability of confronting these assumptions in any meaningful attempt to talk about dynamics and phenomena we consider to be metaleptic in kind. In this respect, part of what makes critical operations with the term 'metalepsis' so productive is that they function like a litmus test: talking about metalepsis brings to the fore a critic's assumptions about narrative scenarios and their preconditions, if not about literature as such (notions of representation, of how texts work, of how author, narrator, text, reader, and reality relate, of how authority and truth claims in narrative settings function, and so on). What otherwise often remains inaccessible here demands some form of more or less explicit articulation and acknowledgement. To study metalepsis therefore means to return to and confront fundamental questions of literary theory and critical practice.

Against the note of scepticism that 'metalepsis' might just be a newfangled term for something that both Classics and classicists have known and talked about all along (as *enargeia*, apostrophe, epiphany, ekphrasis, etc.), we therefore hold that this volume demonstrates instead the value of engaging with this concept, and on several levels. It forces critics to engage visibly with their fundamental and, consequently, often obscured assumptions regarding many central aspects of literary criticism; it brings into view productive parallels, connections, or comparable aspects among otherwise seemingly unrelated phenomena (as the range of phenomena discussed here as metaleptic shows); it refines literary theory and methodology in general by drawing out variables that require historicizing; and it forges new means of dialogue between literary criticism of ancient works and modern literary and cultural studies (as the many moments of diachronic comparison that punctuate this volume illustrate).[33]

Specifically, we wish to draw out the contributions this volume has to offer in three related areas, all of which intersect richly with a range of

---

[33] Cf. the similar aims of the volume on metalepsis in popular culture edited by Kukkonen and Klimek (2011), highlighted particularly in Pier's afterword (2011: 269).

current developments in literary scholarship. Firstly, in making the case that theorizing about metalepsis must be historicized, our voices join those evoked by Grethlein 'that demand a historical narratology'.[34] Like Grethlein, however, we resist calls for a comprehensive study of the diachronic development of metalepsis.[35] Despite the optimism of De Jong, who argues in her foundational article on metalepsis in Greek literature that classicists studying metalepsis might contribute to 'the writing of a history of European storytelling',[36] we suspect that such endeavours might prove too ambitious for the granular work that is required here. It may well be that such large-scale accounts prove less and less fruitful, the more the narrative concepts examined increase in complexity. Attempting to write a history of a narrative phenomenon as slippery and protean as metalepsis seems to us far less promising—and indeed far less viable—than, for instance, the history of 'scene shift' in British literature over several centuries, a project successfully undertaken by Fludernik in the article which first explicitly called for narratology to be 'diachronized'.[37] For metalepsis in all its complexity and diversity, a more productive working out of historical narratology would involve, as we have argued above, the careful consideration of the historical, contextual, and even individual factors at play where metalepsis is identified.

This emphasis on the importance of the many contextual variables that affect interpretation of and theorizing about metalepsis is one reason why the present volume does not fully bear out a conclusion that is drawn both by De Jong's original article and by Eisen and von Möllendorff's introduction to their collection on metalepsis in the literary and visual art of antiquity,[38] and that is cited, presumably as the current orthodoxy on ancient metalepsis, by Pier in his article on metalepsis for *The Living Handbook of Narratology*—namely that 'unlike modern practices, metalepsis in ancient literatures is a serious technique which is used not for comic or anti-illusionistic effects, but rather as a means for increasing the narrator's authority and intensifying the credibility of the narrative.[39] Our volume explores in several different ways the question of how metalepsis can affect readers' or audiences' understanding of the site(s) of authority in a text, and we will return below to the question whether metalepsis may be

---

[34] Grethlein in this volume, p. 54.
[35] See Grethlein in this volume and Grethlein (2018a) on the problems created for modern narratology by the motivation of Homer's Penelope.
[36] De Jong (2009: 115).   [37] Fludernik (2003a).
[38] De Jong (2009: 115), Eisen and von Möllendorff (2013a: 8).   [39] Pier (2016: §3.1).

received by readers or audiences as 'comic', 'serious', or as provoking another kind of emotional reaction.

We would, however, join Eisen and von Möllendorff in highlighting another factor which is important for considering metalepsis in the ancient world: the way in which the plots of ancient literature often belong to a shared narrative tradition which presupposes a real historical background.[40] The fact that so many classical narrative texts concern myth, and that myth is presented as an account of the distant past, gives rise to several related implications for the ontological assumptions relevant to ancient metalepsis. Firstly, Eisen and von Möllendorff go on to argue that 'metaleptic contact...only breaks through an already ontologically permeable boundary';[41] that is to say, the 'ontological boundary' between the real, present world and the 'past' world of a myth narrated in a text is experienced as more open and osmotic to start with, so that pushing further in this direction is a matter of difference in degree but not difference in kind. However, the weakness of this ontological boundary may have consequences other than a presumed weaker effect of ancient metalepses in general. Rather, a sustained investigation of metalepsis in ancient texts raises questions about the very assumption of an obvious distinction between the actual world and a fictional world with which Genettean theorizing about metalepsis begins. If myth is a shared tradition, its stories already known to author and audience, perhaps it is on average less true for ancient texts than modern ones that 'the world of which one tells'[42] is always ontologically dependent on the teller and the act of telling.[43] This should make us question the conclusion of Pier and Schaeffer, in another attempt to summarize key aspects of metalepsis, that 'in short-circuiting the frontier between the world of the narration and the world of what is narrated, [metalepsis] emphasizes the fact that in fictional narrative, as opposed to factual narrative, the narrated world is ontologically dependent on the act of narration which gives rise to it' and that, therefore, metalepsis is particularly important for understanding the specificity of fictional narrative compared with factual.[44] Yet, conversely, we have seen in the case of

---

[40] Eisen and von Möllendorff (2013a: 2).

[41] Eisen and von Möllendorff (2013a: 2) 'Der metaleptische Kontakt...durchschlägt...nur eine als solche schon ontologisch durchlässige Grenze.'

[42] Genette (1972 = 1980: 236).

[43] Compare the arguments (differently calibrated though they are) of Grethlein in this volume (pp. 28–9) against Lorenz's attachment of narrative levels to narrators, and our discussion of this issue above, pp. 251–2.

[44] Pier and Schaeffer (2005a: 4) 'la métalepse semble particulièrement importante pour comprendre la spécificité du récit fictionnel compare au récit factuel... en court-circuitant la

Virgil and Dido, or of Pindar metaleptically apostrophizing heroes at the moments when he is 'correcting' their stories,[45] that once shared myth has been made more author-dependent by becoming the subject matter of a text, it might just begin to behave more like fiction—and Pier and Schaeffer would be right that this can be marked by metalepsis.[46] In such cases, which straddle the border between shared mytho-historical past and individual fictional retelling, it begins to look as if the act of narrating might, after all, be able to move events and characters from the (communally shared) past of the 'world in which one tells' onto the level of the (individually recast) 'world of which one tells', transforming them from myth into something closer to fiction. Following on from such considerations, the study of ancient metalepsis should lead us to ask what power telling a story or creating a text might or might not give narrators and authors, not only over the mythical past but also over the historical past. Can that too be transformed into fiction by the same means?[47]

Putting historical narratology into practice by considering what may be specific to ancient metalepsis thus leads to the second of what we consider to be our volume's three key contributions: the importance of letting metalepsis alert us to a greater awareness of (our and other peoples', periods', cultures') metaphysical assumptions, both about the universe of texts and the universe in general. Following Kennedy's encouragement to 'kick' ourselves into probing the metaphysical implications of theorizing about metalepsis (and, indeed, of any theorizing),[48] we concur with his call for postmodern thinking to make sure that it remains anti-foundationalist even when doing narratology, just as, in a historical dimension, we recognize the need to consider how ancient understandings of divine planes and the multilayered temporality occupied by divinized heroes complicate metalepses involving these figures. To these lines of enquiry we may add the implications of those Greek and Roman default assumptions just discussed, namely that the mythical world is, in some way, our own world at

---

frontière entre le monde de la narration et le monde du narré, elle met l'accent sur le fait que dans le récit de fiction, contrairement au récit factuel, le monde narré est ontologiquement dependant de l'acte de narration qui l'engendre.'

[45] Above, pp. 247–9 and p. 255, n. 18.
[46] Compare also the possibility of transfictionality once mythical elements—in this case, characters—are understood to be dependent on a particular author: Lovatt, p. 168 n. 4, on Diomedes in Homer and Virgil; Kearey, p. 204, on Ariadne in Catullus and Ovid.
[47] See especially Trimble on the epilogue of Catullus 64, pp. 141–2, and Grethlein on Xenophon's *Anabasis* and the potential role of metalepsis in 'non-fictional' historiography, p. 44.
[48] Kennedy in this volume, p. 225.

an earlier period in time, and also the issues of anachronism discussed in Bing's chapter. Culturally and historically contingent notions of time do, after all, also come with metaphysical strings attached, as they shape and structure differently experienced and imagined worlds (including the corresponding opportunities for metaleptic transgressions of such temporal structures and boundaries). Bing shows how anachronism, taken as a purposeful and eye-opening transgression, might be considered a kind of metalepsis because it 'brings...disparate times to bear on each other in a productive and meaningful way', whether the times in question are mythical or historical periods, or different times in someone's own life (as in the case of Socrates in Plato's *Symposium*).[49] One of the ways in which anachronisms are 'productive' is in challenging the audience to consider what kind of temporal and metaphysical frameworks would have to be in place for a metaleptic anachronism to be 'meaningful' (rather than an error out of ignorance).

Several contributors raise the question of where we should locate the contact facilitated by metalepsis: when metalepsis occurs, who moves from where to where? Genette used answers to this question as one of the means by which he divided off various categories of metalepsis, especially 'narrator metalepsis' and 'narratee metalepsis'.[50] In this volume, apostrophe and epiphany prompt Budelmann, De Jong, Trimble, and Fulkerson to ask whether the narrator moves onto the diegetic level to meet a character (often an addressee), or the character is 'pulled' out of the diegesis onto the extradiegetic level of the narrator. As the contributors' discussions demonstrate, this is often difficult or impossible to decide, and this is perhaps precisely the point: it seems to be the shared presence that matters most in metalepsis, not so much where exactly that presence is located. Appreciating this might help us to understand the recurring paradox of alienation *and* immersion that metalepsis seems to evoke:[51] we—characters, narrators, authors, readers alike—are suddenly somewhere else, uncertain where exactly we are, and how we can have (im)possibly got there, but nonetheless very much, very intensely *there*, together. Against the backdrop of the analyses in this volume, we are inclined to conclude that metalepsis creates a moment of communion in a location of its own. We might go on to say that, if we must position this location somewhere, it could perhaps be found on Genette's 'shifting but sacred frontier between two worlds';[52]

---

[49] Bing in this volume, pp. 111–14 (quotation at 114).
[50] See the discussion of Matzner in this volume, pp. 3–6.
[51] See in particular in this volume Lovatt (passim), Trimble (p. 142), and cf. below, pp. 268–9.
[52] Genette (1972 = 1980: 236).

we would thus be adding to the list of spatial metaphors that dominate so much metaleptic theorizing,[53] and even offering the third possibility of 'a meeting on the boundary' to set beside the dominant spatial visualizations in which boundaries are either crossed (thus potentially reaffirming that they are there) or blurred (so that they disappear). Alternatively, we might make an even stronger case and assert that the metaleptic encounter is located somewhere else entirely, in its own dimension. In either case, however, we must interrogate the terms we use when we talk about 'personal encounters' taking place in a metaleptic space. The metaphors we use here—if this is what they are—are highly likely to be tied up with ontological, if not metaphysical, claims.

It is time, therefore, to address head on the question of *whose* metaphysical assumptions should be probed. The third key contribution of this volume that we wish to highlight concerns the role that considerations about the readers of metaleptic texts should play in discussions of metalepsis. Lovatt in particular foregrounds this issue, arguing at the outset of her chapter that '[r]eaders must decide' both what constitutes metalepsis and what effects it can have, noting further that '[i]t is likely that different readers will respond differently to features that have the potential to be metaleptic.'[54]

We may start with the point that whether readers perceive metalepsis at all is dependent on what those readers expect, and what they expect depends to a considerable degree on what they know. Bing's chapter discusses the varying levels of relevant knowledge that audiences must have to pick up on certain metalepses, here anachronisms: at the lower end of the scale, viewers of *A Knight's Tale* recognizing that the music of Queen does not fit a medieval setting; at the upper end, early readers of Theocritus 24 spotting a politically significant date of their present encoded in an astronomical observation set in the mythical past. Somewhere in the middle comes an intra-narrative anachronism in Plato's *Symposium* that is noticed by attentive symposiasts—and readers.[55] Identifying anachronism, however, depends not just on specific knowledge and/or observant

---

[53] See particularly in this volume Matzner (pp. 4–5 and n. 10), Bing (p. 106), Kearey (p. 204).

[54] Lovatt in this volume, pp. 167–8 and n. 5.

[55] Bing in this volume, pp. 111–14. As they recognize the anachronistic allusion in Socrates' account of Diotima's speech, Aristophanes and his fellow guests are examples of what Wolf (2013) calls 'reception figures', that is, characters in a text whose reaction to an embedded metalepsis within that text can serve as a *mise en abyme* for the reaction of the text's readers—and indeed, for Bing, the characters in the *Symposium* provide evidence that ancient readers could understand anachronism as a deliberate effect. Cf. also Lovatt in this volume, p. 168, on Dido's response to Aeneas' narrative of Troy in *Aeneid* 2.

alertness, but on what readers 'know' about how time works (and can be expected to work)—that is, on some of the historically contingent ontological and metaphysical assumptions discussed above. Similarly, what readers 'know' or understand about divine or heroic powers and their ability to intervene in human 'real life' will affect whether the actions of, for instance, Helen vis-à-vis Stesichorus in his *Palinode* are perceived to cross a boundary between text and world, or a boundary between divine and human realms that are both 'known' by readers to have 'real' existence.[56] By drawing attention to the historical (and historically variable) knowledges that co-constitute metalepsis, studies of ancient metalepsis like those assembled in this volume can bring increased nuance to recent theorizations of metalepsis as part of 'unnatural narratology',[57] which is defined by some of its key practitioners as 'the analysis of unnatural texts, that is, texts that feature strikingly impossible or antimimetic elements'.[58] What is (assumed to be) impossible or antimimetic—that is, radically unlike mimetic representation of real-world experience—is of course historically contingent too, and texts featuring divine intervention in the human world would seem to be a good test case for exploring this.[59]

However, it is just as important to avoid the easy 'othering' of ancient audiences as it is to avoid assuming that their ideas of what is physically or even logically impossible were necessarily the same as ours. Wolf's article on 'unnatural' metalepsis and immersion begins by drawing a distinction between a modern and an ancient case of embedded metalepsis: in the modern one, the protagonist of a film-within-a-film in Woody Allen's *The Purple Rose of Cairo* steps out of the screen to meet one of his viewers; in the ancient one, the statue created and then desired by Pygmalion transforms into a woman.[60] Yet although Wolf knows the story of Pygmalion from Ovid's *Metamorphoses*,[61] he works hard, '[f]or the sake of argument', to create for his readers the imaginary scenario of 'a rhapsode in ancient Greece' telling an earlier version of the tale before 'a fascinated audience', to whom the scenario of metaleptic boundary-crossing from artwork to represented reality 'would not necessarily appear as unnatural

---

[56] For Stesichorus and Helen see above, p. 255.

[57] Bell and Alber (2012); Wolf (2013); Bell (2016).

[58] Alber, Iversen, Nielsen, and Richardson (2013: 1). For further introductions to unnatural narratology see also Alber (2014) and, from the perspective of a classicist, Liveley (2019: 246–51).

[59] One of the suggestions listed as 'Topics for Further Investigation' in Alber (2014: §4) is 'the role of impossibilities in...religious texts'.

[60] Wolf (2013: 113–14).

[61] Acknowledged by Wolf (2013: 114 n. 2). The myth is told at Ov. *Met.* 10.243–97.

or impossible'.[62] The implication *ex negativo*—that is, without the false pretences 'for the sake of argument'—would seem to be that Wolf finds it hard to believe that the first readers of Ovid's text in late Augustan Rome could have been quite so innocently 'fascinated'. By choosing to evoke a generalized and simplified scenario involving an audience as different from the audience in a modern cinema as he can imagine, Wolf at the very least misses the opportunity to compare *The Purple Rose of Cairo* with a real text from the ancient world, and its audience with (what can be learned about) a specific ancient readership.

We would urge, then, that diachronic literary criticism should approach metalepsis by means of a historicized narratology, should probe and take into account the metaphysical assumptions in play, and should always give consideration to the identity of the readers whose responses to the text are being discussed. Classicists in particular, we suggest, are well qualified to do so. We are (or should be) aware of the variety of readers and audiences that have engaged and continue to engage with classical texts, both across Greek and Roman antiquity and down the centuries—including, ultimately, ourselves. In studying metalepsis, it seems to us critical to attend to the validity of a range of different reading experiences, from those of a text's first receivers to those taking place much later and in very different cultural contexts. This approach would also align well with the main thrust of Hanebeck's recent book on metalepsis, which rightly places renewed emphasis on the hermeneutic process by which the metaleptic potential of a text is activated, in an 'event of understanding',[63] by individual readers on individual occasions.[64]

Speaking of individual readers: a multi-authored book such as the present volume stages the reading experiences of a number of individual modern readers—namely those of our contributors—within its own pages. Indeed, the volume itself perfectly exemplifies the very point that different readers experience metalepsis differently, which is rendered visible here in part by the way in which contributors take different views on how broadly or narrowly metalepsis as a critical concept should be conceived and used in order to be most productive. Matzner (in the opening chapter) and Lovatt might be taken as marking the two ends of the spectrum, with Matzner urging caution and Lovatt favouring a more all-encompassing, pervasive notion. Lovatt's discussion of the 'interplay between narrative

---

[62] Wolf (2013: 114 n. 2, 114).   [63] Hanebeck (2017: 3).

[64] Cf. Lovatt in this volume, p. 168 n. 5, suggesting that responses to potentially metaleptic features may differ at different times in the same reader's life.

levels'[65] as the *Aeneid*'s narrator quotes Aeneas quoting Sinon telling his own story, or the 'weak metaleptic effect' that she sees in epic similes as they 'evok[e] worlds and ideas outside the narrative time and space', have more in common with the wider approach taken by Whitmarsh, both in his argument for the particularly metaleptic nature of classical Greek drama,[66] and in his article identifying the 'fictional autobiography' of authors such as Apuleius and Lucian as characterized by a perpetually unstable divide between author and character, 'ever susceptible to metaleptic play'.[67] Yet, like Whitmarsh, Lovatt identifies 'metaleptic moments' at which the pervasive metaleptic potential that she sees in Virgil's text is more intensely realized;[68] for instance, the punning allusion to Pompey *Magnus* ('the Great') in the appearance of the word *ingens* 'huge' to describe the dead body of Priam.[69] Readers who experience a less forceful effect in these instances and are, consequently, less certain that they find themselves 'understanding metalepsis' at such moments may want to draw instead on Grethlein's concept of 'elastic metalepsis' or 'metaleptic association' to describe passages or words (such as *ingens* here) 'that can be read literally, but their context strongly suggests further significance'.[70]

For both Lovatt and Grethlein, however, what is at stake in such moments where the relevance of the representation is forcefully extended to the reader is not so much the text as the reader's engagement with the text. Grethlein argues that the reader (or viewer) of an elastic metalepsis 'will not feel a jerk that draws their attention to the mediation' (a 'rupture') but 'will feel that the represented scene also pertains to them' (via a shared 'continuum').[71] Lovatt sees something more double-edged: Virgil's use of the word *testudo* ('tortoise formation') for the Greeks at the fall of Troy can either increase a Roman reader's engagement with the text, or alienate them, depending on whether they notice and interpret the 'tortoise' as an anachronism.[72] Such considerations sharply bring into view how a reader's

---

[65] Lovatt in this volume, p. 168; cf. pp. 174–8.

[66] Whitmarsh (2013b); critiqued by Grethlein in this volume, pp. 33–4.

[67] Whitmarsh (2013a: 245).

[68] Cf. Whitmarsh (2013b: 16) 'vertiginously fleeting moments of theatrical self-awareness'.

[69] Virg. *Aen.* 2.557; Lovatt in this volume, pp. 187–8. Intriguingly, the role played here by the polysemy of a single word brings this example close to the ancient, rhetorical understanding of metalepsis: see Matzner in this volume, pp. 14–17, and cf. above, p. 248.

[70] Grethlein in this volume, p. 33 n. 25. As Grethlein points out, in the terms of Matzner's opening chapter such moments are instantiations of metalepsis as a figure 'that meaningfully foregrounds already present features of narrative acts' rather than a trope that breaks expectations: Matzner in this volume, p. 21.

[71] Grethlein in this volume, p. 55.

[72] Lovatt in this volume, pp. 180–1 and n. 39, discussing Virg. *Aen.* 2.441.

perception or understanding of metalepsis prompts an affective response. This is explicitly highlighted by Budelmann, who, like other contributors, steps away from a classic structuralist approach because it eschews questions of 'the whole gamut of ways in which books affect their readers and play a role in their readers' lives'.[73] If, as discussed above, we are concerned in (at least some forms of) metalepsis less with readerly immersion in a narrative world than with a sympathetic encounter—located somewhere else entirely, perhaps—between readers and characters; then for Budelmann, this kind of 'readerly engagement' is modelled by authorial apostrophe, whose metaleptic force enables it 'to serve as a *mise en abyme*'.[74] We can see elsewhere, too, how what holds for readers likewise holds for authors (who are, after all, readers of their own creations): as Kearey reminds us, Parry noted in a famous article on the *Aeneid* the view of some critics that 'Virgil somehow fell in love with, and was carried away by, his own heroine'.[75] Similarly, ancient scholiasts took apostrophe to be an indication of Homer's sympathy for his heroes.[76] The affective force of metalepsis, then, is often related to its power to create interpersonal connections that can link either the reader or the author (or narrator) to figures from 'inside' the text.

Readers who get entangled in such metaleptic relationships may find themselves at some emotional risk. We have seen that while Genette claimed that metalepsis 'produces an effect of strangeness that is either comical...or fantastic',[77] some studies have concluded that metalepsis in classical texts is, in contrast, 'serious' because the links it forges between text and extratextual world increase the text's 'authority' or 'credibility'.[78] Our volume, however, while certainly acknowledging the potentially comic effects of certain metalepses,[79] often brings out effects that are serious or even tragic, resulting not from (unexpected) continuity across narrative or ontological boundaries, but from the extent to which such boundaries remain in place despite narrative efforts to transgress them. In Trimble's analysis, what is more important is not that Catullus can utter a metaleptic apostrophe to his brother, but that he cannot actually communicate with

---

[73] Budelmann in this volume, p. 76, with reference to contemporary critics such as Felski (2008), Keen (2014), and Moi (2017) who are exploring such questions.

[74] Budelmann in this volume, p. 76.

[75] Kearey in this volume, p. 202, quoting Parry (1963: 77).

[76] See in this volume Grethlein, p. 31 n. 21, Budelmann, pp. 61–5, and De Jong, pp. 79–80, with further references.

[77] Genette (1972 = 1980: 235).   [78] Above, p. 261.

[79] See in particular the contributions of Bing (e.g. pp. 111–14) and Fulkerson (e.g. pp. 156–7) in this volume.

him by this means in the same way as he could have done before the brother was separated from him by death.[80] Similarly, Lovatt's reading of *Aeneid* 2 emphasizes the guilt of the bereaved Aeneas as he attempts to use apostrophe to connect with the dead friends and unhappy events of his own past in a spirit of self-justification, as well as the tragic irony of a story told 'by a character who was actually there, but now can no longer intervene'.[81] In such cases, metalepsis both highlights the frames that it temporarily breaks or poignantly fails to break, and demonstrates the limitations of the power of narrators who are also agents—or sufferers—in the worlds of which they tell ('first-person narrators', usually). In other words, by laying bare the structures involved in narration, metalepsis also lays bare the limits of human agency in shaping the worlds we inhabit. It may thereby prompt readers who are emotionally engaged with characters in the text, especially when such characters are also narrators, not only to sympathize with the often tragic limitations of those characters' agency (or even the author's), but also to begin to wonder about the limitations of their own.

We thus return to the idea that metalepsis draws readers' attention to the possibility 'that the extradiegetic is perhaps always diegetic, and that the narrator and his narratees—you and I—perhaps belong to some narrative'.[82] Whether readers find the contemplation of this possibility worryingly 'troubling',[83] refreshingly provocative, or a fact to be embraced (as Latour and Kennedy would have it), will ultimately depend on their ontological and metaphysical assumptions and beliefs. Crucially, however, the very point of Genette's observation is that such contemplation can 'trouble' or disturb exactly one's assumptions about the world's ontological frameworks and one's own position in relation to those frameworks. Readers' disbelief in a fictional narrative cannot be unproblematically 'suspended' and then restored, because metalepsis—once it has given us a 'kick'—has the potential to cause lasting confusion about the bases for belief and disbelief.[84] Hanebeck argues that thinking about metalepsis can

---

[80] Trimble in this volume, p. 137; see also above, p. 259, on this 'failed metalepsis'.

[81] Lovatt in this volume, p. 174.

[82] Genette (1972 = 1980: 236), discussed specifically in this volume by Trimble, p. 144, and Kennedy, p. 225.

[83] Genette's word (1972 = 1980: 236; 'troublant' in the French original, 1972: 245), despite his preceding characterization of the effect of metalepsis as 'comical... or fantastic' (above, n. 77).

[84] In this volume Budelmann (p. 78) and Kearey (pp. 209, 218–19) articulate reservations about the usefulness in this context of the concept 'suspension of disbelief'.

help to shift us towards a 'hermeneutics of belonging' in which we model a reader's encounter with a text not as the examination of a separate object, but as 'an act of understanding that belongs ontologically to what it understands'.[85] The enquiries into metalepsis in classical literature offered in this volume have shown that readers and critics—from the ancient world through to our own time—are constantly becoming implicated not just in the texts they read, nor even just in the wider narrative worlds to which they gain access through those texts, but in the narratives created by themselves and others about what they understand to be the 'real world'. Examining how fictional worlds tend to open up as readers explore them, Laird demonstrates that they turn out to be much less bounded by the texts that generate them than we might initially expect: he observes that 'perceptions of fictional worlds are conditioned by the view we have of our own world', both in terms of 'ethical and other value judgments' and in terms of our assumption that 'a delimited fictional or diegetic world' can be stably identified in the first place. '[W]hat makes our actual world "actual"', Laird suggests, is merely 'the fact that we are in it'.[86] Kennedy's chapter shows that even being 'in' the 'actual world' involves being 'in' frameworks and narratives, to which metalepsis can alert us.[87] What makes metalepsis so fascinating, challenging, and infuriating, then, is that it fundamentally confronts us with the inevitability of living with such naturalized narratives and necessary fictions. And ancient texts, in particular, give new perspectives on this issue: by increasing our awareness of how human beings from the classical world until today have lived with and by metalepses, they shake up—differently for each of us—our understanding of the relations between the worlds we experience, the texts we read, the stories we tell of ourselves and others (living, dead, or fictional), and the texts we write.

So, what remains to be said and done? Where and how does metalepsis end? Perhaps the most familiar gesture at this point of a scholarly book is to conclude with reflections on avenues of future research opened up by the volume, along with the expression of the hope that other critics will pursue these avenues in their work (as, indeed, we have done above). In other words: academic books have a habit of ending by telling their readers to become writers and to write further (or rewrite), as narrators themselves,

---

[85] Hanebeck (2017: 122).   [86] Laird (2007: 296–7).
[87] See above, pp. 257–8.

the account that has just been narrated to them.[88] πῖνε καὶ σύ ('you too drink!') says, cheerily and metaleptically, the B side of the red-figured cup by Oltos;[89] γράφε καὶ σύ ('you too write!') says the scholarly book—and this one is no exception.

---

[88] Cf. Kennedy in this volume on the hidden metaphysical, frame-changing implications of every endeavour to offer a superior account for an experience or phenomenon 'as it really is'; see above, pp. 257–8.

[89] Discussed by Grethlein in this volume, pp. 35–6.

References

Agócs, P., C. Carey, and R. Rawles (eds.) (2012) *Reading the Victory Ode.* Cambridge: Cambridge University Press

Ahl, F. (1985) *Metaformations: Soundplay and Wordplay in Ovid and Other Classical Poets.* Ithaca, NY and London: Cornell University Press

Alber, J. (2014) 'Unnatural Narrative', in P. Hühn et al. (eds.), *The Living Handbook of Narratology*, Hamburg: Hamburg University. http://www.lhn.uni-hamburg.de/article/narrator [Accessed 15 December 2019]

Alber, J., S. Iversen, H. Skov Nielsen, and B. Richardson (2013) 'Introduction', in J. Alber, H. Skov Nielsen, and B. Richardson (eds.), *A Poetics of Unnatural Narrative.* Columbus, OH: Ohio State University Press, 1–15

Alden, M. J. (2000) *Homer beside Himself: Para-Narratives in the Iliad.* Oxford: Oxford University Press

Allan, R. J., I. J. F. de Jong, and C. C. de Jonge (2017) 'From Enargeia to Immersion: The Ancient Roots of a Modern Concept', *Style* 51.1, 34–51

Allen, D. S. (2010) *Why Plato Wrote.* Oxford: Wiley-Blackwell

Amir, A. (2009) '*Sunt Lacrimae Rerum*: Ekphrasis and Empathy in Three Encounters between a Text and a Picture', *Word&Image* 25, 232–42

Anderson, R. D., P. J. Parsons, and R. M. G. Nisbet (1979) 'Elegiacs by Gallus from Qasr Ibrîm', *JRS* 69, 125–55

Armstrong, R. (2002) 'Crete in the *Aeneid*: Recurring Trauma and Alternative Fate', *CQ* 52, 321–40

Armstrong, R. (2004) 'Retiring Apollo: Ovid on the Politics and Poetics of Self-Sufficiency', *CQ* 54, 528–50

Asso, P. (2008) 'The Intrusive Trope: Apostrophe in Lucan', *MD* 61, 161–73

Athanassaki, L. (2004) 'Deixis, Performance, and Poetics in Pindar's *First Olympian Ode*', *Arethusa* 37, 317–41

Auerbach, E. (1984) *Scenes from the Drama of European Literature.* Manchester: Manchester University Press

Austin, R. G. (ed.) (1955) *P. Vergili Maronis Aeneidos Liber Quartus.* Oxford: Clarendon Press

Austin, R. G. (ed.) (1964) *P. Vergili Maronis Aeneidos Liber Secundus.* Oxford: Clarendon Press

Axelson, B (1960) 'Lygdamus und Ovid: Zur Methodik der literarische Prioritätsbestimmung', *Eranos* 58, 92–111

Baetens, J. (1988) 'Les Dessous d'une planche: Champ censuré et métalepse optique dans un dessin de Joost Swarte', *Semiotica* 68.3–4, 321–30

Baetens, J. (2001) 'Going to Heaven: A Missing Link in the History of Photonarrative?', *Journal of Narrative Theory* 31.1, 87–105

Bakker, E. J. (1993) 'Discourse and Performance: Involvement, Visualization and "Presence" in Homeric Poetry', *ClAnt* 12, 1–29

Bal, M. (1977) *Narratologie: Essais sur la signification narrative dans quatre romans modernes*. Paris: Klincksieck

Bal, M. (1997) *Narratology: Introduction to the Theory of Narrative*, 2nd edn. Toronto: University of Toronto Press

Banfield, A. (1982) *Unspeakable Sentences: Narration and Representation in the Language of Fiction*. London: Routledge

Barchiesi, A. (2001) *Speaking Volumes: Narrative and Intertext in Ovid and Other Latin Poets*, ed. and trans. M. Fox and S. Marchesi. London: Duckworth

Barkan, L. (1991) *Transuming Passion: Ganymede and the Erotics of Humanism*. Stanford: Stanford University Press

Bartsch, S. (2018) 'The *Aeneid* as "Weaker Text" and Fulgentius' Radical Hermeneutics', in S. Matzner and S. Harrison (eds.), *Complex Inferiorities: The Poetics of the Weaker Voice in Latin Literature*. Oxford: Oxford University Press, 225–44

Baron, C. (2005) 'Effet métaleptique et statut des discours fictionnels', in J. Pier and J.-M. Schaeffer (eds.), *Métalepses: Entorses au pacte de la representation*. Paris: Éd. de l'EHESS, 295–310

Barwick, L. (1957) *Probleme der stoischen Sprachlehre und Rhetorik*. Berlin: Akademie Verlag

Baumann, M. (2011) *Bilder schreiben: Virtuose Ekphrasis in Philostrats 'Eikones'*. Berlin: Walter de Gruyter

Baumann, M. (2013) 'Der Betrachter im Bild: Metalepsen in antiken Ekphrasen', in U. E. Eisen and P. von Möllendorff (eds.), *Über die Grenze: Metalepse in Text- und Bildmedien des Altertums*. Berlin: Walter de Gruyter, 257–91

Becker, A. S. (1995) *The Shield of Achilles and the Poetics of Ekphrasis*. Lanham, MD and London: Rowman & Littlefield

Beecroft, A. J. (2006) ' "This Is Not a True Story": Stesichorus's "Palinode" and the Revenge of the Epichoric', *TAPhA* 136, 47–69

Bell, A. (2016) 'Interactional Metalepsis and Unnatural Narratology', *Narrative* 24, 294–310

Bell, A. and J. Alber (2012) 'Ontological Metalepsis and Unnatural Narratology', *Journal of Narrative Theory* 42, 166–92

Belliotti, R. A. (2009) *Roman Philosophy and the Good Life*. Lanham, MD: Lexington Books

Bennett, C. (2001–13) 'Ptolemaic Dynasty', s.v. Ptolemy I. http://www.instonebrewer.com/TyndaleSites/Egypt/ptolemies/genealogy.htm [Accessed 15 December 2019]

Bessière, J. (2005) 'Récit de fiction, transition discursive, présentation actuelle du passé, ou que le récit de fiction est toujours métaleptique', in J. Pier and J. M. Schaeffer (eds.), *Métalepses: Entorses au pacte de la representation*. Paris: Éd. de l'EHESS, 279–94

Bing, P. (1988) *The Well-Read Muse: Present and Past in Callimachus and the Hellenistic Poets*. Göttingen: Vandenhoeck & Ruprecht

Black, M. (1962) *Models and Metaphors: Studies in Language and Philosophy*. Ithaca, NY: Cornell University Press

Block, E. (1982) 'The Narrator Speaks: Apostrophe in Homer and Vergil', *TAPhA* 112, 7–22

Boedeker, D. and D. Sider (eds.) (2001) *The New Simonides: Contexts of Praise and Desire*. Oxford: Oxford University Press

Boehm, G. (2007) *Wie Bilder Sinn erzeugen: Die Macht des Zeigens*. Berlin: Berlin University Press

Boileau, N. (1674 = 2007) 'L'art poétique', in *Selected Poems: Nicholas Boileau*, trans. B. Raffel. New Haven, CT: Yale University Press, 20–61

Bonifazi, A. (2004) 'Communication in Pindar's Deictic Acts', *Arethusa* 37, 391–414

Borges, J. L. (1964) *Other Inquisitions, 1937–1952*, trans. R. L. C. Simms. Austin, TX: University of Texas Press

Bourdieu, P. (1979) *La Distinction: Critique sociale du jugement*. Paris: Éditions de Minuit

Bowie, A. M. (1990) 'The Death of Priam: Allegory and History in the *Aeneid*', *CQ* 40, 470–81

Bowie, A. M. (2008) '*Aeneas narrator*', *PVS* 26, 41–51

Bowie, E. L. (1993) 'Lies, Fiction and Slander in Early Greek Poetry', in C. G. Gill and T. P. Wiseman (eds.), *Lies and Fiction in the Ancient World*. Exeter: Exeter University Press, 1–37

Bowra, C. M. B. (1961) *Greek Lyric Poetry*, 2nd edn. Oxford: Clarendon Press

Braswell, B. K. (1988) *A Commentary on the Fourth Pythian Ode of Pindar*. Berlin: Walter de Gruyter

Bredekamp, H. (2010) *Theorie des Bildakts*. Berlin: Suhrkamp

Bremer, J. M. (2008) 'Traces of the Hymn in the Epinikion', *Mnemosyne* 61, 1–17

Büchner, K. (1965) 'Die Elegien des Lygdamus', *Hermes* 93, 65–112, 503–8

Budelmann, F. (2018) *Greek Lyric: A Selection*. Cambridge: Cambridge University Press

Bürger, R. (1903) 'Eine Elegie des Gallus', *Hermes* 38, 19–27

Burgess, J. (2006) 'Neoanalysis, Orality, and Intertextuality: An Examination of Homeric Motif Transference', *Oral Tradition* 21.1, 148–89

Burnyeat, M. (1982) 'Idealism and Greek Philosophy: What Descartes Saw and Berkeley Missed', *Philosophical Review* 92, 3–40

Burzacchini, G. (2005) 'Fenomenologia innodica nella poesia di Saffo', *Eikasmos* 16, 11–40

Butrica, J. L. (2007) 'History and Transmission of the Text', in M. B. Skinner (ed.), *A Companion to Catullus*. Oxford: Blackwell, 13–34

Cadau, C. (2015) *Studies in Colluthus' Abduction of Helen*. Leiden: Brill

Calame, C. (1999) 'Performative Aspects of the Choral Voice in Greek Tragedy: Civic Identity in Performance', in S. Goldhill and R. Osborne (eds.), *Performance Culture and Athenian Democracy*. Cambridge: Cambridge University Press, 125–53

Camille, M. (1992) *Image on the Edge: The Margins of Medieval Art*. London: Reaktion Books

Campbell, D. A. (ed. and trans.) (1982) *Greek Lyric I: Sappho, Alcaeus*. Cambridge, MA and London: Harvard University Press

Campbell, D. A. (ed. and trans.) (1991) *Greek Lyric III: Stesichorus, Ibycus, Simonides, and Others*. Cambridge, MA and London: Harvard University Press

Caplan, H. (ed. and trans.) (1954) *[Cicero]: Rhetorica ad Herennium*. Cambridge, MA and London: Harvard University Press

Carson, A. (1995) *Plainwater*. New York, NY: Alfred A. Knopf

Carson, A. (1999) *Autobiography of Red: A Novel in Verse*. New York, NY: Vintage Books

Casali, S. (2003) '"Impius" Aeneas, "impia" Hypsipyle: Narrazioni menzognere dall' "Eneide" alla "Tebaide" di Stazio', *Scholia* 12, 60–8

Casali, S. (2010) 'Autoreflessività onirica nell'*Eneide* e nei successori epici di Virgilio', in E. Scioli and C. Walde (eds.), *Sub Imagine Somni: Nighttime Phenomena in Greco-Roman Culture*. Pisa: ETS, 119–42

Catoni, M. L. (2010) *Bere vino puro: Immagini del simposio*. Milan: Feltrinelli

Chadwick, H. (ed. and trans.) (1991) *Saint Augustine: Confessions*. Oxford: Oxford University Press

Clay, J. S. (2011) *Homer's Trojan Theater: Space, Vision, and Memory in the Iliad*. Cambridge: Cambridge University Press

Cohn, D. (2005) 'Métalepse et mise en abyme', in J. Pier and J.-M. Schaeffer (eds.), *Métalepses: Entorses au pacte de la representation*. Paris: Éd. de l'EHESS, 121–30

Colwell, S. M. (1993) *Apostrophe and Audience in the Epinician Odes of Pindar and the Hymns of the Book of Psalms*. Diss. Princeton

Conington, J. and H. Nettleship (1884/1963/2007) *P. Vergili Maronis Opera*. Exeter: Bristol Phoenix Press, 1884, rev. 1963, repr. 2007

Conte, G. B. (1986) *The Rhetoric of Imitation: Genre and Poetic Memory in Vergil and Other Latin Poets*, ed. and trans. C. Segal. Ithaca, NY: Cornell University Press

Conte, G. B. (2007) *The Poetry of Pathos: Studies in Virgilian Epic*. Oxford: Oxford University Press

Conte, G. B. (2009) *P. Vergilius Maro Aeneis*. Berlin: Teubner

Contzen, E. von (2014) 'Why We Need a Medieval Narratology', *Diegesis* 3.2, 1–21

Cornell Way, E. (1991) *Knowledge Representation and Metaphor*. Dordrecht: Kluwer Academic

Cortázar, J. (1964) 'Continuidad de los parques', in *Final de juego*. Buenos Aires: Editorial Sudamericana, 9–11

Cortázar, J. (1967) 'Continuity of Parks', in *End of the Game and Other Stories*, trans. P. Blackburn. New York, NY: Random House, 63–5

Courtney, E. (1985) 'Three Poems of Catullus', *BICS* 32, 85–100

Cowan, R. (2010) 'Virtual epic: Counterfactuals, Sideshadowing, and the Poetics of Contingency in the Punica', in A. Augoustakis (ed.), *Brill's Companion to Silius Italicus*. Leiden: Brill, 323–54

Csapo, E. and M. C. Miller (1991) 'The "Kottabos-Toast" and an Inscribed Red-Figured Cup', *Hesperia* 60.3, 367–82

Culler, J. (1981) *The Pursuit of Signs: Semiotics, Literature, Deconstruction*. London: Routledge

Culler, J. (2015) *Theory of the Lyric*. Cambridge, MA: Harvard University Press

Cullhed, A. (2015) *The Shadow of Creusa: Negotiating Fictionality in Late Antique Latin Literature*, trans. M. Knight. Berlin: Walter de Gruyter

Currie, B. G. F. (2004) 'Reperformance Scenarios for Pindar's Odes', in C. J. Mackie (ed.), *Oral Performance and Its Context*. Leiden: Brill, 49–69

Currie, B. G. F. (2005) *Pindar and the Cult of Heroes*. Oxford: Oxford University Press

Currie, B. G. F. (2013) 'The Pindaric First Person in Flux', *ClAnt* 32, 243–82

D'Alessandro Behr, F. (2005) 'The Narrator's Voice: A Narratological Reappraisal of Apostrophe in Virgil's *Aeneid*', *Arethusa* 38, 189–221

D'Alessandro Behr, F. (2007) *Feeling History: Lucan, Stoicism, and the Poetics of Passion*. Columbus, OH: Ohio State University Press

Daston, L. (ed.) (2000) *Biographies of Scientific Objects*. Chicago, IL and London: University of Chicago Press

Davidson, J. (1998) 'Domesticating Dido: History and Historicity', in M. Burden (ed.), *A Woman Scorn'd: Responses to the Dido Myth*. London: Faber and Faber, 65–88

Davies, M. and P. J. Finglass (2014) *Stesichorus: The Poems*. Cambridge: Cambridge University Press

Davison, J. A. (1968) 'Stesichorus and Helen', in J. A. Davison, *From Archilochus to Pindar: Papers on Greek Literature of the Archaic Period*. London: Macmillan, 196–225

de Man, P. (1979) *Allegories of Reading: Figural Language in Rousseau, Nietzsche, Rilke, and Proust*. New Haven, CT: Yale University Press

Del Bello, D. (2007) *Forgotten Paths: Etymology and the Allegorical Mindset*. Washington, DC: Catholic University of America Press

Denniston, J. D. (ed.) (1957) *Aeschylus: Agamemnon*. Oxford: Clarendon Press

Descartes, R. (2013) *Meditations on First Philosophy: With Selections from the Objections and Replies*, ed. and trans. J. Cottingham. Cambridge: Cambridge University Press

Descola, P. (2013) *Beyond Nature and Culture*, trans. J. Lloyd. Chicago, IL and London: University of Chicago Press

Dietrich, N. (2010) *Figur ohne Raum? Bäume und Felsen in der attischen Vasenmalerei des 6. und 5. Jahrhunderts v. Chr.* Berlin: Walter de Gruyter

Dillery, J. (2003) 'Putting Him Back Together Again: Apion Historian, Apion *grammatikos*', *CPh* 98.4, 383–90

Dillon, J. T. (2004) *Musonius Rufus and Education in the Good Life: A Model of Teaching and Living Virtue*. Dallas, TX and Oxford: University Press of America

Dinshaw, C. (1989) *Chaucer's Sexual Poetics*. Madison, WI: University of Wisconsin Press

Döpp, S. (2013) 'Metalepsen als signifikante Elemente spätlateinischer Literatur', in U. E. Eisen and P. von Möllendorff (eds.), *Über die Grenze: Metalepse in Text- und Bildmedien des Altertums*. Berlin: Walter de Gruyter, 431–65

Dornseiff, F. D. (1933) *Die archaische Mythenerzählung: Folgerungen aus dem homerischen Apollonhymnos*. Berlin and Leipzig: Walter de Gruyter

Dubel, S. (2011) 'Changement de voix: Sur l'apostrophe au personage dans l'Iliade', in E. Raymond (ed.), *Vox poetae: Manifestations auctoriales dans l'épopée gréco-latine*. Paris: De Boccard, 129–44

Dufallo, B. (2013) *The Captor's Image: Greek Culture in Roman Ecphrasis*. Oxford and New York, NY: Oxford University Press

Dumarsais, C. C. (1730) *Des Tropes ou de différents sens*, ed. F. Douay-Soublin, repr. 1988. Paris: Flammarion

Easterling, P. E. (1985) 'Anachronism in Greek Tragedy', *JHS* 105, 1–10

Ebert, A. (1888) *Der Anachronismus in Ovids Metamorphosen.* Ansbach: C. Brügel

Edwards, R. (1976) 'Fulgentius and the Collapse of Meaning', *Helios* 3, 17–35

Effe, B. (2004) *Epische Objektivität und subjektives Erzählen: 'Auktoriale' Narrativik von Homer bis zum römischen Epos der Flavierzeit.* Trier: WVT

Eisen, U. E. and P. von Möllendorff (2013a) 'Zur Einführung', in U. E. Eisen and P. von Möllendorff (eds.), *Über die Grenze: Metalepse in Text- und Bildmedien des Altertums.* Berlin: Walter de Gruyter, 1–9

Eisen, U. E. and P. von Möllendorff (eds.) (2013b) *Über die Grenze: Metalepse in Text- und Bildmedien des Altertums.* Berlin: Walter de Gruyter

Eliade, M. (1967) *Myths, Dreams and Mysteries: The Encounter between Contemporary Faiths and Archaic Reality,* trans. P. Mairet. New York, NY: Harper & Row

Ellis, R. (1889) *A Commentary on Catullus,* 2nd edn. Oxford: Clarendon Press

Elsner, J. (1995) *Art and the Roman Viewer: The Transformation of Art from the Pagan World to Christianity.* Cambridge: Cambridge University Press

Emlyn-Jones, C. and W. Preddy (eds. and trans.) (2017) *Plato: Euthyphro. Apology. Crito. Phaedo.* Cambridge, MA and London: Harvard University Press

Endt, J. (1905) 'Der Gebrauch der Apostrophe bei den lateinischen Epikern', *WS* 27, 106–29

Enk, P. J. (1962) *Sex. Propertii Elegiarum Liber Secundus.* Leiden: Sijthoff

Ercoles, M. (2013) *Stesicoro: Le testimonianze antiche.* Bologna: Pàtron Editore

Évrard-Gillis, J. (1977) 'Le Jeu sur la personne grammaticale chez Catulle', *Latomus* 36, 114–22

Fairbanks, A. (ed. and trans.) (1979) *Elder Philostratus, Younger Philostratus, Callistratus.* Cambridge, MA: Harvard University Press

Faulkner, W. (1990) *Absalom, Absalom!* New York, NY: Vintage International

Fedeli, P. (1983) *Catullus' Carmen 61.* London Studies in Classical Philology 9. Amsterdam: J. C. Gieben

Fedeli, P. (1985) *Properzio: Il libro terzo delle Elegie.* Bari: Adriatica

Feeney, D. C. (1992) '"Shall I Compare Thee…?" Catullus 68b and the Limits of Analogy', in A. J. Woodman and J. G. F. Powell (eds.), *Author and Audience in Latin Literature.* Cambridge: Cambridge University Press, 33–44

Feeney, D. C. (1998) *Literature and Religion at Rome: Cultures, Contexts, and Beliefs.* Cambridge: Cambridge University Press

Feldherr, A. (2000) '*Non inter nota sepulcra*: Catullus 101 and Roman Funerary Ritual', *ClAnt* 19, 209–31

Felski, R. (2008) *Uses of Literature.* Oxford: Blackwell

Felson, N. (1999) 'Vicarious Transport: Fictive Deixis in Pindar's *Pythian* 4', *HSCPh* 99, 1–31

Fernandelli, M. (2012) *Catullo e la rinascita dell' epos: Dal carme 64 all' Eneide.* Spudasmata 142. Hildesheim: Georg Olms Verlag

Ferrari, G. (1986) 'Eye-Cup', *RA* 1, 5–20

Ferrari, G. (2008) *Alcman and the Cosmos of Sparta.* Chicago, IL: University of Chicago Press

Fitton Brown, A. D. (1985) 'The Unreality of Ovid's Tomitan Exile', *LCM* 10.2, 18–22

Fitzgerald, W. (1984) 'Aeneas, Daedalus and the Labyrinth', *Arethusa* 17, 51–65

Fitzgerald, W. (1995) *Catullan Provocations: Lyric Poetry and the Drama of Position*. Berkeley, CA: University of California Press

Fludernik, M. (1994a) 'Introduction: Second-Person Narrative and Related Issues', *Style* 28, 281–328

Fludernik, M. (1994b) 'Second-Person Narrative as a Test-Case for Narratology: The Limits of Realism', *Style* 28, 445–79

Fludernik, M. (1996) *Towards a Natural Narratology*. London: Routledge

Fludernik, M. (2003a) 'The Diachronization of Narratology', *Narrative* 11, 331–48

Fludernik, M. (2003b) 'Scene Shift, Metalepsis, and the Metaleptic Mode', *Style* 37.4, 382–400

Fontane, T. (2015) *Effi Briest*, trans. M. Mitchell. Oxford: Oxford University Press

Fontanier, P. (1818) *Commentaire raisonné sur Les Tropes de Dumarsais*. Paris: Belin-le-Prieur, repr. 1967: *Les Tropes*, vol. 2. Geneva: Slatkine Reprints

Ford, A. (1992) *Homer: The Poetry of the Past*. Ithaca, NY: Cornell University Press

Ford, A. (1994) 'Protagoras' Head: Interpreting Philosophic Fragments in *Theaetetus*', *AJPh* 115.2, 199–218

Fordyce, C. J. (1961) *Catullus: A Commentary*. Oxford: Clarendon Press

Fowler, D. (1997) 'The Virgil Commentary of Servius', in C. Martindale (ed.), *The Cambridge Companion to Virgil*. Cambridge: Cambridge University Press, 73–8

Fowler, R. L. (2011) 'Mythos and Logos', *JHS* 131, 45–66

Fränkel, H. (1962) *Dichtung und Philosophie des frühen Griechentums*. Munich: C. H. Beck

Frontisi-Ducroux, F. (1995) *Du masque au visage: Aspects de l'identité en Grèce ancienne*. Paris: Flammarion

Frontisi-Ducroux, F. and F. Lissarrague (1983) 'De l'ambiguïté à l'ambivalence: Un Parcours dionysiaque', *AION* 5, 11–32

Frye, N. (1957) *Anatomy of Criticism: Four Essays*. Princeton, NJ: Princeton University Press

Fulkerson, L. (2012) 'Pastoral Appropriation and Assimilation in Ovid's Apollo and Daphne Episode', in E. Karakasis (ed.), *Singing in the Shadow…Pastoral Encounters in Post-Vergilian Poetry*. Trends in Classics 4.1. Berlin: Walter de Gruyter, 29–47

Fulkerson, L. (2017) *A Literary Commentary on the Appendix Tibulliana*. Oxford: Oxford University Press

Funke, C. (2003) *Inkheart*. London: The Chicken House

Furley, W. D. and J. M. Bremer (eds.) (2001) *Greek Hymns: Selected Cult Songs from the Archaic to the Hellenistic Period*, vol. 1. Tübingen: Mohr Siebeck

Gabriel, M. (2015) *Why the World Does Not Exist*, trans. G. S. Moss. Cambridge: Polity Press

Gadamer, H.-G. (1990) *Wahrheit und Methode: Grundzüge einer philosophischen Hermeneutik*, 6th edn. Tübingen: Mohr Siebeck

Gagné, R. and M. Hopman (eds.) (2013) *Choral Mediations in Greek Tragedy*. Cambridge: Cambridge University Press

Gaskin, R. (1990) 'Do Homeric Heroes Make Real Decisions?', *CQ* 40, 1–15; here cited from slightly revised version in D. L. Cairns (ed.) (2001) *Oxford Readings in Homer's Iliad*. Oxford: Oxford University Press, 147–69

Gasti, H. (2006) 'Narratological Aspects of Virgil's *Aeneid* 2.1–13', *Acta Classica* 49, 113–20

Gell, A. (1998) *Art and Agency: An Anthropological Theory.* Oxford: Clarendon Press

Genette, G. (1966–2002) *Figures I–V.* Paris: Seuil

Genette, G. (1969) *Figures II.* Paris: Seuil

Genette, G. (1970) 'La Rhétorique restreinte'; here cited from *Gérard Genette: Figures of Literary Discourse*, trans. A Sheridan. Oxford: Blackwell (1982), 103–26

Genette, G. (1972) *Figures III.* Paris: Seuil

Genette, G. (1972 = 1980) 'Discours du récit', *Figures III* (Paris: Seuil): 65–282; here cited from *Narrative Discourse: An Essay in Method*, trans. J. E. Lewin. Ithaca, NY: Cornell University Press (1980)

Genette, G. (2004) *Métalepse: De la figure à la fiction.* Paris: Seuil

Georgacopoulou, S. (2005) *Au frontières du récit épique: L'emploi de l'apostrophe du narrateur dans la Thébaide de Stace.* Brussels: Editions Latomus

Gerber, D. E. (1982) *Pindar's Olympian One: A Commentary.* Toronto and London: University of Toronto Press

Gerber, D. E. (2002) *A Commentary on Pindar, Olympian Nine.* Stuttgart: Steiner

Gerleigner, G. S. (2014) 'Smikros hat's gemalt: Zur Schriftbildlichkeit griechischer Vaseninschriften', in A. Kehnel and D. Panagiotopoulos (eds.) *Schriftträger— Textträger: Zur materiellen Präsenz des Geschriebenen in frühen Gesellschaften.* Berlin: Walter de Gruyter, 209–28

Gildenhard, I. (2012) *Virgil Aeneid 4.1–299: Latin Text, Study Questions, Commentary and Interpretative Essays.* Cambridge: Open Book Publishers

Giles, D. C. (2010) 'Parasocial Relationships', in J. Eder et al. (eds.), *Characters in Fictional Worlds: Understanding Imaginary Beings in Literature, Film, and Other Media.* New York: Walter de Gruyter, 442–56

Gill, C. (1996) *Personality in Greek Epic, Tragedy, and Philosophy: The Self in Dialogue.* Oxford: Clarendon Press

Giuliani, L. (2013) *Image and Myth: A History of Pictorial Narration in Greek Art.* Chicago, IL: University of Chicago Press

Giusti, E. (2018) *Carthage in Virgil's Aeneid: Staging the Enemy under Augustus.* Cambridge: Cambridge University Press

Goethe, J. W. (1950) *Gesamtausgabe der Werke, Briefe und Gespräche*, ed. E. Beutler, 24 vols., Volume 15: *Schriften zur Literatur.* Zurich: Artemis

Goldhill, S. (1991) *The Poet's Voice: Essays on Poetics and Greek Literature.* Cambridge: Cambridge University Press

Goold, G. P. (1970) 'Servius and the Helen Episode', *HSCPh* 74, 101–68

Goold, G. P. (1989) *Catullus*, 2nd edn. London: Duckworth

Gow, A. S. F. (1942) 'Theocritus, *Idyll* XXIV, Stars and Doors', *CQ* 36, 104–10

Gow, A. S. F. (1952) *Theocritus*, 2 vols., 2nd edn. Cambridge: Cambridge University Press

Gowers, E. (1994) 'Persius and the Decoction of Nero', in J. Elsner and J. Masters (eds.), *Reflections of Nero: Culture, History and Representation.* London: Duckworth, 131–50

Gowers, E. (2005) 'Virgil's Sibyl and the "Many Mouths" Cliché (*Aen.* 6.625–7)', *CQ* 55.1, 170–82

Grafton, A. (1990) *Forgers and Critics: Creativity and Duplicity in Western Scholarship.* Princeton, NJ: Princeton University Press

Graziosi, B. (2002) *Inventing Homer: The Early Reception of Epic.* Cambridge: Cambridge University Press

Graziosi, B. (2013) 'The Poet in the *Iliad*', in A. Marmodoro and J. Hill (eds.), *The Author's Voice in Classical and Late Antiquity.* Oxford: Oxford University Press, 9–36

Greene, T. M. (1982) *The Light in Troy: Imitation and Discovery in Renaissance Poetry.* New Haven, CT: Yale University Press

Grethlein, J. (2012) 'Xenophon's *Anabasis* from Character to Narrator', *JHS* 132, 23–40

Grethlein, J. (2013a) 'Choral Intertemporality in the *Oresteia*', in R. Gagné and M. Hopman (eds.), *Choral Mediations in Greek Tragedy.* Cambridge: Cambridge University Press, 78–99

Grethlein, J. (2013b) *Experience and Teleology in Ancient Historiography: Futures Past from Herodotus to Augustine.* Cambridge: Cambridge University Press

Grethlein, J. (2015) 'Aesthetic Experiences, Ancient and Modern', *New Literary History* 46.2, 309–33

Grethlein, J. (2016) 'Sight and Reflexivity: Theorising Vision in Greek Vase-Painting', in M. Squire (ed.), *Sight and the Ancient Senses.* London and New York, NY: Routledge, 85–106

Grethlein, J. (2017) *Aesthetic Experiences and Classical Antiquity: The Content of Forms in Narratives and Pictures.* Cambridge: Cambridge University Press

Grethlein, J. (2018a) 'Homeric Motivation and Modern Narratology: The Case of Penelope', *CCJ* 64, 70–90

Grethlein, J. (2018b) 'Ornamental and Formulaic Patterns: The Semantic Significance of Form in Early Greek Vase-Painting and Homeric Epic', in N. Dietrich and M. Squire (eds.), *Ornament and Figure in Graeco-Roman Art: Rethinking Visual Ontologies in Classical Antiquity.* Berlin: Walter de Gruyter, 73–96

Grethlein, J. (forthcoming) 'Author and Characters: Ancient, Narratological and Cognitive Views on a Tricky Relationship', *CPh*

Grethlein, J. and L. Huitink (2017) 'Homer's Vividness: An Enactive Approach', *JHS* 137, 67–91

Griffith, R. D. (1991) 'Person and Presence in Pindar', *Arethusa* 24, 31–42

Grossardt, P. (2012) *Stesichoros zwischen kultischer Praxis, mythischer Tradition und eigenem Kunstanspruch: Zur Behandlung des Helenamythos im Werk des Dichters aus Himera.* Tübingen: Narr Verlag

Hacking, I. (1994) 'The Looping Effects of Human Kinds', in D. Sperber, D. Premack, and A. J. Premack (eds.), *Causal Cognition: A Multidisciplinary Approach.* Oxford: Oxford University Press, 351–94

Hacking, I. (2002) *Historical Ontology.* Cambridge, MA: Harvard University Press

Hagen, B. (1954) *Stil und Abfassungszeit der Lygdamus-Gedichte.* Diss. Hamburg

Halliwell, S. (2002) *The Aesthetics of Mimesis: Ancient Texts and Modern Problems.* Princeton, NJ: Princeton University Press

Halliwell, S. (2011) *Between Ecstasy and Truth: Interpretations of Greek Poetics from Homer to Longinus.* Oxford: Oxford University Press

Hampel, E. (1908) *De apostrophe apud Romanorum poetas.* Diss. Jena

Hanebeck, J. (2017) *Understanding Metalepsis: The Hermeneutics of Narrative Transgression.* Berlin: De Gruyter

Harris, W. V. (2003) 'Roman Opinions about the Truthfulness of Dreams', *JRS* 93, 18–34

Harris, W. V. (2009) *Dreams and Experience in Classical Antiquity.* Cambridge, MA: Harvard University Press

Harrison, S. J. (2001) 'Picturing the Future: The Proleptic Ekphrasis from Homer to Vergil', in S. J. Harrison (ed.), *Texts, Ideas, and the Classics.* Oxford: Oxford University Press, 70–92

Harrison, S. J. (2005) 'Altering Attis: Ethnicity, Gender and Genre in Catullus 63', in R. R. Nauta and A. Harder (eds.), *Catullus' Poem on Attis: Texts and Contexts.* Leiden: Brill, 11–24

Harrison, S. J. (2010) 'Picturing the Future Again: Proleptic Ekphrasis in Silius' *Punica*', in A. Augoustakis (ed.), *Brill's Companion to Silius Italicus.* Leiden: Brill, 279–92

Harrisson, J. (2013) *Dreams and Dreaming in the Roman Empire: Cultural Memory and Imagination.* London: Bloomsbury Academic

Havelock, E. A. (1939) *The Lyric Genius of Catullus.* New York, NY: Russell & Russell

Hays, G. (2003) 'The Date and Identity of the Mythographer Fulgentius', *Journal of Mediaeval Latin* 13, 163–252

Hays, G. (2013) *Fulgentius the Mythographer: A Bibliography.* http://www.people. virginia.edu/~bgh2n/fulgbib.html [Accessed 26 September 2019]

Heath, M. (2003) '*Metalepsis, Paragraphe* and the Scholia to Hermogenes', *Leeds International Classical Studies* 2.2, 1–91

Hedreen, G. (2007) 'Myths of Ritual in Athenian Vase-Painting of Silens', in E. Csapo (ed.), *The Origins of Theater in Ancient Greece and Beyond: From Ritual to Drama.* Cambridge: Cambridge University Press, 150–95

Hedreen, G. (2017) 'Unframing the Representation: The Frontal Face in Athenian Vase-Painting', in V. Platt and M. Squire (eds.), *The Frame in Classical Arts.* Cambridge: Cambridge University Press, 154–87

Heerink, M. (2015) *Echoing Hylas: A Study in Hellenistic and Roman Metapoetics.* Madison, WI: University of Wisconsin Press

Heidegger, M. (1962) *Being and Time*, trans. J. Macquarrie and E. Robinson. Oxford: Blackwell

Heinze, R. (1993) *Virgil's Epic Technique.* Bristol: Bristol Classical Press

Helgeland, B. (dir.) (2001) *A Knight's Tale*, Special Edition. DVD. Culver City, CA: Sony Pictures.

Helm, R. (1898) *Fabii Planciadis Fulgentii V. C.: Opera.* Leipzig: Teubner

Hendrickson, G. L. and H. M. Hubbell (eds. and trans.) (1939) *Cicero: Brutus. Orator.* Cambridge, MA and London: Harvard University Press

Henrichs, A. (1994/5) '"Why Should I Dance?" Choral Self-Referentiality in Greek Tragedy', *Arion* 3.1, 41–55

Henrichs, A. (1996) 'Dancing in Athens, Dancing on Delos: Some Patterns of Choral Projection in Euripides', *Philologus* 140, 48–62

Henry, J. (1878) *Aeneidea*. Dublin: Dublin University Press

Hexter, R. (1992) 'Sidonian Dido', in R. Hexter and D. Selden (eds.), *Innovations of Antiquity*. New York, NY: Routledge, 332–84

Hill, T. D. (2004) *Ambitiosa Mors: Suicide and Self in Roman Thought and Literature*. London: Routledge

Hinds, S. (1998) *Allusion and Intertext: Dynamics of Appropriation in Roman Poetry*. Cambridge: Cambridge University Press

Hirzel, R. (1895) *Der Dialog: Ein literaturhistorischer Versuch*, 2 vols. Leipzig: S. Hirzel

Hollander, J. (1981) *The Figure of Echo: A Mode of Allusion in Milton and After*. Berkeley, CA: University of California Press

Hooley, D. M. (1997) *The Knotted Thong: Structures of Mimesis in Persius*. Ann Arbor, MI: University of Michigan Press

Hopkinson, N. (ed. and trans.) (2015) *Theocritus. Moschus. Bion*. Cambridge, MA and London: Harvard University Press

Horsfall, N. (1973) 'Dido in the Light of History', *PVS* 13, 1–13

Horsfall, N. (2008) *Virgil Aeneid 2: A Commentary*. Leiden: Brill

Horsfall, N. (2010) 'Pictures from an Execution', in J. S. F. Dijkstra, J. E. A. Kroesen, and Y. Kuiper (eds.), *Myths, Martyrs, and Modernity: Studies in the History of Religions in Honour of Jan N. Bremmer*. Leiden: Brill, 237–48

Howald, E. (1924) 'Meleager und Achill', *RhM* 73, 402–25

Howe, T. P. (1954) 'The Origin and Function of the Gorgon-Head', *AJA* 58.3, 209–21

Howie, J. G. (1983) 'The Revision of Myth in Pindar *Olympian* 1', *Papers of the Liverpool Latin Seminar* 4, 277–313

Hubbard, T. K. (1987) 'The "Cooking" of Pelops: Pindar and the Process of Mythological Revisionism', *Helios* 4, 3–21

Hubbard, T. K. (2004) 'The Dissemination of Epinician Lyric: Pan-Hellenism, Reperformance, Written Texts', in C. J. Mackie (ed.), *Oral Performance and Its Context*. Leiden: Brill, 71–93

Hühn, P. (2004) 'Transgeneric Narratology: Application to Lyric Poetry', in J. Pier (ed.), *The Dynamics of Narrative Form: Studies in Anglo-American Narratology*. Berlin and New York, NY: Walter de Gruyter, 139–58

Hühn, P. (2005) 'Plotting the Lyric: Forms of Narration in Poetry', in E. Müller-Zettelmann and M. Rubik (eds.), *Theory into Poetry: New Approaches to the Lyric*. Amsterdam: Rodopi, 147–72

Hühn, P. (2014) 'The Problem of Fictionality and Factuality in Lyric Poetry', *Narrative* 22, 155–68

Hunter, R. (1996) *Theocritus and the Archaeology of Greek Poetry*. Cambridge: Cambridge University Press

Hunter, R. (1999) *Theocritus: A Selection*. Cambridge: Cambridge University Press

Hunter, R. (2003) *Theocritus: Encomium of Ptolemy Philadelphus*. Berkeley, CA: University of California Press

Hunter, R. (2004) *Plato's Symposium*. Oxford: Oxford University Press

Hunter, R. (2016) ' "Palaephatus," Strabo, and the Boundaries of Myth', *CPh* 111, 245–61

Huttner, U. (1997) *Die politische Rolle der Heraklesgestalt im griechischen Herrschertum*. Stuttgart: Steiner

Immerwahr, H. R. (1990) *Attic Script: A Survey*. Oxford: Oxford University Press

Innes, D. C. (1995) 'Introduction', in D. C. Innes (ed. and trans.), *Demetrius: On Style*. Cambridge, MA: Harvard University Press, 311–42

Jacob, C. G. (1839) *Quaestiones Epicae*. Quedlinburg: G. Bassius, 188–91

Jakobson, R. (1956) 'Two Aspects of Language and Two Types of Aphasic Disturbances', repr. in S. Ruby (ed.), *Roman Jakobson: Selected Writings*, 6 vols., Volume 2: *Word and Language*. The Hague: Mouton, 239–59

Jakobson, R. (1960) 'Linguistics and Poetics', in T. Sebeok (ed.), *Style in Language*. Cambridge, MA: Technology Press of Massachusetts Institute of Technology, 350–77

Janan, M. W. (1994) *'When the Lamp Is Shattered': Desire and Narrative in Catullus*. Carbondale, IL: Southern Illinois University Press

Johnson, W. R. (1982) *The Idea of Lyric: Lyric Modes in Ancient and Modern Poetry*. Berkeley, CA: University of California Press

Jones, J. W. Jr (1964) 'Vergil as *Magister* in Fulgentius', in C. Henderson (ed.), *Classical, Mediaeval and Renaissance Studies in Honor of Berthold Louis Ullman*. Rome: Edizioni di storia e letteratura, 273–5

Jong, I. J. F. de (2004) *Narrators and Focalizers: The Presentation of the Story in the Iliad*, 2nd edn. London: Bristol Classical Press

Jong, I. J. F. de (2009) 'Metalepsis in Ancient Greek Literature', in J. Grethlein and A. Rengakos (eds.), *Narratology and Interpretation: The Content of Narrative Form in Ancient Literature*. Berlin: Walter de Gruyter, 87–115

Jong, I. J. F. de (2013) 'Metalepsis and Embedded Speech in Pindaric and Bacchylidean Myth', in U. E. Eisen and P. von Möllendorff (eds.), *Über die Grenze: Metalepse in Text- und Bildmedien des Altertums*. Berlin: Walter de Gruyter, 97–118

Kacandes, I. (1994) 'Narrative Apostrophe: Reading, Rhetoric, Resistance in Michel Butor's *La Modification* and Julio Cortázar's *Graffiti*', *Style* 28, 329–49

Kambylis, A. (1964) 'Anredeformen bei Pindar', in A. A. Anastasiou, A. D. Skiadas, and A. Kambylis (eds.), Χάρις Κωνσταντίνῳ Ι. Βουβέρῃ. Ἀφιέρωμα τῶν μαθητῶν τοῦ ἐπὶ τῇ ἑξηκονταπενταετηρίδι τοῦ βίου αὐτοῦ. Athens, 95–199

Kannicht, R. (1969) *Euripides Helena*, vol. 1. Heidelberg: Winter

Kantzios, I. (2003) 'Pindar's Muses', *CB* 79, 3–32

Kearey, T. (2018) '(Mis)reading the Gnat: Truth and Deception in the Pseudo-Virgilian *Culex*', *Ramus* 47.2, 174–96

Keen, S. (2014) 'Novel Readers and the Empathetic Angel of our Nature', in M. M. Hammond and S. J. Kim (eds.), *Rethinking Empathy through Literature*. New York, NY: Routledge, 21–33

Kelly, A. (2007) 'Stesikhoros and Helen', *MH* 64, 1–21

Kennedy, D. F. (2008) 'Elegy and the Erotics of Narratology', in G. Liveley and P. Salzman-Mitchell (eds.), *Latin Elegy and Narratology: Fragments of Story*. Columbus, OH: Ohio State University Press, 19–33

Kennedy, D. F. (2013a) *Antiquity and the Meanings of Time: A Philosophy of Ancient and Modern Literature*. London: I. B. Tauris

Kennedy, D. F. (2013b) 'The Political Epistemology of Infinity', in D. Lehoux, A. D. Morrison, and A. Sharrock (eds.), *Lucretius: Poetry, Philosophy, Science*. Oxford: Oxford University Press, 51–67

Kennedy, D. F. (2020) 'Plato and Lucretius on the Theoretical Subject: A Metaphysical Enquiry', in D. O'Rourke (ed.), *Approaches to Lucretius*. Cambridge: Cambridge University Press, 259–81

Kim, L. (2010) *Homer between History and Fiction in Imperial Greek Literature*. Cambridge: Cambridge University Press

Kirchenko, A. (2016) 'The Art of Transference: Metaphor and Iconicity in Pindar's *Olympian* 6 and *Nemean* 5', *Mnemosyne* 69, 1–28

Kiss, D. (2013) *Catullus Online: A Repertory of Conjectures for Catullus*. http://www.catullusonline.org [Accessed 26 September 2019]

Kiss, M. (2012) 'Narrative Metalepsis as Diegetic Concept in Christopher Nolan's *Inception* (2010)', *Acta Univ. Sapientiae, Film and Media Studies* 5, 35–54

Klimek, S. (2010) *Paradoxes Erzählen: Die Metalepse in der phantastischen Literatur*. Paderborn: Mentis

Klimek, S. (2011) 'Metalepsis in Fantasy Fiction', in K. Kukkonen and S. Klimek (eds.), *Metalepsis in Popular Culture*. Berlin: Walter de Gruyter, 22–40

Klooster, J. (2013) 'Apostrophe in Homer, Apollonius and Callimachus', in U. E. Eisen and P. von Möllendorff (eds.), *Über die Grenze: Metalepse in Text- und Bildmedien des Altertums*. Berlin: Walter de Gruyter, 151–73

Kneale, J. D. (1991) 'Romantic Aversions: Apostrophe Reconsidered', *ELH* 58, 141–65

Koenen, L. (1977) *Eine agonistische Inschrift aus Ägypten und frühptolemaische Königsfeste*. Meisenheim am Glan: Hain

Köhnken, A. (1974) 'Pindar as Innovator: Poseidon Hippios and the Relevance of the Pelops Story in *Olympian* 1', *CQ* 24, 199–206

Köhnken, A. (1983) 'Time and Event in Pindar *O*. 1.25–53', *ClAnt* 2, 66–76

Korshak, Y. (1987) *Frontal Faces in Attic Vase Painting of the Archaic Period*. Chicago, IL: Ares Publishers

Koselleck, R. (2002) *The Practice of Conceptual History: Timing History, Spacing Concepts*, trans. T. S. Presner et al. Stanford: Stanford University Press

Kretschmer, P. (1894) *Die griechischen Vaseninschriften*. Gütersloh: Bertelsmann

Krevans, N. (2006) 'Is There Urban Pastoral? The Case of Theocritus' *Id*. 15', in M. Fantuzzi and T. Papanghelis (eds.), *Brill's Companion to Greek and Latin Pastoral*. Leiden: Brill, 119–46

Krischer, T. (1981) 'Die Pelopsgestalt in der ersten Olympischen Ode Pindars', *GB* 10, 69–75

Kristeller, P. O. (1951) 'The Modern System of the Arts: A Study in the History of Aesthetics, Part I', *JHI* 12.4, 496–527

Kristeller, P. O. (1952) 'The Modern System of the Arts: A Study in the History of Aesthetics, Part II', *JHI* 13.1, 17–46

Kroll, W. (1924) *Studien zum Verständnis der römischen Literatur*. Stuttgart: Metzler

Kubiak, D. (1986) 'Time and Traditional Diction in Catullus 72', *Studies in Latin Literature and Roman History* 4, 259–64

Kukkonen, K. and S. Klimek (eds.) (2011) *Metalepsis in Popular Culture*. Berlin: Walter de Gruyter

Kunisch, N. (1990) 'Die Augen der Augenschalen', *Antike Kunst* 33, 20–7

Kunisch, N. (1997) *Makron*. Mainz: P. von Zabern

Kurke, L. (1991) *The Traffic in Praise: Pindar and the Poetics of Social Economy*. Ithaca, NY: Cornell University Press

Kurzweil, R. (2006) *The Singularity Is Near*. London: Duckworth

Labov, W. (1972) *Language in the Inner City: Studies in the Black English Vernacular*. Philadelphia, PA: University of Pennsylvania Press

Laird, A. (2001) 'The Poetics and Afterlife of Virgil's Descent to the Underworld: Servius, Dante, Fulgentius and the *Culex*', *PVS* 24, 49–80

Laird, A. (2007) 'Fiction, Philosophy, and Logical Closure', in S. J. Heyworth et al. (eds.), *Classical Constructions: Papers in Memory of Don Fowler, Classicist and Epicurean*. Oxford: Oxford University Press, 281–309

Laird, A. (2009) 'Virgil: Reception and the Myth of Biography', *CentoPagine* 3, 1–9

Latour, B. (2005) *Reassembling the Social: An Introduction to Actor-Network-Theory*. Oxford: Oxford University Press

Latour, B. (2010) *On the Modern Cult of the Factish Gods*, first chapter trans. C. Porter and H. MacLean. Durham, NC: Duke University Press

Latour, B. (2013) *An Inquiry into Modes of Existence: An Anthropology of the Moderns*, trans. C. Porter. Cambridge, MA: Harvard University Press

Lattimore, R. (1967) *The Odyssey of Homer*. New York, NY: Harper & Row

Laurenti, R. (1989) 'Musoni, maestro di Epitteto', *ANRW* II.36.3: 2105–46

Lavocat, F. (2016) *Fait et fiction: Pour une frontier*. Paris: Seuil

Le Guin, U. K. (2008) *Lavinia*. London: Gollancz

Lear, J. (1988) *Aristotle: The Desire to Understand*. Cambridge: Cambridge University Press

Lee, A. G. (1958–9) 'The Date of Lygdamus, and His Relationship to Ovid', *PCPhS* 5, 15–22

Lehoux, D. (2013) 'Seeing and Unseeing, Seen and Unseen', in D. Lehoux, A. D. Morrison, and A. Sharrock (eds.), *Lucretius: Poetry, Philosophy, Science*. Oxford: Oxford University Press, 131–51

Leigh, M. (2016) '*Illa domus, illa mihi sedes*: On the Interpretation of Catullus 68', in R. Hunter and S. P. Oakley (eds.), *Latin Literature and Its Transmission: Papers in Honour of Michael Reeve*. Cambridge: Cambridge University Press, 194–224

Lennon, J. (2012) ' "The First Man to Whistle": Two Interviews with Colum McCann', in S. Cahill and E. Flannery (eds.), *This Side of Brightness: Essays on the Fiction of Colum McCann*. Oxford: Peter Lang, 149–75

Lerer, S. (1985) *Boethius and Dialogue: Literary Method in The Consolation of Philosophy*. Princeton, NJ: Princeton University Press

Lesky, A. (1961) *Göttliche und menschliche Motivation im homerischen Epos*. Heidelberg: Winter; here cited from 'Divine and Human Causation in Homeric Epic' in D. L. Cairns (ed.) (2001) *Oxford Readings in Homer's Iliad*. Oxford: Oxford University Press, 170–202

Lewis, M. (2013) 'Narrativising Catullus: A Never-Ending Story', *Melbourne Historical Journal* 41.2, 1–19

Lieberg, G. (1982) *Poeta Creator: Studien zu einer Figur der antiken Dichtung*. Amsterdam: Gieben

Lissarrague, F. (1985) 'Paroles d'images: Remarques sur le fonctionnement de l'écriture dans l'imagerie attique', in A.-M. Christin (ed.), *Ecritures II*. Paris: Le Sycomore, 71–93

Lissarrague, F. (1987) *Un flot d'image: Une esthétique du banquet grec*. Paris: Adam Biro

Lissarrague, F. (1990) 'Around the Krater: An Aspect of Banquet Imagery', in O. Murray (ed.), *Sympotica: A Symposium on the Symposion*. Oxford: Oxford University Press, 196–21

Lissarrague, F. (1992) 'Graphein: Écrire et dessiner', in C. Bron and E. Kassapoglou (eds.), *L'Image en jeu: De l'antiquité à Paul Klee*. Lausanne: Institut d'archéologie et d'histoire ancienne, Université de Lausanne, 189–203

Lissarrague, F. (1999) 'Publicity and Performance: Kalos Inscriptions in Attic Vase-Painting', in S. Goldhill and R. Osborne (eds.), *Performance Culture and Athenian Democracy*. Cambridge: Cambridge University Press, 359–73

Liveley, G. (2019) *Narratology*. Oxford: Oxford University Press

Lloyd, G. E. R. (2015) *Analogical Investigations: Historical and Cross-Cultural Perspectives on Human Reasoning*. Cambridge: Cambridge University Press

Lodge, D. (1977) *Modes of Modern Writing: Metaphor, Metonymy, and the Typology of Modern Literature*. London: Edward Arnold

Lorenz, K. (2007) 'The Anatomy of Metalepsis: Visuality Turns around on Late Fifth-Century Pots', in R. Osborne (ed.), *Debating the Athenian Cultural Revolution: Art, Literature, Philosophy, and Politics 430–380 BC*. Cambridge: Cambridge University Press, 116–43

Lorenz, K. (2013) 'Der Große Fries des Pergamon-Altars: Die narratologische Kategorie Metalepse und die Analyse von Erzählung in der Flächenkunst', in U. E. Eisen and P. von Möllendorff (eds.), *Über die Grenze: Metalepse in Text- und Bildmedien des Altertums*. Berlin: Walter de Gruyter, 119–50

Louden, B. (1993) 'Pivotal Contrafactuals in Homeric Epic', *ClAnt* 12, 181–98

Lovatt, H. V. (2013) *The Epic Gaze: Vision, Gender and Narrative in Ancient Epic*. Cambridge: Cambridge University Press

Lovatt, H. V. (2019) 'Meanwhile Back at the Ranch: Narrative Transition and Structural Intertextuality in Statius *Thebaid* 1', in L. Galli Milic, D. Nelis, and N. Coffee (eds.), *Intertextuality in Flavian Epic Poetry*. Trends in Classics Supplementary Volumes 64. Berlin: Walter de Gruyter, 21–42

Lowrie, M. (1997) *Horace's Narrative Odes*. Oxford: Clarendon Press

Lowrie, M. (2006) '*Hic* and Absence in Catullus 68', *CPh* 101, 115–32

Lutz, C. E. (1947) 'Musonius Rufus: "The Roman Socrates"', *YClS* 10, 3–147

MacCormack, S. (1998) *The Shadows of Poetry: Vergil in the Mind of Augustine*. Berkeley, CA: University of California Press

Mack, R. (2002) 'Facing Down Medusa (an Aetiology of the Gaze)', *Art History* 25.5, 571–604

Mackay, E. A. (2001) 'The Frontal Face and "You": Narrative Disjunction in Early Greek Poetry and Painting', *Acta Classica* 44, 5–34

Majola-Leblond, C. (2015) 'Empathy, Mirror Neurons and the Subversion of Certitude: Political Writing and Creative Reading in Short-Stories by Bernard MacLaverty, William Trevor and Colum McCann', *Études irlandaises* 40, 305–24

Malcolm, N. (1959) *Dreaming*. London: Routledge and Kegan Paul

Malina, D. (2002) *Breaking the Frame: Metalepsis and the Construction of the Subject*. Columbus, OH: Ohio State University Press

Maniglier, P. (2014) 'A Metaphysical Turn? Bruno Latour's An Inquiry into Modes of Existence', *Radical Philosophy* 187, 37–44

Margolin, U. (2014) 'Narrator', in P. Hühn et al. (eds.), *The Living Handbook of Narratology*, Hamburg: Hamburg University. http://www.lhn.uni-hamburg.de/article/narrator [Accessed 26 September 2019]

Martelli, F. (2013) *Ovid's Revisions: The Editor as Author*. Cambridge: Cambridge University Press

Martens, D. (1992) *Une Esthétique de la transgression: Le Vase grec de la fin de l'époque géométrique au début de l'époque classique*. Brussels: Académie royale de Belgique

Marx, F. (1893) 'Albius 12', in A. F. von Pauly (ed.), *Real-Encyclopädie der klassischen Altertumwissenschaft*, rev. G. Wissowa et al., Volume 1.1. Stuttgart: Metzler, 1319–29

Masters, J. M. (1993) *Poetry and Civil War in Lucan's Bellum Civile*. Cambridge: Cambridge University Press

Matthews, V. J. (1980) 'Metrical Reasons for Apostrophe in Homer', *LCM* 5.5, 93–9

Matzner, S. (2016a) 'Queer Unhistoricism: Scholars, Metalepsis, and Interventions of the Unruly Past', in S. Butler (ed.), *Deep Classics: Rethinking Classical Reception*. London: Bloomsbury Academic, 179–201

Matzner, S. (2016b) *Rethinking Metonymy: Literary Theory and Poetic Practice from Pindar to Jakobson*. Oxford: Oxford University Press

May, J. M. and J. Wisse (eds. and trans.) (2001) *Cicero: On the Ideal Orator (De oratore)*. New York, NY and Oxford: Oxford University Press

McHale, B. (1987) *Postmodernist Fiction*. London: Methuen

McHale, B. (2009) 'Beginning to Think about Narrative in Poetry', *Narrative* 17, 11–27

McKeown, J. C. (1989) *Ovid: Amores, Text, Prolegomena and Commentary*, vol. 2 (book 1). Leeds: Francis Cairns

McQuail, D. et al. (1972) 'The Television Audience: A Revised Perspective', in D. McQuail (ed.), *Sociology of Mass Communications: Selected Readings*. Harmondsworth: Penguin, 135–65

Meyer-Minnemann, K. (2005) 'Un Procédé narratif qui "produit un effet de bizarrerie": La Métalepse littéraire', in J. Pier and J.-M. Schaeffer (eds.), *Métalepses: Entorses au pacte de la representation*. Paris: Éd. de l'EHESS, 133–50

Miedel, J. (1892) *De anachronismo, qui est in P. Papinii Statii Thebaide et Achilleide*. Passau: F. W. Keppler

Miller, J. F. (2009) *Apollo, Augustus, and the Poets*. Cambridge: Cambridge University Press

Miller, P. A. (1994) *Lyric Texts and Lyric Consciousness: The Birth of a Genre from Archaic Greece to Augustan Rome*. London and New York, NY: Routledge

Miller, P. A. (2004) *Subjecting Verses: Latin Love Elegy and the Emergence of the Real*. Princeton, NJ and Oxford: Princeton University Press

Miller, P. A. (2015) 'Dreams and Other Fictions: The Representation of Representation in *Republic* 5 and 6', *AJPh* 136, 37–62

Moi, T. (2017) *Revolution of the Ordinary: Literary Studies after Wittgenstein, Austin, and Cavell*. Chicago, IL: University of Chicago Press

Morace, R. A. (1989) *The Dialogic Novels of Malcolm Bradbury and David Lodge*. Carbondale, IL: Southern Illinois University Press

Morrison, A. D. (2007a) *The Narrator in Archaic Greek and Hellenistic Poetry*. Cambridge: Cambridge University Press

Morrison, A. D. (2007b) *Performances and Audiences in Pindar's Sicilian Victory Odes*. London: Institute of Classical Studies

Most, G. W. (2016) 'Allegoresis and Etymology', in A. Grafton and G. W. Most (eds.), *Canonical Texts and Scholarly Practice: A Global Comparative Approach*. Cambridge: Cambridge University Press, 52–74

Murray, J. (2014) 'Anchored in Time: The Date in Apollonius' *Argonautica*', in A. Harder, R. Regtuit, and G. Wakker (eds.), *Hellenistic Poetry in Context*. Hellenistica Groningana 20. Leuven: Peeters, 247–77

Murray, O. (ed.) (1990) *Sympotica: A Symposium on the Symposion*. Oxford: Oxford University Press

Myers, T. A. (2019) *Homer's Divine Audience: The Iliad's Reception on Mount Olympus*. Oxford: Oxford University Press

Mynors, R. A. B. (1958) *C. Valerii Catulli: Carmina*. Oxford: Clarendon Press

Mynors, R. A. B. (1969) *P. Vergili Maronis: Opera*. Oxford: Clarendon Press

Nauta, R. (2013a) 'The Concept of "Metalepsis": From Rhetoric to the Theory of Allusion and to Narratology', in U. E. Eisen and P. von Möllendorff (eds.), *Über die Grenze: Metalepse in Text- und Bildmedien des Altertums*. Berlin: Walter de Gruyter, 469–82

Nauta, R. (2013b) 'Metalepsis and Metapoetics in Latin Poetry', in U. E. Eisen and P. von Möllendorff (eds.), *Über die Grenze: Metalepse in Text- und Bildmedien des Altertums*. Berlin: Walter de Gruyter, 223–56

Navarro Antolín, F. (1996) *Corpus Tibullianum III.1–6: Lygdami Elegiarum Liber. Edition and Commentary*, trans. J. J. Zoltowski. Leiden: Brill

Neer, R. T. (2002) *Style and Politics in Athenian Vase-Painting: The Craft of Democracy, ca. 530–460 BCE*. Cambridge: Cambridge University Press

Nehamas, E. and P. Woodruff (eds. and trans.) (1989) *Plato: Symposium*. Indianapolis, IN: Hackett

Nelles, W. (1997) *Frameworks: Narrative Levels and Embedded Narratives*. New York, NY: Lang

Nerlich, B. and Clarke, D. D. (2001) 'Mind, Meaning and Metaphor: The Philosophy and Psychology of Metaphor in 19th-Century Germany', *History of the Human Sciences* 14.2, 39–62

Nietzsche, F. (1873) 'On Truth and Lying in an Extra-Moral Sense', here cited from *Friedrich Nietzsche on Rhetoric and Language*, ed. and trans. S. Gilman et al. Oxford: Oxford University Press (1989)

Nightingale, A. W. (2004) *Spectacles of Truth in Classical Greek Philosophy: Theoria in its Cultural Context*. Cambridge: Cambridge University Press

Ní Mheallaigh, K. (2009) 'The Teleology of Origins in Lucian's *Verae Historiae*', in A. N. Bartley (ed.), *A Lucian for Our Times*. Newcastle-upon-Tyne: Cambridge Scholars Publishing, 11–28

Nisard, D. (1867) *Études de moeurs et de critique sue les poètes latins de la décadence*, vol. 2, 3rd edn. Paris: Hachette

Nolan, C. (2010) *Inception: The Shooting Script*. San Rafael, CA: Insight Editions

Nünlist, R. (2004) 'Homeric Hymns', in I. J. F. de Jong, R. Nünlist, and A. Bowie (eds.) *Narrators, Narratees, and Narratives in Ancient Greek Literature*. Studies in Ancient Greek Narrative 1. Leiden: Brill, 35–42

Nünlist, R. (2009) *The Ancient Critic at Work: Terms and Concepts of Literary Criticism in Greek Scholia*. Cambridge: Cambridge University Press

Obbink, D. (1993) 'The Addressees of Empedocles', *MD* 31, 51–98

O'Brien, F. (1939) *At Swim-Two-Birds*. London and New York, NY: Longmans, Green & Co.

O'Hara, J. J. (1990) *Death and the Optimistic Prophecy in Vergil's Aeneid*. Princeton, NJ: Princeton University Press

O'Hara, J. J. (1993) 'Dido as "Interpreting Character" at *Aeneid* 4.56–66', *Arethusa* 26.1, 99–114

O'Hara, J. J. (1996) *True Names: Vergil and the Alexandrian Tradition of Etymological Wordplay*. Ann Arbor, MI: University of Michigan Press

O'Hara, J. J. (2007) *Inconsistency in Roman Epic*. Cambridge: Cambridge University Press

Olson, S. D. (ed. and trans.) (2007) *Athenaeus: The Learned Banqueters*, Volume II: *Books 3.106e–5*. Cambridge, MA and London: Harvard University Press

O'Sullivan, T. (2009) 'Death *ante ora parentum* in Virgil's *Aeneid*', *TAPhA* 139, 447–86

Parkes, C. M. (1986) *Bereavement: Studies of Grief in Adult Life*. London: Tavistock

Parry, A. (1963) 'The Two Voices of Virgil's *Aeneid*', *Arion* 2.4, 66–80

Parry, A. (1972) 'Language and Characterization in Homer', *HSCPh* 76, 1–22

Parry, H. (1994) 'The Apologos of Odysseus: Lies, All Lies?', *Phoenix* 48, 1–20

Patron, S. (2009) *Le Narrateur: Introduction à la théorie narrative*. Paris: Armand

Pavlou, M. (2012) 'Pindar and the Reconstruction of the Past', in J. Marincola, L. Llewellyn-Jones, and C. Maciver (eds.), *Greek Notions of the Past in the Archaic and Classical Eras: History without Histories*. Edinburgh: Edinburgh University Press, 95–112

Payne, M. (2007) *Theocritus and the Invention of Fiction*. Cambridge: Cambridge University Press

Pedrick, V. (1986) '*Qui potis est, inquis?* Audience Roles in Catullus', *Arethusa* 19, 187–209

Peirano, I. (2012) *The Rhetoric of the Roman Fake: Latin Pseudepigrapha in Context*. Cambridge: Cambridge University Press

Peirano, I. (2013) '*Ille ego qui quondam*: On Authorial (An)onymity', in A. Marmodoro and J. Hill (eds.), *The Author's Voice in Classical and Late Antiquity*. Oxford: Oxford University Press, 251–86

Pelletier, J. (2003) 'Vergil and Dido', *Dialectica* 57.2, 191–203

Pelliccia, H. (1995) *Mind, Body and Speech in Homer and Pindar*. Göttingen: Vandenhoeck & Ruprecht

Pelling, C. (2006) 'Homer and Herodotus', in M. J. Clarke, B. Currie, and R. O. A. M. Lyne (eds.) *Epic Interactions: Perspectives on Homer, Virgil, and the Epic Tradition. Presented to Jasper Griffin by Former Pupils.* Oxford: Oxford University Press, 75–104

Peponi, A.-E. (2012) *Frontiers of Pleasure: Models of Aesthetic Response in Archaic and Classical Greek Thought.* Oxford: Oxford University Press

Pfeiffer, R. (1968) *History of Classical Scholarship: From the Beginnings to the End of the Hellenistic Age.* Oxford: Clarendon Press

Pfeijffer, I. L. (2004) 'Pindar and Bacchylides', I. J. F. de Jong, R. Nünlist, and A. Bowie (eds.), *Narrators, Narratees, and Narratives in Ancient Greek Literature.* Studies in Ancient Greek Narrative 1. Leiden: Brill, 213–32

Phelan, J. (2007) *Experiencing Fiction: Judgments, Progressions, and the Rhetorical Theory of Narrative.* Columbus, OH: Ohio State University Press

Pier, J. (2005) 'Métalepse et hiérarchies narratives', in J. Pier and J.-M. Schaeffer (eds.), *Métalepses: Entorses au pacte de la representation.* Paris: Éd. de l'EHESS, 247–61

Pier, J. (2011) 'Afterword', in K. Kukkonen and S. Klimek (eds.), *Metalepsis in Popular Culture.* Berlin: Walter de Gruyter, 268–76

Pier, J. (2016) 'Metalepsis (revised version; uploaded 13 July 2016)', in P. Hühn et al. (eds.), *The Living Handbook of Narratology,* Hamburg: Hamburg University. http://www.lhn.uni-hamburg.de/article/metalepsis-revised-version-uploaded-13-july-2016 [Accessed 26 September 2019]

Pier, J. and J.-M. Schaeffer (2005a) 'Introduction: La Métalepse, aujourd'hui', in J. Pier and J.-M. Schaeffer (eds.), *Métalepses: Entorses au pacte de la representation.* Paris: Éd. de l'EHESS, 7–15

Pier, J. and J.-M. Schaeffer (eds.) (2005b) *Métalepses: Entorses au pacte de la representation.* Paris: Éd. de l'EHESS

Platt, V. (2011) *Facing the Gods. Epiphany and Representation in Graeco-Roman Art, Literature and Religion.* Cambridge: Cambridge University Press

Platt, V. and M. Squire (eds.) (2010) *The Art of Art History in Graeco-Roman Antiquity.* Baltimore, MD: Johns Hopkins University Press

Porter, J. I. (1992) 'Hermeneutic Lines and Circles: Aristarchus and Crates on the Exegesis of Homer', in R. Lamberton and J. J. Keaney (eds.), *Homer's Ancient Readers.* Princeton, NJ: Princeton University Press, 67–114

Porter, J. I. (2009a) 'Is Art Modern? Kristeller's *Modern System of the Arts* Reconsidered', *British Journal of Aesthetics* 49, 1–24

Porter, J. I. (2009b) 'Reply to Shiner', *British Journal of Aesthetics* 49, 171–8

Porter, J. I. (2010) *The Origins of Aesthetic Thought in Ancient Greece: Matter, Sensation, and Experience.* Cambridge: Cambridge University Press

Powell, J. G. F. (2011) 'Aeneas the Spin-Doctor: Rhetorical Self-Presentation in *Aeneid* 2', *PVS* 27, 185–203

Prioux, E. (2016) 'Theocritus' Astronomical Description in *Idyll* 24.11–12' (paper delivered in Athens, May 2016)

Quinn, K. (1959) *The Catullan Revolution.* Melbourne: Melbourne University Press

Quint, D. (1993) *Epic and Empire.* Princeton, NJ: Princeton University Press

Rabau, S. (2005) 'Ulysse à côté d'Homère: Interprétation et transgression des frontières énonciatives', in J. Pier and J.-M. Schaeffer (eds.), *Métalepses: Entorses au pacte de la representation.* Paris: Éd. de l'EHESS, 59–72

Race, W. H. (1997) *Pindar*, 2 vols. Cambridge, MA and London: Harvard University Press

Race, W. H. (2014) 'Phaeacian Therapy in Homer's *Odyssey*', in D. Konstan and P. Meineck (eds.), *Combat Trauma and the Ancient Greeks*. New York, NY: Palgrave Macmillan, 47–66

Reid, I. (1992) *Narrative Exchanges*. London: Routledge

Relihan, J. C. (1993) *Ancient Menippean Satire*. Baltimore, MD: Johns Hopkins University Press

Richards, I. A. (1936) *Philosophy of Rhetoric*, repr. New York, NY: Oxford University Press (1965)

Richardson, B. (2006) *Unnatural Voices: Extreme Narration in Modern and Contemporary Fiction*. Columbus, OH: Ohio State University Press

Richardson, E. (2016) 'Ghostwritten Classics', in S. Butler (ed.), *Deep Classics: Rethinking Classical Reception*. London: Bloomsbury Academic, 221–38

Richardson, N. J. (1974) *The Homeric Hymn to Demeter*. Oxford: Clarendon Press

Richardson, S. (1990) *The Homeric Narrator*. Nashville, TN: Vanderbilt University Press

Rosen, R. M. and J. Farrell (1986) 'Acontius, Milanion, and Gallus: Vergil, *Ecl.* 10.52–61', *TAPhA* 116, 241–54

Ross, D. (1975) *Backgrounds to Augustan Poetry: Gallus, Elegy and Rome*. Cambridge: Cambridge University Press

Russell, D. A. (1981) *Criticism in Antiquity*. London: Duckworth

Russell, D. A. (ed. and trans.) (2002) *Quintilian: The Orator's Education*, 5 vols. Cambridge, MA and London: Harvard University Press

Russo, J. (2012) 'Re-Thinking Homeric Psychology: Snell, Dodds and their Critics', *QUCC* 101, 11–28

Ryan, M.-L. (2004) 'Metaleptic Machines', *Semiotica* 150.1, 439–69

Ryan, M.-L. (2005) 'Logique culturelle de la métalepse, ou la métalepse dans tous ses états', in J. Pier and J.-M. Schaeffer (eds.), *Métalepses: Entorses au pacte de la representation*. Paris: Éd. de l'EHESS, 201–23

Ryan, M.-L. (2006) *Avatars of Story*. Minneapolis, MN: University of Minnesota Press

Saint-Gelais, R. (2011) *Fictions transfuges: La Transfictionnalité et ses enjeux*. Paris: Seuil

Sarischoulis, E. (2008) *Schicksal, Götter und Handlungsfreiheit in den Epen Homers*. Stuttgart: Steiner

Schenkeveld, D. M. (1964) *Studies in Demetrius on Style*. Amsterdam: Hakkert

Schlickers, S. (2005) 'Inversions, transgressions, paradoxes et bizzareries: La Métalepse dans les littératures espagnole et française', in J. Pier and J.-M. Schaeffer (eds.), *Métalepses: Entorses au pacte de la representation*. Paris: Éd. de l'EHESS, 151–66

Schmid, M. J. (1998) 'Speaking Personae in Pindar's Epinikia', *Cuadernos de Filologia Clásica* 8, 147–84

Schmitt Pantel, P. (1992) *La Cité au banquet: Histoire des repas publics dans les cités grecques*. Rome: Publications de l'École française de Rome

Sedley, D. (2003) *Plato's Cratylus*. Cambridge: Cambridge University Press

Segal, C. P. (1974) 'God and Man in Pindar's First and Third *Olympian* Odes', *HSCPh* 68, 211–67

Segal, C. P. (1981 (1974)) 'Theocritus' Seventh Idyll and Lycidas', in *Poetry and Myth in Ancient Pastoral*. Princeton, NJ: Princeton University Press, 110–66

Segal, C. P. (1982) *Pindar's Mythmaking: The Fourth Pythian Ode*. Princeton, NJ: Princeton University Press

Sharples, R.W. (1983) '"But Why Has My Spirit Spoken with Me Thus?"': Homeric Decision-Making', *G&R* 30, 1–7

Sharrock, A. R. (1991) 'Womanufacture', *JRS* 81, 36–49

Shiner, L. (2009) 'Continuity and Discontinuity in the Concept of Art', *British Journal of Aesthetics* 49.2, 159–69

Shklovsky, V. (1917) 'Art as Technique', repr. in J. Rivkin and M. Ryan (eds.) (2004) *Literary Theory: An Anthology*, 2nd edn. Oxford: Wiley-Blackwell, 15–21

Sicking, C. M. J. (1983) 'Pindar's First *Olympian*: An Interpretation', *Mnemosyne* 36, 60–70

Sider, D. (1989) 'The Blinding of Stesichorus', *Hermes* 117, 423–31

Silk, M. S. (1974) *Interaction in Poetic Imagery: With Special Reference to Early Greek Poetry*. Cambridge: Cambridge University Press

Skinner, M. B. (2007a) 'Authorial Arrangement of the Collection: Debate Past and Present', in M. B. Skinner (ed.), *A Companion to Catullus*. Oxford: Blackwell, 35–53

Skinner, M. B. (ed.) (2007b) *A Companion to Catullus*. Oxford: Blackwell

Slater, W. J. (ed.) (1991) *Dining in a Classical Context*. Ann Arbor, MI: University of Michigan Press

Snell, B. (1960) *The Discovery of the Mind: The Greek Origins of European Thought*, trans. T. G. Rosenmeyer. New York, NY: Harper & Brothers

Sojcher, J. (1969) 'La Métaphore généralisée', *Revue internationale de philosophie* 87, fol. 1, 58–68

Somerville, T. (forthcoming) 'The Problem of Lygdamus and Ovid Reconsidered', *Hermes*

Spearing, A. C. (2005) *Textual Subjectivity: The Encoding of Subjectivity in Medieval Narratives and Lyrics*. Oxford: Oxford University Press

Squire, M. (2013) 'Apparitions Apparent: Ekphrasis and the Parameters of Vision in the Elder Philostratus's *Imagines*', *Helios* 40.1, 97–140

Stanzel, K.-H. (1995) *Liebende Hirten: Theokrits Bukolik und die alexandrinische Poesie*. Berlin and Boston: B. G. Teubner

Steiner, A. (2007) *Reading Greek Vases*. Cambridge: Cambridge University Press

Steinhart, M. (1995) *Das Motiv des Auges in der griechischen Bildkunst*. Mainz: von Zabern

Steinhart, M. (forthcoming) 'Götterepiphanie als Kunstinspiration? Ein Beitrag zur "Legende vom Künstler"', in R. von Haehling, M. Steinhart, and M. Vielberg (eds.), *Prophetie und Parusie in der griechisch-römischen Antike*. Paderborn: Schöningh

Sterne, L. (1769) *The Life and Opinions of Tristram Shandy, Gentleman*, 'new edn.', vol. 6. London: T. Becket and P. A. De Hondt

Stoichiță, V. I. (1993) *L'Instauration du tableau: Metapeinture à l'aube des temps modernes*. Paris: Droz

Stoichiță, V. I. (2013) *Figures de la transgression*. Geneva: Droz

Stroup, S. C. (2013) '"When I Read My *Cato*, It Is as If Cato Speaks": The Birth and Evolution of Cicero's Dialogic Voice', in A. Marmodoro and J. Hill (eds.), *The*

Author's Voice in Classical and Late Antiquity. Oxford: Oxford University Press, 123–51

Struck, P. (2004) *Birth of the Symbol: Ancient Readers at the Limits of their Texts*. Princeton, NJ: Princeton University Press

Sullivan, S. D. (2002) 'Aspects of the "Fictive I" in Pindar: Address to Psychic Entities', *Emerita* 70, 83–102

Tallis, R. (2010) *Michelangelo's Finger: An Exploration of Everyday Transcendence*. London: Atlantic Books

Tambling, J. (2010) *On Anachronism*. Manchester: Manchester University Press

Theodorakopoulos, E. (1997) 'Closure: The Book of Virgil', in C. Martindale (ed.), *The Cambridge Companion to Virgil*. Cambridge: Cambridge University Press, 155–65

Thorne, M. (2016) 'Speaking the Unspeakable: Engaging *nefas* in Lucan and Rwanda 1994', in A. Ambühl (ed.), *Krieg der Sinne—Die Sinne im Krieg: Kriegdarstellungen im Spannungsfeld zwischen antiker und moderner Kultur/War of the Senses—The Senses in War: Interactions and Tensions between Representations of War in Classical and Modern Culture = thersites* 4, 77–119

Thorsen, T. S. (2014) *Ovid's Early Poetry: From his Single Heroides to his Remedia Amoris*. Cambridge: Cambridge University Press

Thorsteinsson, R. M. (2010) *Roman Christianity and Roman Stoicism: A Comparative Study of Ancient Morality*. Oxford: Oxford University Press

Torrance, I. (2013) *Metapoetry in Euripides*. Oxford: Oxford University Press

Townley, R. (2001) *The Great Good Thing*. London: Simon and Schuster

Tränkle, H. (1960) *Die Sprachkunst des Properz und die Tradition der lateinischen Dichtersprache*. Wiesbaden: Steiner

Tränkle, H. (1990) *Appendix Tibulliana*. Berlin: Walter de Gruyter

Trimble, G. C. (2012) 'Catullus 64: The Perfect Epyllion?', in M. Baumbach and S. Bär (eds.), *Brill's Companion to Greek and Latin Epyllion and Its Reception*. Leiden: Brill, 55–79

Venuti, M. (2015) '*Spoudogeloion*: Hyperbole and Myth in Fulgentius' *Mythologiae*', in P. F. Moretti, R. Ricci, and C. Torre (eds.), *Culture and Literature in Latin Late Antiquity: Continuities and Discontinuities*. Turnhout: Brepols, 307–22

Vernant, J.-P. (1990) *Figures, idoles, masques*. Paris: Julliard

Versnel, H. S. (1987) 'What Did Ancient Man See When He Saw a God? Some Reflections on Greco-Roman Epiphany', in D. van der Plas (ed.), *Effigies Dei: Essays on the History of Religions*. Leiden: Brill, 42–55

Vetta, M. (ed.). (1995) *Poesia e simposio nella Grecia antica: Guida storica e critica*. Bari: Laterza

Viveiros de Castro, E. (2014) *Cannibal Metaphysics*, trans. P. Skafish. Minneapolis, MN: Univocal Publishing

Vöhler, M. (2005) '"Ich aber": Mythenkorrekturen in Pindars 1. *Olympie*', in M. Vöhler and B. Seidensticker (eds.), *Mythenkorrekturen: Zu einer paradoxalen Form der Mythenrezeption*. Berlin: Walter de Gruyter, 19–35

Voigt, E.-M. (1971) *Fragmenta: Sappho et Alcaeus*. Amsterdam: Athenaeum-Polak & Van Gennep

Wachter, R. (2001) *Non-Attic Greek Vase Inscriptions*. Oxford: Oxford University Press

Waddell, P. (2013) 'Eloquent Collisions: The *Annales* of Tacitus, the Column of Trajan and the Cinematic Quick-Cut', *Arethusa* 46, 471–97

Wagner, F. (2002) 'Glissements et déphasages: Note sur la métalepse narrative', *Poétique* 33.130, 235–53

Walter-Karydi, E. (2014) 'When the Athenians Liked to Chat', in P. Balabanes and E. Manakidu (eds.), *Egraphsen kai epoiesen: Essays on Greek Pottery and Iconography in Honour of Professor Michalis Tiverios.* Thessaloniki: University Studio Press, 191–204

Wardy, R. (1988) 'Lucretius on What Atoms Are Not', *CPh* 83, 112–28

Waterfield, R. (trans.) (2005) *Xenophon: The Expedition of Cyrus.* Intro. and notes by T. Rood. Oxford: Oxford University Press.

Webb, R. (2009) *Ekphrasis, Imagination and Persuasion in Ancient Rhetorical Theory and Practice.* Farnham: Ashgate

Weber, C. (1983) 'Two Chronological Contradictions in Catullus 64', *TAPhA* 113, 263–71

Wecowski, M. (2002) 'Towards a Definition of the Symposion', in T. Derda, J. Urbanik, and M. Wecowski (eds.), *Εὐεργεσίας χάριν: Studies Presented to Benedetto Bravo and Ewa Wipszycka by Their Disciples.* Warsaw: Fundacaja im. Rafała Taubenschlaga, 337–61

West, S., A. Heubeck, and B. Hainsworth (1988) *A Commentary on Homer's Odyssey.* Oxford: Clarendon Press

White, H. (1973) *Metahistory: The Historical Imagination in Nineteenth-Century Europe.* Baltimore, MD: Johns Hopkins University Press

Whitmarsh, T. (2001a) ' "Greece is the World": Exile and Identity in the Second Sophistic', in S. Goldhill (ed.), *Being Greek under Rome: Cultural Identity, the Second Sophistic and the Development of Empire.* Cambridge: Cambridge University Press, 269–305

Whitmarsh, T. (2001b) *Greek Literature and the Roman Empire: The Politics of Imitation.* Oxford: Oxford University Press

Whitmarsh, T. (2009) 'Reframing Satire: Lucianic Metalepsis', in M. Çevik (ed.), *Uluslararasi Samsatli Lucianus Sempozyumu.* Adıyaman: Adıyaman Üniversitesi Yayınları

Whitmarsh, T. (2013a) 'An I for an I: Reading Fictional Autobiography', in A. Marmodoro and J. Hill (eds.), *The Author's Voice in Classical and Late Antiquity.* Oxford: Oxford University Press, 233–47

Whitmarsh, T. (2013b) 'Radical Cognition: Metalepsis in Classical Greek Drama', *G&R* 60.1, 4–16

Wiesing, L. (2005) *Artifizielle Präsenz: Studien zur Philosophie des Bildes.* Frankfurt: Suhrkamp

Wigodsky, M. (1972) *Vergil and Early Latin Poetry. Hermes Einzelschriften* 24, Wiesbaden: Steiner

Wilamowitz-Moellendorff, U. von (1914) *Aischylos: Interpretationen.* Berlin: Weidmann

Wilamowitz-Moellendorff, U. von (1926) 'Lesefrüchte', *Hermes* 61, 277–303

Williams, B. (1993) *Shame and Necessity*, Sather Classical Lectures 57. Berkeley, CA: University of California Press

Williams, F. (1978) *Callimachus: Hymn to Apollo: A Commentary*. Oxford: Clarendon Press

Williams, G. D. (1994) *Banished Voices: Readings in Ovid's Exile Poetry*. Cambridge: Cambridge University Press.

Willis, I. (ed.) (2016) 'The Classical Canon and/as Transformative Work', *Transformative Works and Cultures* 21. http://journal.transformativeworks.org/index.php/twc/article/view/807/594 [Accessed 26 September 2019]

Wiseman, T. P. (1992) *Talking to Virgil: A Miscellany*. Exeter: University of Exeter Press.

Wolf, W. (2005) 'Metalepsis as a Transgeneric and Transmedial Phenomenon: A Case Study of the Possibilities of "Exporting" Narratological Concepts', in J. C. Meister (ed.), *Narratology beyond Literary Criticism: Mediality, Disciplinarity*. Berlin: Walter de Gruyter, 83–108

Wolf, W. (2009) 'Metareference across Media: The Concept, Its Transmedial Potentials and Problems, Main Forms and Functions', in W. Wolf (ed.), *Metareference across Media: Theory and Case Studies: Dedicated to Walter Bernhart on the Occasion of his Retirement*. Amsterdam: Rodopi, 1–85

Wolf, W. (2013) ' "Unnatural" Metalepsis and Immersion: Necessarily Incompatible?', in J. Alber, H. Skov Nielsen, and B. Richardson (eds.), *A Poetics of Unnatural Narrative*. Columbus, OH: Ohio State University Press, 113–41

Wolff, É. (2003) 'Fulgentiana', in F. Chausson and É. Wolff (eds.), *Consuetudinis amor: Fragments d'histoire romaine (IIe–VIe siècles) offerts à Jean-Pierre Callu*. Rome: L'Erma di Bretschneider, 431–43

Wolff, É. (ed.) (2009) *Fulgence: Virgile dévoilé. Mythographes*. Villeneuve-d'Ascq: Presses Universitaires du Septentrion

Woodbury, L. (1967) 'Helen and the Palinode', *Phoenix* 21, 157–76

Wray, D. (2001) *Catullus and the Poetics of Roman Manhood*. Cambridge: Cambridge University Press

Wright, M. (2005) *Euripides' Escape-Tragedies: A Study of Helen, Andromeda and Iphigenia among the Taurians*. Oxford: Oxford University Press

Wyke, M. (1987) 'Written Women: Propertius' *Scripta Puella*', *JRS* 77, 47–61

Yamagata, N. (1989) 'The Apostrophe in Homer as Part of the Oral Technique', *BICS* 36, 91–103

Zanker, G. (1981) '*Enargeia* in the Ancient Criticism of Poetry', *RhM* 124, 297–311

Ziogas, I. (2017) 'Singing for Octavia: Vergil's *Life* and Marcellus' Death', *HSCPh* 109, 429–81

Ziolkowski, J. M. and M. C. J. Putnam (eds.) (2008) *The Virgilian Tradition: The First Fifteen Hundred Years*. New Haven, CT: Yale University Press

Zyroff, E. S. (1971) *The Author's Apostrophe in Epic from Homer through Lucan*. Diss. Johns Hopkins

Index Locorum

This index lists all passages from Greek and Latin authors that are directly engaged with (or referenced) in the chapters of this volume. For ancient writers and texts mentioned and/or treated more discursively, please see the General Index.

General Index

This index includes key words, topics, concepts, critical terms, characters (historical and literary), and modern writers and critics. It also includes ancient writers and texts where these are mentioned and/or treated discursively in the volume; for engagements with specific passages from Greek and Latin authors, please see the Index Locorum.

prophecy 95–6, 149 n. 7, 151–3, 154–5, 157,
159, 165, 201 n. 25, 236, 254
prosopopoeia 60, 216–220
Ptolemy Philadelphus 115–16
puella 148, 154–60, 164–5, 203 n. 34, 249;
see also Lesbia; Neaera
puns 3 n. 6, 26–7, 169, 176–8, 186, 187–8,
202–3, 219 n. 89, 268

Queen, 'We Will Rock You' 104–6
Quinn, Kenneth 126, 127, 135, 140
Quintilian 8 n. 18, 11 n. 27, 12–13, 15–16, 20

reader(s) *passim*, and more particularly:
reader's expectation(s) 3, 19, 21–3, 114,
129–30, 133, 154–5, 167 n. 3, 169,
171–2, 178–9, 183, 184, 190, 200 n. 17,
251–2, 260, 265–7, 268 n. 70, 269
readerly investment 68, 74–6, 78,
238–40, 243
see also characters: relationships between
readers and; listeners; metalepsis:
effect of; viewing
reality/real life 4, 20–2, 37, 47 n. 63,
53 n. 74, 55, 59–60, 62–3, 75, 76–8,
86 n. 30, 102 n. 12, 127, 142–3, 148,
150, 152, 154, 161, 165, 168, 172,
178, 199–200, 210–12, 213 n. 71,
214–15, 216 n. 81, 224–7, 228,
230–1, 233–5, 237–40, 242–5, 249,
252–8, 260, 262, 266, 271–2;
see also existence; extradiegesis
representation 7–9, 20–3, 25–57, 93 n. 46,
121–3, 128, 136 n. 61, 139, 148–9, 168,
172–3, 181, 184, 196, 210, 211 n. 63,
214, 228–9, 233, 238, 245, 248 n. 2,
251–3, 255, 256, 260, 266, 268
linguistic vs. pictorial 27–32, 34–5, 37–8,
44–7, 53, 54–7
see also mimesis
rhetoric 1–2, 6, 8, 11–18, 33, 55, 61, 73–5,
82 n. 13, 127, 172, 178, 187 n. 46,
197, 248, 268 n. 69; *see also* criticism,
literary; metalepsis: rhetorical
ring composition 133–4
Romanticism 20, 124, 126–7
Rome, history of 152, 169, 186 n. 43, 187–8,
236, 239, 257

Saint-Amant, Antoine Girard 8
Sappho 65–8, 69–70, 102, 249
scene change/scene shift, *see* narration:
narrative transition

scholia 61–5, 75 n. 37, 87 n. 33, 108–10,
213, 269
Servius 8 n. 19, 177 n. 27, 187–8, 190–1,
211, 212 n. 68
shade/shadow 71 n. 28, 157 n. 23, 186 n. 44,
206, 208 n. 55, 209–17, 220–2, 226,
236; *see also* death
Shklovsky, Viktor 10–11
simile 123, 133–4, 136–7, 169, 202 n. 26
as metaleptic 183–5, 268
Sinon 6, 167–9, 174–8, 179, 268
Sophocles, *Electra* 108–9
spectators/spectatorship, *see* viewing;
see also listeners; reader(s)
status (legal case) 14, 23–4
Sterne, Lawrence 3 n. 4, 198–9, 225
Stesichorus, *Palinode* 68 n. 17, 99–103,
255, 266
structuralism 2, 54, 60, 199–200, 259, 269
subjectivity/subject 4, 126–9, 130, 135–8,
140, 142–3, 147, 173, 201 n. 22, 238
substitution 9–10, 200
suspension of disbelief 78, 209, 218,
270 n. 84
'symmetrical anthropology' 227 n. 12
sympathy 31 n. 21, 61–5, 70, 79–80, 83,
140–1, 191, 202, 269–70; *see also*
empathy
symposium 33 n. 27, 36–42, 56, 101 n. 8,
107, 111–14, 118, 265

temporality, *see* time
tense 7 n. 14, 23, 62, 67, 69, 73, 122, 125 n. 20,
133–5, 137, 161, 180, 183, 186,
234–5; *see also* time
theatre 29, 33–5, 37, 253, 268; *see also*
performance; tragedy/tragic
Theocritus 68–71, 76, 114–18, 265
Theophrastus 11 n. 27
theory/*theōria* 235, 237–40, 257
as journey there-and-back-again 232–4,
237–8
in Plato 232–4, 238–9
The Purple Rose of Cairo, film by Woody
Allen 266–7
time 5, 21, 24, 32–5, 37, 56, 62–3, 67–70, 73,
75, 79–80, 82, 92, 94–7, 103–6, 109,
110 n. 27, 112–18, 120–2, 125–7,
134–5, 137, 141–4, 169, 171–3,
178–9, 183–4, 186, 218, 229, 233–7,
240–1, 243–4, 253–4, 257, 259,
262–4, 266; *see also* anachronism;
tense